FROM
CHESTER TO
HOLYHEAD
The Branch Lines

FROM CHESTER TO HOLYHEAD

The Branch Lines

Bill Rear

OPC

An imprint of
Ian Allan Publishing

Front Cover: Stanier 2-6-4T No 42601 of Bangor (6H) shed stands in the Down loop at Dinas with the afternoon Class K goods Caernarvon Yard to Afon wen, in the summer of 1961. The signalman is just visible walking back along the platform with the Single Line Train Staff for the section Caernarvon No 2 to Dinas in his hand. On the Up platform can be seen the signal cabin minus its nameplate over the door. Behind the bush in the right foreground is the former Welsh Highland Railway station building. The Afon Wen branch closed to all traffic in December 1964. Today the scene has changed. Dinas station site has been completely rebuilt and one might now expect to find an ex-South African narrow gauge Garratt heading a train to Waunfawr. *J. Spencer Gilks*

Back Cover, top: Stanier Class 5MT 4-6-0 No 45277 of Llandudno Junction shed stands on the bridge at Pontrhythallt on the Llanberis branch, at the head of a demolition train heading for Caernarvon. In the background can just be seen the trackbed of the mineral line Padarn Railway — a 4ft gauge line that ran from Llanberis Quarry to Penscoins above Port Dinorwic although by the date this photograph was taken in the summer of 1965, that line too had ceased to operate and like its neighbour would soon be ripped up, though now some of the line has been rebuilt as the Llanberis Lake Railway. This bridge however still stands, as does the station building, beautifully restored and in private hands. *Bill Rear*

Back Cover, lower: Ivatt Class 2MT 2-6-2T No 41234 of Bangor shed stands at the head of the 12.54pm Saturdays Only return working from Amlwch to Bangor on a spring day in 1961, awaiting its departure time. By this date most of the passenger workings on the branch line were in the hands of DMUs but on Saturdays this working was still the preserve of steam. The coaching stock on this spring day was unusual inasmuch that the two coaches were of corridor stock, whereas normally non-corridor coaches would have been used. *J. Spencer Gilks*

Title page: This is perhaps my favourite photograph in the book. Ivatt 2-6-2T No 41223 pulls away from Afon Wen with the 7.5pm to Bangor. The working was a Bangor Saturdays Only diagram. The locomotive came off shed and worked first to Amlwch and return, then took the 4.4pm to Afon Wen. Normally, tank engines worked bunker-first out of Afon Wen returning to Bangor, but it was the practice for tank engines working to Amlwch to work out of Bangor bunker-first. There was no reason to go on shed to turn the locomotive between trips, so the working to Afon Wen was also bunker-first. The job was a No 2 link turn. The four coaches were off a working from Liverpool Lime Street and whilst not shown as a through working, the stock in fact worked through. Note the two water tanks, useful when two engines worked coupled, placed so that both engines could refuel at the same time. *Bill Rear*

Half title: The summer months saw a procession of trains between Bangor and Afon Wen, some service trains running under Class B lamps, others working Butlin's Camp specials. Here Stanier 2-6-4T No 42451 heads a six-coach rake on the 3.15pm Saturdays only Bangor to Afon Wen relief in the summer of 1953, coasting into the Up & Down platform at Caernarvon. It is seen passing the 'Rat Hole', alias Caernarvon No 1 Signal Box. The line in the foreground linked the upper and lower goods yards and at one time gave access to the locomotive shed, whose connecting line is just visible beyond the ground disk signal. *Bill Rear*

Acknowledgements

A work of this magnitude would be almost impossible without the help and collaboration of many people.

First and foremost I must place on record my thanks and gratitude to my wife Kate, who has encouraged me throughout and tolerated hours of solitude whilst I worked at this tome. She acted as mentor and guide, checked proofs and latterly 'kept me at it'. Thank you.

Thanks, too, to Norman Jones of Warrington for continued support and Alun Roberts of Penrhyndeudraeth for on-going research, help and advice.

As always, I have leaned on other photographers. It is sad to reflect that I was in the fortunate position to have travelled over every branch line mentioned in this work, but often travelled without the camera. To this end I must record my thanks to the following:
Mike Bentley, R. J. Buckley, C. L. Caddy,
R. M. Casserley, Derek Chaplin, Gordon Coltas,
A. Cooke, Brian Cowlishaw, G. I. Davies, J. J. Davis,
T. J. Edgington, J. S. Gilkes, Larry Goddard,
A. Wyn Hobson, H. Rogers Jones, Norman Jones,
Norman Kneale, Michael Mensing, J. H. Moss,
F. W. Shuttleworth, Arthur Tyson, Martin Welch,
Anglesey Record Office, British Railways London Midland Region, Clwyd Record Office, Gwynedd Archives, The late W. A. Camwell, The late Brian Hilton, The late J. W. T. House, The late J. A. Peden,
The late G. H. Platt, The late E. S. Russell,
Welsh Highland Heritage (David Allen and John Knight).

Finally, thanks to Ian Allan Publishing, and especially to Peter Waller, for the confidence in publishing this work.

First published 2003

ISBN 0 86093 569 8

Published by Oxford Publishing Co

an imprint of Ian Allan Publishing Ltd, Hersham, Surrey KT12 4RG.
Printed by Ian Allan Printing Ltd, Hersham, Surrey KT12 4RG.

Code: 0303/A1

Contents

North Wales Holiday Pleasure Travel by Rail Road and Sea

To SEE the Countryside Travel in Rail Comfort

10th JUNE to 15th SEPTEMBER 1957

BRITISH RAILWAYS

NORTH WALES RADIO LAND CRUISE

SPECIALLY EQUIPPED FOR ACTUAL RADIO RECEPTION AND DESCRIPTIVE COMMENTARY ON FEATURES OF INTEREST EN ROUTE.

FOR MAP OF ROUTE PLEASE SEE OVERLEAF.

TUESDAYS and THURSDAYS
27th JUNE to 20th JULY, 1961 (inclusive)

ALSO

MONDAYS to FRIDAYS
24th JULY to 8th SEPTEMBER, 1961 (inclusive)

FARE s. d.	Time of departure a.m.	FROM	Arrival on Return p.m.
20/- FROM EACH STATION	10 10	PWLLHELI	5 C28
	10 18	PENYCHAIN	5 C13
	10 33	CRICCIETH	5 14
	10 43	PORTMADOC	5 23
	10 50	PENRHYNDEUDRAETH	5 34
	10 55	TALSARNAU	5 42
	11 0	HARLECH	5 42
	11 6	LLANBEDR & PENSARN	5 46
	11 12	DYFFRYN ARDUDWY	5 58
	11 15	TALYBONT HALT	6 0
	11 25	BARMOUTH	6 3
	11 45	PENMAENPOOL	6 10
	11 50	DOLGELLAU	7 *36
	11 25	BALA...	7 *41
	p.m. 12 50	CORWEN	8 ‡*42
RHYL arrive 1-58 p.m.		RHYL depart 3-30 p.m.	9 * 2

*—Change at Barmouth.   C—Change at Afon Wen.
‡—Change at Bala Junction and Corwen. †—Change at Bala Junction.
Children under Three years of age, Free; Three and under Fourteen years of age, Half-fare.

LIGHT MEALS AND REFRESHMENTS, MAY BE OBTAINED FROM THE CAFETERIA CAR ON THE TRAIN.

HOLIDAY RUNABOUT TICKETS ARE NOT AVAILABLE BY THIS TRAIN

For conditions of issue of these tickets, also luggage allowances, see the British Transport Commission's Regulations and Conditions of Issue of Tickets, etc.

Further information will be supplied on application to the Stations, or to Mr. O. VELTOM, District Traffic Superintendent, Shrewsbury (Telephone Shrewsbury 3614, Extn. 42); or to Mr. W. R. STEVENS, Divisional Traffic Manager, Marland House, Central Square, Cardiff.

BRITISH RAILWAYS

1957 North Wales Holiday Pleasure Travel.   1961 North Wales Radio Land Cruise.

Chester
Fairburn 2-6-4T No 42061 propels its stock out of the Denbigh bay platform at Chester General station in November 1961 after working a train from Ruthin. The bay platform was tucked out of the way, alongside the Western Region platforms, and has since been demolished. The area is now used as a car park. This view was taken in the last winter of the line's passenger service. *Brian Cowlishaw*

Introduction

When approaching a work of this magnitude, an author is faced with a number of decisions in order to ensure comprehensive coverage within an acceptable specification. From an early stage it was decided to concentrate on the period post-Nationalisation in 1948 through to the early 1960s for a number of reasons. Firstly, this is increasingly the most popular period for railway modellers and, undoubtedly, many of the locations featured in this book would be ideal for those seeking inspiration for a new layout.

Secondly, I thought that little would be gained by a repetition of basic information. The likelihood is that prospective readers of the book will probably have this information already to hand, either in the David & Charles 'Regional History' volume covering North Wales or in earlier books on specific branches. If there is one criticism levelled at railway authors is it that they repeat endlessly material already in the public domain. I have, as far as is possible with this volume, sought to avoid this accusation by approaching the subject from an alternative angle, incorporating for example anecdotal evidence where it is of interest.

Again, with reference to the photographic content, I have, wherever possible, endeavoured to use photographs that will be unfamiliar. Inevitably, particularly on the lines that were less well known, there were only ever a limited number of photographs taken and as a result some will have been published before. I also think that it's important to try and illustrate all the stations and locations mentioned in the text and, again, this has required the occasional pre-published photograph.

Whilst the majority of photographs come from the period outlined above, this has been to exclude, where interest or context requires, photographs that are from an earlier or later period. For this reason the reader will find photographs taken about the time of the Grouping around Denbigh, and more recently in the case of the line between Caernarfon and Dinas, scenes taken in the 1950s are compared with the present day set-up where the Welsh Highland Railway now occupies the same track formation.

Concerning placenames used in this work, until 1925 the London & North Western Railway (LNWR) and its predecessors spelt the town name as 'Carnarvon', then the London, Midland & Scottish Railway (LMS) changed it to 'Caernarvon'. The current spelling, 'Caernarfon', became the official spelling, being formally recognised after the 1969 Investiture. Unless the former spelling is necessary, I have used the current version. Concerning the spelling of the junction station on the Cambrian Coast line, the Cambrian Railways, Great Western Railway (GWR) and British Railways (BR) Western Region spelled the station name as 'Afonwen'. The LNWR, LMS and BR London Midland Region spelled it as two words — 'Afon Wen'. Because this work is linked to the Chester & Holyhead Railway, I have spelled the station as two words, namely 'Afon Wen'.

I have tried to standardise on the summer period of 1955 for the extracts from working timetables, but there are exceptions. Where the line closed to passenger traffic before 1955, I have taken the last summer period of operation. Where the branch timetable was included with the Chester & Holyhead Railway main line working timetables, I have decided to use an equivalent public timetable extract.

Bill Rear
Conwy
January 2003

A 1950 BR North Wales travel guide.

THE CHESTER & HOLYHEAD RAILWAY

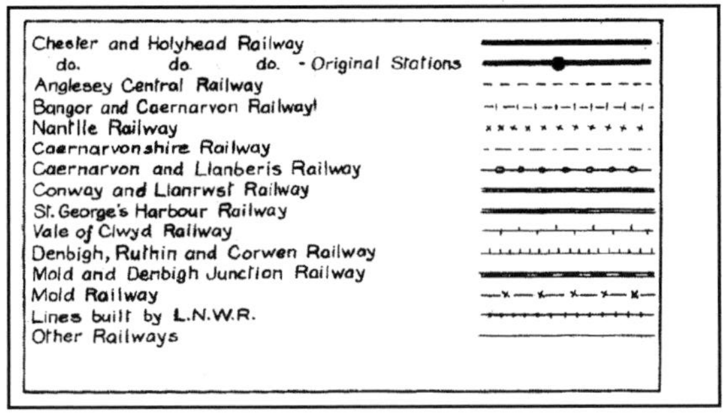

Legend:

- Chester and Holyhead Railway
- do. do. - Original Stations
- Anglesey Central Railway
- Bangor and Caernarvon Railway
- Nantlle Railway
- Caernarvonshire Railway
- Caernarvon and Llanberis Railway
- Conway and Llanrwst Railway
- St George's Harbour Railway
- Vale of Clwyd Railway
- Denbigh, Ruthin and Corwen Railway
- Mold and Denbigh Junction Railway
- Mold Railway
- Lines built by L.N.W.R.
- Other Railways

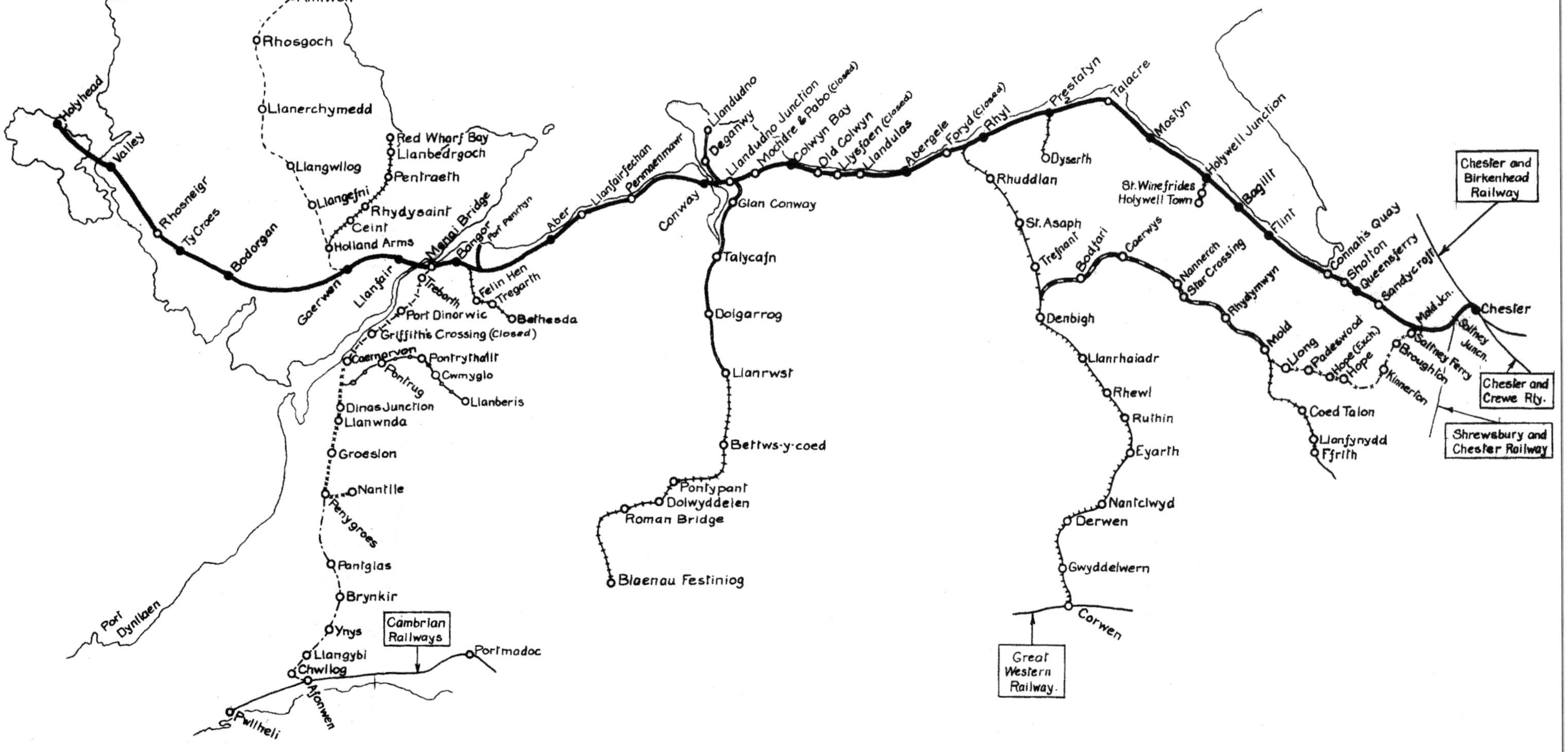

Chester and Birkenhead Railway
Chester and Crewe Rly.
Shrewsbury and Chester Railway
Great Western Railway
Cambrian Railways

Chester — Saltney Junc. — Saltney Ferry — Broughton — Kinnerton — Mold (Coed Talon) — Llong — Padeswood — Hope — Llanfynydd — Fyrth — Coed Talon

Sandycroft — Queen's Ferry — Shotton — Connah's Quay — Flint — Bagillt — Holywell Junction — Mostyn — Talacre — Prestatyn — Rhyl — Foryd (Closed) — Abergele

St Winefrides — Holywell Town — Bodfari — Caerwys — Nannerch — Star Crossing — Rhydymwyn — Mold

Llanrhaiadr — Rhewl — Ruthin — Eyarth — Nantclwyd — Derwen — Gwyddelwern — Corwen

Denbigh — Trefnant — St Asaph — Rhuddlan — Dyserth

Llanddulas — Llysfaen — Old Colwyn (Closed) — Colwyn Bay — Mochdre & Pabo (Closed) — Llandudno Junction — Deganwy — Llandudno

Glan Conway — Talycafn — Dolgarrog — Llanrwst — Bettws-y-coed — Pontypant — Dolwyddelen — Roman Bridge — Blaenau Festiniog

Conway — Penmaenmawr — Llanfairfechan — Aber — Bangor — Port Penrhyn — Treborth — Menai Bridge — Llanfair

Bethesda — Felin Hen — Tregarth

Griffiths Crossing (Closed) — Port Dinorwic — Caernarvon — Pontrythallt — Pontrug — Cwmyglo — Llanberis

Dinas Junction — Llanwnda — Groeslon — Penygroes — Nantlle — Pantglas — Brynkir — Ynys — Llangybi — Chwilog — Afonwen — Pwllheli — Portmadoc

Valley — Tycroes — Rhosneigr — Bodorgan — Tyn Croes — Gaerwen — Holland Arms — Ceint — Llangefni — Llangwillog — Rhydysaint — Pentraeth — Llanbedrgoch — Red Wharf Bay — Llangwyllog — Llanerchymedd — Rhosgoch — Amlwch — Holyhead

Port Dynllaen

Chester to Mold

History

The Mold Railway Company constructed a line of double track from Saltney Ferry to Mold, a distance of 10 miles, under an Act of 9 July 1847. The Chester & Holyhead Railway was to subscribe £30,000 and the cost of the connection between the two lines was borne by the Mold Railway Company. The authorised capital was £180,000. A tender for its construction was made by Edward Ladd Betts, of Peto, Brassey & Betts fame, in November 1846.

By July 1848 work had slowed down, and consequently the Chester & Holyhead Railway Company began to show signs of impatience. As a result, work on the Ffrith branch was abandoned beyond the junction at Coed Talon, although this portion was eventually built 33 years later.

Route Description

Chester to Mold

The line parted company with the Chester & Holyhead Railway main line on the down side at Saltney Ferry (where Mold Junction No 1 box still stands), 3¼ miles from Chester General station.

Saltney Ferry

Saltney Ferry station was 3¼ miles from Chester General on the up and down slow lines. Only trains to and from Mold used the single-island 200ft-long platform. Passengers accessed the platform off Sandycroft Lane, which passed over the tracks at the eastern end of the complex, down a flight of stairs. The platform was latterly

Saltney Ferry (Mold Junction)
This short island platform at Saltney Ferry (Mold Junction) was on the up and down slow lines out of Chester and served trains only to and from the Mold line, although nominally main line trains could access the short platform. Passenger access was off Sandycroft Lane, down a flight of steps. At one time there was a canopy extending some way along the platform. The small shed on the platform served as a booking office and a waiting room. Mold Junction locomotive shed (6B) stood on the down side. *Bill Rear collection*

Broughton & Bretton
Looking towards Mold, the main buildings at Broughton & Bretton were on the down side. The signalbox controlled the level crossing gates over the Chester to Hawarden road. Note the brick-built up-side shelter with the overhanging roof, giving some protection to passengers. The station served the de Havilland aircraft factory nearby, and much traffic derived from this source, even to the extent that an unadvertised service for the workers operated for several months after official closure of the line from Chester General. *Bill Rear collection*

devoid of shelter. A small hut served as a booking hall and waiting room. There were no facilities for freight. The platform stood alongside Mold Junction (6B) locomotive shed. The station closed to passengers on 30 April 1962, when passenger services on the branch were withdrawn.

The line turned southwest, passing the sorting sidings on the right-hand side with access to the motive power depot and yard on the down side. After a short distance the line ascended a gradient of 1 in 270 to reach Broughton & Bretton station, 4¾ miles from Chester.

Broughton & Bretton

Originally the station was named 'Broughton' but was renamed 'Broughton Hall' in April 1861. A further name change to 'Broughton & Bretton' was made on 1 July 1908. The station closed to all traffic on 4 July 1964, latterly being served by unadvertised workmen's trains from Chester for the adjoining aircraft factory.

Broughton & Bretton was 4¾ miles from Chester General. The line was double tracked with platforms on both sides. The main station building was on the down side, built to the same design by Francis Thompson as others constructed for the Mold Railway. The two-storey station building incorporated the usual facilities, with living quarters for the stationmaster. Despite closure and removal of the tracks, the building still stands to this day, albeit in private hands. The station dealt with passenger and goods traffic, the goods yard on the down side having cattle pens and a landing stage,

together with a shed for storing small freight items and animal foodstuffs. Passengers were provided with a single-storey brick-built shelter on the up platform. Access was via a barrow crossing at the Mold end of the station. A standard LNWR-design all-brick signal cabin with a set of 25 levers stood at the Mold end and controlled the level crossing gates where the line crossed the A549 road. Sidings were added to the up side to serve the Vickers aircraft factory during World War 2. The Premier Artificial Stone Company Ltd also had a private siding off the goods yard.

After the line crossed the main A55 road on the level it resumed climbing to Kinnerton.

Kinnerton

Kinnerton station was 6¼ miles from Chester General and located on the steeply graded Kinnerton bank which continued at 1 in 43 towards Mold. The station itself was of simple construction, the platforms on the up and down lines being given scant protection against the elements. The main buildings were located on the up side and consisted of a standard LNWR portable wooden building which constituted the station office and a second wooden structure which served as a waiting room. There was a milk stage at the Mold end. The down platform had an equally small wooden waiting hut of LNWR design. Passengers crossed the line by means of a subway but could also access either platform off the highway via gated paths and steps. The station was demolished after closure.

Kinnerton
The platforms at Kinnerton were located on a severe gradient that sometimes caused problems to down passenger trains on restarting. Added to this was the fact that the platforms were of short length and care was necessary to ensure that the train did not stop short and that the guard was able to access the platform. Facilities were somewhat basic and creature comforts for passengers were limited. This view was taken looking down the bank towards Chester. The station platforms and buildings were removed after the line closed. *R. J. Buckley*

There was a station yard on the up side, with a single siding with a capacity for 14 wagons, that served cattle pens adjoining the passenger platform. Further into the yard it became a coal siding. The yard contained a public weighbridge and weigh-office at the gated entrance.

The line passed over the public road on a standard metal bridge at the Mold end of the site. The bridge was removed after the line closed. There was once a small signal cabin located on the down side which controlled three points and six signals. The signalbox was removed at an unknown date, and replaced by a ground frame alongside the yard siding.

Some freight traffic facilities were withdrawn from 5 December 1955. Down and up trains were booked to call as required at Kinnerton until September 1961, by which time the closure notices for the line had been published.

The line continued climbing out of the station, the gradient stiffening to 1 in 43 and then easing slightly to 1 in 50, before swinging in a westerly direction to Hope & Penyffordd station. At the summit of the line, up-direction unfitted trains were required to stop and pin down brakes. Banking of down line freight trains up the gradient was normal. Mold Junction shed had several diagrams allocated to this work.

Hope & Penyffordd
The station was centrally located in the village of Penyffordd and was 9 miles from Chester General.

The main station building, which provided accommodation for the stationmaster, was on the down side and was uniform with other buildings on the Mold Railway. Passengers crossed the line over a footbridge that stood at the Mold end of the platforms, alongside the main road. A wooden building on the down platform served as a goods shed. At one time there was a single siding off the down line at the Chester end of the site. The station buildings stood in a small open yard that contained the usual weighbridge and office. The main station building survives as a private house.

The site was split by the A550 Queensferry to Wrexham road which crossed on the level, and the gates were worked from the signalbox that stood on the up side, beyond the crossing at the Mold end. Originally, the signalbox had been a standard LNWR-design all-brick cabin which controlled 11 points and nine signals, but this was replaced in 1943 by an LMS-design 'ARP' version with a flat roof and a 25-lever tappet-design frame.

Beyond the level crossing were two sidings off the down line via a trailing connection which could hold 16 wagons. Another trailing siding was located on the up side which could hold six wagons. A small hand-operated yard crane stood adjoining No 2 siding which also extended back and served as a coal siding.

The Kinnerton banker came off the trains at this point. After crossing over to the up line it ran back light to Mold Junction.

The line followed the course of the River Alyn and continued climbing at 1 in 124 to its first summit, at 324ft above sea level near Hope Exchange Low Level station.

Hope Exchange

Hope Exchange (renamed Hope Exchange Low Level from 7 December 1953) was 9½ miles from Chester. At this point the line, now on a falling gradient of 1 in 108, passed under the Wrexham, Mold & Connah's Quay Railway (WM&CQR). The station had no road connection and existed merely to provide passengers with a convenient transfer point between the respective lines, the two stations (the other station being Hope Exchange High Level on the WM&CQR line) being connected by a footpath. Facilities were very basic. A wooden booking office and slightly larger wooden general waiting room were located on the up platform, whilst a wooden waiting shed and a separate ladies' waiting room graced the down platform. Passengers crossed the line on a barrow crossing. A porter was on duty during the day to deal with interchange parcels traffic and advise the passengers. There were no freight facilities. Most passenger trains between Chester and Mold called at the station, but traffic was always light and the station closed on 1 September 1958. It is now demolished, with all traces removed.

The spur line from the WM&CQR saw regular interchange of traffic between the two lines. When the Mold Junction to Mold & Denbigh Junction Railway line closed to regular traffic in 1962 the spur line came into increased use, eventually enabling the tracks between Hope Low Level and Mold Junction to be uplifted. There was regular traffic from Padeswood cement works which continued until the 1990s although the track was uplifted from beyond this point in 1983.

Continuing west, the line maintained the falling gradient for nearly a mile. Just before Padeswood & Buckley station on the up side, Padeswood colliery branch was encountered. This siding was listed in the 1904 working timetables but not afterwards and it is presumed that the colliery had ceased working after this date.

A short distance further on was Ffrith Junction where a double-track freight-only branch used to leave the down line to connect with the Mold to Brymbo branch line near Coed Talon. This branch had closed to traffic following the derailment of a freight train in 1934. The junction was controlled from an LNWR-design composite construction signal cabin. When the Ffrith Junction to Coed Talon line

closed, the signalbox was removed. Points controlling a crossover on the main line were then worked from a ground frame.

Padeswood & Buckley

The station was 10¾ miles from Chester General. The main station building was different to others elsewhere on the line and was suspended over the tracks adjoining a minor road at the Mold end of the station. Passengers descended to the platforms from the booking hall. There were open shelters on both short-length platforms with small canopies for protection.

The station was some distance away from Padeswood village and even further from Buckley. Consequently, passenger traffic was light, which hastened the station's closure on 6 January 1958. The station buildings were demolished almost immediately and the platforms removed within months.

There was a small yard on the down side at the Chester end of the station which contained a covered warehouse and a goods shed, a second dead-end siding passing through the warehouse. A short landing stage and siding with facilities for offloading cattle into pens adjoined the down platform ramp at the Chester end of the station. The station yard included the stationmaster's house, which still survives, and four surfacemen's cottages. Inside the yard was a weighbridge and office, and a general purpose store.

On leaving Padeswood the line crossed the River Alyn on a cast-iron bridge and then crossed a minor road via a hand-operated level crossing.

Llong

Llong station was 11¾ miles from Chester General. The main building was on the down side. A minor road level crossing bisected the line at the Chester end of the station. The station buildings at Llong were designed by Francis Thompson and were similar architecturally to some small stations on the Chester & Holyhead main line. The building contained the usual offices for station business and accommodation for the stationmaster. The platforms were of low height, necessitating portable steps being on hand. The up platform had two small wooden sheds, one of which was designated a 'waiting shed', whilst the other was specified as a 'ladies waiting room'.

At one time a signalbox of standard LNWR design stood on the down side on the Chester end of the site. This controlled six points and seven signals, and access to

Padeswood & Buckley

Long after Padeswood & Buckley station closed. Fairburn 2-6-4T, believed to be No 42236, approaches the site of the station, heading a two-coach local from Chester to Denbigh on the last day of service on 28 April 1962. These tanks took over some of the passenger services only in the last days of operation, although they had appeared from time to time in the preceding 10 years. *M. Mensing*

sidings also on the up side, but these were removed in the 1930s and the signalbox demolished. The crossing was then operated from a small eight-lever frame mounted on the down platform, which also controlled the gate lock and protecting signals.

Traffic was always sparse and the station was closed from 1 January 1917 until 5 May 1919 as a wartime economy measure. Despite its isolated location, it remained open until passenger services were withdrawn on 30 April 1962. The station building survives to this day.

The line then crossed the Alyn river twice before Tryddyn Junction was reached. The Mold to Tryddyn branch came in on the down side from a trailing direction. The junction signalbox controlled access to the line to Coed Talon and Brymbo, to private sidings and a minor road level crossing. The building was of all-brick construction and housed an LNWR 24-lever tumbler frame. The LNWR's 1910 list of all its signalboxes states that it controlled 14 points and 10 signals. By 1962 the number of working levers had been reduced to 11. The signalbox was demolished when the track was lifted.

Mold

Half a mile further on, 13¼ miles from Chester, was Mold station, which was, for the first 20 years, the terminus of the line. It was also the terminus of the Mold & Denbigh Junction Railway (M&DJR), the two concerns meeting at an end-on junction. Whilst the Mold Railway was later incorporated into the LNWR, the M&DJR remained nominally independent until the Grouping in 1923.

The main station building was on the down side and was constructed of red brick. There was a canopy that extended over the platform to the edge of the track and gave protection in inclement weather. The station forecourt was accessed from Chester Road and that road passed over the line just beyond the platform ramps on the Denbigh side of the station. For many years Crosville Motor Services Ltd's main bus stands were on either side of Chester Road bridge and were convenient for any passenger interchange that might happen. The up platform had a small general waiting room, a ladies' waiting room and toilets, and was protected by a canopy that extended to the platform edge. A covered footbridge linked the two platforms. This was located at the

Llong
BR Standard Class 4MT 4-6-0 No 75010, sporting a 6G (Llandudno Junction) shed plate on the smokebox, draws to a halt at Llong station on the last day of service between Chester, Denbigh and Ruthin, with the 6.35pm Chester to Ruthin working. The station still stands today, slightly modified. Note the low platforms which were a feature of the Mold Railway stations.

At one time there was a signalbox on the down side which controlled the level crossing gates but this was removed when the box became life-expired in LMS days. *M. Mensing*

Mold Tryddyn Junction
This signalbox controlled the connection of the main Chester to Mold line with the Coed Talon branch, as well as protecting a minor road crossing. It was closed on 3 March 1965, some time after the main line closed to passenger services. This view was taken from an SLS rail enthusiasts' special, seen here coming off the Coed Talon line. The signalman is waiting outside the box to collect the single-line token. Beyond the box can just be seen the sidings on the approach to Mold station. *G. H. Platt*

Denbigh end of the station. At the Chester end of the up platform was a goods warehouse with a covered unloading canopy. Adjoining this was a second siding with a horse landing stage and an end-on facility for the loading/unloading of carriages. This siding extended back, passing through a second goods warehouse which contained an agricultural store. This was originally the Mold Railway engine shed which had been modified after the locomotive department closed and the engines and men moved to Mold Junction or Denbigh.

Behind the goods warehouse a single siding extended back into the up side yard and was used as a coal siding by local merchants.

According to the 1910 list, the first signalbox was a standard LNWR all-brick construction controlling eight points and 13 signals. It was located on the down side and was replaced in late LMS days by a modern flat-roof structure containing a standard 4½ in centre frame of 35 levers. This was still standing when the line finally closed in 1983 and was subsequently demolished.

There were extensive facilities here, with siding provision for 127 wagons on the down side and 104 on the up.

After closure of the through route to Denbigh the line became an extended siding of 4¾ miles from a spur off the Wrexham to Bidston line, and associated sidings were in use until March 1983. The track was lifted in the summer of 1985 and the site is now a Tesco supermarket.

1914-18 Ordnance Survey map showing Mold station layout.
Crown Copyright

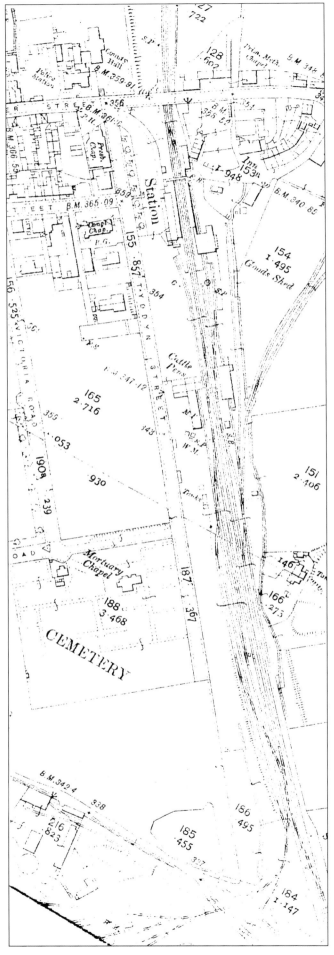

Mold to Denbigh Junction

History

The Mold & Denbigh Junction Railway opened for traffic on 12 September 1869, and despite having been worked from the outset by the LNWR, remained independent until the Railways Act 1921, when it was grouped as a subsidiary company in the London, Midland & Scottish Railway. In 1948 it became part of British Railways London Midland Region (Western Division).

Route Description

On leaving Mold the line passed the Alyn tinplate works siding, one mile from the station. A signalbox to standard LNWR design of composite construction stood on the up side controlling access into the works on the down side.

The works closed some time before the outbreak of World War 2. Ordinarily, the box would have been closed,

Mold
Standard Class 4MT 4-6-0 No 75034 runs into Mold with the 12.49pm (SO) Chester to Denbigh working. Behind the circular water tank on the up side are many wagons which give some indication of the amount of freight traffic handled at this station and which enabled the station to remain open for goods traffic after passenger services ceased in 1962. The white-painted fencing stands out, indicating the pride that the station staff took in the workplace. The locomotive was nominally attached to Rhyl (6K) shed, although the working was diagrammed for a Chester 2-6-4T (Turn 6A/8). The traincrew was also from Rhyl (Turn 6K/123). After the remaining traffic ceased, the site was cleared and today a supermarket stands where platforms once stood. The trackbed is used as an alternative exit from the supermarket.
Bill Rear collection

Mold

Fowler Class 4 0-6-0 No M4065 runs round the single coach after working the 4.50pm from Brymbo on 9 May 1949. At the time this was one of Mold Junction (6B) shed's few passenger turns. The passenger service between Mold and Brymbo ceased on 27 March 1950 and freight traffic services were cut back to Coed Talon. The numbering and wording on the tender indicate that the engine had been in the workshops for overhaul in the earliest days of British Railways, when details of a nationwide locomotive renumbering scheme and logo were still under discussion. Note, too, the tender has coal rails fitted, a feature not found on every member of this freight class of engine. *E. S. Russell*

but a new chemical plant was built on the same site and rail access was controlled from the box.

The line passed under the Mold to Denbigh road. After the track to Rhydymwyn had been uplifted, road improvements in the 1980s bypassed the bridge.

The line was then on a rising gradient and headed generally in a northerly direction, following the course of the valley.

Rhydymwyn

Rhydymwyn station was 16¼ miles from Chester General and was centrally located in the village. The Mold to Denbigh road crossed the line on the level, the gates being hand operated, locked from a two-lever ground frame on the down platform where the main station buildings, which incorporated the stationmaster's house, were located. This building still stands and is now a private dwelling.

The up platform had a rudimentary passenger shelter and a small wooden store shed. Passengers crossed the line at the level crossing.

The main goods yard on the up side contained two sidings, one of which served as a coal siding. A second siding ran alongside a loading wharf with a yard crane located near the conjunction of the sidings; an access road ran between the sidings. At the entrance to the yard was a weigh machine and an office. A second goods yard was located on the down side. Rail access to both yards was controlled from Rhydymwyn signalbox located at the Mold end of the site on the down side. The Ministry of Defence built an extensive collection of government buildings on the down side in 1940 with separate rail access, to sidings dealing with MoD or government freight traffic during World War 2. The complex remained rail-connected until the freight services to Mold were finally withdrawn and the tracks lifted in 1985. The sensitive nature of the work done at Rhydymwyn ensured that the site was classified, and retained as a site of strategic importance well into the 1970s.

On leaving the station, the Alyn valley closed in and became quite narrow.

Mold

On the last day of passenger services between Chester, Mold and Denbigh, Standard Class 4MT 4-6-0 No 75033, hauling two non-corridor coaches, runs into Mold station with the 5pm (SO) from Denbigh to Chester. The engine was attached to Mold Junction (6B) shed Turn 6B/10, which involved three engines of this class on a three-day diagram. Rhyl men (Turn 6K/33) were in charge for this trip which returned from Chester with the 8.50pm to Ruthin. Note that the down starter and distant for Alyn tinplate works was pulled off, for the tinplate works box would have been switched out. Today, this section of track is a private relief road for the Tesco supermarket which stands on the station site. *M. Mensing*

Rhydymwyn

The main station building stood on the down platform, ahead of a level crossing. The building stands today in private ownership, not very much altered from this view taken in April 1957, although the track, up platform and wooden buildings have all been removed in the intervening years. The train was a traditional special, organised by the Merseyside Ramblers' Association for Easter Monday, when the walkers would have an enjoyable day out, and would be picked up at this and other stations on the line. The train comprised seven non-corridor coaches hauled by Stanier 2-6-0 No 42977, a Speke Junction engine at the time, seen here heading for Denbigh, where it would lay-over until the time of the return working. It is likely that Chester men would be in charge, as Speke men did not sign for the road to Denbigh. *W. A. Camwell*

Dolfechlas Crossing

This box controlled freight sidings for the Olwyn Goch lead mine and Ruby brick and tile works which were adjoining the line and from which considerable quantities of freight were transported. Beyond the box was a minor road but which carried sufficient road traffic to and from both works and mine to justify the box being manned during daylight hours. Latterly it was worked by a porter signalman on an 'as required' basis. It was 1,149yd from Rhydymwyn station. This view was taken from a Chester-bound train. *Brian Cowlishaw*

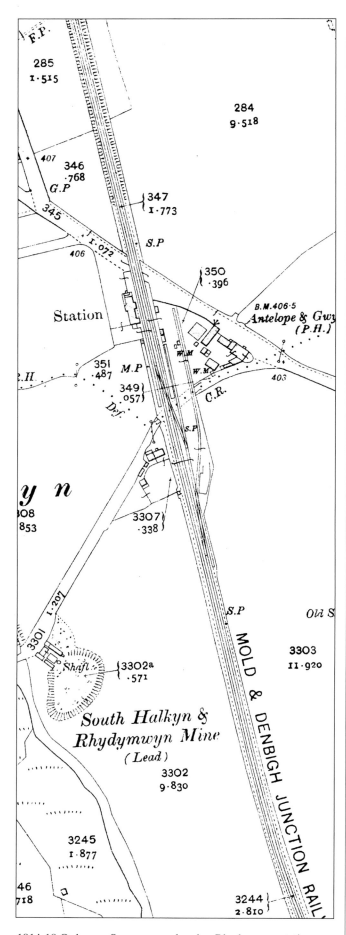

1914-18 Ordnance Survey map showing Rhydymwyn station layout. *Crown Copyright*

Dolfechlas Crossing

Three quarters of a mile from Rhydymwyn was Dolfechlas Crossing signalbox. Located on the up side, it protected a minor road leading to the Olwyn Goch lead mine, and controlled sidings which were located on the up side for the Olwyn Goch mine and Ruby brick and lime works. The box was a standard LNWR-design Type 'E' of composite construction housing a set of 22 levers controlling six points and 10 signals. The crossing gates were hand operated by the signalman on duty.

Hendre Siding

1,100yd beyond Dolfechlas Crossing was Hendre siding signalbox on the up side. The line and box were on an embankment at the narrowest point of the valley, with road, rail and river hemmed in by rocky outcrops on either side. The railway crossed over the Mold to Denbigh road twice in quick succession on plate girder bridges. The signalbox controlled access to a Hendre Quarries private siding on the down side and Hendre lime works located on the up side. Hendre signalbox was of standard LNWR design, of composite construction with a frame of 20 levers. Both sidings were worked by trains heading

Star Crossing Halt
This halt opened in 1914 only to be closed again from 1 January 1917 until 1 July 1919 as a temporary wartime measure. The platforms were short, and the down side had no shelter at all, although the stationmaster's house adjoining the site provided some shelter in its booking office. This view shows the waiting shed on the up side, passengers having to cross the line by a barrow crossing alongside a minor road level crossing, which was hand operated. The station remained open until the line closed to all traffic in April 1962. The platforms were removed but the house remains in private ownership. *Bill Rear collection*

towards Mold. Latterly, the box opened only between 1.25pm and 1.45pm on Mondays to Saturdays. A porter signalman from Rhydymwyn attended and switched the box into the circuit.

The summit of the line was reached on the Mold side of Star Crossing halt. It then started to descend at 1 in 80.

Star Crossing Halt

18½ miles from Chester General station was Star Crossing halt, which comprised simple short wooden platforms on both sides. The up side boasted a wooden shelter, whilst the down side had no protection whatsoever. The stationmaster's house, which survives to this day as a private house, stood at the Denbigh end of the down platform ramp. A room in the house served as a booking office and waiting room. The hand-operated gates were normally kept across the tracks.

There were two surfacemen's cottages nearby, on the down side nearer Hendre (both of which are now in private hands and one boasts a miniature steam railway in the garden). The nearest village to Star Crossing is Cilcain, some two miles distant. Despite the sparseness of habitation, the station remained open until the line closed in 1962.

Nannerch

The station was about ½ mile from Nannerch village, where the line levelled out from a falling gradient of 1 in 80, resuming at 1 in 73 after the station.

The station approach was off the Mold to Denbigh road just beyond a road bridge that passed over the line, between an avenue of mature trees creating an idyllic setting which epitomised the rural branch railway station. The main station building was on the up side and included the stationmaster's house. The down platform had a very basic shelter open to the elements and was devoid of comfort. Passengers crossed the line on a barrow crossing off the ramp at the Caerwys end of the platforms. A short trailing siding off the up line led to a cattle dock controlled by a two-lever ground frame. Four points and eight signals were controlled from an LNWR-design 'K1'-type eight-lever open frame which stood on the up platform.

There was a small yard with a siding off the up line, access to the up line being via a trailing point, together with a wooden store shed at the Mold end.

After closure and removal of the tracks, the station building was converted into a delightful private house but, sad to say, shortly after the conversion was completed, it was compulsorily purchased and demolished by the

Nannerch

An idyllic view which, in the author's opinion, typifies the rural LMS branch line station. The station buildings were similar in design to others on the line. The small goods yard stood beyond the platforms on the Chester side of the line. A solitary wagon stands in the coal siding, awaiting uplifting by the daily pick-up goods. A small office is situated at the entrance to the yard. The approach was along a private road flanked by mature trees. Sadly, the station building and site were cleared to make way for road improvements. Today, only some of the trees stand in silence to remind us of what was once a private road. *Bill Rear collection*

Nannerch

Another view of Nannerch station, now long gone, swept away for the all-conquering motor vehicle in the name of progress. The station had an air of timelessness about it but appearances were deceptive. After the tracks were removed, the building and yard were purchased and the building was converted to a delightful dwelling. After 18 months the house was compulsorily purchased and demolished in a glut of road improvements. On still summer evenings, though, one can almost hear the hoot of a Stanier 2-6-4T as it whistles up a warning to the staff of the approaching train. In the summer evening twilight the station had a magical air about it as oil lamps flickered while the last train of the day was awaited. *Bill Rear collection*

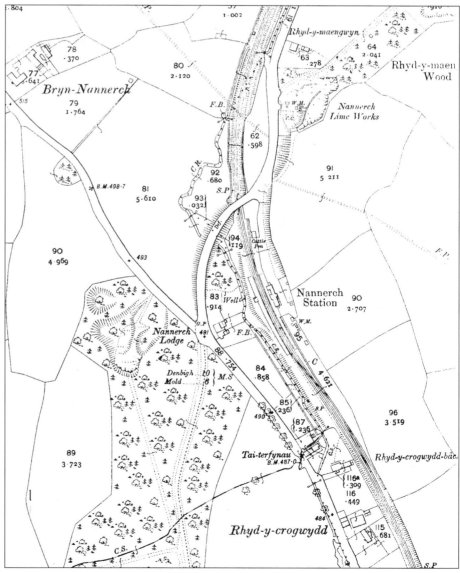

1914-18 Ordnance Survey map showing Nannerch station layout. *Crown Copyright*

Council, as was the road overbridge, to make way for a road widening scheme. Only the remnants of the wooden shed and half the avenue of mature trees remain to this day.

About ½ mile from the station, heading towards Denbigh, a public footpath crossed the line near the Rising Sun pub. In the last weeks of service a fatal accident occurred here when a young wife was knocked down and killed by a passenger train as she crossed the tracks on her way to meet her husband.

Caerwys

The line kept to the Wheeler valley floor for most of the way, the gradient varying from 1 in 73 to 114 falling for the next eight miles, and headed northwest until it reached Caerwys station, 23 miles from Chester. True to form, Caerwys village was about a mile from the railway. There were houses around the station and this settlement is known as 'Afonwen'.

The station was one of the busiest on the line. It consisted of platforms on the up and down sides. The station forecourt and main buildings were on the up side, similar in design to those at Nannerch and Bodfari. The down platform had a rudimentary shelter. Passengers crossed the tracks on the barrow crossing located at the Mold end of the platforms.

An eight-lever open frame on the platform to the standard LNWR design controlled four points and eight signals. There was a siding on the up side behind the up side platform with another connection off the down side to a dock landing, controlled from the station frame. The local sawmill operated in the station yard, as it still does, and used this siding to load timber. Another siding was located on the down side at the Mold end, operated by the down siding frame controlled by Annett's key. The main goods

yard was on the up side at the Mold end and was controlled from the yard frame. A trailing connection led to a single road through the goods shed before terminating at stops by the platform ramp. A second siding was used for coal traffic, with a third line leading to two private sidings, serving a cement shed owned by British Portland Cement Manufacturers Ltd.

There was always substantial freight traffic despatched from here, mainly timber. A large goods shed stood on the down side at the Mold end of the platform. After closure, the yard was expanded as the timber store. The station building became the timber firm's offices, and is still used for this purpose.

Bodfari

Bodfari, 25½ miles from Chester, opened to traffic from 12 September 1869. The line ran into the station under the Mold to Denbigh road bridge (since demolished). The main building was on the up side platform and the structure survives to this day as a private house. It has not lost its character and is in very good condition.

The station building, which included the stationmaster's house, was of similar style and construction to those at Caerwys and Nannerch. The down platform had the usual basic shelter. There was no footbridge and passengers travelling to Denbigh crossed the line after calling at the booking office via the road overbridge and down a long footpath.

An LNWR standard design open frame located on the up platform between the station building and the bridge abutments controlled three points and six signals.

A small goods yard was situated on the up side at the foot of the climb to Blue Hand bridge. The yard, which had two sidings and held 21 wagons, included a weighbridge and an office, a coal merchant's office and a small yard crane. At one time a private siding left the goods yard through gates and across a minor road to the village, to a quarry owned by the Partington Iron & Steel Co Ltd.

Immediately on leaving the station in the Denbigh direction, the line commenced a climb of 1½ miles. Passing over an elegant three-arch stone viaduct spanning Afon

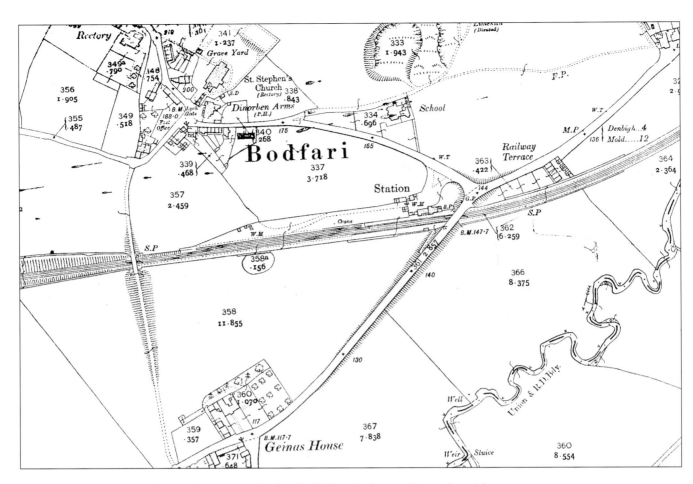

1914-18 Ordnance Survey map showing Bodfari station layout. *Crown Copyright*

Bodfari
A Stanier 2-6-4T with a three-coach local from Denbigh to Mold and Chester descends the 1 in 96 bank from Blue Hand bridge to Bodfari in the spring of 1961. The train is about to pass over an elegant stone viaduct crossing the Afon Clywedog. Today, the upper section of the embankment is covered in coniferous trees which conceal the trackbed. The viaduct is visible briefly from the Denbigh to Mold road. *Norman Jones*

Clywedog, it continued up to Blue Hand bridge, which carried the St Asaph to Bodfari road over the line. Beyond the bridge the line levelled off before descending for a mile towards Denbigh, then climbed at 1 in 96 to the junction with the Vale of Clwyd line. The section from Bodfari was double track until 28 April 1957 when the down line from Bodfari to Mold & Denbigh Junction box was lifted. The layout at the junction was modified to two single lines running parallel as far as the station throat where a new signalbox controlled all Denbigh station movements. When Denbigh station finally closed, the station building was demolished and a Kwik Save supermarket now stands on the site.

The line had an uneventful life, never achieving its full potential. After the passenger traffic ceased on 30 April 1962, the tracks were lifted between Denbigh and Dolfechlas signalbox and the remaining double track was singled from Dolfechlas to Penyffordd where the spur connecting the line with the Wrexham Central to Bidston line came into regular use. The track from Hope Junction to Mold Junction was subsequently lifted. Some traffic to Mold persisted but finally the last freight train ran on 15 March 1983. The track was lifted back to the Padeswood cement works siding in 1985, which remains connected to this day, although little used.

Bodfari
This station building still survives in private hands, largely unchanged, although the road bridge from which this photograph was taken has been demolished and the Mold to Denbigh road lowered. The main buildings were on the up side. At one time the track was double from here to Mold & Denbigh Junction signalbox, but in 1957 this section was singled, the down line being taken out and single-line working with miniature train staff equipment instituted. In the distance, beyond an overbridge, the track commences to climb up a steep bank to Blue Hand bridge. The small goods yard lay between the platform ramp and the bridge on the up side. At one time a private siding took off from the yard to the Partington Iron & Steel Co's quarry, but the track was removed some time after 1951 and the only survivor of that siding is the fencing in which the small building stands. *Bill Rear collection*

Blue Hand Bridge, Bodfari
The climb out of Bodfari to Denbigh was up a steep 1 in 96 climb almost immediately after leaving the station. The severity of the climb is accentuated by the straight line of track which extended for nearly a mile. Ivatt Class 2MT 2-6-0 No 46423, seen here with a three-coach local from Chester to Denbigh, nears the top of the bank with steam to spare. This engine was a resident of Rhyl (6K) shed from 28 April 1956 until transferred away to Springs Branch on 22 March 1958. In 1957 the down line between Bodfari and Mold & Denbigh Junction was taken out of use and single-line working instituted. *Bill Rear*

Train Services

Chester to Mold
Mold to Mold & Denbigh Junction
The Ffrith Branch
Mold to Brymbo

The working timetable dated August 1862 shows passenger and coal traffic between Chester and Mold listed separately. Passenger trains ran daily in each direction, leaving Mold at 8am, 11am, 4.30pm and 7.15pm, taking 40 minutes for the journey and calling at Llong, Padeswood, Hope, Broughton Hall and Chester. Departures from Chester were at 9.30am, 2.30pm, 5.40pm and 8.15pm. A pick-up goods train left Chester at 10.40am daily, arriving at Mold at 11.31am. It returned from Mold at 1.15pm and arrived back in Chester at 2.20pm. On Sundays there were two passenger trains in each direction, departing Mold at 8.50am and 6.15pm, and Chester at 9.45am and 7.20pm. Passenger services were worked from Mold where the locomotive depot was situated.

Seven coal trains in each direction are shown working between Chester and Padeswood, with another two coal trains each way to and from Broncoed colliery at Mold. Four of the trains started from or finished at Mold Junction, where there were extensive siding facilities. There never were any Sunday freight trains over the branch.

Until Mold Junction locomotive depot opened on 1 October 1890, engines worked to and from Chester shed to take up, and on finishing their rostered work. There was limited local passenger work based at Mold Junction, principally covering the service between Mold and Brymbo through Coed Talon.

When the Mold & Denbigh Junction Railway was opened, the timetable structure was recast; Mold shed was closed and the work transferred to Denbigh or Chester. The locomotive shed was converted into a warehouse which was demolished after closure in the 1970s.

No passenger trains worked over the Padeswood Junction to Coed Talon line.

By July 1904 all the branch lines were operational. There were seven passenger trains daily in each direction but only six SO (Saturdays Only). There was one working SX (Saturdays Excepted) and two SO between Mold and Denbigh; one passenger SX and two SO between Mold and Chester. Most of the down freight workings were shown as 'conditional' with four trains running from Mold Junction to Denbigh, the remaining workings terminating at Mold. The up freight workings were similar.

Two goods trains each way were shown working over the Padeswood, Coppa and Coed Talon branches for the same period, although the timings of the up trains varied between weekdays and Saturdays. On the Mold, Coed Talon & Brymbo branch there were four passenger trains each way daily, and an extra train each way on Wednesday and Saturday evenings.

By July 1919 the passenger service over the line remained largely unchanged, with seven trains each way between Chester and Denbigh and return. A 'motor train' ran twice daily between Denbigh and Mold, the listed freight workings were fewer, and the 'conditional' prefix had been removed from most of them. One ordinary goods and one 'fast goods' worked through from Mold Junction to Denbigh. There were two freight workings to Coed Talon daily. The early morning empties trip worked first to Mold where it reversed and proceeded along the branch from Tryddyn Junction; the second train worked via Padeswood Junction and the Coppa line.

A goods train left Denbigh at 1pm and shunted all sidings and stations to Nannerch, then the Ruby brickworks if required. It then called at Rhydymwyn and Mold, where it waited 50 minutes before working forward to Padeswood to pick up, then non-stop to Mold Junction. On the Brymbo branch, there were five passenger trains daily each way between Mold and Brymbo and return. An interesting feature at this time was the daily working of a GWR light engine which came off Wrexham Croes Newydd shed at 3.50am and arrived at Mold at 4.17am to work the early morning train for workmen to Brymbo at 4.32am. It repeated the working in reverse in the afternoon, departing Brymbo with the workmen's train at 3.15pm SX (3.10pm

SO), arriving at Mold at 3.45pm (3.36pm SO). The locomotive then worked back LE (light engine) at 4.8pm to Brymbo, being due there at 4.33pm. There were no through freight or mineral workings.

On the Padeswood, Coppa and Coed Talon branch, by 1919 traffic had dwindled to one train each way daily, departing Mold Junction at 11.40am, and reaching Coed Talon at 1.30pm, after a wait of 45 minutes at Coppa. It then worked a short trip back to Coppa at 2.40pm, returning to Coed Talon after 15 minutes for traffic purposes. It then departed Coed Talon at 3.30pm for Mold Junction, pausing for 10 minutes at Coppa to uplift any wagons, and another 10 minutes at Padeswood, before working through to Mold Junction with no booked stop en route.

The first summer season under LMS control in 1923 showed an increase in the service, with 11 trains each way between Chester and Denbigh, one between Chester and Mold and three between Denbigh and Mold, with some of the workings extended to and from Ruthin or Corwen. A 'motor' train worked from Denbigh, on the 8.7am to Mold, returning at 9am, then the 9.55am to Chester and the 11.55am return. Next it worked the 2.7pm and 5.15pm to Mold, returning from there at 4.7pm and 6.15pm.

The period of the General Strike in 1926 saw the service drastically curtailed to five trains each way between

Denbigh
An unidentified Riddles Class 2MT 2-6-0 in the '78xxx' series pulls away from Denbigh on 25 November 1961 with a train for Mold and Chester. It is possible that the locomotive was No 78032 of Chester shed as this working was attached to Chester (6A) shed at this time. The coal siding was still in use at the time of the photograph. Beyond the wagon can be seen the yard crane and in the distance the modern outline of Denbigh two-road locomotive shed, out of use since 1955, in front of which was a rectangular water tower. The locomotive yard was, nevertheless, still in use for short-stay visits by locomotives needing to clean fires and, until just before closure, to access the 50ft turntable that was located behind the shed. A brake van stands on the short siding that was all that remained of the siding to Graig quarry.
Norman Jones

RUTHIN TO CHESTER — WEEKDAYS (UP)

	Mileage																					
					B	B	B	B	C	B	B	B	G	C	C	B	B	B	G	B	B
	M C	M C						ECS					LE	ECS	Pch					LE	
					am	am	am	am	am	am	am	am	am	am	am	PM	am	PM	PM	PM	PM PM
0 0		0 0	RUTHIN ... dep				6 45		7 50	8 46	9 32					11 41					1 20
1 39			Rhewl ...				6 49		7 54	8 50						11 45					1 24
6 52		0 0	DENBIGH ... arr				6 59		8 4	9 2	9 42					11 57					1 36
			...dep	5 58	6 15	7 15		8 11		9 5	9 48		11 40			12 8	12 4	12 13		12 46
7 58	1 6	Denbigh Jn.	6 1	6 18	7 18		8 14		9 8	9 51		11 43			12 11	12 7	12 16		12 49
	2 60	Trefnant ... arr	6 5						9X12						12 11	12 16	12 20		
	5 19	St. Asaph ... arr	6 8						9 13						12 12	12 21			
		...dep	6 11						9 18						12 17	12 26			
	7 60	Rhuddlan ... arr	6 12						9 19						12 18	12 27			
	10 6	Foryd Jn.	6 17						9a24						12a23	12a32			
	11 8	RHYL ... arr	6 21						9 28						12Y27	12 42			
			6 23						9‡30						12Y29	12 44			
10 32		Bodfari ... dep	6 23		7 23		8 19		9 56					12 16		12a54
12 78		Caerwys	6 30		7 30		8 26	10 3						12 23		1a 1
16 27		Nannerch	6 38		7 38		8 34	10 11						12 31		1 9
17 22		Star Crossing	6 42	7.10 am			8 38	10a15								1a13
19 50		Rhydymwyn	6 48		7c45		8a43	10a20					12c38				1a18
22 52		MOLD ... arr	6 53		7 50		8 48	10 25			12‡10		12 43				1 23
		...dep			7‡15	7 53	8 50	10 27					12 47	12 51			1 26
24 26		Llong			7 19	7 57	8 54	10 31					12 51				1 30
25 15		Padeswood and Buckley		7 22	8a 0	8a57		10a34					12a54				1a33
26 49		Hope Low Level		7 29				10 38					12b59				1 37
27 0		Hope and Penyffordd		7 31	8a 5	9a 2		10 40					1 1				1 39
29 56		Kinnerton		7 36	8 10	9 7		10 45					1 6				1 44
31 25		Broughton and Bretton		7c41	8c15	8c55	9a11	10a49					1a10				1a48
32 30		Mold Jn. No. 2						10 53		11‡p6	12p38		1c15		1‖p20		1c53
32 52		Saltney Ferry		7 45	8a19	9e17		10X54	11X8		12X40		1X16		1X25		1X54
32 61		Mold Jn. No. 1		7X46	8X20	9X19		SL	SL		SL		SL		SL		SL
				SL	SL	SL										
34 12		Saltney Jn.		7 48	8 25	8 51	9 21	10 56	11 11		12 42		1 18		1 27		1 56
35 79		CHESTER ... arr		7 52	8 29	8‡56	9 25	11‡ 0	11‖16		12p46		1 22		1‖32		2 0

RUTHIN TO CHESTER — WEEKDAYS (UP) continued

	B	B	B	B	G	B	B	B	B	B	B	B	G	B	G	B	G	G
	12.55 pm from Mold				LE									LE		LE	LE	LE
	SO PM		PM	SX PM	SX PM	FO PM	FSX PM	SO PM	SO PM	SO PM	SX PM	SX PM	SX PM	SO PM	SO PM	SO PM	SO PM	SO PM
RUTHIN ... dep			3 0						4 30	5 31	5 35			7 25		9 10	10‖30
Rhewl			3 4						4 34	5 35	5 35			7 29		9 14	
DENBIGH ... arr			3 14						4 44	5 45	5 45			7 39		9 24	10‖43
Denbigh Jn. ...dep	1 42		3 22	3 32	4 15			4 50	4 55	5 50	5 50	5 55	6‖25	7 43	7 50	8‖10	
Trefnant ... arr	1 45		3 25		4 18			4 53	4 58	5 53	5 53	5 58	6 28	7 46	7 53	8 13	
	1X49			3 39				4 57		5 57		6 2			7 57		
St. Asaph ... arr	1 50			3 40				4 58		5 58		6 3			7 58		
	1X55			3 45				5 4		6 4		6 8			8X3		
Rhuddlan ...	1 56			3 46				5 4		6 4		6 9			8 4		
	2a 1			3aX51				5a 9		6a 9		6a14			8a 9		
Foryd Jn.	2 6			3 55				5 17		6 13		6 18			8 13		
RHYL ... arr	2 10			3 57				5‡20	5a 3	6 15	5a58	6 20			8 15		
Bodfari ... dep			3a30	4a23					5a10		6a 5			7a51		
Caerwys			3a37	4a30					5 18		6 13			7a58		
Nannerch			3 45	4 38							8				
Star Crossing			3 49					5 24 pm			8 10				
Rhydymwyn			3a54	4c46					5c26		6a20			8a15		
MOLD ... arr			3 59	4 51					5 31		6 25			8 20		
Llong ... dep			4 2						5 37		6 28		6 56	8 24		8 45
Padeswood and Buckley			4 6						5 41		6 32		6 28	8 28		
Hope Low Level			4a 9						5a44		6a35			8a31		
Hope and Penyffordd			4 13						5 47		6 39			8 37		
Kinnerton			4 15						5 49		6 41			8 42		
Broughton and Bretton			4 20				5 30	5 39	5 54		6 46			8a46		
Mold Jn. No. 2			4a24		4p‖32				5a58		6a50		8p‖10			9‖p36
Saltney Ferry			4a28				5a34	5a43		6c 3		6c55		8c51		
Mold Jn. No. 1			4X29		4X35		5X35	5X44		6X 5		6X56		8X13	8X52	9X10	9X38
			SL		SL		SL	SL		SL		SL		SL	SL	SL	SL
Saltney Jn.			4 31		4 37		5 37	5 46		6 7		6 58		8 15	8 54	9 13	9 41
CHESTER ... arr			4 35		4‖41		5 41	5 50		6 11		7 2		8‖20	8 58	9‖18	9‖46

Chester and Denbigh. The Brymbo branch was reduced to three trains daily, with four trains in the reverse direction. Passenger services reverted to their pre-strike situation after the strike was called off, but freight traffic remained subdued.

By May 1934 the passenger service frequency had increased to 13 trains daily (SX) between Chester and Denbigh, with an additional late night train on Saturdays. The Brymbo branch had five return journeys on weekdays and six on Saturdays. Freight services remained virtually unaltered.

As Britain emerged from the Depression, the services increased again and by the summer of 1939 reached a peak frequency. On Saturdays there were 15 trains each way, and there were five through trains each way on Sundays. On the Brymbo branch the weekday frequency remained at five trains each way, with eight on Saturdays. Freight traffic had increased slightly and the same period showed three

DOWN

Mileage M	C	M	C			B	B	B		B (SX)	B (SX)	B	B (SX)	B (SX)	G (L E)		B (SO)	B (SO)	B (TTh FO)	C (SO, To Rhyl)	B (ThSO, 11.20 am Pcls from Grange Lane)
						am	am	am		am			am				am	PM	am	PM	PM
0	0			CHESTER	dep	5 40				7 20	7 40	9 0	9‖54				10 25		11V48	12 45	
1	67			Saltney Jn.		SL				SL	SL	SL					SL		SL	SL	
3	18			Mold Jn. No. 1		5 44				7 24	7 46	9 4	9 58				10 29		11 53	12 49	
3	27			Saltney Ferry		5 46				7 26	7 47	9 7	10 0				10 31		11 55	12 51	
3	49			Mold Jn. No. 2		5b48				7b28							10 32			12 52	
4	54			Broughton and Bretton		5a52				7c33	7 50	9a11	10‖pl				10a36		11p58	12a56	
6	23			Kinnerton						7a38		9a16					10a41			1a 1	
8	79			Hope and Penyffordd						7c49		9b27					10b52			1b12	
9	30			Hope Low Level		6j11				7c53		9a30					10a55			1a15	
10	64			Padeswood and Buckley						7a56		9a33					10a58			1a18	
11	53			Llong						8c 0		9a36					11a 1			1a21	
13	27			MOLD	arr	6 20				8 4		9 39					11 5			1 25	
16	29				dep	6 35				8 10		9 42					11 7	12 55		1 28	
18	57			Rhydymwyn		6j46				8b17		9b49					11b14	1b 2		1b35	
19	52			Star Crossing													11 21	1 9			
23	1			Nannerch						8 25		9b58					11a25	1a13		1a46	
25	47			Caerwys						8a32		10a 5					11a32	1a20		1a53	
				Bodfari	arr	7 4				8 36		10 9					11 36	1 24		1 57	
					dep	7 6				8 37		10 10					11 37	1 25		1 58	
		0	0	RHYL	dep	5 20 SL				7 40 SL	8 25 SL						11 45 SL				
		1	2	Foryd Jn.		5 23				7 43	8 28						11 48				
		3	28	Rhuddlan		5c29				7a48	8a33						11a53				
		5	69	St. Asaph	arr	5 34				7 53	8 38						11 58				
					dep	5 36				7 54	8 39						12 0				
		8	28	Trefnant	arr	5 41				7 59	8 44						12 5				
					dep	5 42				8 0	8 45						12 8				
28	21	10	2	Denbigh Jn.		5 46	7 10	8 4		8 41	8 49		10 14				11 41	12 12	1 29		2 2
29	27	11	8	DENBIGH	arr	5 49	7 13	8 7		8 44	8 52		10 17				11 44	12 15	1 32		2 5
34	40				dep	6 5	7 25			9 5			10 45				12 5				2 10
35	79			Rhewl		6 16	7 36			9 16			10 56				12 16				2-21
				RUTHIN	arr	6 19	7 39			9 19			10 59				12 19				2 24

WEEKDAYS   CHESTER TO RUTHIN

DOWN

		B (SX)	B (SO)	B (SO)	B (SX)	B (SX)	B (SX)	B (SO)	C (ECS)	B (SX)	B	B	B (SO)	B	B (SO)	B	B
		PM	PM	PM	PM	PM	PM	PM	PM	PM		PM	PM		PM	PM	PM
CHESTER	dep	1 30				3 35		4 25	5†0	5 42		6 20		8 25		9 35	
Saltney Jn.		SL				SL		SL	SL	SL		SL		SL		SL	
Mold Jn. No. 1		1 34				3 39		4 29	5 4	5 46		6 24		8 29		9 39	
Saltney Ferry		1 36				3 41		4 31	5 6	5 48		6 26		8 31		9 41	
Mold Jn. No. 2		1 37				3 42		4 32		5b50		6b28		8b33		9b43	
Broughton and Bretton		1a41				3a46		4a36	5 11	5a54		6a32		8a37		9a47	
Kinnerton		1a46				3a51		4a41		5a59		6a37		8a42		9a52	
Hope and Penyffordd		1b57				4b 2		4b52		6 9		6d49		8b53		10b 3	
Hope Low Level		2a 0						4a55		6a12		6a52					
Padeswood and Buckley		2a 3				4a 6		4a58		6a15		6a55		8 57		10 7	
Llong		2a 6				4a 9		5a 1		6a18		6a58					
MOLD	arr	2 10				4 13		5 5		6 22		7 2		9 4		10 14	
Rhydymwyn	dep	2 14				4 15	5 5	5 9		6 25		7 6		9 6		10 17	
Star Crossing		2a21				4a22	5a12	5a16		6a32		7a13		9a13		10a24	
Nannerch		2 28				4 29	5 19	5 23		6 39				9D20			
Caerwys		2 32				4 33	5 23	5 27		6 43		7 21		9 24		10 32	
Bodfari		2 39				4 40	5 30	5 34		6 50		7a28		9 31		10 39	
	arr	2 43				4 44	5 35	5 38		6 54		7 32		9 35		10 43	
	dep	2 44				4 45	5 36	5 39		6 55		7 36		9 36		10 45	
RHYL	dep		4 12	4 20								7 10 SL		9 25 SL		10 30 SL	
Foryd Jn.			4 15	4 23								7 13		9 28		10 33	
Rhuddlan			4aX20	4aX28								7a18		9a33		10a38	
St. Asaph	arr		4 25	4 33								7 23		9 38		10 43	
	dep		4 26	4 34								7 24		9 39		10 44	
Trefnant	arr		4 31	4 39								7 29		9 44		10 49	
	dep		4 32	4 40								7 30		9 45		10 51	
Denbigh Jn.		2 48	4 36	4 44		4 49	5 40	5 43		6 59		7 34	7 40	9 49		10 55	
DENBIGH	arr	2 51	4 39	4 47		4 52	5 43	5 46		7 2		7 37	7 45	9 43	9 52	10 52	10 58
RUTHIN	dep		4 0			5 0				7 5		7 54		10 5			
Rhewl			4 11			5 11				7 16		8 5		10 16			
RUTHIN	arr		4 14			5 14				7 19		8 8		10 19			

Extracts from summer 1955 BR passenger timetable for the Chester to Ruthin line.

through freight workings between Mold Junction and Denbigh, and two in the reverse direction.

The outbreak of World War 2 saw a drastic reduction in passenger services. From 11 September 1939 the service was cut back to six trains each way between Chester and Denbigh, with seven on Saturdays. There was one train each day between Chester and Mold and return. The Brymbo branch was reduced to three trains each way. By 28 October 1940 this had eased slightly, with seven trains each way weekdays and 10 on Saturdays. The Chester to Mold and return working had gone, and the Brymbo branch was reduced to two trains each way. By 1943 the weekday frequency had increased

Denbigh
Ex-Midland Railway Class 3F 0-6-0 No 43618, a Johnson design rebuilt by Fowler, is seen here shunting the goods shed road with vans. This engine was transferred to Rhyl from Barrow in April 1958 and was withdrawn from service in March 1962. The locomotive, despite its age, was considered a good steamer and strong puller by Rhyl men, and was preferred to the allegedly stronger Fowler Class 4F. The engine is seen here working Rhyl Turn 60 which had worked light engine off Rhyl shed at 6am and, on arrival at Denbigh, shunted the yard until 8.10am, when it worked a Class K trip to Ruthin. After shunting there from 8.30am until 9am, it worked the daily freight to Corwen and return, arriving back at 2.15pm. It next shunted the goods yard from 3.40pm until 6pm, when it returned, coupled to another engine, to Rhyl shed and disposal. *Norman Jones*

to eight trains each way, but there was no change on the Brymbo branch.

The summer of 1946 period saw an increase in journeys along the line. There were eight trains daily (Mondays to Fridays) in the down direction between Chester, Mold and Denbigh, three being extended to Corwen, with two short workings between Chester and Broughton & Bretton serving the aircraft factory, one short empty stock working between Mold and Rhydymwyn for the MoD factory workers at 5pm, with another at 5.20pm between Mold and Denbigh. On the Mold to Brymbo line there were only two passenger trains each way, catering for pupils who attended Mold Grammar School. In the up direction the pattern was broadly similar. On Saturdays there were 10 trains between Chester, Mold and Denbigh.

The first summer after nationalisation in 1948 saw 11 passenger trains between Chester and Denbigh each weekday, but only nine in the reverse direction. The Brymbo branch service survived with two trains each way, Mondays to Fridays, purely for schoolchildren. Two freight trains ran each way between Mold Junction and Denbigh,

with an additional two return workings between Mold Junction and Mold. There was one freight working along the Brymbo branch.

Passenger traffic between Mold and Brymbo ceased in March 1950. Services between Ruthin and Corwen ended on 23 January 1953 but some Chester to Denbigh trains were then extended to Ruthin. The summer 1954 working timetable showed 10 trains from Chester to Denbigh or Ruthin, and one between Mold and Denbigh during the week. There was one working from Mold to Rhyl via Denbigh on Saturdays. In the reverse direction there were nine between Denbigh and Chester, with one working from Denbigh to Mold SX and an ECS (empty carriage stock) working on Saturdays Only to take up the Mold to Rhyl working. Two freight trains ran daily each way between Mold Junction and Denbigh. There were three freight workings between Mold Junction and Mold, one of which worked a trip to Coed Talon and back, whilst a second working ran between Mold and Hendre quarry.

The summer service for 1960 saw nine trains daily between Chester and Denbigh or Ruthin, with an extra

Denbigh
The 12.46pm to Chester stands at the through platform with an unidentified BR Standard Class 4MT 4-6-0 at the head of the two-coach train. Interestingly, the leading coach is an ex-LNER Thompson steel-sided non-corridor design. The goods yard is full of stock, giving some indication of the traffic handled. A postman is hidden by the finger post that once indicated the destination of trains. Note the totems on the gas lamp posts, nowadays worth a small fortune. Note, too, the four-arm bracket signal at the platform ramp, only four years old and destined to be removed within a few months. *Bill Rear collection*

working between Mold and Denbigh and return. In the opposite direction there was one train fewer. From 1961 the line was under threat but because an objection to closure was lodged, services continued to operate.

The passenger services finally ceased on Saturday 28 April 1962, although freight continued to be worked to and from Mold. The September 1963 Freight Book shows two trains daily. The summer of 1964 saw the Coed Talon trip omitted; the locomotive remained shunting at Mold. By 1965 these freight workings were omitted from the working timetables. Traffic finally ceased in 1983.

Country Lorry Service

The LMS had its 'Country Lorry' service which operated a collection and delivery service from most of the stations along the line, and this continued after nationalisation. Some of the specialist traffic was hived off to British Road Services. The railway continued to operate its own lorry service, dealing with parcels traffic for several years, until the staffing levels at stations was reduced. It eventually disappeared during the mid-1960s.

Freight Traffic

All but the smallest stations were provided with facilities for handling some types of freight traffic. In the early days, there was considerable coal traffic from the Mold area, but as the pits became worked out the traffic fell away and had all but disappeared at the time of the Grouping. Surviving freight traffic was of a mixed variety, livestock and agricultural produce, with some timber, mineral and domestic coal constituting the principal commodities carried.

The July 1904 working timetable showed paths for 17 mineral or empties trains. By July 1919, freight traffic had dwindled to a shadow of its former self, down to three trains daily during the week and an extra early morning train on Saturdays, mainly due to the drastic reduction of interchange traffic at Hope Junction.

The summer 1939 working timetable showed little change from that of 20 years earlier. Two trains worked between Mold Junction and Denbigh each way each day, and there were five trains each way between Mold Junction and Hope Junction for interchange with the London & North Eastern Railway (LNER ex-GC, WM&CQ) line.

There was little variation after the war. The summer 1949 freight timetable showed two through trains each way between Mold Junction and Denbigh, although the trip from Mold to Caerwys had been cut back to Hendre siding but now ran daily.

By June 1954 the services had modified somewhat. The Brymbo branch had been truncated just beyond Coed Talon. The first train of the day, a through freight or Class H working, reporting number 40, departed Mold Junction at 5.15am, halted briefly at Hope Junction and Mold and then worked through to Denbigh. The crew returned home with the 8.35am Class K working, departing at 8.35am and calling briefly at most yards, reaching Mold Junction at 11.49am.

By June 1957, traffic had dwindled to four trains between Mold Junction and Mold. Two of them worked through to Denbigh and return, in much the same timings as 1954. The second freight train of the day ran to Mold, where it shunted, and worked the Coed Talon trip. The same arrangement for working exchange traffic off the LNER line persisted.

MOLD JUNCTION TO CORWEN		WEEKDAYS					H103		
		H	H	G	G	K	K	K	K
DOWN				5.1 am LE from Saltney	5.55 am LE from Holywell Jn.				6.20 am from Rhyl
		41	40				65	65	37
					MX	SX	SO		
MOLD JUNCTION		am	am	am	am	am	am	am	am
No. 1	1	..	..	5 10	6 23	..	..	..	..
No. 2	2	..	..	5 p12	6 p25	..	..	..	..
No. 3	3	5 15	5 55	..	..	..	..	..	..
Broughton and Bretton arr	4	..	6 0	..	..	..	..	..	..
dep	5	..	6 10	..	..	..	..	..	..
Kinnerton	6	..	..	..	..	..	..	..	..
Kinnerton Siding	7	..	..	..	..	..	..	..	..
Hope and Penyffordd arr	8	..	..	..	..	..	..	..	..
dep	9	..	..	..	..	..	..	..	..
Hope Junction arr	10	5 40	6 29	..	..	..	..	..	..
dep	11	5 45	6 42	After working 3.25 am from Warrington	After working 2.20 am from Wallascote Sidings	..	..	..	..
Padeswood and Buckley arr	12	..	..			..	..	..	..
dep	13	..	..			..	..	..	..
Coed Talon dep	14	..	..			..	..	..	..
Tryddyn Junction	15	..	..			..	..	..	..
MOLD arr	16	5 55	6 57			..	..	..	..
dep	17	6 5	..	..	..	..	..	..	..
Alyn Tin Plate Siding	18	..	..	..	..	..	..	..	..
Rhydymwyn	19	..	..	..	Suspended	Suspended	..	Llanerch Sidings	..
Hendre Siding	20	..	..	..			..		..
Nannerch arr	21	..	..	..			..		..
dep	22	..	..	..			..		..
Caerwys arr	23	..	..	..			..		..
dep	24	..	..	..			..		..
Bodfari arr	25	..	..	..			..		..
dep	26	..	..	..			..		..
Foryd Junction	27	..	..	..	..	..	..	6 26	..
Foryd Pier arr	28	..	..	..	..	..	..		..
Rhuddlan arr	29	..	..	..	..	..	..	6 35	..
dep	30	..	..	..	..	..	..	6 45	..
St. Asaph arr	31	..	..	..	..	..	..	6X55	..
dep	32	..	..	..	..	..	..	8 5	..
Trefnant arr	33	..	..	..	..	..	..	8X15	..
dep	34	..	..	..	..	..	..	8 25	..
Denbigh Junction	35	..	..	..	..	..	..	8 31	..
DENBIGH arr	36	6 45	..	..	..	..	..	8 35	..
dep	37	..	..	..	8 6	8 10	8 10	..	..
Llanrhaiadr	38	..	..	..	..	..	..	..	..
Rhewl arr	39	..	..	..	..	R	..	..	..
dep	40	..	..	..	..	..	..	..	..
Ruthin Line Siding arr	41	..	..	..	..	R	R	..	..
dep	42	..	..	..	..	..	..	..	..
Ruthin arr	43	..	..	..	8 25	8 30	8 30	..	..
dep	44	..	..	..	..	9 0	..	..	..
Eyarth arr	45	..	..	..	..	9 5	..	..	..
dep	46	..	..	..	..	9 15	..	..	..
Nantclwyd arr	47	..	..	..	..	9 25	..	..	..
dep	48	..	..	..	..	9 41	..	..	..
Derwen arr	49	..	..	..	..	9 47	..	..	..
dep	50	..	..	..	..	9 52	..	..	..
Craig Lelo Siding	51	..	..	..	..	R	..	..	..
Gwyddelwern arr	52	..	..	..	..	10 12	..	..	..
dep	53	..	..	..	..	10 32	..	..	..
CORWEN arr	54	..	..	..	..	10 42	..	..	..

Extract from summer 1955 BR freight timetable for the Mold Junction/Foryd Junction to Corwen line.

Ffrith Branch

The Ffrith branch left the Mold Railway main line 71 chains west of Hope Junction on the down side at Padeswood Junction and then proceeded south through Coppa Wood to Pontblyddyn, before curving right for Leeswood and Coed Talon East Junction.

The branch opened on 14 September 1849 and served the Coppa colliery. The line was short, only 2⅜ miles in length on a rising gradient of 1 in 33. It was double track between Ffrith Junction and Coppa.

The working timetable lists the train staff stations as Coppa and Leeswood Crossing. The section of line between Coppa and Coed Talon is marked as 'single line'.

As a freight-only branch, details have had to be extracted from the available working timetables to hand.

For trains heading to Coed Talon, the first provisional stop was at Ratcliffs siding, 220yd from Padeswood Junction. In the 1904 working timetable it was not given a booked time and it has to be presumed that traffic to and from this siding was spasmodic. The siding was still listed in the working timetables for 1919, 1921 and 1922 but not in the LMS working timetable for the summer of 1923 and subsequent issues. It was worked by down direction (Padeswood Junction to Coed Talon) trains only.

The next siding listed was at Alyn Bank siding, also provisional. It is shown in the 1904 working timetable, but is missing from the next available issue to hand, dated 1 July 1919, and subsequent timetables onward. This siding, too, was worked by only down direction trains. Alyn Bank siding was only yards from Coppa.

Coppa itself was ½ mile from Padeswood Junction and an undated but probably 1927, side strip (a scale representation of the line showing gradients and mileages along the length of the line, whether the line is single or double and, in some cases, a station track layout plan) indicates that there were substantial sidings here on either side of the line. It was shown as operational in all editions of the Freight working timetable up to and including the September 1935 book. Interestingly, the branch and the Coppa facilities are listed in the 1 May 1935 publication *Loading of Passenger and Freight Trains*, although by the time the booklet appeared the line had suffered an accident in 1934 and all services had been suspended.

All trains were booked to call at Coppa, and the aforementioned book in the section 'Loading of Mineral Trains' gave the loading for the section between Padeswood Junction and Coppa as 44 wagons in the up direction, 39 in the Down, and between Coppa and Coed Talon as 25 in the up direction and 39 in the down. Between five and eight minutes were booked for trains between Padeswood Junction and Coppa, but only five minutes for the return journey.

Trains departing Coppa for Coed Talon were allowed between eight and 10 minutes for the 1½ miles to Leeswood Crossing, with another two minutes allowed for the ¼ mile to Coed Talon. Up trains were allowed eight minutes between Leeswood Crossing and Coppa. Little is known of Leeswood Crossing other than it was a timing point in the timetable and presumably was included because the crossing keeper needed to know when trains were due.

The main entry in this book on Coed Talon will be found in the Mold to Brymbo chapter, but the station was closed following an accident on 29 July 1934. LMS Standard 0-6-0T No 7374 was working the 4.5pm goods from Coed Talon to Mold Junction which comprised 17 wagons of minerals and two of earthenware drainpipes, together with the brake van, when the third wagon suffered derailment as the train approached the bridge over the Mold to Wrexham road at Pontblyddyn. In an endeavour to straighten out the train, the driver applied steam and passed over the bridge safely, but having done so, discovered that he had only two wagons left attached to the locomotive. All the others, including the brake van, had left the rails and gone down the bank, fortunately without injuries but damaging the road underbridge beyond repair. It transpired that the track had spread. The pile-up was cleared over subsequent weeks by the breakdown train, but it was the last working to use the branch, and track lifting took place in the spring of 1935, although the entire branch was still listed in the Freight working timetable for 30 September 1935, albeit with no traffic booked to pass over the line. The next available issue of the Freight book removed references to Padeswood Junction, Coppa and the branch in its entirety.

For many years traffic over the branch had been steady with three trains of empties worked to Coed Talon, balanced by three trains of minerals (coal) returning to Mold Junction daily. From the terminus at Coed Talon, a private standard gauge line, known as the Nerquis Private Railway, extended to the collieries of the Nerquis Coal and Canal Company.

Traces of the line are now hard to find. Apart from some earthworks where Coppa colliery used to be, there is nothing visible. The embankment where the gradient commenced is still traceable but at Pontblyddyn, where the line crossed the Mold to Wrexham road, the embankment has been recently removed and a housing development now occupies the site. Nearby, a house at Pontblyddyn crossroads has a peculiar low hedge which is trimmed topiarily to read 'PONTBLYDDYN' and is similar to those at Levens Hall near Kendal in Cumbria. It is very attractive and it is the second time the owner of the property has developed this feature. For the first occasion, after 30 years of trimming and clipping, his work was demolished by an out of control lorry that careered down the hill opposite circa 1970. Undeterred, the owner replanted the shrubs and started trimming and clipping all over again. His handiwork is there for all to see. The line continued to climb at the back of this property, and the embankment is now heavily wooded. There are some traces left at Leeswood Crossing and at Coed Talon, but one has to search diligently.

Apart from a photograph in a private collection of Padeswood looking back towards Chester, which shows Padeswood Junction signalbox in the distance, no photographs of sidings on the branch have surfaced.

Extract from July 1919 LNWR timetable for the Padeswood, Coppa and Coed Talon line.

PADESWOOD, COPPA & COED TALON BRANCH.

Train Staff Stations—Coppa and Leeswood Crossing.   Single Line—Coppa to Coed Talon.

		1	2	3	4	5	6 Goods 11.40 a.m. from Mold Junction	7 Mineral For Mold Jct.			8	9	10 Engine and Van.	11 Mineral to Mold Jct.	12
Miles.	WEEK DAYS. Down Trains.								Miles.	WEEK DAYS. Up Trains.					
							p.m.	p.m.					p.m.	p.m	
...	Padeswood Jc. dep.	...	...	...	...	...	12 30	...	—	Coed Talon — dep.	...	...	2 40	3 30	...
⅛	Ratcliffs Siding.	...	...	...	...	...	...	...	—	Leeswood Crossing	...	...	...	3§32	...
½	Coppa { arr.	...	...	...	...	...	12 35	...	1¾	Coppa — { arr	...	...	2 50	3 40	...
	{ dep.	...	...	...	...	...	1 20	3 5		{ dep	...	...		3 50	
—	Leeswood Crossing arr.	...	...	...	...	...	...	...	2¾	Padeswood Junct.	...	...	...	...	...
2¼	Coed Talon arr.	...	...	...	...	...	1 30	3 15	—	Padeswood & Buckley arr.	...	...	...	3 55	...

4

Mold to Brymbo

History

The Mold to Brymbo line had its origins in 1849 when the Ffrith branch was opened from Padeswood Junction to Coed Talon, where it joined a private railway to Nerquis colliery (see previous chapter). In 1865 the Wrexham & Minera Railway was authorised to construct a 2¾-mile extension to its line from its line to Coed Talon. Both lines were built primarily for freight. In 1866 the extension became the LNWR and GWR 'Wrexham & Minera Joint Railway' (W&MJR) which opened to freight on 27 January 1872. The gradients on the original Ffrith branch were fearsome, and to avoid using this line, a new line 4½ miles long was authorised by an LNWR Act of 1866 from Tryddyn Junction near Mold, over part of the Nerquis Railway, and opened to Oak Pits colliery in 1869 and to a triangular junction at Coed Talon in 1870. A Mold to Coed Talon passenger service was commenced in 1892 which was extended over the W&MJR to Brymbo in May 1898.

Route Description

The Mold to Brymbo branch was single track. The train staff sections were Tryddyn Junction to Coed Talon, and Coed Talon to Brymbo (GWR). The timetables indicate that the 'Down' direction was from Mold to Brymbo whilst, confusingly, the side strip for 1927 indicated that it was the opposite direction.

Tryddyn Junction

The branch left the main line in a trailing direction at Tryddyn Junction, ⅜ mile from Mold, and proceeded due south on a rising gradient for approximately two miles, first on an embankment and subsequently in a cutting. After 1½ miles the gradient eased from 1 in 70 to 1 in 200 for half a mile, during which it crossed the River Terrig on a one-arch brick-built bridge.

Nerquis Siding

Nerquis siding was 1¾ miles from Mold. Details of this siding are sparse, the only reference being an entry in the 1904 working timetable. The 1927 side strip suggests that a siding facing Tryddyn Junction on the up side was still extant then. The summit of the branch was reached at Milepost 3 and then it descended in a southeasterly direction at 1 in 130 to Coed Talon station.

Plas ym Mhowys Siding

Plas ym Mhowys siding was located 3½ miles from Mold on the up side. This must have been installed after 1904 and was included in the timetables from 1919, and was shown on the side strip.

Celyn Wood Siding

Another siding was listed in 1904. This was Celyn Wood siding, 3¾ miles from Mold on the down side, but it had been removed from later issues of the timetable.

Cae Blyddyn Siding

At 4 miles from Mold came Cae Blyddyn siding on the up side, shown in the 1904 working timetable but removed from the later editions, although still shown on the side strip.

At this point the branch was utilising the formation of the Nerquis Private Railway, and it continued to Coed Talon West Junction where it joined the Ffrith branch.

Alongside the West Junction to East Junction line was Leeswood sidings, which held 141 wagons.

Coed Talon

The station was 4⅝ miles from Mold and was a train staff token station. The station's short single platform was on the up side. The station buildings were two storey and incorporated the stationmaster's house, which still stands,

Mold, Tryddyn Junction
The joint GWR/LNWR line from Mold to Coed Talon and Brymbo started 525yd from Mold station. It took off at the down side and at one time the connection was a double-junction formation. It was singled at some unspecified date, probably after passenger services ceased in 1950. The box also controlled the hand-operated level crossing gates and remained open to traffic until 3 March 1965. Despite its rickety appearance, the box was watertight and snug. The 'Hours of Opening of Signalboxes' booklet for Crewe & North dated 11 September 1961 shows the box was open from 6am until 9.30pm daily (not Sundays). *Bill Rear collection*

Coed Talon
This small station was at one time a junction. At the station ramp the freight-only line from Padeswood, known as the 'Ffrith Branch', met and connected with the line from Mold Tryddyn Junction to Brymbo. The station was well patronised until shortly before the outbreak of World War 2, when buses working a circular route from Mold abstracted most of the local traffic. The passenger service survived until 1950, depending mostly on children travelling to and from Mold. The stationmaster's house stands alongside the level crossing, whilst the station building faces the platform. The goods yard was always busy and the truncated line from Mold remained in use until 1965. *Bill Rear collection*

and the booking office. There were a couple of LNWR-design wooden 'portable'-type buildings on the platform. The line from Padeswood Junction met the line from Mold at the platform ramp. Behind the passenger platform was the goods yard in which a siding ran alongside a landing stage which contained a small warehouse and a yard crane. A second siding ran into the yard, used as a coal siding. A weigh machine and office completed the contents of this yard.

At one time there was a small signal cabin here. The 1910 list gives the dimensions of the box as 8ft x 8ft and it housed a frame which controlled 10 points and signals. Presumably, it must also have housed the single-line staff token equipment. This was removed at an unspecified date and latterly the token equipment was kept in the station office.

Immediately beyond the station was a hand-operated level crossing followed by Stuart Colin's siding, a trailing connection on the up side, latterly called 'Welsh Coal & Cannel Co', and also serving 'Alyn Brick and Terracotta Works' which used the line's facilities until the branch finally closed.

When the line to Brymbo was truncated, a couple of track panels beyond the siding entrance were left, but the remaining track was lifted for a distance of 2¾ miles, as far as Bwlchgwyn siding.

Four hundred yards after the Alyn Brick and Terracotta Works sidings on the main line, another siding took off on

the up side, serving Wood Pit colliery. It was not listed in the timetables and so, presumably, it was covered by trip workings from Coed Talon.

The line then continued towards Brymbo. It formed an end-on junction, known as the LNWR & GWR Wrexham & Minera Extension Joint Railway Junction at 1 mile 15 chains from Coed Talon. At 5¼ miles from Mold came a siding on the down side known as Cefn-y-Coed. It is not known whether this siding served a colliery or a works. It was still included in the Freight working timetable for summer 1939 but presumably was closed during World War 2 and was not listed in the summer 1947 issue.

Llanfynydd

This station was 6½ miles from Mold and consisted of a small single wooden platform on the up side with a couple of wooden huts which served as a booking office and a waiting shelter. A trailing siding ran behind the platform. The station was not a block post.

Between Llanfynydd and Ffrith were two colliery sidings. Crown Dale siding was 6¾ miles from Mold on the down side; ¼ mile further on was Trimley Hall siding, again on the down side. It is understood that both sidings served collieries. Both were shown as operational in the October 1947 freight timetable.

Ffrith

Ffrith station was 7¼ miles from Mold and was located near

Llanfynydd

One of the two intermediate stations between Coed Talon and Brymbo, facilities at Llanfynydd were somewhat basic. This poor photograph shows the station about 1920, although the date might be several years out. There was a small siding behind the timber passenger platform. The station was some distance from the village and traffic returns were low. At one time the freight traffic was worked to Mold from Brymbo by a GWR locomotive, but this duty was handed over to the LMS before World War 2. Latterly, there were only two passenger trains a day which called, and freight from the station was virtually non-existent.
Bill Rear collection

Brymbo

The station in happier days when the GWR still operated regular passenger services to Brymbo. The LMS and later BR London Midland Region continued to use the station until 1950, after which the buildings were demolished, the footbridge removed and the track between Brymbo and Coed Talon lifted. *Bill Rear collection*

an old lime works and the intended terminus of the Ffrith branch. Facilities here were even more basic than at Llanfynydd and comprised a short wooden platform on the up side with a small wooden shed that doubled up as a booking office and a waiting room. The station was some distance from the village on a ledge on the hillside; access was by a footpath. Immediately on leaving the station towards Brymbo, the line ran over an imposing stone viaduct crossing Nant Ffrith valley that stands to this day. Beyond the viaduct was Ffrith Fire Clay siding, serving a brick and tile works, which had ceased to be operational by 1920.

Next came Glascoed siding on the up side via a trailing connection. This was not listed in the 1904 working timetable but was shown in the 1 July 1919 issue and subsequently until the BR London Midland (LM) Region issue of summer 1950.

The line then climbed at 1 in 50 for 1¾ miles in a southeasterly direction, crossing another viaduct which is still in situ near Ffrith Hall, before finally making a junction with the GWR Coedpoeth and Wrexham line 9 chains north of Brymbo station, located 600ft above sea level on a hillside.

Brymbo

This station shared the facilities with the GWR, which owned the site, maintained the station and provided the staff. The station was cut into the hillside and overlooked Brymbo steelworks, now closed, across the valley. It was demolished in the 1990s.

There were two brick-edged platforms with a wooden hut on what was the GWR up side. The down platform was devoid of any structure. Passengers crossed the line on a barrow crossing. It was merely a convenient point where the trains from Mold and Coed Talon terminated. The GWR was reluctant to allow the LNWR to get a toe-hold into Wrexham.

The passenger service was never more than basic. In 1922 there were four trains in each direction daily, with an extra train each direction on Saturdays. By 1947 this had been reduced to two trips daily in each direction for schoolchildren travelling to and from Mold. Traffic rarely justified more than one coach. Passenger services ceased over the whole of the branch from 27 March 1950. The line between Tryddyn Junction and Coed Talon survived until 1964 when it closed and the track was subsequently lifted. A few traces of the line still remain.

Brymbo

Photographs of LMS passenger trains at Brymbo are very rare. On 9 May 1949 Mold Junction's Class 4F 0-6-0 No M4065 stands at the head of the single-coach return working, 4.50pm to Mold, one of only two passenger workings daily. The service was maintained for the use of schoolchildren attending Mold Grammar School, but after 1950 the work was handed over to Crosville Motor Services. The station was the property and responsibility of the GWR, which had discontinued its passenger services from Wrexham in 1931. As a consequence, the wooden buildings were in poor condition. *E. S. Russell*

5

Holywell Town Branch

The Holywell Town branch was constructed by the London & North Western Railway and opened in 1912. The line was constructed mostly on the course of an earlier line — the Holywell Railway — part of which had itself been constructed on the course of a mineral tramway which it had taken over. Detailed information about the earlier mineral tramway can be found in *The Tramways and Railways to Holywell* written and published by J. R. Thomas. The Holywell Railway (1860) was built to transport stone from quarries near Holywell, and had ambitions to tap the Denbighshire coalfield, but these were unfulfilled. The line was out of use by the late 1870s and the company went into liquidation. The LNWR purchased the derelict line in 1891 (some sources state 1895) but did little or nothing with its acquisition beyond instituting lorry and bus services to connect the town with Holywell station on the coast main line until it decided to open a new branch on the old trackbed in the early 1900s.

As constructed, the branch line was 1½ miles in length, most of it on a ruling rising gradient of 1 in 27 from the main line station, which was renamed Holywell Junction upon the opening of the branch line. There was a private siding at 1 mile entitled Crescent Factory siding and one intermediate station, St Winefrides, 1¼ miles from the junction. The opening of the branch was conducted with the usual pomp and ceremony on 1 July 1912. The inaugural special train departed Holywell Junction station at 12.50pm.

The line posed special problems for operation and the Sectional Appendix to the working timetables (Western Division — Crewe and North Thereof) has special instructions for working the branch:

'Freight trains are run as laid down with the traffic for Crescent sidings or Holywell Town station, but in no case must such trains in either direction exceed three loaded

Holywell Junction
Whilst strictly speaking this view is of the main line platforms at Holywell Junction, the reason for including it here is to show the bay platform at which trains to and from Holywell Town arrived and departed. This view is looking towards Holyhead and shows the short bay platform on the down side. There was some interchange traffic to the branch from here but traffic up the hill was restricted to five wagons only, which had to include two 20-ton brake vans marshalled into the formation. The locomotive propelled all trains up to Holywell Town at all times, such was the severity of the climb. *BRM*

Opening of the Holywell Branch Line.

JULY 1st, 1912.

DEAR SIR,

I am desired to inform you that Guests for the Opening Ceremony can assemble at HOLYWELL JUNCTION (GREENFIELD) STATION, at 12.45 p.m. on JULY 1st, and travel by the Special Train leaving about 12.50 p.m. to Holywell Town, or they can meet at Holywell Town Station about 1.0 p.m.

On arrival of the train from Holywell Junction, the Guests are invited to take Luncheon with the Directors and Officers in the tent which will be placed in a field adjoining the New Town Station.

Attached hereto are tickets to cover the rail journey and also for admission to the Luncheon Tent.

G. T. PHIZACKERLEY,

Chester,
June 24th, 1912.

District Traffic Superintendent.

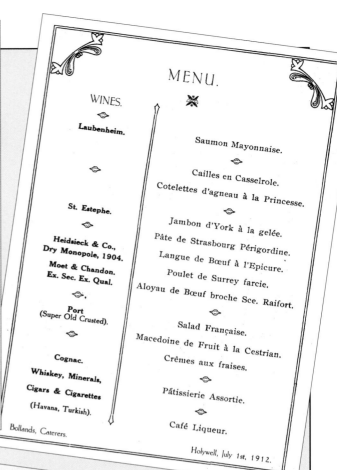

MENU.

WINES.

Laubenheim.

St. Estephe.

Heidsieck & Co.,
Dry Monopole, 1904.

Moet & Chandon.
Ex. Sec. Ex. Qual.

Port
(Super Old Crusted).

Cognac.

Whiskey, Minerals,
Cigars & Cigarettes
(Havana, Turkish).

Saumon Mayonnaise.

Cailles en Casserole.
Cotelettes d'agneau à la Princesse.

Jambon d'York à la gelée.
Pâte de Strasbourg Périgordine.
Langue de Bœuf à l'Epicure.
Poulet de Surrey farcie.
Aloyau de Bœuf broche Sce. Raifort.

Salad Française.
Macedoine de Fruit à la Cestrian.
Crêmes aux fraises.

Pâtissierie Assortie.

Café Liqueur.

Bollands, Caterers.

Holywell, July 1st. 1912.

L. & N. W. Rly.

RAILWAY TICKET.

No 37

Pass the Holder between
HOLYWELL JUNCTION
AND
HOLYWELL TOWN...

Available only on 1st July, 1912.

FRANK REE,
General Manager.

Opening of the

Holywell Branch

of the

L. & N. W. RAILWAY,

July 1st, 1912.

HOLYWELL TOWN

Formal invitation to the opening of the Holywell Town branch in 1912, showing the menu, and an invitation travel pass. Also, a leaflet showing the officers of the LNWR at the time.

Holywell Junction
Until 1950 ex-LNWR Class 1F auto-fitted 0-6-2T engines provided the power for all trains on the branch. The ruling gradient of 1 in 27 necessitated the engine to face uphill. The engine, provided by Rhyl shed, worked out in the early mornings and returned after the last train. The coach was normally parked in a siding off the platform overnight or when the engine was working a freight trip. Here No 58889 stands at the platform coupled ready for the next trip, in this case the 7.37pm to Holywell Town on 9 May 1949. This engine transferred to Rhyl from Bangor on 8 May 1948 and was sent to Abergavenny on 23 December 1950. *E. S. Russell*

goods or mineral wagons, or five empty wagons, and two 20-ton brake vans, one van at each end of the train. The engine must always be at the Holywell Junction end of the train.

'When working at Crescent sidings, the whole of the train must be backed inside one of the sidings before shunting is commenced, and guards and shunters must leave the sidings when work is finished in such a state that there is room for the next train to back in.

'Should any shunting be required from one siding to another which necessitates the use of the main lines, not more than four wagons and break van must be attached to the engine at a time.

'Before starting to descend the branch line the side brakes of all wagons on the train must be properly secured, and the hand brake of the van next to the engine must be applied. In addition the guard or shunter working the train must apply the hand brake in his van.

'A safety siding is on the single line, about 440 yards from the terminus of Holywell Junction. From Holywell Town to the Junction, all trains must come to a stand at

these points, and the fireman must operate the safety points for the train to pass over. As soon as the last vehicle of the train has passed the points, they must be replaced, the staff withdrawn, and the train must be stopped clear on the station side of the points for the fireman to rejoin the train. A signal is provided at the points leading to the station, which must only be lowered when the points have been set for the single line.'

Being a single line, it was necessary to be worked under the working conditions on such a line. The short length of the line meant that it was not envisaged that more than one train would be on the branch and the 'One Engine in Steam' method of working was practised. Nevertheless, because there were sidings that had to be kept locked, a train staff was necessary. The Sectional Appendix to the working timetables dated March 1937 stated that the train staff was round in shape, coloured 'Brass' and the staff station was at Holywell Junction.

Despite its draconian gradient, the line was capable of accommodating most LMS designs of engines. The more

HOLYWELL JUNCTION and HOLYWELL TOWN—Single Line

WEEK DAYS ONLY. Passenger Service worked by Motor Train, one class only.

‡—Goods Trains.   WK—Workmen's train.

		ETY	ETY																						
Down Trains.	a.m	a.m	a.m	a.m	a.m	a.m	a.m	a.m	a.m	p.m	p.m		p.m	p.m	p.m	p.m		p.m	p.m	p.m	p.m	p.m			
HOLYWELL J. dep	4 25	5 55	6 40	7‡30	8 20	9 0	10 10	10‡45	11 45	12 35	1 30	...	2 45	3‡20	4 8	4‡45	...	5 50	6 20	6 45	7 40	9 0			
Crescent Factory Sdg	...	S	...	7‡33									3‡25												
St. Winefrides	......	...	...	6 46	—	8 26	9 6	10 16	..	11 51	12 41	1 36	...	2 51	—	4 14	...	...	5 56	6 26	6 51	7 46	9 6		
HOLYWELL T. arr	4 35	6 5	6 50	...	8 30	9 10	10 20	11‡ 0	11 55	12 45	1 40	...	2 55	...	4 13	5‡ 0	...	6 0	6 30	6 55	7 50	9 10		

		WK	WK																						
Miles.	**Up Trains.**	a.m	a.m	a.m	a.m	a.m	a.m	a.m	a.m	p.m	p.m	p.m		p.m	p.m	p.m	p.m		p.m	p.m	p.m	p.m	p.m		
	HOLYWELL T.dep	4 45	6 15	7 5	...	8 33	9 35	10 25	11‡15	12 0	1 5	2 15	...	3 0	...	4 20	5‡15	...	6 5	6 32	7 10	8 10	9 25	
¼	St. Winefrides	4 50	6 18	7 8	...	8 36	9 38	10 28	...	12 3	1 8	2 18	...	3 3	...	4 23	...	...	6 8	6 35	7 13	8 13	9 28	
	Crescent Factory Sdg	...	S	...	7‡50									3‡40										
1¾	HOLYWELL J. arr	4 53	6 25	7 15	S‡ 0	8 43	9 45	10 35	11‡30	12 10	1 15	2 25	...	3 10	3‡50	4 30	5‡30	...	6 15	6 42	7 20	8 20	9 35	

normal power in regular use was limited up to Class 2 tank engines. The Ivatt Class 2MT 2-6-2T engines based at Rhyl shed were the last regular performers on the line, replacing LNWR 0-6-2T Class 1F engines, and they worked the freight trains when not working the pull-push motor-fitted passenger trains. Passenger and freight services were withdrawn on 6 September 1954 although the line remained in use as far as Crescent sidings on an 'as required' basis as a private siding for three more years, finally closing on 11 August 1957.

Partly due to the severity of the gradient towards the Town station, no through working of coaches or trains was ever undertaken. For the same reason freight traffic on the branch was always worked from or to Holywell Junction yard and wagons working forward were remarshalled, being taken back to Mold Junction yard or onward to Rhyl.

Holywell Junction station, which is a listed structure of Thompson design, closed on 14 February 1966, became a private house and is well maintained, in contrast to that at the former Mostyn station site, which despite also being listed has been allowed to fall into disrepair, is derelict and now almost beyond renovation.

Part of the Holywell Town branch trackbed is now a walkway, albeit overgrown in parts. The former tramway bridge leading to the harbour that passed over the main road still stands and appears to be in reasonable shape.

Holywell Town

The terminus was a simple affair, with one platform, wooden office buildings and a corrugated-iron waiting shed, open to the elements. The gradient in the station was 1 in 200 and at the platform ramp stiffened to 1 in 27. Here Webb '2F' auto-fitted 0-6-2T No 27585 of Rhyl shed stands, blowing off, ready to work the 5.45pm to Holywell Junction on 27 May 1947. *W. A. Camwell*

Holywell Town

The line terminated in a cutting beyond the passenger platform. Access to the goods yard was from a loop off the platform road but space was at a premium and only a limited number of wagons could be held in the small yard at any one time. Here a passenger train stands in the platform, headed by Ivatt Class 2MT 2-6-2T No 41276. In the goods yard beyond the bridge a few wagons stand on the sidings. *Derek Chaplin*

Holywell Town
In January 1950 Ivatt Class 2MT 2-6-2T No 41210 was received from Plodder Lane and immediately put to work on the Holywell Town branch. Its spacious cab and modern controls, as well as being a strong engine, made it a firm favourite with traincrews. It is seen here awaiting departure time, the driver standing on the platform. The locomotive was transferred temporarily on 29 September 1951 to Crewe North, returning on 20 October of the same year. Its stay was brief, merely a month before it was transferred back to Plodder Lane on 17 November.
Derek Chaplin

Holywell Town
A general view of the passenger platform at Holywell Town. Access to the station was by a ramp which zigzagged up the steep slope. Note the chalk board advertising the times of departures. Note, too, the station seat with 'Holywell Town' inscribed on the back support. The station looks tidy and was probably repainted after the war. The date of this view is unknown but believed to be in 1954. *Bill Rear collection*

6

Prestatyn to Dyserth

Historical

Quarries at Dyserth in the Clwydian range of hills in North Wales experienced difficulties in transporting their materials to the nearest railhead, which was either Prestatyn or Rhuddlan. The quarry owners were at a disadvantage without direct rail connection, their goods costing more than their rail-connected competitors. At a public meeting on 17 November 1860 held at Prestatyn, it was decided to consider the implications of privately

constructing a line from Cwm via Dyserth, to make a connection with the LNWR at Prestatyn. It was left to the LNWR to lay before Mold's Clerk of the Peace its own plans and sections entitled 'Prestatyn & Cwm Railway'. Parliament eventually approved the scheme for the 2¾-mile line between Prestatyn and Dyserth, although the actual distance to Dyserth terminus is quoted in the working timetables as 3¼ miles from Prestatyn. The Act of Incorporation was dated 16 July 1866 and five years were granted for completion of the line. There was a delay in starting construction due to land disputes. It was in the

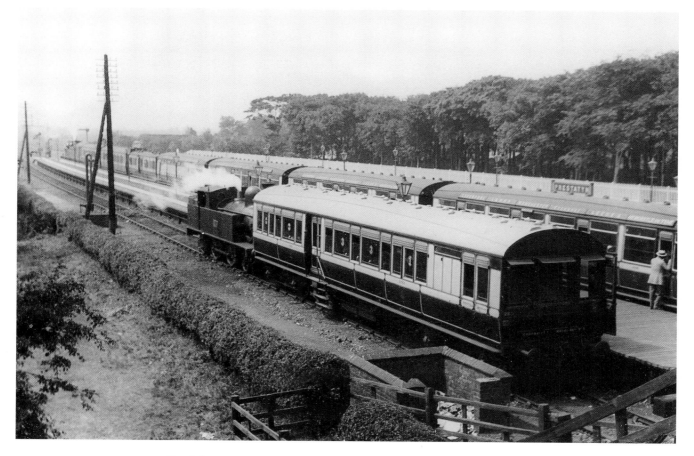

Prestatyn
An early view of Prestatyn station, taken by the author's father in summer 1923. In the main down platform stands a train of pure LNWR stock with the carriage board on the nearest two coaches reading 'Liverpool, L&NWR, Manchester, Exchange, Leeds & Newcastle on Tyne', which suggests the coach is some way off its diagram. In the bay platform is a 2-4-2T, number unidentifiable, with a pull-push motor coach. Note the retracting steps for use where the platform was minimal. At one time steam railcars were used, but were replaced by the more conventional arrangement. The possible explanation is that the locomotive was required to perform shunting duties when not on passenger workings. *D. J. Rear*

47

Prestatyn
The back of Prestatyn signalbox, showing Fowler Class 4F 0-6-0 No 44389, with tender cab, hauling a Western Region brake van, coming off the Dyserth branch some time in the early 1960s. The engine was at one time allocated to Rhyl shed but at the time this photograph was taken it was allocated to Llandudno Junction (6G) shed, moving to Skipton shed in January 1965. The signalbox is still in use today, although it is switched out for long periods. *Bill Rear collection*

summer of 1868 that work commenced and then the line was completed in 16 months.

Originally the line opened for stone and mineral traffic to Trecastell, near Dyserth, on 1 September 1869. The connection at Prestatyn was by means of a trailing point on the down side. The line was steeply graded and had severe curves. The line was upgraded to passenger-carrying status in 1905 but the passenger facilities provided were somewhat basic. From the start, trains were steam railcars and latterly pull-push railmotors. Intermediate halts, such as they were, were very basic indeed.

Before the LNWR took over the building of the line, various proposals were made to extend the branch to 'Newmarket' which came to naught. In November 1905 the LNWR deposited plans and sections at Mold for a 'Dyserth and Newmarket Light Railway'. Flintshire County Council and St Asaph Rural District Council, however, objected to the proposed method of crossing the main road at Dyserth, and wanted a bridge constructed. The LNWR would not concede and stalemate occurred. Ironically, by 1910 Flintshire County Council withdrew its objection as did St Asaph Council in 1913, but then World War 1 intervened and the proposal was put on hold. It was resurrected in 1921, but not proceeded with, and the development of road transport saw off the scheme.

Initially seven halts were decided upon, and the initial four were located at Prestatyn, Rhuddlan Road, Meliden and Dyserth. The latter three were more substantial than that at Prestatyn, which was merely an extension on the

ramp of the down slow platform. By 1910 it included some form of shelter. All the platforms were short, mostly 63ft. A halt was erected at Chapel Street, Prestatyn, in 1906, whilst that at Allt-y-Graig near Dyserth opened for public use in 1929. Facilities at Dyserth were more substantial than those at the other halts on the branch, and boasted a ticket office, a waiting room, toilets and a general store, all contained in two wooden huts that had been cascaded from elsewhere. The introduction of passenger services meant that some modifications to the track and infrastructure had to be made to satisfy the Board of Trade before passenger services could operate.

Despite phenomenal passenger support in the early days, the coming of the motor car (and buses) signalled the end of passenger traffic on the branch and public services were withdrawn as early as 20 September 1930. Freight continued but the remaining mineral traffic also started to decline about this period. The remaining freight traffic continued until 1 December 1951, when the parcels traffic ceased. Coal traffic survived until 4 May 1964. The outward stone products continued until 7 September 1973 when the line was declared closed, but there is evidence that a couple of special trains worked stone away in 1974.

Route Description

The branch trailed off the down line and passed behind the present Prestatyn signalbox. When passenger traffic started

Prestatyn

Even in the mid-1960s there was a large quantity of freight traffic over the Dyserth branch, and latterly Class 5 engines were authorised to work over the line. Here Stanier Class 5MT 4-6-0 No 45285 of Llandudno Junction shed propels wagons up the branch. The engine was transferred to Llandudno Junction shed from Woodford Halse in November 1963 and went to Shrewsbury in October 1965. This photograph is dated 2 May 1964. *J. Hobbs*

on the branch on 28 August 1905, the platform for branch trains was a short bay off the down slow line platform. It was necessary for the train to draw forward past the station signalbox before reversing and proceeding on to the branch. Almost immediately the line started to climb at 1 in 55 for about a quarter of a mile, when it stiffened to 1 in 45 for a further mile. At 2¼ miles from Prestatyn the line levelled out briefly for Meliden. Once clear of the station

limits the line continued climbing, this time at 1 in 65 for about ¼ mile before briefly easing to 1 in 100, then 100yd or so further on stiffening to 1 in 76 until Dyserth station was reached, where the climb then levelled off.

The line swept round on a right-hand curve of 13 chain radius on leaving Prestatyn station and at ¼ mile a private siding serving Prestatyn gasworks forked off left. Parallel to the main line, a long refuge siding on the Rhyl side of

Meliden

This photograph was taken in July 1963, by which time intermediate halts and sidings had largely disappeared. Seen here is the former goods shed, having lost its rail connection, although the building looks in remarkably good condition despite its boarded up windows and the patch on the door. This view is looking towards Dyserth. Note the track is laid with concrete sleepers. *R. M. Casserley*

the branch kept company for about a quarter of a mile. Gas production here ceased in 1955 and the siding was lifted in 1964. Unstaffed halts were provided on the down side at Chapel Street (¾ mile), Woodlands Park (originally called Rhuddlan Road Halt) (1 mile) and St Melyd Golf Links Halt (1½ miles) before Meliden station was reached.

Meliden

Meliden platform, 2¼ miles from Prestatyn, was on the up side, but before the platform was reached two sidings took off again on the up side. Between Meliden and Dyserth another halt — 'Allt-y-Graig' — was located on the down side and it must have been used very intermittently. A

siding to Dyserth Castle quarry took off on the down side shortly after Allt-y-Graig halt.

The gradient and curves on the line demanded that a speed restriction of 25mph be placed on all trains, reduced to 10mph through the junction at Prestatyn. As with the Holywell Town branch, it was decreed that all trains be propelled up the grade to Dyserth, the engine to be at the Prestatyn end at all times.

Signalling on the branch conformed to standard practice, the signals initially provided being to LNWR design and pattern. Two protected the level crossing at Bryn Rhosyn, near Woodlands Park, and a third protected the junction and platform line at Prestatyn. At one time there were two fixed distant signals at Meliden.

Dyserth

The terminus at Dyserth still showed a few signs of its former passenger station use in this view dating from 1950. The wooden passenger waiting hut was still standing, with a very low, short platform in front of it. Beyond it stands a goods shed with a coal stage between the hut and the shed. A solitary wagon stands on one of the yard sidings beyond the Vale of Clwyd Farmers' store, adjacent to which was a loading bank. There were no run-round facilities and all trains were propelled up the grade to Dyserth. *Bill Rear collection*

Near Dyserth

A railmotor is seen here at Allt-y-Graig, believed to be in 1913. The remains of Dyserth castle are visible on the horizon, right. The castle was demolished by the quarry company which was expanding its operations to extract stone. The railcar is working in the down direction. This view is well known, the photograph having been used commercially. *J. A. Peden collection*

PRESTATYN and DYSERTH BRANCH—Single Line. (One class only.)

Train Staff Stations—Prestatyn No. 2 Box and Dyserth.

	WEEK-DAYS. Down Trains.	1 Goods	2 Motor Train	3 Motor Train	4 Motor Train	5	6 Goods Empt.	7 Motor Train	8	9 Motor Train	10 Motor Train	11 Motor Train	12 Motor Train	13	14 Motor Train	15	16, 17 Motor Train	18 Motor Train	19
Miles		a.m.	a.m.	a.m.	a.m.		a.m.	p.m		p.m	p.m.	p.m.	p.m.		p.m.		p.m.	p.m.	
...	PRESTATYN ......dep	5 15	6 45	7 35	8 45	...	10 15	12 10	...	12 52	2 30	3 55	5 20	...	6 40	...	8 40	9 45	...
...	Chapel Street ..... ,,	...	6 49	7 39	8 49	...	‡See note	12 14	...	12 56	2 34	3 59	5 24	...	6 44	...	8 44	9 49	...
1¼	Rhuddlan Road ... ,,	...	6 52	7 42	8 52	...		12 17	...	12 59	2 37	4 2	5 27	...	6 47	...	8 47	9 52	...
2¼	Meliden .... ,,	5 35	6 57	7 47	8 57	...		12 22	...	1 4	2 42	4 7	5 32	...	6 52	...	8 52	9 57	...
3¼	DYSERTH ....arr	5 45	7 2	7 52	9 2	...	10‡25	12 27	...	1 9	2 47	4 12	5 37	...	6 57	...	8 57	10 2	...

	WEEK-DAYS. Up Trains.	20 Goods	21 Motor Train	22 Motor Train	23 Motor Train	24	25 Goods	26 Motor Train	27	28 Motor Train	29 Motor Train	30 Motor Train	31 Motor Train	32	33 Motor Train	34	35 Motor Train	36	37 Motor Train	38
Miles		a.m.	a.m.	a.m.	a.m.		a.m.	p.m.		p.m.	p.m.	p.m.	p.m.		p.m.		p.m.		p.m.	
...	DYSERTH ....dep	6 15	7 15	7 55	9 45	...	...	12 30	...	1 35	3 0	4 20	5 40	...	7 20	...	9 0	...	10 5	...
...	,, Castle Quarry S.	...	...	...	...	10 50	...			...	...			...		...				...
1	Meliden ....dep	X	7 20	8 0	9 50	...		12 35	...	1 40	3 5	4 25	5 45	...	7 25	...	9 5	...	10 10	...
2¼	Rhuddlan Road ... ,,	...	7 25	8 5	9 55	...		12 40	...	1 45	3 10	4 30	5 50	...	7 30	...	9 10	...	10 15	...
...	Chapel Street .... ,,	...	7 28	8 8	9 58	...		12 43	...	1 48	3 13	4 22	5 53	...	7 33	...	9 13	...	10 18	...
3¼	PRESTATYN ......arr	6 35	7 32	8 12	10 2	...	11 0	12 47	...	1 52	3 17	4 37	5 57	...	7 37	...	9 17	...	10 22	...

No. 6—‡ Runs to Dyserth, Castle Quarry Siding.

When wagons are left in the Talargoch Co.'s Sidings the goods guard will be held responsible for seeing that the breaks are securely pinned down.

Extract from July 1919 LNWR timetable for the Prestatyn and Dyserth branch.

Train Services

The railway was built primarily for freight and it carried considerable quantities of limestone which was used in the steel-making industry, and baked limestone (used in steel making). Considerable quantities of limestone were sent to Mostyn Ironworks and John Summers Shotton steelworks over the years and the quarries latterly supplied baked limestone to Round Oak steelworks at Brierley Hill near Stourbridge in the Midlands. The baked limestone traffic ceased when the lime kilns became life-expired and due for major renewals and the quarry owners closed the kilns in 1977.

Latterly, the main customer for limestone was Shotton steelworks, but the market had been lost by the time that that works ceased steel production in 1981. The dwindling limestone market hastened the end of the branch. The line had remained intact for stone rail traffic, albeit as a private siding to Dyserth quarries, until 1973 and even after this date irregular amounts of stone were worked away. Inevitably, even this occasional stone traffic declined and fell to nothing. Some agricultural traffic had always been carried, but this too had fallen after 1962. The track was eventually lifted in 1980.

The initial proposal was to work passenger trains with conventional locomotives and rolling stock, but this was deemed too extravagant by the LNWR for this branch line service so they designed a steam railcar which was constructed at Crewe and Wolverton. The first unit went into service on the Dyserth branch and was deemed a success, so much so that a total of seven were eventually built and operated on various branches on the LNWR and later LMS. Unit No 1 arrived at Rhyl on the evening of 24 August 1905. Its modern equivalent is the Class 153 unit.

An inaugural service was run for invited guests, civic dignitaries, the local MP, journalists and Mr (later Sir) Frank Ree, the LNWR Chief Goods Manager, on Saturday 26 August. Regular passenger services started two days later.

The passenger service in LNWR days was initially a success. The first service worked eight passenger trains, reduced during the winter months to five trains, each way daily, with an extra working each way on Saturday evenings. By the summer of 1911 this had increased to 16 trains daily and demand was high, so much so that from 1911 a trailer car with a driver's compartment was attached. The winter period saw the service frequency reduced to nine trains each way. After World War 1 the railmotors were replaced with locomotive-propelled pull-push trains. The rise in road transport and competition from the bus industry ate into the branch line's profitability. The General Strike of 1926 did not help matters and passenger numbers declined significantly, to the extent that the LMS decided to close the line to passenger traffic from 1930, although from time to time the occasional private charter train worked along the branch. As already stated, freight traffic lingered on until the 1960s when general services were withdrawn. The Locomotive Club of Great Britain and the Railway Correspondence & Travel Society ran a special trip over the line on Saturday 11 October 1969 just before the official closure became effective.

The only features to remain are the earthworks, used by a public country walk which is pleasant, and not too steep.

Rhyl

The 'North Wales Radio Land Cruise' trains were part of the holiday ritual for visitors to the North Wales coast in the 1950s, but by the end of the decade the interest was waning. To foster interest, the London Midland Region introduced an observation car to the Rhyl-based working and the former 'Devon Belle' car was transferred for this purpose. In the summer of 1960 it is seen here standing near the carriage shed at the eastern end of the station, not yet lettered but ready for service. It became necessary to turn this coach on the locomotive shed turntable after each trip, which was a bit of a chore, but necessary. The 'Devon Belle' observation car was sold out of service to the Paignton & Dartmouth Railway, where it still operates. *G. H. Platt*

Foryd Junction

This view actually shows the main line, looking towards Rhyl. The bridge in the foreground carried the main lines over the Foryd Harbour branch. The signalbox stood in the fork between the down lines and the Vale of Clwyd branch to Rhuddlan and Denbigh. The two-arm bracket signal on the branch indicates which line trains will take: the taller post signal arms indicate the up fast line, the lower post signal arms indicate the up slow line. In the distance, underneath the up line signals, can be seen the junction signals for the down fast and slow lines, and for the branch. *BRM*

7

Vale of Clwyd

Historical

Denbigh was the hub for the routes up the Vale of Clwyd to Ruthin and on to Corwen on the River Dee; towards the coast through St Asaph; and through a gap in the Clwydian range of hills to Mold. The establishment of the Chester & Holyhead Railway (C&H), which opened to traffic as far as Bangor on the north Wales coast on 1 May 1848, ensured that the apparent prosperity that followed in the wake of the opening of the main line inspired local communities to consider ways of establishing their own lines.

The Vale of Clwyd Railway

The Vale of Clwyd Railway was incorporated by an Act of 23 June 1856. The line as built was single track throughout, with provision made for doubling if traffic justified the expense, which sadly it never did. Connection was made with the C&H at Foryd Junction to the first station at Denbigh, which was a temporary structure, with intermediate stations at Foryd (near the junction), Rhuddlan, St Asaph and Trefnant. The line was formally inspected on 22 September 1858, but permission to open was initially refused because of unfinished works. These were completed within a week.

Ultimately, the Vale of Clwyd Act of 30 June 1862 authorised an extension which provided an improved junction and a new pier at the Foryd terminus. Goods traffic along the harbour branch commenced after the official inspection in August 1864, but it never had a regular passenger service. It survived as a freight-only line until as late as 6 April 1959.

The Vale of Clwyd (VofC) purchased three 0-4-2 saddle tank engines from Sharp, Stewart of Manchester. Rolling stock was supplied by John Ashbury of Openshaw, Manchester. Signals were supplied by Stevens & Son and the electric telegraph was completed and put into use at the end of 1862.

The railway formally opened to traffic on 5 October 1858 with four weekday stopping trains. The permanent station at Denbigh came into use in December 1860. The interest shown by the GWR in the nascent Denbigh, Ruthin & Corwen Railway (DR&C) line prompted the LNWR to take control of the VofC, with LNWR directors joining the VofC

board in September 1861. The LNWR agreed to work the VofC and DR&C lines into Denbigh as one undertaking. The LNWR assumed operational control of the VofC in 1864 and The Vale of Clwyd Railway Company was finally absorbed by the LNWR by an Act dated 15 July 1867.

Route Description

Foryd Junction

Foryd Junction signalbox stood on the down side of the Chester & Holyhead Railway main line. It had a total of 56 levers, of which 43 were working. It was located in the fork

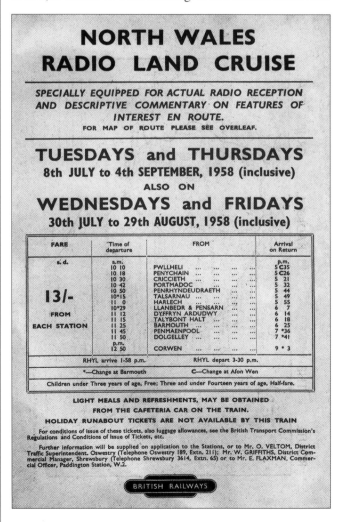

1958 North Wales Radio Land Cruise.

Rhuddlan
The first station on the original Vale of Clwyd line was Foryd but this closed to traffic in 1885. Next was Rhuddlan, which was a staff token station, although there was only one platform and two passenger trains were not authorised to cross here. The loop was added later and was used exclusively by freight trains. Beyond the station can be seen a small goods yard with an interesting collection of private-owner mineral wagons, including one belonging to Barton & Co. The platform appears to have an extensive range of parcels and other items ready for uplifting. The station building and site were cleared to make way for the Rhuddlan bypass road and no traces remain. *Bill Rear collection*

between the branch and the down slow main line. The slow lines were ultimately removed although the four-track bridge remains intact, minus its tracks on the inland side.

From Foryd Junction the line assumed single-track working to Rhuddlan, the gradient along this stretch being almost level for 2¾ miles. A connection with the Foryd branch and Kinmel Park private railway was made at Foryd station, at the foot of a short climb, where a small signalbox was once located which controlled access to the Foryd Pier line. This was 40yd north of the Vale of Clwyd line station. It was replaced by ground frames after 1883, becoming a double line which climbed up to Foryd Junction on a 12-chain curve to meet with the Chester to Holyhead main line, the course of which can still be seen from passing trains.

Rhuddlan

The single platform and station buildings were located on the down side. The station was designated a crossing point, with token exchange facilities, but passenger trains were not permitted to cross here. Between Foryd Junction and Rhuddlan the single-line train staff was coloured red. An eight-lever ground frame was mounted on the platform at the northern end of the station building which controlled signals in both directions, together with two points. The station buildings were constructed of local brick, the stationmaster having a house on the site. A wooden goods store was mounted on the platform at the southern end of the platform. A forecourt gave vehicular access to the station, beyond which was the goods yard at the northern end of the site, containing a cattle dock, a horse landing and a coal wharf. Four camping coaches were stationed on the

site from 1948 until the early 1960s.

Freight traffic consisted chiefly of timber and livestock away from Rhuddlan, with domestic coal inward.

Nothing remains of the station today. The road overbridge, station platform and buildings were all swept away in a road improvement programme in the 1960s or 70s.

On leaving the platform, the line passed under the Rhuddlan to Abergele road bridge, then it resumed as single track towards St Asaph on a rising gradient of varying steepness. For the last mile to St Asaph the gradient stiffened to 1 in 78 before the line crossed the old A55 road by a plate girder bridge, since removed. The bridge was built for a single line of track but sufficient land for doubling the line had been provided for.

St Asaph

St Asaph station was located in the older part of the city, at the upper end close to the cathedral. The Rhyl end of the up platform commenced almost at the bridge abutment and contained the main station building and stationmaster's house. The structure survives in private hands, still very attractive and little changed, and in contrast to Trefnant, it is an elegant building and was the largest intermediate station on the line.

The down platform, which was staggered, was added in 1877. It boasted an open shelter which faced the track. When passenger services were withdrawn in 1955, the down loop was removed, although the platform and shelter remained for several years (but have since been demolished). Passengers crossed the line by an open footbridge at the Denbigh end.

Near St Asaph

The 'Cambrian Radio Cruise' is seen in August 1960, with BR Standard Class 4MT 4-6-0 No 75053 crossing the River Elwy, roughly halfway between Rhuddlan and St Asaph, heading for Denbigh. This engine arrived at Rhyl shed from Chester with its fellow shed mate, No 75054, on 18 June, and after the season had finished, transferred away to Mold Junction. This and the next but one photograph were taken on successive days. The last vehicle in the consist was one of the former 'Coronation' train sets' brake coaches that had no corridor connection, making it difficult for the coach to be included in normal-use formations. The engine looks in need of a clean — normally they were turned out in sparkling condition on this particular working. *Bill Rear collection*

St Asaph

The station was on a high point above the town and somewhat exposed to the elements. This 1951 view shows the main building on the up side, built of red brick faced with local stone surrounds to the windows and doors, to good advantage. The down platform shelter was spartan and devoid of any comfort, although a bench seat was provided. Signals were controlled from a ground frame on the platform. The station was a staff token exchange point and the line crossed over the former A55 road on a single-span bridge wide enough for only one line of track, hence the need to commence the down side loop once the bridge had been cleared. The main building still stands in private ownership, but the up-side shelter has long since gone. *Bill Rear collection*

St Asaph

Regular passenger trains ceased to run between Rhyl and Denbigh in September 1955 and the intermediate staff token sections were replaced by a single miniature staff from Foryd Junction to Denbigh, and the down-side loop and connecting footbridge taken out. Nevertheless, the down-side platform and the passenger shelter were left intact and remained in a pristine state until demolition. BR Standard Class 4MT 4-6-0 No 75054 is seen here heading for Denbigh working the 'Cambrian Radio Cruise', a successor to the land cruise trains of the previous decade, with a motley collection of coaches in August 1960. To the left of the locomotive can be seen part of the goods shed which still stands to this day. No 75054 was transferred to Rhyl (6K) shed from Chester specifically for the land cruise workings in June 1960 and remained for the summer, transferring away in September to Mold Junction. *Bill Rear collection*

Near St Asaph

On 1 September 1961 Standard Class 4MT 4-6-0 No 75020 approaches St Asaph with an unnamed land cruise train that started from Pwllheli. This engine was a long-time resident of Machynlleth (89C) shed, of which Pwllheli was a sub-shed. This engine was based at Pwllheli specifically for the summer workings. Unlike the London Midland Region, the Western Region used BR Standard Mk 1 stock. Pwllheli men worked this working throughout.
Bill Rear collection

Trefnant

This 1965 view shows the closed Trefnant station after the down-side passenger loop had been taken out. Here Stanier Class 5 No 45275, a long-time resident of Mold Junction, is seen working a Denbigh to Rhyl freight. Note the simple design of the station building, in contrast to St Asaph. Unfortunately, the building was demolished and the site cleared after the line was taken up and today the area is a housing estate. The road bridge, from which this photograph was taken, was also removed, requiring the Mold to Rhyl road to wind round a 90° curve at this point. *Bill Rear collection*

Between Rhuddlan and St Asaph the section of single line was worked by train staff, coloured blue. The single-line token equipment was located in the booking office, the large Webb & Thompson tokens in use on the section to Trefnant being replaced by miniature tokens in 1949. On the main platform, an open ground frame of 15 levers was located close to the passenger footbridge, which controlled up and down signals and the loop and horse landing points.

Some local milk and fish traffic was handled by the platform staff and there was a steady income from sundries and small parcels, in addition to the handling of Post Office traffic. Until the withdrawal of passenger services, it was a token exchange point. A goods yard was located on the up side, containing a horse and carriage landing siding parallel with the up platform, with a 5-ton crane alongside in the yard, which contained a goods warehouse with a single track passing through. A second siding off the warehouse road served as a coal siding. The weigh machine and office stood at the yard entrance. Livestock traffic accounted for a high proportion of the freight traffic revenue, and Vale of Clwyd Farmers, an agricultural co-operative association, established a depot at the station and provided the station with a regular income. North Wales Agricultural Engineers also imported implements and machinery. Domestic coal was distributed by several merchants from the yard.

Between St Asaph and Trefnant the line kept to the eastern side of the Elwy valley and commenced climbing to Llanerch siding, a mile from Trefnant.

A set of sidings was constructed at Llanerch by the Royal Engineers in the later stages of World War 2 to service a military stores depot. These sidings gradually fell into disuse, latterly being used for the storage of coaching stock, or supplies of locomotive coal for Rhyl shed. A final moment of glory came when the royal train was stabled here overnight on 10 July 1953, when the Queen visited parts of North Wales following her Coronation.

From St Asaph the 2½ miles to just before the road overbridge at the north end of Trefnant station, the track had been single. At this point the track diverged, forming a passing loop.

Trefnant

The community of Trefnant was clustered around the crossroads where the Denbigh to St Asaph road met roads from Mold and Henllan. The station was centrally placed in the village.

The line ran under the St Asaph to Mold road bridge, since demolished, into Trefnant station. Here a passenger loop was provided, the main building being on the up platform.

Denbigh
On 1 September 1960 Standard Class 4MT 4-6-0 No 75054 pulls away from Denbigh on the final leg of the journey back to Rhyl with the 'Welsh Chieftain' land cruise train. Worked by Rhyl men throughout, this was the last week of operation for the season. Most of the coaching stock appears to be LMS Period II and at the tail of the train can be seen the former 'Devon Belle' observation car. The first, fourth and sixth coaches bear the carriage board 'The Welsh Chieftain'. *Bill Rear collection*

Extract from July 1925 LMS timetable for the Rhyl, St Asaph and Denbigh line.

RHYL, ST. ASAPH, AND DENBIGH. Week Days only.

		Saturdays only. One class only.		Saturdays excepted One class only.					S	SO			Th S		One class only.			Saturdays only			Thursdays and Sats. only
Rhyl ....dep.	7 25		7 30		8 31	9 0	10 55	12 58	2 40	2 45	4 23	6 5	7 0	8 3		9 10	9 51		10 45	
Rhuddlan.........	7 33		7 38		8 39	4 8		1 6		2 53	4 31	6 13	7 8	8 11		9 18				
St. Asaph.........	7 40		7 45		8 46	9 15	11 10	1 13	2 55	3 0	4 38	6 20	7 15	8 18		9 25	10		11	
Trefnant.........	7 46		7 57		8 53	9 25	11 16	1 19	3 1	3 6	4 44	6 26	7 22	8 24		9 31	10 12		11	
Denbigh ....arr.	7 55		8 0		9 3	9 33	11 25	1 28	3 10	3 15	4 55	6 35	7 33	8 33		9 41	10 21		11 16	
		SO	S							S	SO									
Denbigh ....dep.	6 28	7 42	7 47		9 6	10 0		11 55	1 24		2 55	3 0	4 53		6 5		7 0		8 5	9 12	
Trefnant.........	6 34	7 48	7 53		9 12	10 6		12 1	1 30		3 1	3 6	4 59		6 11		7 6		8 11	9 18	
St. Asaph.........	6 40	7 55	8 0		9 18	10 12		12 7	1 36		3 8	3 13	5 5		6 17		7 12		8 17	9 24	
Rhuddlan.........	6 46	8 2	8 7		9 24	10 18		12 13	1 45		3 14	3 19	5 11		6 27		7 21		8 25	9 32	
Rhyl ....arr.	6 55	8 11	8 16		9 33	10 29		12 24	2 1		3 25	3 30	5 22		6 42		7 31		3 36	9 42	

S—Saturdays excepted.   SO—Saturdays only.   Th S—Thursdays and Saturdays excepted.

Denbigh
An unidentified LNWR 2-4-2T pulls away from Denbigh with a train for Rhyl in 1923. The first coach is a 'modern' bogie vehicle, the rest of the stock being five six-wheel local stock. There is an abundance of locomotive power visible: 'Cauliflower' No 3136 stands on one of the shed roads in front of the water tank, whilst two tank engines shunt wagons on the up side in the yard. The old No 1 signalbox is visible in the distance. The line off to the right in the foreground of the picture led to the Graig quarry, which provided much revenue for the line. *Bill Rear collection*

The platforms were low and short. The main building was a two-storey square-shaped structure of brick construction containing the usual offices with the stationmaster's house at the south end. The station was demolished after the line closed and the track lifted, a housing estate being built on the site.

A ground frame of 11 levers stood on the up platform at the north end controlling the signals in each direction, the loop points and the horse landing connection. The single-line token instruments were located in the ticket office.

Passengers crossed the line via the road overbridge that stood at the north end of the platforms.

The down platform itself was devoid of shelter and it is uncertain whether there ever was protection provided.

A small goods yard stood on the up side comprising a line to a landing stage and cattle dock, parallel to the running lines, and a second siding with a loop which terminated close to the goods yard entrance. The yard contained a small 5-ton crane, a weighbridge and an office. The down platform line extended beyond the loop, ending in a headshunt.

Freight and parcels traffic played a significant part in the station's viability, with domestic coal the principal commodity. There was a store on the up platform, but no goods warehouse. In 1939 and up to the summer of 1948, Passenger working timetables indicated that two minutes were allowed at Trefnant on Rhyl to Denbigh trains for ticket collecting purposes. The note had disappeared by the September 1948 issue.

The line departed from Trefnant, resuming as a single track with occasional and gradual changes of gradient, falling then rising across farming countryside.

The section of line between Trefnant and Mold & Denbigh Junction was controlled by a train staff, coloured blue and of special make. Latterly, this was worked by miniature train staff, also coloured blue and of special make.

Mold & Denbigh Junction

Near the settlement of Denbigh Green, a standard LNWR-design signalbox stood on the down side.

At this point the track was on level ground. Here the Mold and Chester line came in from the east, worked as a double line until 1957. The single-track Vale of Clwyd line became a double line beyond the junction at this point.

Until the 1957 Denbigh signalbox was commissioned, the running lines south were worked under absolute block regulations. The lines continued to fall on a very slight gradient for the next ¼ mile. After the new box was commissioned the lines were worked as separate up and down lines as far as the divergence of the lines to Rhyl and Mold.

Denbigh

Within the station limits but before the goods yard on the up side was a private siding belonging to the Ruthin & Denbigh Tarmacadam Company Ltd, formerly the Denbigh Lime & Stone Co, from the Graig quarry which made a connection with the shunting neck. Within the quarry itself was a 2ft 0in gauge tramway, which was abandoned by 1960. At one time there was a 36ft turntable located alongside the quarry siding, but this was replaced by a larger turntable located behind the engine shed on the down side during LMS days.

Denbigh

Until 1957, movements at the north end of Denbigh station were controlled from Denbigh No 1 signalbox, which was located at the north end of the platform on the up side. It was falling into a serious state of decline before World War 2 but plans to replace it were shelved during the conflict. However, it is understood that it was given a coat of paint about 1946. By the mid-1950s it was becoming difficult to maintain and the decision was ultimately taken to replace it with a modern box. It was decommissioned in 1957 and demolished almost immediately, to no one's regret. *BRM*

Vale of Clwyd Branch (Single Line) and Kinmel Park Camp Military Railway (Single Line).

Train Staff Stations—Foryd Junction, Rhuddlan, St. Asaph, Trefnant, and Denbigh Junction.

Passenger Trains can cross each other only at Denbigh Junction, Trefnant, St. Asaph and Foryd Junction.

Miles.	DOWN TRAINS. Week Days.	1	2	3	4	5	6	7	8	9	10	11	12	13
		Mails	Goods	Goods	Pass.	Pass.	Pass.	Goods TThO	Pass.	Pass.	Pass.	Pass	Pass.	Pass
		a.m.	a.m.	a.m.	a.m.	a.m.	a.m.	a.m.	a.m.	a.m.	p.m.	p.m.	p.m.	p.m.
...	RHYL dep.	5 40	5 50	6 25	7 28	8 10	8 55	10 10	11 0	11 18	1 25	2 15	4 10	4 35
1	Foryd Jct. arr.	5§43	5§55	6§30	7§31	8§15	8§58	10§14	11 §3	11§23	1§28	2§20	4§13	4§38
	,, ,, Pier Line dep.	...	6 5	...	...	8 22	...	10 20	...	11 30	...	2 27	...	4 47
...	Kinmel Park Camp arr.	...	6 25	...	...	8 33	...	...	...	11 41	...	2 38	...	4 58
3 3/8	Rhuddlan arr.	5 48	...	6 50	7 36	...	9 3	...	11 8	...	1 33	...	4 18	...
	Rhuddlan dep.	5 49	...	7 25	7 37	...	9 4	...	11 9	...	1 34	...	4 20	...
5 7/8	St. Asaph arr.	5 55	...	7 35	7 43	...	9 10	...	11 15	...	1 40	...	4 25	...
	St. Asaph dep.	5 57	...	8 20	7 46	...	9 12	...	11 17	...	1 42	...	4 29	...
7 3/8	Llanerch Siding	...	...	X	...	...	...	...	...	...	...	...	...	...
8 3/8	Trefnant arr.	6 2	...	8 30	7 51	...	9 17	...	11 22	...	1 47	...	4 34	...
	Trefnant dep.	6 3	...	9 5	7 54	...	9 20	...	11 25	...	1 53	...	4 38	...
10	Denbigh Junction	6 §7	...	9§11	7§58	...	9§24	...	11§29	...	1§57	...	4§42	...
11 1/8	DENBIGH arr.	6 10	...	9 15	8 1	...	9 27	...	11 32	...	2 0	...	4 45	...

DOWN TRAINS. Week Days.	14	15	16	17	18	19	20	21	22	23	24	25	26	27
	Pass.	Pass SO	Pass.	Pass.	Pass.	Pass. SO	Pass S	Pass SO	Pass. S	Pass SO	SUNDAYS.	Pass	Pass	Pass
	p.m.	p.m.	p.m.	p.m.	p.m.	p.m.	p.m.	p.m.	p.m.	p.m.		p.m.	p.m.	p.m
RHYL dep.	5 57	6 5	6 55	7 20	8 55	9 5	10 0	10 20	11 10	11 35		3 0	8 0	10 20
Foryd Jct. arr.	6 §0	6§10	6§58	7§25	8§58	9§10	10 §5	10§25	11§15	11§40		3 §5	8 §5	10§25
,, ,, Pier Line dep.	...	6 17	...	7 32	...	9 17	10 12	10 32	11 22	11 47		3 12	8 12	10 32
Kinmel Park Camp arr.		6 28	...	7 43	...	9 28	10 23	10 43	11 33	11 58		3 23	8 23	10 43
Rhuddlan arr.	6 5	...	7 3	...	9 3	...	...	...	...	...		...	...	...
Rhuddlan dep.	6 6	...	7 4	...	9 4	...	...	...	...	...		...	...	...
St. Asaph arr.	6 12	...	7 10	...	9 10	...	...	...	...	...		...	...	...
St. Asaph dep.	6 14	...	7 12	...	9 12	...	...	...	...	...		...	...	...
Llanerch Siding	...	...	...	...	...	...	...	...	...	...		...	...	...
Trefnant arr.	6 19	...	7 17	...	9 17	...	...	...	...	...		...	...	...
Trefnant dep.	6 23	...	7 20	...	9 20	...	...	...	...	...		...	...	...
Denbigh Junction	6§27	...	7§24	...	9§24	...	...	...	...	...		...	...	...
DENBIGH arr.	6 30	...	7 27	...	9 27	...	...	...	...	...		...	...	...

UP TRAINS. Week Days.	28	29	30	31	32	33	34	35	36	37	38	39	40	41
	Goods	Pass	Pass.	Pass	Pass.	Goods	Pass.	Pass.	Pass		Pass.	Pass	Goods	
	a.m.	a.m.	a.m.	a.m.	a.m.	a.m.	p.m.	p.m.	p.m.		p.m.	p.m.	p.m.	
DENBIGH dep.	...	...	7 25	...	9 24	TThO	12 3	...	1 45	...	2 55	...	3 30	
Denbigh Junction	...	...	7§28	...	9§27	...	12 §6	...	1§48	...	2§58	...	3§34	
Trefnant arr.	...	...	7 32	...	9 31	...	12 10	...	1 52	...	3 2	...	3 40	
Trefnant dep.	...	...	7 33	...	9 32	...	12 11	...	1 55	...	3 3	...	4 10	
Llanerch Siding	...	...	...	...	...	...	...	...	...	...	...	...	...	1.0 p.m. from Ruthin.
St. Asaph arr.	...	...	7 38	...	9 37	...	12 16	...	2 0	...	3 8	...	4 20	
St. Asaph dep.	...	...	7 44	...	9 39	...	12 18	...	2 2	...	3 10	...	5 25	
Rhuddlan arr.	...	...	7 50	...	9 45	...	12 24	...	2 8	...	3 16	...	5 35	
Rhuddlan dep.	...	...	7 51	...	9 48	...	12 27	...	2 12	...	3 19	...	6 43	
Kinmel Park Camp dep.	4 20	7 22	...	9 15	...	...	...	1 35	...	...	...	3 20	...	
Foryd Jct. Pier Line arr.	4 40	7 33	...	9 26		10 40		1 46	...	...	...	3 31	...	
,, Junction dep.	4§55	7§40	7§56	9§33	9§53	10§50	12§32	1§53	2§17	...	3§24	3§40	6§50	
RHYL arr.	5 0	7 45	7 59	9 38	9 56	10 55	12†35	1 58	2 20	...	3 27	3 45	6 55	

UP TRAINS. Week Days.	42	43	44	45	46	47	48	49	50	51	52	53	54	55
	Pass.	Pass.	Pass	Pass.		Pass	Pass.	Pass.	Pass	Pass	SUNDAYS.	Pass	Pass	Pass
	p.m.	p.m.	p.m.	p.m.		p.m.	p.m.	p.m	p.m.	p.m.		p.m	p.m.	p.m.
DENBIGH dep.	5 2	SO	...	5 55	...	...	8 2	SO	S	SO		...	...	...
Denbigh Junction	5§ 5	...	...	5§58	...	...	8 §5	...	...	...		...	...	...
Trefnant arr.	5 9	...	...	6 2	...	...	8 9	...	...	...		...	...	...
Trefnant dep.	5 10	...	...	6 3	...	...	8 10	...	...	...		...	...	...
Llanerch Siding	...	...	...	...	...	...	...	...	...	...		...	...	...
St. Asaph arr.	5 15	...	...	6 8	...	...	8 15	...	...	...		...	...	...
St. Asaph dep.	5 18	...	...	6 13	...	...	8 17	...	...	...		...	...	...
Rhuddlan arr.	5 24	...	...	6 19	...	...	8 23	...	...	...		...	...	...
Rhuddlan dep.	5 27	...	...	6 22	...	...	8 26	...	...	...		...	...	...
Kinmel Park Camp dep.	...	5 25	5 45	...	...	7 55	...	9 40	10 30	10 55		1 50	5 20	9 0
Foryd Jct. Pier Line arr.	...	5 36	5 56	...	...	8 6	...	9 51	10 41	11 6		2 1	5 31	9 11
,, Junction dep.	5§32	5§43	6 §3	6§27	...	8§13	8§31	9§58	10§48	11§13		2 §8	5§38	9§18
RHYL arr.	5 35	5 48	6 8	6 30	...	8 18	8 34	10 3	10 53	11 18		2 13	5 43	9 23

The Kinmel Park Camp Service is worked throughout by the Military Railway.

No. 34—†Public Bills 12.37 p.m.

Denbigh Tickets of all Down Trains to be collected at Trefnant.

Tickets of all Up Trains from Denbigh to be examined at Rhuddlan.

Extract from July 1919 LNWR timetable for the Vale of Clwyd branch and the Kinmel Park military railway.

Denbigh

The replacement signalbox was to a British Railways standard design and replaced the former No 1 and No 2 boxes on either side of the station platform, and the Mold & Denbigh Junction box at the end of the site, where the Rhyl and Mold lines parted company. At the same time the signals through the station were replaced. The decision to replace the box was taken because it was believed at the time that the line had a secure future. Unfortunately, because of a lemming-like attitude by the higher management of the region, this decision was reversed and the decline of the lines to Denbigh became inevitable. With the closure of the line to Rhydymwyn, and from Ruthin to Corwen, the box became largely surplus to requirements although it staggered on until services between Rhyl and Ruthin were withdrawn and the line closed completely. The box, with other railway features, was demolished and the site cleared. *Jim Parry*

Denbigh

The station building was a striking structure, constructed of local limestone. It was in a prominent position, raised above the lower level of Denbigh town at the foot of, and on the corner of, Vale Street. The building was the headquarters of the Vale of Clwyd Railway and the spire may have been built to emphasise its importance. It will be seen that there is only one through platform, which caused some minor traffic problems, but in the main, things worked smoothly as there was rarely more traffic than could be handled by the station staff. Trains terminating at Denbigh from Rhyl usually pulled into the bay platform on the right of the main platform, whilst trains from Chester and Mold would stop at the main platform face. If a train was working through to Ruthin or Corwen, and the main face was part occupied, trains would pass by the station on the left-hand line and set back into the platform under the watchful eye of a station inspector or the stationmaster. The canopy over the platform gave some shelter to passengers and survived until the station was demolished. *Norman Jones*

Denbigh

In September 1961 a Chester-bound train pulls away from the through platform. On the bay line stands a Stanier 2-6-4T, probably awaiting a path to go on shed for servicing. The buildings in the centre of the picture were used as an agricultural foodstuffs store and beyond them is the two-road goods shed. Some mineral wagons stand on the cattle pen line. The scene has an air of tranquility about it, but the view is deceptive. Already closure notices have been published and within 12 months all would be changed. *Bill Rear collection*

Denbigh

When this photograph was taken in 1923 locomotives were used indiscriminately for shunting purposes whether they were designated passenger engines or not. Here an ex-LNWR 2-4-0 of the 'Precedent' class, No 1194 *Miranda*, shunts mineral and cattle wagons in Denbigh yard. The locomotive is carrying a '38' shed plate on its roof indicating that it was attached to Llandudno Junction shed, of which Denbigh was a sub-shed at the time. This locomotive was a long-time resident of Denbigh shed. Note the stack of timber in the background, which was a regular commodity carried by the railway. In the immediate foreground are some wagons loaded with granite from the Graig quarry, standing on their private siding line. *Bill Rear collection*

8

Foryd Pier Line

The Foryd Pier line led off the Vale of Clwyd line and passed under the Chester & Holyhead line, following the west bank of the Clwyd estuary for 1¼ miles. There had been high hopes of establishing a passenger station in Rhyl Harbour at Foryd Pier Quay, but these plans came to naught and the branch remained a freight-only line until final closure on 6 April 1959. It was a single line from the junction with the Vale of Clwyd line until shortly before the line crossed the Rhyl to Abergele road, where a run-round loop line ran parallel, giving the appearance of a double-track line. Facilities listed in the Railway Clearing House (RCH) 1929 *Handbook of Stations* indicate that it was a goods station. There was one private siding, listed as Jones & Son's siding.

The traffic carried over the line consisted mainly of timber and coal, and in early LMS days the turn worked only on Tuesdays, Thursdays and Saturdays. The daily trip working was restored in the mid-1930s and this frequency continued until closure. The job was designated a Class K freight working, and for most of the time departed Rhyl about 11am, taking 15 minutes to reach the pier, which included running round its train at Foryd Junction. It remained at the pier for half an hour, undertaking what shunting was necessary, before returning, usually departing just before midday. Running round the train at Foryd Junction was repeated, this movement taking place on the Vale of Clwyd branch, under the control of the signalman at Foryd Junction.

Foryd Pier

The line to Foryd Pier took off at a connection with the Vale of Clwyd line beyond Foryd Junction signalbox. The line passed underneath the main Chester & Holyhead line, seen here. The track appears to have some growth between the sleepers but at the time of photographing (1957) was still in active use, one train a day working a short trip from Rhyl yard to the pier and back. Coaches can be seen through the bridge, stored on a siding parallel with the line to Denbigh, which was a short-term measure. Ultimately, they would be removed and stored on the up or down slow lines between Abergele and Llandulas which were taken out of regular use during the winter months. *BRM*

Foryd Pier

The Foryd Pier line never opened for passenger trains. The original intention had been for the privately constructed line to convey people to the harbour, from where they would get a steamer to Liverpool. A large goods shed was installed, which survives to this day, although the rail service was discontinued after 1959. Prior to that date a daily trip worked out from Rhyl yard and delivered or collected wagons off the pier. This view, dated 1956, whilst not showing a locomotive, does show a mineral wagon outside the goods shed and it is understood that a regular movement of both wagons and vans took place. *G. H. Platt*

Kinmel Park Military Railway

A second branch took off the Vale of Clwyd line, to Kinmel Park Camp, a complex set up by the War Office in early 1915 where basic training was undertaken.

According to Peter E. Baughan, in his work *A Regional History of the Railways of Great Britain, Vol 11, North & Mid Wales*, the first connection between the camp and the main line was made at the site of the 1885 Foryd station on the Chester & Holyhead main line in 1915 where it formed a trailing connection with the down slow main line. This arrangement must have proved unsatisfactory to the military and the line was diverted to join the Vale of Clwyd near Foryd Junction on the Foryd Pier line. A deviation to the northern section of line was provided by the LNWR in April 1917, the connection being made first with the Foryd Harbour branch and then quickly modified to provide through running to and from Rhyl.

The line was officially opened for passenger traffic on 14 June 1917 by Sir Pitcairn Campbell, General Officer Commanding-in-Chief of Western Command. Foryd station on the main line was closed on 2 July 1917, but reopened in July 1919. After the cessation of hostilities in 1918 the camp was used to house Canadian soldiers awaiting repatriation, but conditions at the camp were so bad that in early 1919 a series of mutinies broke out, resulting allegedly in the deaths of five men on Wednesday 5 March 1919. It appears that this has been covered up for over 80 years. The men were buried in Bodelwyddan churchyard where their graves can still be seen.

The working timetable for 1 July 1919 shows a regular service of trains still running between Rhyl station and the camp. A footnote states 'The Kinmel Park Camp Service is worked throughout by the Military Railway'. The military authorities cleared and closed the camp as quickly as possible after the 1919 mutiny, and for the next few years the line was worked 'as required' from Rhyl by Rhyl shed men.

In February 1923 the line was taken over by Lime Firms Ltd of Llandebie and worked by an associate company — Limestone Products Ltd, of St George limeworks, which extended the original military line to its quarry at St George and worked it as a private siding using its own locomotive, an Avonside-built 0-6-0ST named *Margaret*, replaced in May 1960 by a diesel-mechanical locomotive. In the early days, according to a Mr Hindley, the LMS worked the original line as far as the level crossing over the St Asaph to Abergele road. This practice was discontinued during the 1930s when the quarry company took over the working as far as Foryd Junction. Traffic finally ceased in February 1965, the track being lifted two months later. The RCH 1929 handbook makes no mention of the St George quarry as a separate entry, but lists the positions of Kinmel Park estate and the Royal Army Service Corps under 'Rhyl — Limestone Products Ltd Siding', and Jones & Son's siding and Limestone Products Ltd siding under 'Rhyl and Foryd'. Bass breweries had a depot adjoining the line where it crossed the A55 road, and also made use of the rail facilities in the late 1930s. After World War 2 a timber yard was located alongside the line, which necessitated a spark arrester being fitted to the steam locomotive.

Very little remains of the trackbed today. The site of Kinmel Park camp became absorbed into Bodelwyddan industrial estate and was subsequently built over.

Denbigh, Ruthin & Corwen Railway

History

The Denbigh, Ruthin & Corwen Railway had an inauspicious start. It was essentially a contractor's railway. The first sod was turned by Miss Florence West of Ruthin Castle on 4 September 1865 but differences between the contractors caused the partnership between Thomas Savin and David Davies of Llandinam to terminate in November, leaving Thomas Savin to wield power on the DR&C board.

By early 1862 the DR&C had been constructed as far as Ruthin (6¾ miles), and was opened to traffic on Saturday 1 March, operated by the LNWR. Intermediate stations were provided at Llanrhaiadr and Rhewl.

The 9¾-mile section of line to Gwyddelwern was passed as satisfactory in March 1863. Stations were provided at Eyarth, Nantclwyd and Derwen. The route included some heavy earthworks at Eyarth and gradients of 1 in 50 on the climb beyond Derwen to the summit en route to Gwyddelwern.

Differences between Savin and the LNWR board delayed the official opening of the final 2-mile section from Gwyddelwern to Corwen until 6 October 1864. DR&C trains terminated at a temporary station.

By July 1878 a working agreement with the LNWR came into force, and full vesting into the LNWR was authorised by an Act of 3 July 1877, taking effect from 1 July 1879.

Route Description

Denbigh to Corwen

Between Denbigh and Corwen the intermediate station buildings, with the exception of Derwen, were generally

Denbigh

An unidentified LNWR 2-4-2T hauling a rake of six six-wheel coaches approaches the outskirts of Denbigh with a working from Corwen. Note the close-cropped embankment sides, with what appear to be allotments and immaculate fencing, a far cry from today's overgrown tracksides. The tank engines were used by the LNWR in order to avoid paying the GWR for the use of its turntable at Corwen. Locomotives could face Corwen or Denbigh: there was no hard and fast rule as to which direction was 'correct' for the branch, unlike some other branches. *Bill Rear collection*

similar in design. Platforms were short and low. Single-line staff token was in use, with the equipment located in the station offices. Other than at Ruthin, no signalboxes were provided. Towards Corwen was the Down direction.

Denbigh

Denbigh station was an imposing two-storey structure constructed of local stone, surmounted by a spire, befitting the headquarters (albeit briefly) of the Vale of Clwyd Railway. Facilities included a single through platform and a passenger bay at the Rhyl end with the usual arrangements for dealing with freight. A two-road locomotive shed with a 36ft turntable was located on the down side, north of the station.

Throughout the station's existence, traffic working followed a broadly similar pattern, with up and down direction through trains both using the main platform.

The signalling arrangements were simplified in early 1957 with the commissioning of a new signalbox of typical 1950s British Railways design, located on the down side. It took over the functions previously undertaken by Mold & Denbigh Junction box on the down side, Denbigh No 1 (at the north end of the station on the up side) and Denbigh No 2 box located at the south end of the main platform, again on the up side. The new box was 45ft 4ins x 13ft 0in and contained a set of 70 levers. The revised track layout which came into use on the same date dispensed with separate up and down lines between the station and Mold & Denbigh Junction, both lines becoming bi-directional single lines. The Mold & Denbigh Junction signalbox had been located 1 mile north of the station where the Vale of Clwyd line parted company with the Mold and Chester line. The former up line became the up and down single track to Foryd Junction near Rhyl, whilst the former down line became the up and down single line to Bodfari and Mold.

On leaving Denbigh station the line continued, falling at first for a short distance then undulating to just beyond Milepost 2 then stiffening for about half a mile before easing slightly to 1 in 354 to run into Llanrhaiadr station.

Llanrhaiadr

Llanrhaiadr station, 3½ miles from Denbigh, was an intermediate halt on the single-line section from Denbigh to Ruthin.

The station building was of brick construction two storeys high, with a low, short platform located on the up side. There was some protection offered by a canopy that extended over the platform in front of the building. The facilities were somewhat excessive for the amount of traffic

Llanrhaiadr

This commercial postcard produced in LNWR days shows the station at its peak condition, looking towards Ruthin. Note the canopy over the platform, all the woodwork in immaculate condition, and the gathering of people. It is assumed that this was the station staff and the family of the stationmaster, seen on the extreme right of the group and identified by his uniform. Out of sight behind the platform was a solitary siding for the freight traffic handled. There was no goods warehouse, although a shed on the platform acted in this capacity. The loop would have been rarely used, and was taken out after the LMS took over. *J. A. Peden*

generated. There was a goods loop on the down side with a facing siding on the up. These were removed after the station closed to all traffic on 2 February 1953, as was the canopy over the platform. The building was demolished in the 1970s.

After closure it remained necessary to have a member of staff on duty to control the hand-operated level crossing. The line was protected by signals controlled from Llanrhaiadr station frame of five levers mounted on the platform adjoining the crossing gates.

On leaving the station the line continued to rise at 1 in 354 briefly before levelling out for half a mile. At about 3¾ miles the line started to climb at 1 in 196 for the next ½ mile where it then stiffened to 1 in 130 before levelling out.

Rhewl

Rhewl station was 5¼ miles from Denbigh and on the level. There was a rarely used goods loop located on the down side with a facing siding on the up side before the passenger platform, which extended to a loading bank on which a yard crane was mounted. Access to the loop and a siding on the up side at the north end was controlled from the trackside by a two-lever ground frame locked by the train staff. Rhewl level crossing, north of the station, was controlled by signals worked from the four-lever crossing frame.

The station building and platform were on the up side. The station was not designated a passing point and the loop, which was rarely used, was lifted after the line closed to passenger traffic in 1962. At one time some passenger protection was provided by a canopy, but this had been removed some years earlier. The station building survives to this day as an attractive and well-preserved private house. At the Ruthin end of the station a road bridge over the line was removed in the 1970s.

The station lost its freight traffic from 1 September 1958, but passenger trains continued to call until 30 April 1962 when all services were withdrawn. The station was quite close to the village, and the community, which was very supportive, tried to retain passenger services on the line.

The railway then maintained roughly a straight course in the centre of the valley for nearly five miles towards Ruthin.

Approximately three quarters of a mile north of Ruthin station, Ruthin Lime & Limestone Co, Craig-y-Ddywart quarry and works were located on the up side, about half a mile off the main line and served by freight trains heading towards Ruthin. This traffic survived until freight services were withdrawn in 1963. The traffic was sometimes

Rhewl
This is the only photograph so far located that shows Rhewl and the track looking towards Ruthin in later days. The original negative has been lost and this print is a copy from a small contact print held in Denbighshire Archives, taken by a member of the County Council after the closure notices had been posted. Note the two tanks in the siding, although it is not clear who would have taken delivery of fuel. Possibly they were for a local farmer for his tractors. After the track was lifted the road bridge was demolished and the road levelled. The building still stands, in private hands. *Denbighshire Archives*

worked to the main line by the quarry's own locomotive. Storage hoppers were located alongside the Ruthin to Denbigh main road and discharged into the standard gauge wagons standing on the siding. The Denbigh to Ruthin trip engine had to work the sidings when the quarry's locomotive was unavailable and I recall seeing '3F' 0-6-0 No 43396 from Rhyl shed standing on the side of the main road at the head of a raft of wagons being loaded, the rails being submerged by lime dust.

Ruthin

The town of Ruthin stands at the southern end of the Vale of Clwyd, at the foot of Llantysilio Mountain, behind which lies Llangollen and the valley of the River Dee.

Facilities comprised the station buildings, the up and down platforms, a signalbox, a goods warehouse and small yard with public weighbridge facilities. In addition to the normal facilities, the goods department could deal with livestock, including horse and cattle traffic. Coal was also catered for, and the yard offered crane lifting capacity up to 3 tons. The main platform, buildings and station forecourt were on the up side, the platform line signalled for 'Up & Down' working. The building was of two-storey brick construction with a slate roof. A canopy extended over the

full width of the platform and for the length of the building, although this was subsequently cut back, giving only partial protection. The attractive station building was demolished in the 1970s to make way for road improvements.

A large goods warehouse adjoined the platform at the Denbigh end, with the goods yard road access off the forecourt. The yard contained four sidings, made up of a group of three (the centre road of which passed through the warehouse), and a fourth siding running alongside the cattle pens. On the down side was a second shorter platform, used only occasionally for passenger services. An open sheltered area was provided, with a canopy that extended over the full width, and a bench seat. This was removed after passenger services to Corwen were discontinued in 1953. Installed on the platform was a standard LNWR-design 12ft x 8ft signal cabin housing a 22-lever frame, which controlled points and signals in the station limits and housed the single-line token instruments. Passengers who detrained on the down side platform crossed the line by the barrow crossing at the Denbigh end, under the watchful eye of the signalman. A goods loop ran behind the platform and signal cabin, together with a short siding that terminated at the platform ramp. This siding was removed and the goods loop cut back after the line to Corwen was closed. The

Ruthin

BR Standard Class 4MT 2-6-4T No 80086 of Chester (6A) shed stands at the head of a two-coach local at Ruthin on 22 April 1957. The train had been the 9am from Chester to Denbigh which then worked forward to Ruthin at 10.45am. This was now the terminus for passenger trains and the locomotive would run round its stock to form the 11.41am through to Chester. The station building was at one time the headquarters of the Denbigh, Ruthin & Corwen Railway and was constructed on a grand scale, befitting the head office of a major employer in a rural area, but with the take-over by the LNWR the station was downgraded to ordinary status. The stationmaster lived 'over the shop' but the building was draughty and for much of its time the living quarters were unoccupied. It was demolished after the tracks were uplifted and today a roundabout stands on the site. *W. A. Camwell*

Ruthin

The signalbox at Ruthin was a small wooden structure on the former down platform. The box housed a 22-lever frame of which 15 were working levers. The platform was rarely used as train services were modest and usually the single main up platform sufficed. Here No 78038 of Rhyl shed, with Driver E. Evans at the regulator, runs round its train on the down loop on 10 September 1959. Two months later the engine was transferred to Northwich. *Norman Jones*

Ruthin

Before the line to Corwen closed for regular passenger services from 2 February 1953, some trains used the down platform, which necessitated shelter and protection from the elements. In 1947 the Bangor shedmaster took this photograph, looking towards Denbigh, which shows the shelter and the canopy over the main platform. Note the wooden post lower quadrant-type signals in the foreground. The whole station area is spotless and one can imagine the stationmaster expressing disapproval if anything littered his platforms. *J. M. Dunn*

Ruthin

This view, taken in 1949, shows the platforms and track looking towards Corwen. The down-side shelter and seating are clearly visible. The deserted air suggests that perhaps this was taken on a Sunday when there was no traffic to disturb the peaceful atmosphere. The footbridge replaced a level crossing which was sealed off at the turn of the century. *Bill Rear collection*

Ruthin

On the penultimate Saturday before passenger trains ceased to run to Ruthin, Standard Class 4MT 4-6-0 No 75010 stands at the head of the 3pm to Chester, is taken from the main up platform looking towards Corwen. The locomotive displays a 6G shed plate, showing it was attached to Llandudno Junction shed. In the following October it was transferred away to Nuneaton. Note that the canopy over the platform has been cut back and no longer gives shelter to the platform edge. Nevertheless, the barge boards remain, and it is reputed that the design was unique to Ruthin. *Keith Smith*

Ruthin

The same day, the same train and the same photographer: Despite the impending closure and wet conditions, the station is still kept in tidy condition. The station staff maintained their pride in the site, although few, if any, found alternative employment on the railway. Just visible is the down starter which had replaced its lower quadrant predecessor. Note the signal arm is pivoted away from the post, mounted on a bracket. The reason for this is unknown. *Keith Smith*

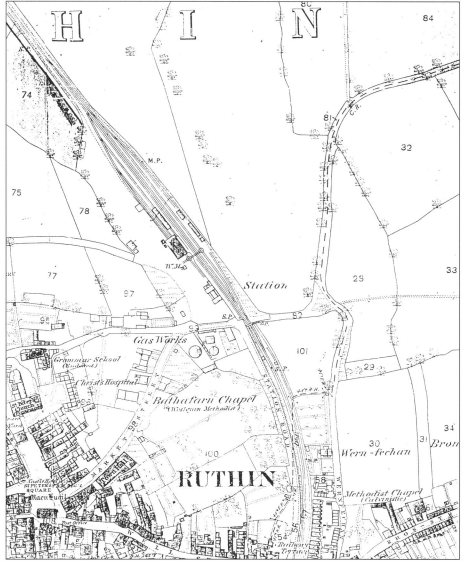

1914-18 Ordnance Survey map showing Ruthin station layout. *Crown Copyright*

Ruthin
Ruthin signalbox was in the charge of Mr R. Williams on 10 September 1959, seen here (left) with an unknown colleague. Note the miniature train staff equipment for the section to Denbigh, as well as the usual signalbox fittings, the clock and the vintage telephone. The desk behind Mr Williams was standard equipment and probably contained old timetables as well as the register. Note, too, the gas lamp suspended from the ceiling and the working timetable pinned above the telephone. In the foreground can be seen three of the Webb-pattern levers in the frame. *Norman Jones*

single-line token instruments were moved to the station office at this time and the section was extended from Ruthin to Corwen, with no intermediate post. A public footbridge crossed the tracks from Market Street at the Corwen end, with a second set of steps off the up side ramp.

Trains departing for Corwen started on a rising gradient. At ¾ mile from Eyarth the line passed through Eyarth Gorge, where road and rail followed the course of the river through spectacular scenery, twisting, turning and squeezing along the very narrow and picturesque deep cutting through solid rock with extremely sharp curves. A speed restriction was in force through the rock cutting: 20mph for up trains and 35mph for down. The cutting marked the change of gradient until the summit of the line beyond Gwyddelwern, from falling to Eyarth station then rising in the cutting to the summit.

Eyarth
The single platform and buildings in the 1930s. Despite the presence of a loop, Eyarth was not a token exchange point but an intermediate stop on the section from Ruthin to Nantclwyd. The platforms were of low height and whilst this was acceptable in the days of six-wheel carriages, they were too low for the modern LMS stock and portable steps had to be on hand. The small wooden shed in the foreground was the waiting shelter with the porters' room and lamp room adjoining. The main building was the stationmaster's house and was not used for railway business. The small brick building beyond was another waiting room, behind which was a well. Presumably there was no piped water to the site! A single siding terminated behind the platform, trailing off the platform line. It was little used. *Bill Rear collection*

Eyarth

On the last Saturday of passenger service between Corwen and Ruthin, 31 January 1953, the 11.10am from Corwen to Denbigh pulls away from the station, with the stationmaster watching the photographer from the doorway to his house. Note that five years after nationalisation the poster boards still carry the heading 'LMS' although they are devoid of any information. The station nameboard has disappeared, presumably in readiness for the closure. The train normally consisted of two coaches but, possibly anticipating some enthusiasts, was strengthened by an additional coach. The motive power was different, too. The usual type on this duty would have been a Fowler Class 2P 4-4-0, but on this day a Stanier 2-6-4T was substituted. *W. A. Camwell*

Eyarth Gorge

BR Standard Class 4MT 4-6-0 No 75020 threads through the narrow gap where road, river and rail compete for the space available. The road is above the line. The safety valves are lifting, showing that the fireman is on top form, ready for the climb that follows. This was the Land Cruise that started at Pwllheli and was heading for Denbigh and Rhyl. The engine carried an 89C (Machynlleth) shed plate but was out-stationed at Pwllheli for three days at a time, returning to the parent shed for servicing, when it was replaced by another for the diagram. Pwllheli men were on the footplate. The last season that the Land Cruise trains worked was in 1961. *Bill Rear collection*

Eyarth

Eyarth station was 8½ miles from Denbigh. The line through the station was located on a slight falling gradient. Trains could not cross here.

The single passenger platform was of low height on the down side and it was necessary to provide portable steps for passengers.

Eyarth Gorge
Another view of the track through the gorge, this time looking towards Corwen. The track was climbing at this point and would continue to do so for the next seven miles. Note the method of securing the telegraph poles into the rock face. The unstable nature of the rock meant that vigilance was necessary by all concerned and speed was restricted to 20mph for up trains and 35mph for down workings. Milepost 9 can be seen in the distance. *J. M. Dunn*

A goods yard was located at the Corwen end of the site behind the passenger platform. The yard also contained a weigh machine and an office. A goods loop was located on the up side and two sidings were situated at either end of the platform ramp off the main line, controlled by the usual two-lever ground frame.

Domestic coal was dealt with from the siding at the Corwen end and the station was listed as open for goods traffic until final closure on 30 April 1962.

In its heyday the station boasted a stationmaster, who lived on the premises, assisted by two porters. The station building was sold and is now a private hotel and restaurant set in delightful surroundings and has not lost its character.

From Eyarth the line continued to fall for about a quarter of a mile before the gradient changed to rising before levelling out briefly at Nantclwyd.

Nantclwyd

Nantclwyd station was a staff token station with the instruments located in the station office. A short platform was located on the down side. There was a goods loop provided for the commencement of services, but this was removed after passenger services ceased. There was a gated siding on the down side at the Corwen end of the platform, served by down trains. The siding contained a loading bank and a coal siding which survived until the line closed, although all other freight traffic apart from coal was discontinued from 2 December 1957. The platform road at the Ruthin end was extended back beyond the loop point to provide a second siding, with a loading gauge. Points were controlled from two-lever ground frames locked by the train staff. A six-lever frame controlled signals.

The building remained unchanged until closure, although the platform canopy was removed after regular passenger traffic ceased. The station building was demolished in the 1970s.

Derwen

Derwen station consisted of a single short, low platform on the up side. The station buildings were different in design to others between Ruthin and Gwyddelwern, and incorporated a canopy built over the station offices at the Corwen end. Although it was not a staff token station, there was a goods loop on the down side, which was cut back to a trailing siding served by down trains after regular passenger services ceased. When passenger services ended in February 1953 the station remained open to goods traffic until the line closed. The loop was still in place during the summer of 1953. There was also a trailing siding with a loading wharf located at the Ruthin end of the platform. Access to the loop and siding was controlled from two-lever ground frames, locked by the train staff. After the loop was severed at the Ruthin end, the track was lifted for about half its length and rail-built buffer stops installed. This section was also used as a coal siding until the line closed to all traffic.

The station building passed into private hands and is an attractive private residence. Its location is somewhat isolated, being some distance from the village, but the building is beautifully preserved. Between Derwen and Gwyddelwern the gradient continued to rise steeply.

1¼ miles from Derwen on the up side and connected to the line whilst still on the rising 1 in 138 gradient came the Craig-Lelo Quarry Co's siding and Dee Clwyd Granite Quarries Co's siding.

Gwyddelwern

Gwyddelwern station was 2 miles 1,104yd from Derwen. Initially, the station was the southern terminus of the line. The single platform and station building were on the down side, with a goods loop on the up. A small four-lever frame, controlling signals, was mounted on the platform at the Corwen end. Points were locked by Annett's keys. There was a small yard on the down side at the Denbigh end, with a coal siding and weighing machine, off which ran a second siding parallel to the main line which ended in buffer stops at the platform ramp. Access to the sidings was controlled by small lever frames on the trackside, locked by the train-staff. The siding at the Corwen end was removed between the wars.

Following withdrawal of passenger services on 2 February 1953, the station remained open for goods traffic until 2 December 1957. It was subsequently demolished in the 1970s and no trace remains.

On departing towards Corwen, the single line was resumed, the Webb & Thompson train staff for the section of line between Gwyddelwern and Corwen being coloured blue.

Nantclwyd

Stanier Class 4MT 2-6-4T No 42568 of Chester LM (6A) shed deputises for the usual Fowler Class 2P 4-4-0 on the last day of services from Ruthin to Corwen. Anticipating an increase of travellers, the authorities had added an extra coach to the formation for the working. In the event, not many enthusiasts travelled over this line, for in 1953 such melancholy events went by largely unnoticed by the fraternity. The 10.25am from Chester to Corwen is seen here pausing at Nantclwyd with little sign of public support. The station closed to traffic the following day although the goods siding, seen passing through the gate, remained open for business until traffic ceased altogether. *W. A. Camwell*

Derwen

This 1963 view shows how little the station had changed since passenger services ceased in 1953. The loop had been cut back and a buffer stop installed halfway. The siding, as it now was, was used by a local coal merchant. There was a second siding at the Ruthin end, behind the platform, which had a loading ramp alongside, but it saw little use. The station survived the dismantling of the track and was converted into a delightful private house which stands to this day. *Brian Cowlishaw*

Gwyddelwern
Gwyddelwern station was a staff token exchange point and the two instruments for issuing the staffs for the respective sections of line were located in the station office. These were of the long Webb & Thompson type. On the shelf can be seen the lever collars and covers to protect instruments if 'blocking back'. The left-hand instrument has a token already removed for the freight train, resting in the instrument. On the desk can be seen the train register and immediately above the desk is the signal light indicator. The whole scene is one of spartan existence and few creature comforts can be seen. *Norman Jones*

Gwyddelwern
BR Standard Class 2MT 2-6-0 No 78056 pauses at Gwyddelwern station on its journey back to Denbigh to exchange the single-line token. The timings on this daily freight working were relaxed and it was the norm to pause at each station and pass the time of day with the staff on duty. Note in the far distance the up starter is pulled off, with the up home signal on the same post. In the foreground can be seen the six-lever ground frame which controlled the goods loop point lock and signals. Note, too, the 'Jim Crow' rail bending/straightening tool. At one time there was a canopy over the platform but this was removed after regular passenger services ceased in 1953. *Norman Jones*

Gwyddelwern

An unusual feature at Gwyddelwern was this concrete post signal with the down starter and up home signal arms. It is believed that this concrete post signal was one of the first to be produced by the LNWR and was installed about 1919. At the foot of the signal post can be seen a small two-lever ground frame, controlled by rodding and locked from the station ground frame Annett's key. The DMU standing at the platform was working an RCTS special over the line in the winter prior to complete closure of the line. *G. H. Platt*

Corwen Dee Bridge

On 19 May 1961 Norman Jones travelled with the crew of the daily Denbigh to Corwen goods. He photographed Class 3F 0-6-0 No 43618 traversing the gradient from the Dee Bridge towards Gwyddelwern. The return working train consisted of five mineral wagons and the brake van. By arrangement, the guard, Arthur Davies, stood on the verandah of the brake van, seen here silhouetted against the sky as the locomotive plods on towards Ruthin and Denbigh. *Norman Jones*

Corwen Dee Bridge
An atmospheric scene, as Class 3F 0-6-0 No 43618 trundles onto the bridge with its train of mineral wagons (five empty and one of coal) and brake van on the return journey to Denbigh with the daily working on 19 May 1961. This working had departed Corwen at 12.20pm (Saturdays Excepted). The start out of Corwen was vigorous as the climb was unremitting, about 1 in 58 at this point, and it continued to the summit beyond Gwyddelwern. *Norman Jones*

Corwen Dee Bridge
Class 2P 4-4-0 No 40629 of Denbigh shed commences the climb out of Corwen to Gwyddelwern, seen here passing over the Dee Bridge with a through working to Denbigh, Mold and Chester. The locomotive is displaying the wording 'BRITISH RAILWAYS' on the tender which suggests that it had been through the works on overhaul during the first months after nationalisation. The weather must have been warm for every drop-light in the carriage doors is down. The locomotive is steaming well with no trace of black smoke, which would satisfy even the sternest of locomotive inspectors. The bridge was removed after the track was uplifted. *Bill Rear collection*

Corwen

The line from Denbigh met up with the Great Western Railway line from Llangollen about ¼ mile from the station, and the two single lines ran parallel into the station. At the approach to the platforms a scissors crossover permitted trains to reach their designated platform. Here, on 7 August 1948, LMS Class 2P 4-4-0 No 675 negotiates the crossover to access the down platform with the 5.12pm working from Denbigh. Note the GWR token catcher in the foreground, of no use to the LMS traincrew who would hand over their single-line train staff to the Corwen East box signalman on the platform.
W. A. Camwell

Corwen

Ex-Midland Railway Class 3F 0-6-0 No 43396 was a long-time resident of Rhyl shed, having arrived there on 3 May 1947 from Warrington Dallam shed. It was normally out-shedded at Denbigh specifically for the daily freight working to and from Corwen. It was withdrawn from Rhyl shed on 17 August 1958. Although Corwen station was a GWR/ Western Region station, the LMS and London Midland Region maintained a presence here. Freight trains off the LMS line worked through the station to the yard on the west side and disposed of their trains under the eyes of the yard foreman. After turning on the shed turntable, they proceeded to make up the train for the return journey. Departure time was booked for 2.5pm but because the traincrew had been on duty for several hours, they changed footplates with another Denbigh set who had worked a passenger train out. Here, on 9 May 1949, the locomotive pulls a lengthy train out of the up-side yard and proceeds along the platform road to collect the train staff from the signalman at East box, before starting the journey back to Denbigh. *E. S. Russell*

Half a mile before Corwen station on the down side was the siding belonging to E. Jones & Sons of Bryn Eglwys, served by Corwen-bound trains which had to set back into the siding to set down or pick up wagons.

The climb from Corwen to Gwyddelwern was unremitting, with sections of the line rising for short stretches at 1 in 58 and 1 in 48, and a half-mile length at 1 in 71. There were also some very severe curves on this section which inhibited up freight trains immediately on leaving Corwen.

Just before Corwen the railway crossed the River Dee on an attractive lattice girder bridge of six spans, each of 50ft. The bridge is no longer with us, being demolished in about 1969. The line then swung right through 90° and ran parallel to the Llangollen line for the last ¼ mile before Corwen station was reached.

Corwen

Corwen station was 2½ miles from Gwyddelwern. Initially station facilities were provided by the Denbigh, Ruthin & Corwen Railway at a temporary platform on its own line at Corwen when services commenced in the autumn of 1864, until the Corwen & Bala Railway station opened the following year. The single line from Denbigh was then extended, running parallel with the Llangollen & Corwen line into the station.

The Denbigh, Ruthin & Corwen line platform was located on the up (towards Llangollen) side. Goods traffic to and from the Denbigh line ran through the platform road to the up-side yard, west of the platform, although terminating passenger trains from Denbigh discharged on the down-side platform. The passenger stock was then shunted to the up side for the return journey.

The main station building survives as an industrial trailer centre, and although the middle section containing the former booking hall and barrier to the down platform was removed in the 1980s, a new section was inserted in-between in 2002.

Corwen

It was somewhat unusual to find an LMS Compound at Corwen, but on 9 May 1949 No 40933 of Chester shed was working the 10.25am from Chester. Denbigh men took over the controls at Denbigh and worked the train to Corwen where they changed footplates with another Denbigh crew who had worked the 9.50am Class K freight out. Two coaches were the normal stock for this working which was booked to depart at 2.25pm all stations to Chester. The train is standing awaiting departure time outside Corwen East box, which would issue the single-line train staff at the appropriate time. The locomotive had by this time acquired its permanent British Railways number on the smokebox and the cab sides, but the tender still wears the LMS on the sides. *E. S. Russell*

Working the Line

Corwen to Denbigh

Initially the LNWR commenced working trains between Denbigh and Ruthin in 1862. The service (worked by the DR&C) was extended to Gwyddelwern (March 1863) and finally to Corwen. The LNWR ultimately worked the line with locomotives based at Denbigh, Ruthin and Corwen.

It was the practice for most passenger trains from Corwen to terminate at Denbigh, although some workings from the Mold and Chester line were extended to and from Ruthin. All workings were of a local nature, and no through working of coaches took place.

The earliest LNWR timetable to hand is a public passenger issue dated January 1875. Trains departed on Mondays to Saturdays from Corwen at 7.30am to Denbigh, 10.35am through to Chester, 2.40pm to Denbigh and 5.20pm to Denbigh, with additional departures from Ruthin at 8.20am to Denbigh and 2.50pm through to Chester. Three passenger trains worked to Corwen: 7.20am from Chester, arriving at 9.55am; 12.00pm from Denbigh, due 1.15pm; and the 3.40pm from Denbigh, due 4.40pm. There were departures for Ruthin at 4.35pm and 7.30pm from Denbigh. The unbalanced working into Corwen was probably offset by a freight working.

The July 1904 issue of the working timetable lists five passenger and one goods arrival at Corwen, with the same number of departures. Between Ruthin and Denbigh additional trains ran: two passenger, one mixed, one goods (MX — Mondays Excepted) and one empty stock (ThSO — Thursdays and Saturdays Only).

Local needs were adequately catered for, with five passenger trains and one freight train daily in each direction. Additional trains ran as far as Ruthin, usually formed by extending the Chester and Mold line trains.

The train services along the line remained broadly the same throughout World War 1 and until 1926, with minor variations in timings.

The General Strike of 1926 saw a reduction in the passenger services to three passenger trains each way between Corwen and Denbigh, with an additional two trains between Ruthin and Denbigh. It is understood that a freight train ran daily between Corwen and Denbigh. Afterwards, traffic reverted to its normal pattern of five passenger trains each way.

The following season saw an increase to six passenger trains each way between Corwen and Denbigh, with a further four trains running between Ruthin and Denbigh on weekdays and an extra train on Thursday and Saturday evenings.

Freight traffic also took an upturn, and the September 1927 working timetable shows three workings daily.

Despite the increase in passenger traffic, by September 1936 the freight traffic had fallen off and one train each way again sufficed.

The summer of 1939 was probably the busiest in the line's whole history, although the basic six trains per day in each direction were sufficient, with two additional trains to Corwen on Wednesdays and Saturdays. There were eight trains each way between Ruthin and Denbigh on weekdays and an extra train on Saturdays, together with the relevant empty stock workings back to Denbigh. On Sundays there were seven passenger workings between Denbigh and Ruthin, and five passenger workings, one empty stock and one light engine working between Ruthin and Denbigh. Most Sunday workings started or finished at Rhyl. The freight traffic service remained at one train each way between Denbigh and Corwen and return, in the same approximate timings as in previous years.

The outbreak of World War 2 saw a reduction in services. Four trains ran daily from 11 September 1939, departing Corwen at 8.10am, 10.50am, 6.50pm and 9.10pm. The first worked through to Rhyl, the last to Denbigh, the others

DENBIGH, RUTHIN & CORWEN BRANCH.—(Single Line.) 65																		
Train Staff Stations—Denbigh, Ruthin, Nantclwyd, Gwyddelwern, and Corwen. Passenger Trains can cross each other only at Ruthin.																		
Miles.	**WEEK DAYS Down Trains.**	**1**	**2**	**3**	**4**	**5**	**6**	**7**	**8**	**9**	**10**	**11**	**12**	**13**	**14**	**15**	**16**	**17**
		Goods		Pass			G'ds.		G'ds.	Pass.		Pass.	Pass.	Pass		Pass.		
		a.m.		a.m.			a.m.		a.m	a m		p.m.	p.m.	p m		p.m.		
...	DENBIGH dep	6 25	...	8 40	...	...	9 25	..	10 0	11 55	...	3 25	5 5	6 38	...	8 10	...	...
3½	Llan-rhaiadr arr	...	...	8 47	...	...	...	...	10 10	12 2	...	3 32	5 12	6 45	...	8 17	...	...
	Llan-rhaiadr dep	...	...	8 48	...	...	...	...	10 20	12 3	...	3 33	5 13	6 43	...	8 18	...	...
5¾	Rhewl ...... „	...	...	8 53	...	...	...	...	10 45	12 8	...	3 38	5 18	6 51	...	8 23	...	...
6	Ruthin L.S. „	...	...	...	...	...	...	...	11 0	...	...	...	...	...	...	...	...	...
6¾	Ruthin ... arr	6 40	...	8 57	...	...	9 45	...	11 5	12 12	...	3 42	5 22	6 55	...	8 27	...	...
	Ruthin ... dep	...	...	9 0	...	...	10 5	...	...	12 15	...	3 45	5 25	...	...	8 30	...	...
8¾	Eyarth ...... „	...	...	9 6	...	...	10 35	...	...	12 21	...	3 51	5 31	...	...	8 36	...	...
11¾	Nantclw'd arr	Conveys Mail Bags.	...	9 15	...	...	10 45	...	...	...	...	...	...	...	...	8 45	...	...
	Nantclw'd dep		...	9 16	...	...	11 25	...	...	12 31	...	4 1	5 41	...	...	8 46	...	...
13½	Derwen...... „		...	9 22	...	...	11 55	...	...	12 37	...	4 7	5 47	...	...	8 52	...	...
16½	Gwydwrn arr		...	9 29	...	...	12 15	...	...	12 44	...	4 14	5 54	...	...	8 59	...	...
	Gwydwrn dep	...	...	9 32	...	...	12 20	...	...	12 47	...	4 17	5 57	...	...	9 2	...	...
17¾	Bryn Egw S „	...	...	...	...	...	X	...	...	...	...	...	...	...	...	...	...	...
18¾	CORWEN arr	...	...	9 40	...	...	12 30	...	...	12 55	...	4 25	6 5	...	...	9 10	...	...

WEEK DAYS Up Trains.	**18**	**19**	**20**	**21**	**22**	**23**	**24**	**25**	**26**	**28**	**29**	**30**	**31**	**32**	**33**	**34**	**35**	**36**
		Pass		Pass	Pass.	Go'ds		Pass.		Min.	Minrl		Pass.		Exp. Go'ds		Pass.	
		a m		a m	a m	p m		p m		p.m.	p m		p m		p.m.		p.m.	
CORWEN...dep	...	...	...	8 15	10 50	...	...	1 45	...	2 0	2 40	...	4 45	...	TO	...	6 45	...
Gwyddel-wern arr	...	...	...	...	...	...	...	...	...	2 10	2 50	...	...	...	Runs first Tuesday of each month. Conveys Cattle.	...	...	...
Gwyddel-wern dep	...	...	...	8 24	10 59	For Rhyl.	...	1 54	...	2 30	2 55	...	4 54	...		...	6 54	...
Dee Clwyd S. „	...	...	...	...	...		...	...	...	X	...	...	...	...		...	...	...
Derwen ...... „	...	...	...	8 32	11 7		...	2 2	...	2 45	...	...	5 2	...		...	7 2	...
Nantclwyd arr	...	...	...	8 38	11 13		...	2 8	...	2 55	3 10	...	5 8	...		...	7 8	...
Nantclwyd dep	...	...	...	8 39	11 14		...	2 9	...	3 10	3 20	...	5 9	...		...	7 9	...
Eyarth ...... „	...	...	...	8 48	11 23		...	2 18	...	3 25	...	...	5 18	...		...	7 18	...
Ruthin ... arr	...	...	...	8 54	11 29	...	...	2 24	...	3 32	3 35	...	5 24	...		...	7 24	..
Ruthin ... dep	...	7 55	...	8 58	11 32	1 0	...	2 27	...	4 40	4 40	...	5 27	...	6 15	...	7 27	...
Rhewl......... „	...	7 59	...	9 2	11 36	1 30	...	2 31	...	See note	See note	...	5 31	...		...	7 31	...
Llan-rhaiadr arr	...	8 3	...	9 6	11 40	1 40	...	2 35	...			...	5 35	...		...	7 35	...
Llan-rhaiadr dep	...	8 6	...	9 9	11 43	2 5	...	2 38	...	...	...	...	5 38	...		...	7 38	...
DENBIGH arr	...	8 13	...	9 16	11 50	2 15	...	2 45	...	5 0	5 0	...	5 45	...	6 30	...	7 45	...

Denbigh Tickets of all Up Trains to be collected at Llanrhaiadr.

No. 28—Does not run on Corwen Fair Days.

No. 29—Runs on Corwen Fair Days only.

Extract from July 1919 LNWR timetable for the Denbigh, Ruthin and Corwen branch.

working through to Chester. The pattern was unchanged for freight trains during 1940, although some of the timings were slightly different.

By October 1940 the passenger service had reverted to five trains daily to Corwen and, interestingly, two Saturdays Only workings to Gwyddelwern, the latter working back to Denbigh as empty stock. There were three trips between Denbigh and Ruthin and return.

By October 1943 the Saturdays Only trips to Gwyddelwern had been cut, and in addition to the five trains daily over the line, three trains worked to Ruthin and return during the week and an extra two on Saturdays. The first train out from Denbigh to Ruthin worked as empty stock at 5.45am, and the last train on Saturdays from Ruthin (off the 8.50pm from Rhyl) worked back ECS to Denbigh. This pattern remained broadly similar until the railways were nationalised.

The summer issue of the working timetable, dated May 31 to September 26 1948, showed six passenger trains daily each way, with a late 9pm Saturdays-Only train from Rhyl to Corwen, balanced by an empty stock train working to Denbigh. There were three additional workings to and from Ruthin, the first down and last up workings run as empty stock. The freight train pattern remained at one through working each way, daily, and one afternoon working from Denbigh to Ruthin and back.

The last season of passenger working was the winter of 1952-3, which provided five trains daily each way between Corwen and Denbigh. Three of the Corwen departures worked through to Chester via Mold; the other two worked through to Rhyl. The one freight working each way remained in the same paths as previously.

The summer of the following year (1954) saw passenger services between Denbigh and Ruthin cut back from the previous season, with 11 trains daily.

There was little change to the pattern of services until 19 September 1955 when regular passenger services between Rhyl and Denbigh were withdrawn, closure of Denbigh motive power depot (MPD) taking place on the same day. Whilst Denbigh shed was no longer functional, it was still used for the servicing of locomotives or turning on the turntable. Four drivers (but no firemen) still booked on at Denbigh station, nominally attached to Rhyl shed, firemen being obliged to travel by bus or on light engines. This arrangement persisted until the Mold line closed to traffic on 30 April 1962.

There were no changes to regular passenger and freight workings during the summer of 1960. The next year, 1961, saw the final summer for the DR&C line, closure notices having been posted before the summer season commenced.

Final closure came on 1 March 1965. No real protest was made by local people to retain the lines to Rhyl or Mold and accordingly they passed away quietly into history.

Llandudno Junction to Blaenau Ffestiniog

Historical

In early days several proposals were made for a branch. The Conwy & Llanrwst Railway received its Royal Assent on 23 July 1860 and the first sod was cut on 25 August of the same year at Llanrwst Abbey. The Chester & Holyhead Railway was involved and had also submitted proposals for a line which found favour. Ultimately the all-powerful LNWR, which absorbed the C&H, was behind construction as confirmed by the Act of 1863.

The Conwy Valley line extends from Llandudno Junction, on the North Wales coast, to the original terminus at Blaenau Ffestiniog, a distance of 27 miles.

As built, the 11¼ miles of line to Llanrwst were single throughout, with sidings at Llanrwst and intermediate stations at Llansantffraid (subsequently named Glan Conwy) and Tal-y-Cafn. Connection with the main line was effected at Llandudno Junction, with the branch line trains having their own separate line and platform.

On 16 June 1863 a special inaugural train left Llandudno for Llanrwst with all the usual ceremony that befitted such an important event in a rural community. Public services began the following day. The initial train service consisted of three trains each way each day, which was increased to five by June 1864.

The LNWR was authorised to extend the railway to Betws-y-Coed by an Act of 5 July 1865. The 3¾-mile extension left the Conwy and Llanrwst formation north of Llanrwst old station, which was replaced by a new building south of the junction. The line opened for goods traffic on 18 October 1867. At Betws sidings were provided, with slate earning much revenue for the line. Passenger services started on 6 April 1868 and the station refreshment rooms opened that summer. A service of five trains worked to and from Betws on weekdays.

During the construction of the Betws extension the quarry owners at Blaenau Ffestiniog made approaches to the LNWR with a view to extending their line to the quarries. As a result, the LNWR surveyed various routes, but the inescapable fact of requiring a long tunnel to reach Blaenau caused the company to consider both narrow (1ft 11⅝in) and standard gauges for an acceptable route via the Lledr or Penmachno valleys.

By August of that year work had already commenced on a narrow gauge line, but by May 1873 it was decided that despite the advanced state of the works, it would be necessary for the LNWR to construct special locomotives and rolling stock to work this line, so the decision was taken to reconstruct to standard gauge, which involved a number of alterations having to be made to the curves, earthworks and bridges. Hand boring of the long tunnel began in January 1874 and so the Betws Extension Railway was authorised, which continued the new line for nearly one mile to a new terminus, near Blaenau market hall. By January 1878, single-platform stations at Roman Bridge and Pont-y-Pant were put to contract, and a loop with an island platform at Dolwyddelan was authorised.

The line to Dolwyddelan was in use for local freight by February 1879, and at Blaenau a temporary station was erected immediately south of the tunnel mouth in order that the line might open for traffic whilst the Betws Extension Railway was completed. The 11½-mile line was inspected in June 1879; the inspector tested the width of the single-line 3,726yd tunnel by walking in front of a locomotive propelling a coach at walking speed with doors open on both sides from end to end.

The summit of the line is reached inside the tunnel about ¼ mile from the Ffestiniog end. There were four other tunnels of short length on the line. The Lledr viaduct (Gethin's Bridge) with seven stone arches is the other major feature, with 17 bridges of lesser size constructed mainly from undressed stone, a detail with which the inspecting Colonel found fault. After a reinspection, the railway between Betws and the temporary station at Blaenau was opened on 22 July 1879. The extension to the permanent station opened on 1 April 1881, after which the temporary station was closed and removed. At Blaenau, a combined locomotive and carriage shed was built which contained one and three roads respectively. This shed was closed on 14 September 1931 and afterwards was demolished.

The original junction with the Chester & Holyhead line of the LNWR was almost opposite the junction of the Llandudno branch and at the point where the first Llandudno Junction station stood. The line, which was single throughout, followed close along the shore between the engine shed and the waterline. The present Llandudno Junction station was opened on 1 October 1897 when the first station was closed and demolished. The branch junction was moved further east and ½ mile of new track was built. The original branch line was retained as a long siding, although the last hundred yards towards Glan Conwy was taken up.

The line was controlled by block working from 1879, a system replaced in 1894 by electric staff, coincidental with the signalbox at Dolwyddelan being replaced by a frame mounted on the island platform. In July 1898 the goods

Llandudno Junction
Class 2F 0-6-2T No 27593 (LNWR No 3748) stands in No 4 bay platform at the head of the 2.47pm (SO) to Betws y Coed. The LMS used these small tank engines on the shorter journeys up the Conwy valley line for many years until they were superseded by the larger, more modern LMS 2-6-2T Stanier design. Trains working through to Blaenau Ffestiniog were usually hauled by tender engines at this time. The normal load on the short journeys was three coaches. Note the wooden platform extension and the overhead cross-bracing between the platform canopies, necessary with the high winds experienced blowing off the Conwy estuary. *G. H. Platt*

loop on the down side at Betws became the down passenger line with the construction of a new platform reached by a footbridge. The up line was signalled for up and down working by the LNWR in contravention of the Board of Trade requirements, although an exception was permitted for trains that terminated at Betws and worked back to Llandudno Junction.

When the 'Dolgarrog Light Railway Order of 1910' was authorised, it was built as 'Government Works' during World War 1 from the branch to the aluminium works at Dolgarrog, crossing the River Conwy. A new halt on the branch, with the name of 'Dolgarrog', was opened in 1917.

The scenery along the line was recognised as a major tourist attraction from the start and was publicised from early days to encourage holiday traffic in the area. In September 1911 the LNWR introduced a third class 'Observation' car on the morning down journey to Blaenau, returning in the afternoon, with a supplementary fare for passengers. This facility was increased when two more cars were built in 1913, and was extremely popular. They were used on a seasonal basis continuously until World War 2, when they were withdrawn for the duration of the war.

Reinstatement after the war continued every summer until the introduction of the Derby 'Lightweight' DMUs in 1956, the large panoramic windows in the new units rendering the steam-hauled stock surplus to requirements.

Description of the Line

Llandudno Junction

Llandudno Junction station is better known as a main line junction on the Chester & Holyhead line. The first station was located in the fork where the Llandudno Town branch diverges from the main line to Bangor, and opened to traffic in 1848. It was somewhat cramped. Conwy Valley line trains worked from a separate platform on the south side of the original station, which was inconvenient for passengers. The present station was opened on 1 November 1897 and consisted of six through lines and two bays at either end. When the replacement station opened, the original structure was demolished. Because the new station was on a different site, the original Conwy valley line had to be diverted. The branch connection with the main line was realigned a second time in 1984.

Llandudno Junction
In 1956 the first of the 'Lightweight' DMUs appeared in regular service in North Wales. Most units were based at Llandudno Junction and operated up the Conwy valley line, replacing the majority of the steam services. They were an immediate 'hit' with the public and traffic receipts grew; the panoramic windows at the front enabled travellers to see the line ahead as well as watching the driver at work, a fact which was sometimes resented and blinds were dropped to prevent such a thing happening. Here in the summer of 1956 one such unit off the branch pulls into No 4 bay platform. In the receding distance a Class A working for Chester passes under Queen's Road bridge. *Bill Rear*

Glan Conwy
Originally called Llansantffraid, the station was renamed Glan Conway in 1865. As with other branch line stations in North Wales, the platforms were low and portable steps were necessary. Facilities were limited. The single platform was on the down side, facing the Conwy estuary, and at times of high wind and rain passengers were liable to get soaked. The main building provided accommodation for the stationmaster as well as a combined booking hall and waiting room. At one time there was a single siding behind the platform which saw minimal use as a freight facility and which after World War 2 housed a camping coach in the summer months. The station closed to all traffic in 1964 and the building was sold off into private hands. It survives to this day as a house. Public pressure nevertheless caused the platform to be reopened in 1970 as an unstaffed halt and so it remains. *J. J. Davis*

Glan Conwy

After leaving Glan Conwy the line keeps to the shoreline of the Conwy estuary. Here a new Derby 'Lightweight' DMU skirts the shoreline on an afternoon working to Blaenau Ffestiniog, believed to be in the summer of 1956. Note the 'whiskers' on the end panel of the unit; the block yellow warning panel had not yet appeared. The trackside is clear of growth, unlike today when it is difficult to see through the vegetation in places. These units were very popular, especially with tourists, and local traffic was boosted by imaginative marketing. Note the features that have now disappeared from the railway scene, namely telegraph poles and in the distance a permanent way hut.
Bill Rear collection

Glan Conwy

In fact this location is midway between Glan Conwy and Tal-y-Cafn. Here Stanier 2-6-2T No 40130, hauling a standard set of three non-corridor coaches, skirts the estuary with a train for Blaenau Ffestiniog. This type of locomotive was introduced to Llandudno Junction in 1935 when five locomotives were transferred in or received new, and put to work on the branch with immediate effect. They were considered superior to what had been used before, although they quickly acquired a reputation for being indifferent steamers. Nevertheless, they worked practically all the traffic on the branch until they were superseded by the Ivatt Class 2MT 2-6-2Ts which, although a lower power class, were superior in every respect. *H. Rogers Jones*

Tal-y-Cafn
Stanier Class 3P 2-6-2T No 40133 of Llandudno Junction (6G) shed coasts into Tal-y-Cafn station with a three-coach non-corridor empty stock working to Blaenau Ffestiniog in the winter of 1956. This train, running under the reporting number W954A, was to form a football supporters' special from Blaenau although the venue is not known. The 'A' suffix on the headcode denotes that the train was running in two parts, but it is not known where the second part originated. *W. A. Camwell*

The branch leaves the Chester & Holyhead main line on the down side and turns through 90° to run alongside the River Conwy, today passing through the edge of the freight yard and crossing a minor service road to the industrial estate, before passing under the A55, where it rejoins its original formation.

Access to the branch is now controlled from the power signalbox, the single-line token equipment being held in the station office.

Conwy Valley trains worked either through from Llandudno, or started from either No 3 or No 4 down-side bay platform at Llandudno Junction. These platforms were taken out of use when the station layout was simplified.

Originally, the single-line train staff was the large Webb & Thompson type and controlled the section between Llandudno Junction No 1 and Tal-y-Cafn. The train staff for this section was coloured blue.

Once the single line is accessed, the track keeps the river company for much of the way, rarely deviating from the riverbank by more than a few yards before Llanrwst.

Glan Conwy

The first station, originally called Llansantffraid but renamed Glan Conway in 1865, is 1½ miles from Llandudno Junction. The single low platform and the former station building are located on the down side, the line being built on the sea wall. No goods accommodation was provided, but a small siding south of the platform on the down side sufficed, access being controlled by the train staff. During the summer months after World War 2, a camping coach was situated here. There was not enough revenue to justify

the station's retention during the purge of the 1960s so it closed in December 1964. The station building is now an attractive private house with a fine view over the River Conwy towards the castle. The station reopened on 4 May 1970.

On leaving the station the line closely follows the River Conwy — which is tidal up to Trefriw. The first crossing loop was at Tal-y-Cafn & Eglwysbach, 5¼ miles from Llandudno Junction and close to the National Trust's Bodnant Gardens.

Tal-y-Cafn & Eglwysbach

The settlement of Tal-y-Cafn has historic links. Nearby is the estate of Lord Aberconway at Bodnant, near Eglwysbach. His home and gardens are now owned by the National Trust, the ornamental gardens being world famous.

Tal-y-Cafn was one of the original stations on the line when it first opened. The main station had two platforms. On the down-side platform was a two-storey structure that included the stationmaster's house and a booking office. The train staff token machines for both sections were located in the station office. The general waiting room and porters' room were detached from the main building and a small wooden hut served as a lamp room.

A minor road crosses the track which is protected by hand-operated level crossing gates south of the station. Passengers crossed the line from the station office to the up platform across the level crossing.

The up platform had a 15-lever ground frame which stood on a raised plinth adjoining the level crossing. It was open to the elements until 1950, when a cover was

Tal-y-Cafn

A gleaming new DMU stands at the up platform at Tal-y-Cafn awaiting the arrival of a down train. The unit was on a through working to Llandudno, as the destination indicator states. Note that every window seat appears to be occupied, and it is known from personal observations at the time that the line enjoyed an enormous boost to its revenue with the introduction of these units. Note, too, the pristine appearance of both platforms. There is not a scrap of litter to be seen, in contrast to the neglected appearance of the station in later years. In the late 1960s the loop was taken out and the up-side shelter removed. The station site in general took on a bedraggled appearance despite the fact that the station was manned. In late 2000, however, the Llandudno & Conwy Valley Railway Society was given permission to landscape the now-trackless up platform, with the support of Railtrack and Bodnant Gardens, and the general appearance is much improved. *W. A. Camwell*

Tal-y-Cafn

This 1949 view shows the immaculate state of the station platforms and buildings in steam days. Approaching the platform is an up Class K freight hauled by an unknown Class 2MT 2-6-2T. The fireman can just be seen leaning out of the cab with the long Webb & Thompson train staff, ready to hand it over to the porter signalman standing with hand outstretched at the top of the ramp. Note the up-side shelter with its extended roof to give passengers some cover. Other features include the Hawkeye sign on the down platform that remained until the 1960s although the yellow background was painted maroon in early BR days. Long-burning oil lamps can be seen on the down platform. Beyond the level crossing was a small goods yard, but only the loading ramp can be seen. *Derek Chaplin*

provided. When the crossing loop was taken out the frame was removed, replaced by a small five-lever frame mounted on the down platform which controlled signals protecting the level crossing and the gate lock. The up platform had a semi-open passenger shelter, a station nameboard and long-burning oil lamps.

Beyond the crossing on the down side was a small goods yard, serving the local livestock market, now closed and sold. The yard was really an extension of the down-side loop. In the yard were cattle pens with a cattle shed close by. On a short neck was a 5-ton yard crane and beyond that were timber wharves. Access to the goods loop was by a small two-lever ground frame, whilst a second ground frame of two levers, which was locked by the train staff, controlled access on to the single line.

In 2001 a local rail enthusiasts' group, the Llandudno & Conwy Valley Railway Society, refurbished the up platform, including an LNWR-type new sign and an extensive display of plants provided in part by Bodnant Gardens, a gesture which was promoted by both Railtrack (the station is still manned for crossing keeper duties) and the local community council. The station building is now an attractive private house, still being converted.

On 5 July 1904 an accident occurred between Tal-y-Cafn and Dolgarrog. The 10.25am Llandudno to Betws-y-Coed ran off the rails two miles south of Tal-y-Cafn. The locomotive, 2-4-2T No 891, hauling seven coaches, overturned. Bad weather was blamed, but the LNWR was criticised for timing this and other trains on the branch to cover six miles in eight minutes, which was deemed too tight for the line.

Dolgarrog

A small wooden platform halt was built at Dolgarrog (8¼ miles) in 1917 on the down side serving the aluminium works across the river. The platform had two small huts which provided shelter, together with station nameboards and electric lights. A handrail at the back of the platform ran the entire length.

Beyond the platform was a loop on the up side with a connection to the private branch. This was controlled by two ground frames at either end of the loop, locked by the train staff. A siding off the loop led to the aluminium works across the river and to a hydro-electric station. The connection from the works fell out of use by 1960 and was taken out and lifted in 1963.

Between Tal-y-Cafn and Dolgarrog
On 5 July 1904 the 10.25am Llandudno to Betws y Coed ran off the rails two miles south of Tal-y-Cafn. The engine, a Webb 2-4-2T, No 891, and the seven coaches overturned, the locomotive turning through 180° in the process. Fortunately there were only six passengers on board and none of them was injured although the driver, Charles Jones of Llandudno Junction shed, was badly injured, and his fireman, John Williams, was badly scalded. The recovery of the engine, a fortnight later, took the power of eight other locomotives to drag it free. At the resulting enquiry it was shown that the cause was excessive speed, but there were mitigating circumstances; then train timings for this and other workings required the driver to cover the six miles in eight minutes and the LNWR was criticised for this fact which required speeds of 60mph to be achieved. The timings were relaxed the following September. *Bill Rear collection*

Dolgarrog

Dolgarrog halt was some distance away from the village of the same name, on the opposite bank of the river, so traffic potential was minimal. There were few facilities, with little protection other than a wooden shelter, and declining passenger receipts (there were no freight facilities) meant that the halt was closed in the purges of 1964. Somewhat surprisingly, the local authority pressed for its reopening, which it did in 1965 with even fewer facilities, and it remains open to this day. Here a new DMU is seen approaching the halt on its outward trip to Blaenau Ffestiniog. It had one passenger waiting although it is suspected that this was a railway employee going on duty! *W. A. Camwell*

Llanrwst & Trefriw (now Llanrwst North)

Immediately beyond Tan Lan siding came the point where the extension to Betws-y-Coed diverged on the down side from the Conwy & Llanrwst Railway, forming the down line of the passing loop. The original line continued straight on here for about 200yd to a terminus in what became Llanrwst goods yard. Llanrwst signalbox on the up side stands in the 'V' between the entrance to the goods yard and the up-side loop line. The signalbox still remains, attractively modernised, today controlling the only passing loop on the branch.

The first station at Llanrwst was the terminus of the Conway & Llanrwst Railway, authorised under an Act of 23 July 1860. The station was formally opened on 16 June 1863 and public services commenced the following day.

The signalbox consisted of a composite structure to standard LNWR design with a set of 20 levers. It contained the single-line token equipment for the sections in either direction, as it still does.

The Betws-y-Coed extension had its new station some 200yd from the junction with the old line into the terminus. The station is 11¼ miles from Llandudno Junction. Facilities on the new line consisted of a single platform with station buildings constructed of local dressed stone with a slate roof on the up side. The building is two-storey and included the stationmaster's house. A passing loop was incorporated on the down side and a platform was added

later at an unknown date on which a matching stone-built shelter with overhanging slate roof was constructed. This had waiting rooms at each end, separated by an area covered by the overall roof but open to the platform edge.

Passengers used to cross the line by the open footbridge but this was removed in the 1970s and replaced by a boarded crossing.

The goods yard itself was located on the up side. It contained four sidings with two tracks on either side of the access road. One road passed through the goods shed, with a second line running parallel but outside the shed. The outer line of the second pair of lines in the yard ran alongside cattle-loading pens. There was a 10-ton yard crane. The yard was extremely busy until traffic was diverted on to the roads in the mid-1960s. A siding remains for use by the permanent way gang based here.

The main building is unfortunately in a rather dilapidated condition and is now boarded up.

Half a mile beyond the station is a short tunnel, 85yd long, under a portion of the town centre.

An unusual incident occurred in 1954 or thereabouts. A freight train heading back to Llandudno Junction was setting back into the down-side loop to permit an up passenger train to pass when the locomotive became derailed. The points controlling the loop had not moved over completely. Examination of the track revealed that a kitten had become trapped between the point blades and

Llanrwst

The goods yard at Llanrwst was on the site of the first terminus of the line, but when the branch was extended to Betws y Coed the platform was resited and the old formation became the goods yard. Here Stanier Class 5MT 4-6-0 No 45348 of Llandudno Junction (6G) shed waits at the neck of the yard with a freight working for Llandudno Junction. The fireman and guard stand on the signalbox steps talking to the signalman, presumably awaiting the train staff and authority to proceed. The signalbox remains and is in use to this day, having recently had a coat of paint and new windows. The sidings and track have been uplifted and the yard is an industrial estate. The signalman's bike, his mode of personal transport of the time, rests under the steps. Today the signalmen on duty park their cars near where the locomotive is standing. *Brian Cowlishaw*

Llanrwst

The station was fully operational and staffed at the time of this photograph in 1956. A new DMU stands in the down platform, heading for Blaenau Ffestiniog. A platform trolley full of mail bags is seen being loaded into the guard's van. A couple of passengers cross the footbridge. The up platform canopy is in place and people can be seen near the booking hall entrance. Note, too, the station seats and gas lamps, one illuminating the footbridge steps. *W. A. Camwell*

Llanrwst
The exterior views of stations are often ignored and yet can be full of interesting detail. This building was the second station on the site, erected for the opening of the Llanrwst & Betws y Coed Railway. The nearest portion of the building resembles a small chapel, apart from the smoke stack. The first railway terminated in the what is now the yard and its building was modified to become part of the goods shed, seen here on the left. In front of the shed was the body of a 50ft full brake brought in to provide additional storage space. In the distance can be seen the signalbox and up starter signal. The station building is intact in 2002 but boarded up. The goods shed is now demolished and the site is an industrial estate. *W. A. Camwell*

Llanrwst
This view shows the station as it was in the 1950s, looking towards Llandudno Junction. Note the clean approach to the cutting slopes, unlike today when the houses on the left cannot be seen for shrubby growth. Apart from the removal of the up platform canopy, the footbridge and the platform furniture, the scene is little changed. The down platform shelter survives; passengers cross the line by the barrow crossing shown here. *Bill Rear collection*

Llanrwst

In 1989 a new station was built, more centrally located to the town than formerly. The platform and shelter were part financed by the local county council and the station was opened on 29 July, in time for the National Eisteddfod which was held on the outskirts of the town. The old station remains, renamed Llanrwst North, retaining the loop and the signalbox. Here a 'Heritage' DMU calls at the station on its way to Blaenau Ffestiniog. The new station sees more use than the older station but traffic is mainly confined to schoolchildren travelling to and from the local comprehensive near the station. *Larry Goddard*

prevented them from closing properly. As a consequence the engine trailing truck became derailed and the line was blocked for several hours whilst the engine was re-railed. The kitten had been crushed to death.

Llanrwst

The new Llanrwst station platform is in the town centre. It was funded by the County Council and British Rail and opened in 1989. It is located 48 chains beyond Llanrwst North. The platform is on the down side just south of the tunnel and consists of a short platform with a bus shelter for protection. Access is off the Nebo road via a footpath. Today, trains call here upon request, as they still do at Llanrwst North.

The line heads south and passes underneath the main road to Betws-y-Coed then follows the course of the River Conwy, which it crosses on a very photogenic metal viaduct midway between Llanrwst and Betws, before continuing

along the hillside of Gwydyr Forest to Betws. Just prior to Betws station the line crosses the Afon Llugwy on a short three-span bridge which is difficult to access or to photograph.

Betws-y-Coed

The line from Llanrwst was opened to traffic for freight in October 1867 and for passengers the following April. It became the second temporary terminus of the line from Llandudno Junction. Originally the main platform on the up side was much shorter and straight, ending in buffer stops. When the line was extended to Blaenau Ffestiniog, the track in the station was realigned to pass under a new road bridge that gave access to the goods yard. The up platform was extended at this time.

The goods yard was established on the down side and could be accessed from either end of the main line. It had a goods shed through which one siding road passed. There

Between Llanrwst and Betws-y-Coed
After leaving Llanrwst the line keeps company with the river, cutting across the valley floor. The valley at this point has always been at risk from the river overflowing its banks and the engineers constructing the line made allowances for this by providing extra spans on land. Since this photograph was taken in 1956 the river has eroded further and some shrub growth has been allowed to get a foothold on the rail embankment sides, to the annoyance of photographers! Here a new two-car DMU heads south up the valley to Blaenau Ffestiniog with an afternoon working. *Bill Rear collection*

were cattle pens and a weigh machine, and the office was at the road entrance.

North of the up platform was an engine shed with a siding and turntable road. The shed was rarely used for its original purpose, becoming surplus to requirements when the line was extended to Blaenau Ffestiniog. It was demolished before World War 2 but the siding and inspection pit remained until the 1980s.

Betws-y-Coed was the largest station on the line and lavishly equipped. The stationmaster had accommodation on the first floor of the large main station building. There were eight employees' cottages on the up side.

The station itself consisted of two lengthy platforms which were rarely utilised to the full. Canopies were provided over the station buildings on both platforms. A refreshment room and the station offices were incorporated into the structure. The attractive canopies on the up side were removed in the late 1960s.

The down platform contained a semi-open wooden building which provided some shelter. Passenger access was by a covered footbridge at the southern end of the platforms.

The down-side loop and platform buildings were demolished in the 1970s, but the main station building remains in use. Although in private ownership, the station still has refreshment facilities.

No 1 signalbox was located at the Llanrwst end of the down platform, just off the ramp. This was a standard LNWR Type 4 composite design with a set of 30 levers.

When the line was extended to Blaenau Ffestiniog a second small signal cabin was installed on the down side at the end of the loop, just beyond the road overbridge at the commencement of the single line to Dolwyddelan. No 2 signal cabin housed an 18-lever frame. This box controlled entrance to the goods yard and could release a train staff for trains proceeding south.

Half a mile beyond the station, the line begins to climb in earnest, initially at a gradient of 1 in 50, changing to 1 in 69 halfway up, where Beaver Pool Tunnel (117yd long) is located. The gradient continues at 1 in 56 and the line turns west, leaving the Conwy valley to enter the Lledr valley, high above the A470 road. Levelling off to 1 in 220, the line passes over the road and river crossing on Gethin's Bridge (17¼ miles). This viaduct crosses over the Lledr, a tributary of the Conwy. The line takes a somewhat tortuous course in a generally westerly direction on a still rising gradient of 1 in 47, the steepest on the line and which extends for a distance of 1¾ miles past the notorious 'Milepost 19' deep in the woods amongst a succession of reverse curves, mostly check-railed. In the past, countless trains, and in 1998-9 two steam railtours, came to grief here. It must be pointed out that regular service trains were not immune from grinding to a halt at this point and consequently a phone box is located here at the milepost for drivers in emergencies! Near the end of the climb is the 148yd, wet, Pont-y-Pant Lower Tunnel.

Between Llanrwst and Betws-y-Coed

The same location as the previous photograph but 30 years later. Here Class 31 No 31201 working a Maentwrog Road to Llandudno Junction freight disturbs the peace of the valley as it crosses over the river bridge. The growth is now becoming apparent on both the embankment and the riverbank. The train was one of the short-lived workings carrying explosives from the Cookes explosives factory at Penrhyndeudraeth that had been carried to Maentwrog Road in lorries and transferred to vans at the former station. This working ceased shortly after the factory closed. Today, not even the nuclear flask trains run on the branch. However, it is possible that a new working carrying slate waste from Blaenau Ffestiniog to southern England will develop late in 2003. It is also rumoured that some timber traffic is under consideration from the forestry near Roman Bridge or Maentwrog Road and there is talk of some residual material at Trawsfynydd nuclear power station that will need to be moved to Sellafield in the near future. *Larry Goddard*

95

Near Betws-y-Coed
Stanier 2-6-2T No 40133 skirts the river about a mile from Betws-y-Coed in 1953, with a three-coach working to Blaenau Ffestiniog. Three coaches was the maximum load for a Class 3 engine and at the time this was the power limit for the line. This was subsequently relaxed and by 1963 Class 5 engines were authorised to work through to Blaenau Ffestiniog. It will be noted that most of the steam workings on the branch used non-corridor coaches for regular trains. These generally stayed on the same circuit and through coach working on or off the Conwy valley line was virtually unknown. *Bill Rear collection*

Betws-y-Coed

Ivatt 2-6-2Ts took over many workings on the Conwy valley line from the Stanier Class 3P tank engines and were preferred by drivers and firemen alike. Despite the lower power classification, the Ivatt engines were regarded as the stronger of the two classes. The sentiment was not solely the preserve of Llandudno Junction men, for Bangor drivers and firemen preferred the more modern design too. Here No 41236 of Llandudno Junction shed coasts into Betws-y-Coed with the 12.30pm from Llandudno to Blaenau Ffestiniog. The safety valves are lifting, slight smoke emerging from the chimney and, if I remember correctly, the train was a minute early. A solitary wagon stands on what was once the shed road. *Bill Rear*

Betws-y-Coed

No 1 signalbox at Betws-y-Coed was just off the down-side platform ramp. It was a traditional LNWR Type 4 Design G composite building dating from 1879, containing an LNWR tumbler frame with a set of 30 levers, of which nine were spare in 1955. The LNWR list of signal cabins issued in 1910 expected it to be life-expired in 1939, but in fact it survived in full working order until 1966. Note that the spelling of the box adhered to the old form of 'Bettws', although the rest of the station had changed to the preferred version with one 'T' by 1939. *J. H. Moss*

Betws-y-Coed
In 1949 passenger services were still in the hands of the Stanier Class 3P 2-6-2T engines. Here No 40209 of Llandudno Junction coasts into Betws-y-Coed station with the normal load of three non-corridor coaches. The entrance to the goods yard on the down side passes to the right of the camera. It was located behind the down platform and is now the site of the Conwy Valley Railway Museum. The water tank on the up side was the survivor of the locomotive shed that stood here, although, apart from a few years when the line terminated at Betws, was never operational. The shed building was demolished between the two world wars although the tank survived until the end of steam. *E. S. Russell*

Betws-y-Coed
The exterior of the station was unchanged in appearance over the years, although some cosmetic alterations were undertaken from time to time. The restaurant has now been privatised but the passenger entrance to the platform is the same. The stationmaster's house was on the left of the building and is now in private hands. *C. L. Caddy*

Betws-y-Coed

This 1965 view shows the daily freight returning from Blaenau Ffestiniog, which was the only remaining regular steam working on the branch at the time. The passenger traffic was in the hands of DMUs and, although trains were busy, the station staff had been depleted and the buildings were assuming an unkempt appearance. Freight traffic timings over the branch had been taken out of the Freight working timetables book and details were listed in the Chester Divisional Manager's shunting engine and local trip notice. The Trawsfynydd nuclear power station had been commissioned in 1964 and the details of the freight working for train 9T47 showed the working in the photograph for a Class 2 tank (ex-LMS 2-6-2T) departing Llandudno Junction at 8.20am and reaching Blaenau Ffestiniog at 10.35am, where it was booked to shunt. It had the note 'also trip to Trawsfynydd as necessary' added. The return journey was booked to depart from Blaenau Ffestiniog at 12.40pm. Steam was also booked to work conditional trips to Trawsfynydd the following year, when the motive power for trip 8T47 was changed to an ex-LMS Class 2 2-6-0. A retired Llandudno Junction driver stated recently that he drove Class 5 steam locomotives to and from Trawsfynydd while working the nuclear traffic before steam was replaced by diesel locomotives, adding that Class 40 diesels were also used on these trains until replaced by Class 24 locomotives. *C. L. Caddy*

Betws-y-Coed

Another view of the same train as the previous picture, taken on the same occasion. This view shows the station building behind the freight, the down platform, the water tank on the up side and No 1 signalbox. The consist of wagons could have been almost any time after the war, and on this occasion no nuclear flask traffic was included. Note, too, the well-kept appearance of the down-side shelter with its canopy stretching to the platform edge. The cast-iron brackets holding the up-side canopy were the same pattern as those used at Llanberis. Perhaps the same builder was used? *C. L. Caddy*

Betws-y-Coed
The footbridge at Betws-y-Coed was the standard lattice pattern with wooden covering in typical LNWR style. Here a DMU enters the platform, bound for Llandudno. In the yard a camping coach stands on one of the sidings in front of the former slate wharf. Today the down platform and the footbridge covering have been removed, and the Conwy Valley Railway Museum stands in the goods yard. The camping coach was replaced by an assortment of coaches and vans serving as a café and living accommodation for the museum staff. *Bill Rear collection*

Betws-y-Coed
In happier times, steam reigned supreme on the Conwy Valley line. Here Stanier 2-6-2T No 40133 stands at the down platform with the 10.53am Llandudno Junction to Blaenau Ffestiniog working. The up-side platform station sign still shows the prewar spelling of 'Bettws' but this would be changed in the next few months, and a platform seat still has the same spelling on its back support. Note, too, beyond the covered footbridge the large vitreous enamel sign for 'Palethorpes Sausages', once a familiar feature of hundreds of stations. Today commercial buildings back on to the platform that has been shortened. *E. S. Russell*

Betws-y-Coed
Ivatt Class 2MT 2-6-2T No 41228
heads south with the daily pick-up
goods for Blaenau Ffestiniog on
9 August 1960. The locomotive had
arrived only the previous week at
Llandudno Junction shed from Rugby
shed and its stay was to be brief. On
12 November the same year it was
transferred away to Lancaster on loan
but returned on 18 February the
following year for the summer. In
September 1961 it moved to Leicester.
The up platform was at one time
capable of holding 22 coaches but the
southern end was rarely used. It was
originally designated an excursion
platform, and at one time had a
separate access gate to a minor road.
Derek Cross

Gethin's Bridge
A Blaenau Ffestiniog DMU crosses the
bridge on its southbound trip. The
bridge was numbered 34 on the line
and consisted of seven arches, the first
of which was skew. The original
specification called for nine arches but
this was modified at some stage of the
negotiations. The LNWR specified that
local stone be used wherever possible
to blend in with the landscape and over
the years this has weathered
harmoniously. The castellated refuges
are barely visible from the lineside but
are very obvious when seen from the
train. The origin of the name is
unknown but is believed to be that of
the builder. *Bill Rear collection*

Pont-y-Pant

The main station building and platform are on the down side and constructed of local stone, now painted white. The valley at this point is subject to severe weather conditions at times and the buildings were necessarily sturdy. Some measure of the cost of travelling at this time can be made out on the poster indicating that a cheap day return to Llandudno could be had for 4s 6d (22½p) and to Blaenau Ffestiniog for 1s 9d (8½p). Note the small canopy over the entrance to the booking hall. Most of the building was the stationmaster's house, with the general waiting room and station office being in the right-hand end. The small wooden shed was the ladies' waiting room. As with some other station buildings on the line, the site is now in private hands and tastefully restored. Today's passengers have a bus shelter in which to wait.
Bill Rear collection

Pont-y-Pant

Another view of the station, looking towards Llandudno Junction, with a new Blaenau Ffestiniog-bound DMU in the platform. Note the unit destination blind states 'Blaenau Festiniog North', to distinguish its destination from the former GWR line's station, Blaenau Festiniog Central. The gradient at the station had eased from 1 in 47 to 1 in 304.
W. A. Camwell

Pont-y-Pant

Pont-y-Pant Station is 19¼ miles from Llandudno Junction on a rising gradient of 1 in 47. The community around the station is sparse and somewhat isolated.

The station is similar in design to Roman Bridge, both being constructed by the same builder. Local stone was used in the construction of the attractive station building, now a private house, with a single platform 270ft long on the down side. At one time there was a wooden hut at the Blaenau end of the platform, containing a ladies' waiting room and a toilet.

The station once had a down-side siding and an up-side passing loop for goods trains only, but these were taken out on 28 July 1957. At one time the loop, sidings and signals were controlled from a signalbox on the up side, but this was removed before World War 2. Freight facilities were withdrawn in 1966 when the station became unstaffed.

On leaving Pont-y-Pant station the line changes direction, heading southwest, and the gradient eases out to 1 in 304, on which is Pont-y-Pant Upper Tunnel. Beyond this the line falls at 1 in 330 for 500yd through predominantly agricultural country. The fall in gradient gave the fireman a brief respite before running into Dolwyddelan station (24 miles).

Pont-y-Pant
Beyond Pont-y-Pant the valley widens out and the line continues climbing at 1 in 304 for ¾ mile before it eases. The scene is tranquil and the line keeps Afon Lledr company for some distance. In the winter, though, this stretch of line can be very bleak and wind channelled down the valley caused down direction trains to have to work hard. Today, scrub growth obscures the view of the line from the roadside but recently Railtrack started a programme of cutting it back, making views of the line and from the train more open. *Bill Rear collection*

Dolwyddelan

This station was laid out differently to others on the line, comprising an island platform. Passenger access to the platform was off a minor road, down a footbridge and a flight of stairs, since removed. The building was an elaborate affair as can be seen from the other photograph. A goods yard with a shed stood on the up side but is long since gone. When rationalisation of the line took place the up loop line through the platform was taken out, leaving only the down line, the brick building was demolished and the platform was shortened. In 2003 it is suggested that due to the introduction of freight trains conveying slate waste from Blaenau, a loop will be reinstated here. It will be interesting to see whether this takes place and, if so, how it will be achieved.
Derek Chaplin

Dolwyddelan

The station name was persistently incorrectly spelt until 1980 when it was changed from 'Dolwyddelen' to 'Dolwyddelan'.

The station was operational by February 1879. Its layout was to an unusual arrangement, consisting of a single island platform similar in style to some stations on the West Highland line. The platform was about 300ft long with a single-storey building of brick construction. The roof was the dominating feature of the building, extending over both platforms and the ends, with two chimney stacks and a large ornate vent at the Betws end. It contained the usual facilities. Passengers' access was by stairs off the public road overbridge that crossed the tracks and down steps at the Blaenau end. The stationmaster's house was nearby, but off the station site.

The goods yard was on the up side and contained a siding which divided, one track passing through a large goods shed, the other passing outside the building, the tracks rejoining beyond the shed and ending in a coal siding. The goods shed was constructed of brick with a 1½-ton crane inside the building and a loading platform. It was demolished in the mid-1950s and replaced by a small concrete slab building on a raised platform. The yard also contained a weigh machine and an office, and two small offices used by local coal merchants.

At one time there was a separate signal cabin but this was removed in the 1930s, replaced by a 15-lever frame mounted on a raised plinth at the Blaenau end of the station building facing the passenger steps. The frame controlled points and signals. Until about 1950 the frame was open to the elements, but was subsequently enclosed to give some shelter and privacy. The single-line token equipment was located in the station office.

In the late 1960s the up-side passing loop was removed, as was the goods siding and shed, and the lever frame. The station building was demolished and replaced by a bus shelter. For a while, access via the steps off the road bridge

Dolwyddelan
Some idea of the elaborate nature of the building on Dolwyddelan platform can be gained from this view looking towards Llandudno Junction. The original goods shed has been demolished, replaced by a very basic concrete structure on a plinth. At one time there was a signalbox here, located where the loop lines converge by the down home signal, but this was demolished before World War 2 and replaced by a lever frame mounted on the platform, seen here with a wooden covering for shelter and privacy. Note, too, the running-in board's spelling of the station name. To ensure political correctness, the spelling was changed to Dolwyddelan in 1980, which it still retains. The station is, like all others on the branch, unstaffed and guards act as conductors on the DMUs. *Bill Rear collection*

was retained but ultimately this was removed and passengers now access the platform by a path through the edge of what was the goods yard. The yard became the site of the village primary school.

Beyond Dolwyddelan the line crosses a bridge over a river. The scenery becomes wild and desolate as the line climbs at 1 in 62 for about a mile and a quarter, past the 11th-century Dolwyddelan castle on its rocky crag overlooking the valley, before easing slightly to 1 in 90 for a short distance at Bertheos Tunnel (47yd), shortly after which a new road overbridge was constructed over the line as part of a road improvements scheme south of Dolwyddelan village in the late 1990s. After this a levelling off occurs approaching Roman Bridge station.

Roman Bridge

Roman Bridge is 22½ miles from Llandudno Junction and has a single platform on the down side. Modern travellers get the feeling that this station would never have done a lot of business, even in the early days, not unlike stations in the remoter areas of the Settle-Carlisle line like Ribblehead, or on ScotRail's West Highland lines at Corrour or Rannoch. The station, like Pont-y-Pant, is now an attractive private house, albeit in a much more desolate and wild location.

The station was built in about 1878 by D. & E. Jones of Betws-y-Coed. The main building was a two-storey stone structure which incorporated the stationmaster's house. The ground floor offices consisted of a station office, a booking office, and a combined booking hall and waiting room. The low platform face was built of local stone and apart from the section immediately in front of the booking hall, which was faced in brick, the rest of the platform was infilled with rubble and soil. The platform is 270ft in length.

A short siding used to be located here on the down side just before the platform but this, like at Pont-y-Pant, was removed in 1957.

Beyond this station is a short, wet 'Roman Bridge Tunnel', 43yd long, on which the date 1891 is inscribed.

Roman Bridge
This train was photographed on the outward journey at Tal-y-Cafn. It is seen here heading north with the football supporters' special, reporting number W954A, shortly after passing through Roman Bridge station, the roof which can be seen above the first coach. The portal of Roman Bridge Tunnel is just visible above the bunker of the engine. No 40133 was transferred to Llandudno Junction from Bangor shed on 8 May 1948 and remained there until withdrawn on 21 October 1961. Of the Stanier 2-6-2T engines, this was probably the most successful, although it too suffered from steaming problems throughout its working life. *W. A. Camwell*

Roman Bridge
Some DMUs did not have 'whiskers' on the unit ends, the thin yellow lining band passing instead under the windows. Here car No 50398, a Class 103 Park Royal-built unit, pauses at the platform with the 11.20am from Blaenau Ffestiniog to Llandudno. The station building is similar in design to Pont-y-Pant and was probably built by the same contractor. At one time there was a siding on the down side but this was removed before nationalisation. There is talk in 2003 that this siding may be reinstated soon to facilitate loading of timber from the nearby forestry plantation. *Bill Rear collection*

Blaenau Ffestiniog
Stanier 2-6-2T No 40130 is seen here running round its train, reversing towards Blaenau Ffestiniog Tunnel. On the right is one of Llandudno Junction's ex-LNWR 'Cauliflower' locomotives on the daily freight working, standing in the yard. On the left is the small signal cabin that replaced a very tall cabin in the 1930s that had been located nearer the tunnel mouth than its successor, which had stood at the platform ramp. Beyond the box can be seen three sidings ending in buffer stops. At one time there was a combined carriage and locomotive shed here but the building became unsafe and was demolished. On the right of the picture can be seen the slate transhipment wharves with an assortment of narrow gauge wagons. *Bill Rear collection*

This causes some confusion to railway historians as the long 'Festiniog' tunnel carries the date 1879. The explanation is that originally the long tunnel was built unlined and quite literally was just a hole in the rock, originally intended to be for a narrow gauge line. Twelve years later, in 1891, it was necessary to add lining and the original date of completion on the coping stone was added to commemorate this.

Beyond Roman Bridge Tunnel the gradient stiffens to 1 in 60 for about a mile and a half through barren, desolate upland sheep country with only a few farms visible from the train before reaching the northern portal of the long Festiniog Tunnel (2 miles 206yd) where it abruptly turns to the southeast. The tunnel is straight apart from the first few yards at the north end and passengers in an old-fashioned 'Heritage' DMU (but not in the modern Classes 153 or 156 units) can see through to the southern end over two miles distant. This tunnel was the eighth longest bore in Britain and, apart from Standedge between Manchester and Huddersfield and Blea Moor between Ribblehead and Dent on the Settle-Carlisle line, this must be one of the most sinister or scary of tunnels in Britain, certainly in Wales, because it seems to go on for so long!

About a quarter of a mile before the Blaenau end of the tunnel the line reaches its summit, 790ft above sea level and 26½ miles from Llandudno Junction. It then falls at 1 in 600 just beyond the southern tunnel mouth where Greaves and Oakeley Sidings were located, before being taken up in the 1960s. Here, amongst the wild mauve rhododendrons

which flower in their season in this desolate wilderness amongst the dour slate tips of Blaenau, the gradient drops at 1 in 43 and 1 in 144, followed by a short rise of 1 in 100, before coming level to the point at the terminus 2¼ miles from Llandudno Junction.

Blaenau Ffestiniog

In British Railways' parlance the LNWR station was known as 'Blaenau Festiniog North'.

The first permanent standard gauge station at Blaenau consisted of a single, wide platform some 160yd long on the up side, which was subsequently extended. A locomotive release road and two sidings ran parallel to the platform road. The original building was an ugly Victorian two-storey structure constructed of buff-coloured brick with timber cladding and a slate roof, which had a canopy that extended over the immediate platform area.

The high altitude above sea level ensured that rainfall and adverse weather conditions prevailed for most of the year — a fact for which Blaenau is notorious! The weather affected the appearance of the buildings and despite regular maintenance the station presented a depressing sight even on sunny days. Due to the enforced neglect brought about by World War 2 the structure deteriorated rapidly and was demolished in 1951, replaced by wooden huts that served for a few years before they were replaced in turn in about 1956 by an even uglier block-built building which is now boarded up, vandalised and desolate.

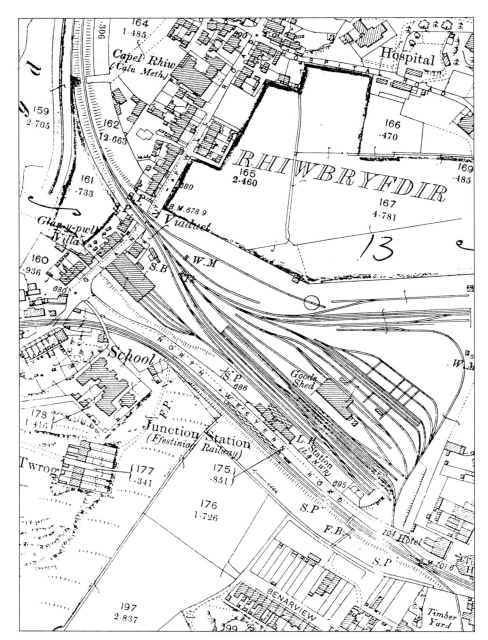

1914-18 Ordnance Survey map showing Blaenau Ffestiniog station layout. *Crown Copyright*

There was an extensive goods yard and a goods shed on the down side. Narrow gauge lines ran on to a raised tranship platform which was parallel to the passenger platform, with standard gauge lines on either side. The narrow gauge lines were at standard gauge wagon floor height which facilitated easier loading and reduced breakages to roofing slates. Beyond the tranship platform was a large goods warehouse with standard and narrow gauge lines passing through. At the back of the goods yard was a locomotive turntable with a water tank at the neck where the tracks in the goods yard converged and met the run-round road from the passenger loop line. There was a coal merchant's set of offices in the yard, which also contained a weigh machine and an office at the road entrance. A standard gauge wagon weighbridge was located near the turntable. The goods shed survived until the 1980s although it had been out of use for some time. Most of the tracks in the yard were lifted about this time and the site sold.

The closure of the former GWR branch line from Bala Junction to Blaenau Festiniog Central in 1960 was authorised on condition that a new connection was made from the former LMS line to the GWR line by means of a linking spur and an end-on junction. This enabled the GWR line to be truncated north of Trawsfynydd station, close to the lake where a nuclear power station was being built. A condition of the siting of the power station was that the nuclear material could be conveyed by rail to and from its processing base at Sellafield in Cumbria.

Another factor which was instrumental in the closing of the GWR branch was the controversial decision to flood the Tryweryn valley east of Trawsfynydd to provide water for Liverpool. This would have meant diverting the line, which in fairness Liverpool Corporation was prepared to pay for, but the railway powers-that-be, in the closure mania that existed at the time, preferred to sever the line and create the link line at Blaenau Ffestiniog, which extended the Conwy valley branch by another seven miles but curtailed passenger traffic and abandoned the beautiful Cwm Prysor viaduct in the process. The nuclear flask traffic was worked up and down the Conwy valley for the duration of the life of the power station.

Blaenau Ffestiniog

The original LNWR station at Blaenau Ffestiniog was demolished in the 1950s and for a while a wooden hut served as a replacement. However, it was deemed unsatisfactory and it in turn was replaced with a single-storey block construction of remarkable ugliness. The station was renamed 'Blaenau Festiniog North' on nationalisation. The track layout remained basically the same as previously but, when the decision was made to extend the line to connect up with the former GWR station, the connecting line was slewed round and, after passing under a rebuilt Tanygrisiau road bridge, cut across the former Ffestiniog track and made an end-on connection with the GWR line. When the standard gauge station was relocated in 1982, the former Blaenau Festiniog North station closed and passenger trains passed through to the new terminus without stopping. The station building was boarded up and now looks depressingly decrepit. *BRM*

Blaenau Ffestiniog
The present station opened on 22 March 1982 and consists of a single platform on the down side with modern functional buildings on the platform. A run-round loop was provided for the occasional locomotive-hauled train. In 1990 the Ffestiniog Railway built a new island platform adjoining the standard gauge line, and interchange facilities were then available. The nuclear flask traffic was still running from Trawsfynydd to Sellafield at this time, tripped from and to Blaenau Ffestiniog in special workings once or twice a week according to needs. In October 1990 flooding severed the Conwy valley line north of Llanrwst and stranded a nuclear flask working and a DMU. Here, in the background, can be seen Class 31 No 31275 with a flask, behind a DMU on the run-round road. Also in the photograph, the Ffestiniog Railway is still running a late-season service with ex-Penrhyn Railway locomotive *Linda* standing at the platform. Today the Ffestiniog has added another track to the opposite face of its platform although it is rarely used. The line beyond the standard gauge platform is stopped by a temporary buffer stop, although the line is intact as far as the terminus at Trawsfynydd in the event of a need to convey away any residual materials at the power station. *Larry Goddard*

In 1982 Gwynedd County Council agreed to participate in the resiting of the passenger station at Blaenau Ffestiniog, replacing it with a new station built on the site of the former GWR station. The new building is a rather desolate modern structure, busy only during the height of the tourist season. It has an interchange facility with the Ffestiniog Railway and remains in use to this day.

With the closure of the Trawsfynydd power station in 1999, the rail link was no longer required after removal of all the nuclear waste so the line south from the passenger station was declared 'surplus to requirements' and traffic suspended. In October 1998 a railtour run by Hertfordshire Railtours, entitled 'The Trawsfynydd Lament', was the last diesel-hauled train to pass over the Blaenau Ffestiniog to Trawsfynydd section of the branch. The train was hauled up to Trawsfynydd by No 56108 and tailed by No 47785. Typically, as with many railtours, time was lost and the up path from Blaenau was sacrificed. Returning from Trawsfynydd the train was prevented from accessing Blaenau Ffestiniog station and the passengers were obliged to spend a couple of hours off the platform, unable to get refreshments which had run out on the train. Arrival

back in Euston was in the very small hours of a Sunday morning!

By 2000 the line was severed by the insertion of a buffer stop 60yd beyond the point where the loop merged, whilst the rest of the track to Trawsfynydd remains in place. The former station at Maentwrog Road also remains and has been pleasantly preserved, alas without any passing trains.

On 17 November 2002 trials were conducted on the branch to test the viability of conveying slate waste. Freightliner locomotives Nos 66606 and 66514 worked two trains of loaded JNA wagons.

Train Services

The initial train service consisted of five through trains daily between Blaenau and Llandudno Junction, the workings being manned by traincrews from Llandudno Junction or the small sub-shed at Blaenau. There were also two intermediate workings between Llandudno Junction and Betws-y-Coed. The first trains in each direction crossed at Llanrwst, with the second workings crossing at Dolwyddelan. Mail trains first appeared on the line on 1 May 1880 and subsequently ran daily, including Sundays.

The earliest working timetable to hand is dated July, August and September 1904, when seven passenger trains worked each way between Llandudno Junction and Blaenau. There were additional trains that worked from the Junction or from Blaenau to Betws-y-Coed.

In the public timetables for 1 April to 10 July 1915 seven trains ran daily in each direction, with two additional down trains on a Saturday, but with no balancing up passenger journeys.

By July 1919 there were seven through journeys in each direction forming the passenger service, with four down and three up trips between the Junction and Betws. There was one through freight in each direction, and one goods in each direction from the Junction to Betws.

The July 1921 working timetable shows an increase to nine trains each way, which included a seasonal excursion that did not run on Saturdays, and two through freight trains each way daily. In addition, there were four down trains to Betws but only one in the up direction. The last down train daily ran to Betws, where it parked the stock and worked

back LE to the Junction. The Saturday times were later than the weekday ones.

By July 1923 the through journeys had become nine down trips and eight up trips, with two goods trips each way; five passenger trains worked from the Junction to Betws, but only two worked back. The final train of the timetable, which ran only on Thursdays, Fridays and Saturdays, worked back empty stock. An additional freight worked south to Betws, where it shunted for 90 minutes before working back with an up freight. There was little change by 1926. Blaenau Ffestiniog shed closed in September 1931, the men and work being transferred to Llandudno Junction.

In April 1934 the number of weekday trains on the branch was at nine in each direction, with four extra trains on a Saturday. There were five trains between Llandudno Junction and Betws and return during weekdays, some of which were motor trains, and an additional late train on Saturday nights.

By the summer of 1939 traffic on the line was at its peak with 11 trains each way on weekdays (and an additional late train on Thursdays), some of which worked from and to Llandudno. There were also seven trains to and from

Extract from July 1939 LMS timetable for the Llandudno Junction, Betwys-y-Coed and Blaenau Festiniog line.

LLANDUDNO JN. TO BLAENAU F. N.

DOWN

Note (vertical column): Mails. V—Stops to set down only on notice being given to the guard at Betws-y-Coed.

Mileage M	C	Station		B	B	B	B (SO)	B (SX) 10.35 am from Llandudno
				am	am	am	am	am
0	0	LLANDUDNO JN. ... dep	1	4 55	5 40	7 55	10 53	10 53
1	31	Glan Conway	2	....	5 51	8c 1	10a58	10a58
4	78	Tal-y-Cafn and E. .. .. arr	3	5 6	5 51	8X 8	11 4	11 4
		.... dep	4	5 8	5 52	8 15	11 5	11 5
8	3	Dolgarrog	5	5D15	6aD0	8a23	11 12	11 12
11	9	Llanrwst and Trefriw .... arr	6	5 22	6 7	8 30	11 19	11 19
		.. .. dep	7	5 26	6 9	8 34	11 21	11 21
14	76	Betws-y-Coed .... arr	8	5 33	6 16	8 41	11X28	11X28
		.. .. dep	9	5 36	6 19	8 46	11 31	11 31
19	22	Pont-y-pant	10	V	6a32	8a59	11a44	11 44
20	55	Dolwyddelen .. .. .. arr	11	5 53	6 36	9X3	11 48	11 48
		.. .. dep	12	5 55	6 38	9 7	11 50	11 50
22	40	Roman Bridge	13	6Dc2	6c45	9c14	11c57	11c57
27	19	BLAENAU F. N. .... arr	14	6 14	6 57	9 26	12 9	12 9

BLAENAU F. N. TO LLANDUDNO JN.

UP

Mileage M	C	Station		B (To Llandudno)	B (To Llandudno Jn. SX, Llandudno Jn. SO)	B (To Llandudno Jn. SX, Llandudno Jn. SO)	B (To Llandudno Jn. SX, Llandudno Jn. SO)	B (To Llandudno)	B (To Llandudno) SX
				am	am	am	PM	PM	PM
0	0	BLAENAU F. N. ... .. dep	1	7 5	8 45	10 54	12 27	2 18	..
4	59	Roman Bridge	2	7c19	8c59	11c 8	12c41	2c32	..
6	44	Dolwyddelen .. .. .. arr	3	7 24	9X4	11 13	12X46	2 37	..
		.... dep	4	7 25	9 5	11 14	12 47	2 38	..
7	77	Pont-y-pant	5	7a29	9a 9	11a18	12a51	2a42	..
12	23	Betws-y-Coed .... arr	6	7 40	9X20	11X29	1X2	2 53	..
		.. .. dep	7	7 44	9 22	11 33	1 6	2 56	4 9
16	10	Llanrwst and Trefriw .... arr	8	7X51	9 29	11 40	1 13	3 3	4X16
		.. dep	9	7 52	9 30	11 41	1 14	3 4	4 20
19	16	Dolgarrog	10	7 59	9 37	11 49	1 21	3 11	4 28
22	21	Tal-y-Cafn and E. .. .. arr	11	8X 7	9X44	11 56	1 28	3X18	4 35
		.... dep	12	8 10	9 45	11 57	1 29	3 19	4 36
25	68	Glan Conway	13	8a17	9a52	12a 4	1a36	3a26	4a43
27	19	LLANDUDNO JN. .. arr	14	8 21	9 56	12 8	1 40	3 30	4 47

Extract from summer 1955 BR passenger timetable for the Llandudno Junction to Blaenau Festiniog line.

LLANDUDNO JN. TO BLAENAU F. N. WEEKDAYS

	B	B	B	B	B	B	B	B	B	B
		2.0 pm from Llandudno						8.10 pm from Llandudno	10.50 pm from Llandudno	10.50 pm from Llandudno
		SX			SX	SO			ThO	SO
	PM	PM	PM	PM	PM	PM	PM	PM	PM	PM
1	12 30	2 16	3 5	3 52	4 48	4 48	6 0	8 28	11 2	11 2
2	12a35	2a21	3a10	3a57	4a53	4a53	6a 5	8a33		
3	12 41	2X27	3X16	4X 3	4X59	4 59	6 11	8X39	11X13	11X13
4	12 42	2 28	3 20	4 4	5 0	5 0	6 12	8 43	11 16	11 16
5	12 49	2 35	3 27	4 11	5 7	5 7	6 19	8 50		
6	12X56	2X42	3X34	4X18	5X14	5X14	6X26	8 57	11 29	11 29
7	12 57	2 43	3 35	4 19	5 18	5 18	6 29	8 58	11 30	11 30
8	1X4	2 50	3X42	4 26	5 25	5 25	6 36	9 5	11 37	11 37
9	1 8		3 43	4 29		5 38	6 39	9 6		11 40
10	1a21		3a56	4a42		5a51	6a52	9a19		
11	1X25		4 0	4X46		5X55	6X56	9 23		11 57
12	1 30		4 3	4 51		6 0	6 58	9 26		11 59
13	1c37		4c10	4e59		6c 7	7e 6	9c33		
14	1 49		4 22	5 11		6 19	7 18	9 45		12 16

BLAENAU F. N. TO LLANDUDNO JN. WEEKDAYS SUNDAYS

	B	B	B	B	B	B	B	C	C
	To Llandudno		To Llandudno	To Llandudno	To Llandudno			ECS	ECS
			SX	SO		SX	SO	ThO	
	PM	PM	PM	PM	PM	PM	PM	PM	am
1	4 30	5 39		6 36	7 40	10 15	10 15		12†37
2	4c44	5c53		6c50	7c54	10c29	10c29		
3	4X49	5X58		6X55	7 59	10 34	10 34		12 53
4	4 50	5 59		7 0	8 0	10 35	10 35		
5	4a54	6a 3		7a 4	8a 4	10a39	10a39		
6	5 5	6 14		7 16	8 15	10 50	10 50		1* 8
7	5 9	6 17	7 10	7 19	8 18	10 54	10 54	11†55	1*11
8	5X16	6X24	7 17	7 26	8 25	11 1	11 1	12 2	
9	5 17	6 29	7 18	7 27	8 27	11 2	11 2		1 18
10	5 25	6 37	7 27	7 36	8 35				
11	5 32	6 44	7 34	7 43	8X42	11X15	11X15		1 30
12	5 33	6 45	7 35	7 44	8 44	11 16	11 16	12 12	
13	5 40	6 52	7 42	7 51	8 51		11 23		
14	5 44	6 56	7 47	7 56	8 55	11 25	11 27	12†22	1†40

Mails to Llandudno Jn.

Betws, again some working from Llandudno. On Saturdays this increased to 16 for Blaenau, but only 14 from there to Betws, Llandudno or the Junction, the balance being worked back as empty stock workings. On Sundays there were five trains to Blaenau, of which two worked from Llandudno, and another four as far as Betws, balanced by four up trains to Llandudno from Blaenau, two empty stock trains to the Junction, and three from Betws to Llandudno.

The wartime Emergency working timetable, issued on 11 September 1939, curtailed services drastically although the line fared better than some branches, with seven through workings in each direction. There were no extra Saturday workings or Sunday trains.

By October 1940 there was a more even distribution of trains, the last down train departing Llandudno Junction at 8.50pm and returning as empty stock during the week, but a Class B passenger on Saturdays, running in the same times, departed Blaenau at 10.20pm.

By 1943 this had been reduced by one train daily each way; the last train from Blaenau now worked back as passenger on weekdays as well as Saturdays. The freight service was also cut back to one train per day to Blaenau and return in the morning, and a midday freight to Llanrwst and return. By June 1947 there was a daily through freight which departed Llandudno Junction at 6.45am and arrived at Blaenau at 10.30am. It returned at 12.45pm, arriving at the Junction at 4.20pm.

By the summer of 1948 the passenger service had increased to 10 down trains through to Blaenau, from Llandudno or the Junction, but only nine up trains during the week, with a daily empty stock and SX passenger working to Betws, balanced by two return passenger workings to Llandudno Junction. Freight services were the same as 1947.

The winter service for 1951 showed nine trains daily each way with an additional SX working from Llandudno Junction to Betws and return. The freight pattern was similar to 1947.

The summer season commencing 14 June 1954 gave nine weekday departures daily to Blaenau and return, with two additional trips to Betws and return in the afternoon at 2.1pm, 4.48pm and 6pm. On Thursdays there was an extra late departure from Llandudno at 10.50pm to Betws which returned as empty stock. On Saturdays there were two extra workings to Blaenau and return, the first of these running in the same path as the 4.48pm which returned as the 6.36pm from Blaenau. The late train on Saturdays departed Llandudno at 10.50pm and worked back as empty stock from Blaenau at 12.37am on Sunday mornings. The freight workings for the same period had been reduced to one train each way daily.

The introduction of diesel multiple-units (DMU) to the line in March 1956 showed no significant alteration to the service either in frequency or in running times, although an additional train ran from the Junction to Betws and return in the evening.

By the summer of 1958, there was an additional working in the morning from Llandudno Junction to Betws and return, as well as the three short workings previously mentioned. However, an innovation was the introduction of four Sunday workings from Llandudno to Betws and return, which ran for eight Sundays. There was no change to the freight workings.

In 1960 there was a modest increase, 10 trains running to Blaenau daily, with an additional three to Betws and return. There was the usual late train at 11pm to Blaenau on Thursday nights, returning as ECS, whilst on Saturdays the 5.3pm to Betws was extended as previously to Blaenau, returning from there at 6.30pm, and the 11pm ran as on Thursdays. On Sundays there were now five trains to Betws and return from Llandudno.

The winter 1960 working timetable showed 10 trains daily to Blaenau and return, and one evening train to Betws and return during the week. On Saturdays there was an additional DMU to Betws at 4.42pm, returning from there at 5.40pm. There was no late train on Saturdays as previously.

By the summer of 1961 there had been an increase in the number of trains run during the week, with 12 trips Mondays to Fridays to Blaenau and return, and two trips to Betws and return. On Saturdays there were 13 to Blaenau and return, but only one to Betws. The extra working was the 10.50pm from Llandudno, which returned early Sunday morning as an empty DMU. There were once again five trips from Llandudno to Betws and return on Sundays, but for only five weeks.

On 11 September 1961 the service had been reduced to 10 trips to Blaenau with one additional working to Betws during the week. and an additional trip to Betws and return at 4.42pm on Saturdays. However, the freight traffic was increased to three trains daily between Llandudno Junction and Blaenau, with one trip working in a 'Q' path, as required.

The summer 1962 passenger service was similar to the previous year, with the Sunday trains running on five days. The freight working was the same as the previous winter. The winter 1962 timetable saw the passenger service reduced to nine trains to Blaenau and return, and one afternoon working to Betws and back. The freight service was altered with two trains running to Blaenau with a 'Q' path for a train mid-morning, which was suspended.

The summer services which commenced on 17 June 1963 saw a drastic reduction of trains on the line, only six DMUs working daily between Llandudno Junction and Blaenau, with an early morning short trip from Blaenau to Dolwyddelan and return. There was no variation on Saturdays. Sunday services were reduced to four trains between Llandudno and Betws and return, but the season was extended over nine weeks. The freight timetable remained the same as the previous winter. There was no change with the introduction of winter services on 9 eptember 1963 to passenger or freight workings.

The new link line connecting Blaenau Festiniog North with the GWR line was officially opened on 20 April 1964, and extended to a point close to the Trawsfynydd nuclear power station.

The summer services for 1964 introduced on 15 June showed a slight improvement on the passenger workings, with seven trains each way daily, and four workings for the nine Sundays from July 5 between Llandudno and Betws. The freight service was reduced to one train daily from the Junction to Blaenau and return. 7 September 1964 saw the introduction of winter services, with a reversion to six trains daily. The solitary freight appeared for the last time in freight working timetables. Dolarrog halt was taken out of use in 1964, only to be reinstated the following year.

June 1965 saw a midday train reinstated, together with three Sunday trains from Llandudno to Betws for nine weeks. Freight traffic was removed from the working

DOWN

Mileage M	C	Station		23 (am)	am			
0	0	LLANDUDNO JN.	dep	6 30	..	..	..	
1	48	Glan Conway	arr	6 35	..	..	..	
			dep	6 45	..	..	..	
5	16	Tal-y-Cafn and	arr	6 55	..	..	..	
		Eglwybach	dep	7 16	..	..	..	
8	20	Dolgarrog	arr	7 26	..	..	..	
			dep	7 36	..	..	..	
11	18	Llanrwst and Trefriw	arr	7X46	..	..	..	
			dep	8 47	..	..	..	
15	0	Betws-y-Coed	arr	8X57	..	..	..	
			dep	9 45	..	..	..	
19	38	Pontypant			..	..	..	
20	71	Dolwyddelen	arr	10 5	..	..	..	
			dep	10 25	..	..	..	
22	60	Roman Bridge			..	..	..	
26	46	Greave's Siding			11 40	..	..	
27	19	BLAENAU F.N.	arr	10 45	11 45	..	..	

UP

Mileage M	C	Station		28 (am)	PM			
0	0	BLAENAU F.N.	dep	11 20	12 50	..		
0	53	Greave's Siding		11 25	..	..		
4	39	Roman Bridge		..	..	..		
6	28	Dolwyddelen	arr		1X10	..		
			dep	..	1 44	..		
7	61	Pontypant		..	..	..		
12	19	Betws-y-Coed	arr	..	2 4	..		
			dep	..	2 25	..		
16	1	Llanrwst and Trefriw	arr	..	2X35	..		
			dep	..	3 36	..		
18	79	Dolgarrog	arr	..	3 46	..		
			dep	..	3 52	..		
22	3	Tal-y-Cafn and	arr	..	4X2	..		
		Eglwybach	dep	..	4 7	..		
25	51	Glan Conway	arr	..	..	..		
			dep	..	..	..		
27	19	LLANDUDNO JN.	arr	..	4 22	..		

Extract from summer 1955 BR freight timetable for the Llandudno Junction and Blaenau Festiniog line.

timetables and was shown as a trip working, to be found in the Chester District shunting and trip working notices.

The 1966 train service remained as previously, with the 13.19 from Llandudno Junction to Blaenau and the 14.25 return working running from 27 June to 3 September only. From 1 September, however, the 20.17 Llandudno Junction to Blaenau and corresponding 21.55 Blaenau to Llandudno Junction ran on Saturdays only and the Sunday services did not appear. This was repeated with only minor timing changes in the two succeeding years.

In 1969 the usual middle day seasonal working had advanced to 13.35pm from Llandudno Junction and 14.35 from Blaenau. The rest of the passenger working was as for previous years.

From 4 May 1970 five trains daily sufficed for the greater part of the year, with an extra late evening working on Saturdays. During summer months, this was expanded to seven trains.

In 1971, the station at Glan Conwy reopened. In 1973 there was no change to the weekday pattern of services in winter or summer, but three Sunday trains ran from Llandudno unadvertised , two to Blaenau and the middle one to Betws from 1 July to 2 September inclusive.

The 1974 timetable saw a reduction during the winter period from five trains daily to four during the week, with

the Saturdays Only evening train running in the same times. There was a very large gap between the 08.17 departure and 15.45 from 6 October onwards. As before, the summer Sunday trains remained unadvertised.

1975 followed the same pattern with only four trains on weekdays in the winter. The summer Sunday Only workings, running from 29 June to 31 August, were increased to four trains from Llandudno: at 11.00, 14.05 and 15.55 to Blaenau, and the 18.30 to Betws-y-Coed.

1976 issues saw a relapse, with only four weekday trains in the winter months. The Saturday Only evening train no longer ran. The Sunday trains did not appear either.

The timetable commencing 2 May 1977 showed the number of trains increased to five daily during the winter months, and seven from 27 June to 3 September. There were no Sunday trains. The following year the winter period remained the same, but the summer period, from 19 June to 9 September, indicated eight trains on weekdays but only seven on Saturdays.

1979 saw nine trains daily, Mondays to Fridays, in each direction with seven trains on a Saturday in the summer period from 18 June to 7 September. The winter period remained as before, with five trains each way. The 1980 summer period from 16 June to 5 September saw nine trains each way from Mondays to Fridays and seven on Saturdays, reverting to five for the winter period.

The traditional passenger and freight working timetable books were replaced by mandatory and conditional issues after 1970, but these were deemed unsatisfactory and from 1 June 1981, separate passenger and freight working timetables were reintroduced. The service was unchanged from the previous year. The same was true for 1982 and 1983, but in the case of the latter the summer season 11.05 SX from Llandudno and the 13.30 from Blaenau Ffestiniog to Llandudno were locomotive-hauled stock and not DMU.

From 14 May 1984 the train frequency remained the same with nine trains on weekdays, with the 11.05 and 14.53 SX from Llandudno, returning with the 13.30 and 16.25 SX from Blaenau worked by locomotive hauling vacuum-braked stock. On Saturdays in the summer period, the seven trips were worked with DMUs. The winter period reverted to five trains daily.

The 1985 issue, dated 13 May to 11 May 1986, showed the summer weekday period with two of the nine weekday workings running as locomotive-hauled vacuum-braked trains and in approximately the same timings as in past years. On summer Saturdays, there were eight DMU workings each way. Sunday trains were reintroduced from 21 July to 25 August with three trains between Llandudno and Blaenau. The winter service remained unchanged.

A revised passenger working timetable was issued dated 30 September 1985 to 11 May 1986. The Llandudno Junction to Blaunau Ffestiniog service was no longer shown separately but was included within the main Crewe to Holyhead pages. 'Sprinter' units were appearing on the North Wales coast but none was scheduled to work to Blaenau Ffestiniog. The normal five trains per day persisted for this period.

The passenger working timetable dated 12 May 1986 introduced 'Sprinter' DMUs to the line, but there were technical problems and their appearance was spasmodic. Their replacements were old DMUs, mainly Class 101 units and without working toilets! Some of the workings emanated from points further afield than Llandudno Junction. The summer season 10.52 to Blaenau Ffestiniog departed from Manchester Victoria at 08.42. There were eight trains between Llandudno Junction and Blaenau Ffestiniog in the summer period, with the 14.40 Llandudno to Blaenau and the 16.05 to Llandudno worked SX by locomotive-hauled stock in lieu of the 'Sprinter'. The winter workings were reduced to five trains daily. Gwynedd County Council paid for the three Sunday trains that worked from and to Llandudno for the six peak weeks in July and August. The following year saw the same eight train workings, mostly using 'Sprinter' units. The 10.51 from Llandudno Junction, 2D15, started from Crewe at 9.19. whilst the 17.47 from Blaenau Ffestiniog attached to the front of the 18.10 from Holyhead and worked to Crewe. The winter service reverted to five trains daily. Three Sunday trains from Llandudno to Blaenau Ffestiniog and return, sponsored by Gwynedd County Council, ran from 26 July to 30 August.

The services from 16 May 1988 had a few changes in the timings, but the trains were worked by the older DMUs and not 'Sprinters'. There was the same frequency of five winter and eight summer journeys in each direction. The summer 12.23 working from Llandudno Junction originated at Birmingham New Street at 9.28 and worked

via Crewe and Chester. The same Sunday service operated from 17 July to 4 September — two weeks longer than the previous year.

In the 15 May 1989 issue the Wednesday-and-Friday-only nuclear freight from Llandudno Junction to Trawsfynydd, 6D38, was shown for the first time. The 'Sprinters' were then not rostered to work on the line. There was a change to the winter schedules from 5 October. The 20.42 from Llandudno Junction to Blaenau and the corresponding 21.49 return working, which was daily during the summer period, continued to run on Thursdays, Fridays and Saturdays. There was a variation of the Gwynedd County Council sponsored Sunday trains, which ran from 9 July until 10 September. Two trains ran to Blaenau and back, but the 14.45 from Llandudno worked only to Betws, arriving there at 15.22. It returned at 15.28 to Llandudno.

The working timetables issued on 14 May 1990 now contained the freight workings and from this date Saturday services along the coast were shown separately. Seven trains ran daily during the summer months. The 20.49 from Llandudno to Blaenau ran until 28 September and came off for the winter.

After 1990 the service settled down to an all-year frequency of five trains each day. The Class 101 units survived until 1998, although Class 150 and 153 units increasingly appeared. The last 'Heritage' units made occasional appearances until April 1998. Bizarrely, amongst the last workings were Class 101 units in Strathclyde orange and black livery. There is now some 'bustitution'.

Occasional special steam workings have ventured over the branch in the last few years, the sound of steam roaring away on the climb to Pont-y-Pant bringing music to one's ears. Past Time Rail tried to run a six-coach special with Class 4MT 2-6-4T No 80079 in 1999, which repeatedly stalled spectacularly at Milepost 19. As water levels became critical, it had to propel its stock back to Betws where water was taken on and the train was dragged unceremoniously back to Llandudno Junction by a Class 47 off another private charter. The blockage and delay caused a regular service train to terminate short and did not endear the enthusiasts to the locals. The following day with a reduced load the same engine made it to Blaenau. The exercise was then repeated, the eight-coach train hauled by two Standard Class 4MT 2-6-4Ts being split into two four-coach units at Llandudno Junction. Alas, the first train failed before reaching Pont-y-Pant and the second 2-6-4T had to be detached from its stock at Llanrwst North and worked up to the stranded train to assist all the way to Blaenau, the two engines returning coupled to Llanrwst North to work the second portion to its destination. Earlier, in April 1999, a solitary working by a Stanier Class 5 took place, but steam has avoided the Conwy valley line ever since. There have been several diesel locomotive-hauled excursions, including one which made the 'last ever' journey to Trawsfynydd before the section beyond Blaenau Ffestiniog was severed. On this occasion the train made the journey to Trawsfynydd without problems, but delays on returning caused the path to be lost and the train was not allowed to enter Blaenau Ffestiniog station for a couple of hours, causing much distress to the passengers who were obliged to sit in the train, wait and starve. Arrival back in Euston was about four hours late.

12

Llandudno Town Branch

One of many proposals to construct a railway line to Llandudno was a scheme entitled the 'Ormes Bay' proposal, which was mooted in 1836. A private group asked William (later Sir William) Cubitt, civil engineer, to make a survey for a new harbour at Ormes Bay and a connecting railway. The scheme was defeated by the decision to construct the line to Holyhead which, in the opinion of the Commissioner's report, better suited the need for the Dublin to London traffic.

The St George's Harbour Act of 20 August 1853 authorised, amongst other things, the building of a 3¼-mile railway from Llandudno to join the Chester & Holyhead main line at Llandudno Junction.

It was decided in April 1860 to develop Llandudno Junction station to provide interchange facilities as the opening of the line to Llanrwst was imminent. For the winter of 1860-1 services on the Llandudno Junction to Llandudno line were suspended. The LNWR took a lease

Llandudno Junction
Congestion at Llandudno Junction was becoming a problem soon after World War 2, one of the cited reasons being the delays at the level crossing where the Llandudno Town line crossed the then A55. On a summer Saturday there were about a hundred train movements which snarled up the road traffic. On 9 March 1949 British Railways commissioned a set of views showing the layout where the Chester to Holyhead main line diverged from the Llandudno line. This scene, taken from a high viewpoint, possibly a signalpost, shows the crossing gates with the controlling signalbox beyond, behind the footbridge, hemmed in with the Junction Hotel. The crossing was removed in 1956 when a flyover was installed and the blockage moved elsewhere. The Junction Hotel, the signalbox and the footbridge were removed but otherwise the railway infrastructure was unchanged until the rationalisation scheme simplifying the rail layout was effected in the 1980s. *BRM*

Llandudno Junction

The old footbridge by the level crossing was a good vantage point from which to survey the railway scene in the 1950s. Here Ivatt 2-6-2T No 41224 of Rhyl (6K) shed propels the 'Welsh Dragon' pull-push working that operated between Llandudno and Rhyl in the summer months over the level crossing through Llandudno Junction station, where it did not stop, on its journey to Rhyl. This was, I believe, the only non-corridor pull-push named train on British Railways at the time. The three coaches were always well patronised and eventually a DMU took over the working. *Bill Rear collection*

on the line in early 1862 and worked trains with a locomotive for the summer season, replacing the locomotive with a horse and two old coaches over the winter. In July 1863 the small station platform at Llandudno was lengthened.

In May 1866 Deganwy station appeared in the timetables. Between 1869 and 1872 the platform at Llandudno was further extended with a run-round loop put in and a waiting shed built. The line passed into LNWR ownership in 1873. By 1876 the branch had been doubled and Deganwy station rebuilt. New connections were put in at Llandudno Junction, enabling through running to the resort town.

Station growth at Llandudno had been piecemeal and, with the rapid development of Llandudno as a tourist resort, the station had become congested and complaints were becoming ever more vociferous. In October 1890 contracts were let for a new station to be built which had five platforms and a centre carriage drive. That opened in the summer of 1892.

There was some local freight work. A yard behind the main station served the needs of the town. Generally, freight traffic was tripped from Llandudno Junction yard.

In summer months in the heyday of the line's operation there was sufficient traffic to justify the use of a station pilot, which shunted stock into and out of the platforms, and into extensive carriage sidings on the down side. With upwards of 20 excursion trains working into and out of the station on summer Saturdays there was insufficient space to store all the stock so empty stock workings were made to the slate quay at Deganwy. To keep line occupancy at a manageable level, a 60ft turntable was located in the carriage sidings and facilities were on hand for cleaning fires and taking water.

LLANDUDNO JUNCTION AND LLANDUDNO.

Extract from July 1925 LMS timetable for the Llandudno Junction and Llandudno line.

The 'Welsh Dragon' 1956 booklet.

Llandudno Junction

The first station at Llandudno Junction was located west of the present site and the Llandudno Town branch platforms started at the level crossing gates. When the new station was built the old buildings and platforms were demolished and completely removed. The area around the level crossing developed quickly and the open fields opposite the station gave way to industrial and residential properties. Note the three-arm bracket signal beyond the footbridge in front of a signal cabin. Note, too, the signal arm suspended from the footbridge. The photographer is under surveillance from station staff on the platform including an enterprising lad porter performing a balancing act with a sack truck and a station trolley. *BRM*

Llandudno Junction
Rebuilt 'Patriot' Class 4-6-0 No 45523 *Bangor* eases its way round the curve approaching Llandudno Junction station with the 1.5pm Llandudno to Euston working on Wednesday 10 August 1960. The train is routed into the up passenger loop platform where stock from the 12.50pm from Bangor will be attached. The locomotive was based at Camden and the enginemen were from Llandudno Junction. They would work the train as far as Crewe. Today the A55 expressway road occupies the space beyond the tracks and the shoreline has been diverted to give the necessary space. *Derek Cross*

Deganwy
Between the wars there was a lot more auto-train working on local services along the North Wales coast. This formation comprised a Webb auto-fitted Class 1F 0-6-2T sandwiched between four coaches, and operated a frequent interval service between Llandudno and Rhyl, the forerunner of the 'Welsh Dragon'. The fireman would see his driver as he changed ends at each terminus, but would mostly be left to his own devices on the footplate. The work with four-coach workings was not very popular. Here No 6666 is seen departing Deganwy station, bound for Rhyl. Note the motor coach parked on a siding near the entrance to Deganwy slate quay, which was used to store carriages. *Gordon Coltas*

Deganwy

The station buildings at Deganwy were located on the up side, the site being protected by two signal cabins at either end of the station. The cabin at the Llandudno end controlled a level crossing which is still operational to this day. Here Stanier 2-6-0 No 42964, sporting a hand-painted 8C (Speke Junction) shed code, working under light engine lamps, stands on the down line. The movement is unusual and it is presumed that it had worked a coaching set into the slate quay sidings for storage, although it could be travelling to Llandudno to turn on the turntable in the carriage sidings at Llandudno, near Maesddu bridge. *E. S. Russell*

Deganwy

Stanier 2-6-2T No 40083 stands at the down platform while working an afternoon local to Llandudno in the summer of 1954. This view was taken from a footbridge over the tracks by Deganwy No 2 signalbox. In the distance can be seen coaches in store on the slate quay, whilst in the extreme distance across the estuary can be seen coaches parked on the siding alongside the Holyhead to Chester main line. *Bill Rear*

Between Llandudno Junction and Llandudno stations there were six signalboxes. First came Llandudno Junction No 2 signalbox, which controlled all movements at the west end of the station, including the connections to and from Llandudno.

Then came Llandudno Junction Crossing box, which stood on the down side just north of the junction with the main line to Holyhead. This was removed shortly after the crossing was replaced by a flyover bridge in 1956. At the Llandudno Junction end of Deganwy station stood No 1 box, now demolished, on the up side, which controlled another level crossing to a boatyard and also the sidings on the slate quay on the down side. Next came Deganwy No 2 on the down side, which still stands, controlling the level crossing, as it does to this day. The box was given a face-lift by Railtrack in February 2002 in anticipation of a residential development being built on the former slate quay at Deganwy. Llandudno No 1 box was at Maesddu bridge, now closed, again on the down side, where the carriage sidings converged. Lastly is Llandudno No 2 box, which was at the station platform end, and is still in place today, albeit with most of its levers being spare.

After 1978 two of the platform roads were taken out, as were the carriage sidings near Maesddu bridge. The land was sold off and is now a housing estate.

Certain facilities remain today. Llandudno signalbox, formerly No 2 box, at the throat of the station, survives, controlling some manually operated semaphore signals mounted on a gantry. The train shed was cut back and the station has a very down-at-heel appearance. Locomotive-hauled trains rarely appear here. On those instances when steam trains have traversed the branch it has been necessary to attach a diesel locomotive to haul the train back to Llandudno Junction to release the locomotive.

In the summer of 2000 Class 37 locomotives regularly hauled a four-coach set into the town from Manchester Piccadilly. This necessitated sending a shunter by road from Holyhead to uncouple and recouple after the locomotive had run round the stock for the journey back to Manchester. Needless to say, this working was extremely popular with the rail fans, and First North Western Trains took record receipts for the duration of the working.

One incident comes to mind. In 1956 a DMU working the 10.20pm Llandudno to Llandudno Junction pulled into the up-side bay road where it terminated and parked up for the night. A new and raw young passenger guard was in charge. He had few passengers for the 10-minute journey, who got out and shuffled along the platform to the barrier. One woman remained seated and motionless. The guard approached her, and was alarmed when she made a lunge for his trousers and made clear her desires and intentions. She was known to both railway and Crosville staff as 'Midnight Mary' and was more or less in a permanently intoxicated state. She also had a reputation for being 'on the game' and, being past her prime, found 'trade' difficult to come by. The guard, finding his trousers and his virginity under attack, fended her off and his cries for help were eventually heeded. She was 'persuaded' to abandon her seduction which she did with some reluctance. The guard had to suffer the indignity of taunts until he eventually had enough and left the railway service.

The 'lady' in question nevertheless continued to molest railway and Crosville bus staff with regular monotony. She ultimately descended into meths drinking and her behaviour grew more outrageous until she was banned from travelling. Finally the authorities caught up with her and she was spirited away, never to be seen again.

Llandudno

Trains to Llandudno passed a complex of sidings on the final approach to the station. Access to the sidings was controlled from two signalboxes. At the Deganwy end was Llandudno No 1 box which stood close by Maesddu bridge. Here, in this 1938 view, an abundance of motive power can be seen. In the foreground ex-LNWR 'Cauliflower' No 8337 pulls an assortment of coaching stock out of the up side relief road onto the main line. On the down line a train of eight coaches heads for the station. Standing in the neck behind the box can be seen another 'Cauliflower'. A 'Patriot' stands close by, and behind it in the distance a Fowler 0-6-0 is visible carrying a reporting number plate on the smokebox door. Behind the signalbox can be seen another Fowler 0-6-0 and a Horwich 'Crab', both with reporting number plates on the smokebox. They are standing in front of the turntable. Today all this land is occupied by housing, and the signalbox has long gone. *Gordon Coltas*

Booklet issued to LMS staff for the sixth annual company outing, 1932.

Llandudno

'Jubilee' class 4-6-0 No 45599 *Bechuanaland* stands at the head of a return excursion at Llandudno station on 6 August 1962. Details of the working have not been traced but the reporting number 1B30 suggests that the train originated on and worked entirely within the London Midland Region. The locomotive was nominally attached to Nuneaton (2B) shed. Why the train is composed in part of ex-LNER stock is uncertain, but it is possible the train came off the former Great Central line. The scene at Llandudno has changed radically from what can be seen here. The overall train shed roof has been cut back and now the platforms are uncovered. The sidings beyond the railings have gone and the site, derelict for 20 years, is to be redeveloped. Two platforms and their associated tracks out of shot here have been taken out of use and the station generally has an air of dereliction about it. The No 2 signalbox and gantry spanning the tracks however survive and are in regular use. *A. Tyson*

Penrhyn Sidings Box

Penrhyn sidings signalbox was a Saxby & Farmer composite-construction 12-lever frame built in 1870. The box was located on the down side shortly after emerging from Llandegai Tunnel and it was taken out of use on 23 August 1954 and replaced by a ground frame, controlled by Bethesda Junction signalbox. There was no connection from the down line into the siding; trains to the branch were worked out from Bangor or Menai Bridge on the up line and had to set back into the access line before they could work down to the quay. After the frame had been taken out it was sent to the National Railway Museum at York where the indicator plate is sometimes on display. *J. M. Dunn*

Penrhyn Sidings

The view from Penrhyn sidings signalbox, looking towards Bethesda Junction: in the distance can be seen the portal of Bangor Tunnel. The next signalbox in the down direction was Bethesda Junction, only 500yd away, and its protecting signals can be seen in the middle distance. Note the lay-by siding on the up side which was sometimes used to store wagons awaiting movement down to the port. *J. M. Dunn*

Cegin Viaduct

The late J. M. Dunn exploited his position as shedmaster at Bangor and visited many of the private lines in his parish. He had the good fortune to travel on a narrow gauge slate train from Bethesda quarry to Port Penrhyn with his private party, being provided with one of the quarry's open passenger coaches attached to the rear of an empty wagon train and hauled by the locomotive *Blanche* in 1953. This view shows the train approaching Cegin viaduct, the standard gauge main Holyhead to Chester line passing overhead. *J. M. Dunn*

13

Port Penrhyn Branch

History

Despite the existence of the Penrhyn Railway, which was a narrow gauge line carrying the slate from the Penrhyn quarries to Port Penrhyn, it was felt that a standard gauge connection was needed to carry slate from this quarry to a distribution depot at Saltney, near Chester. With Chester & Holyhead Railway approval, a line was constructed from sidings on the up side of the main C&H line just over a mile from Bangor station, 791yd from Bethesda Junction signalbox. The line was constructed by the C&H, although it was never owned by that railway. The line passed through part of the Penrhyn estate, and met up with the narrow gauge line about a mile from Penrhyn sidings. The two lines ran parallel for the remainder of the route to the port. The branch closed to all traffic on 2 March 1963, the official closure date having been given as 30 June 1965, and the track was lifted in 1965-6.

Description of the Line

The line was comparatively unknown outside the local area. Penrhyn sidings were located on the up side, between Bangor Tunnel and Llandegai Tunnel. The line down to the port was single and worked under the 'One Engine in Steam' principle. Nevertheless, a train staff was deemed necessary. The shape of staff was square, it was coloured red, and issued from the Penrhyn Siding signalbox which controlled three sidings from a 12-lever Saxby & Farmer locking frame. The cabin was called 'Penrhyn Sidings' and was located on the down side. Penrhyn Sidings box was manned by a single shift when in use, being switched out

Port Penrhyn
It was not usual in 1956 to find Fowler 2-6-4T engines at Port Penrhyn; the more usual motive power was one of Bangor shed's Aspinall Class 27 0-6-0 tender engines. Here No 42416 pauses during shunting operations so that the shedmaster could take the group's picture. Note the narrow gauge slate wagon on the extreme right. *J. M. Dunn*

Port Penrhyn Branch—Single Line. (Week Days).

Miles	Down Trains.	S a.m.	Mineral.	10.35 a.m. from Menia Bridge.			Up Trains.	S p.m.	Mineral for Bangor.				
...	Penrhyn Siding......dep	11 30			...	...	Port Penrhyn.........dep.	12 40		...	...	...	...
¼	Port Penrhyn ......arr	11 40			...	...	,, ,, ...arr.	12 50		...	...	...	...
							,, ,, ...dep.	2 15					

Port Penrhyn.
A view of the tracks on the quayside at Port Penrhyn. Of particular interest are the narrow gauge points with the pivoting frogs, and the narrow gauge crossing (literally) over the standard gauge track, being pivoted to swing clear when necessary. This narrow gauge line led to the engine shed and was in regular use until the end of services.
J. M. Dunn

outside working hours. It was closed on 23 August 1954, being replaced by a ground frame electrically controlled from Bethesda Junction box. The line was then reclassified from a branch to a siding. There was no crossover from the up to the down line on the main line at this point so down trains working under special instructions back from Penrhyn sidings had to travel 'wrong line' as far as the crossover at Bethesda Junction before regaining the correct track.

Access to the Port Penrhyn line was off two of the sidings and through a pair of gates, which marked the entrance to private land. The two tracks combined and the branch was single all the way to the port. The gradient was somewhat steep, falling at a rate of 1 in 50 and 1 in 64 for a third of the distance. A mile from the gate, the line passed under the main A5 road at the turnpike road bridge, at which point the narrow gauge line drew alongside. The two lines crossed the Afon Cegin on a pile bridge, and recrossed it again a

short distance further on. After passing under the private road bridge to Port Penrhyn, the two lines ran on to the quay and then fanned out.

On the quayside the lines crossed each other at several places. The narrow gauge tracks were laid on top of the standard gauge lines, and pivoted so that the narrow gauge track swung clear of the broader gauge when the latter was in use. With the decline in slate traffic, standard gauge traffic to the port diminished.

According to J. I. C. Boyd in his work *Narrow Gauge Railways in North Caernarvonshire Volume 2 — The Penrhyn Quarry Railways* the last narrow gauge steam slate train ran on 28 June 1964, with an official closure date given as 24 July. The narrow gauge tracks were lifted by the end of 1965.

Initially traffic was sufficiently heavy to justify its own timetable but as traffic diminished, the timetabling was

Port Penrhyn

Penrhyn Railway 0-4-0ST *Linda* departs from Port Penrhyn with a train of empty slate wagons on the narrow gauge line for Bethesda quarry, seen here passing under the private access road bridge on 31 March 1959. The standard gauge line from the port to Penrhyn sidings is seen alongside. The gate across the tracks had to be unlocked by the quarry office staff before trains could pass onto the quayside. The reason quoted was that the port was private land. Note, too, the rudimentary signal protecting the narrow gauge line. It is understood that trains from the quarry also had to stop here and report to the office seen through the bridge arch, before proceeding to the quayside. *J. A. Peden*

combined with the freight working timetable for the Llandudno Junction to Holyhead section. The trip engine which shunted at the port worked through from Menai Bridge to the sidings, then propelled its train down to the quayside and, according to the printed instructions, was required to 'whistle all the way (for the 1½ miles) down to the Port'. The line was worked from the gate to the quay by train staff, although only one engine, or two coupled together, was allowed on the branch at any one time. Wagon brakes were pinned down and the guard rode on the leading wagon, carrying a lamp or a flag. In 1927 working was limited to a train to the port every other day (Mondays, Wednesdays and Fridays), but traffic improved and this working became daily (Saturdays excepted) until closure.

The operating procedure was that the first trip down would then shunt the quayside. When a load had been made up, the loaded wagons were taken up to Penrhyn sidings. The locomotive returned to the quay for a second load and, if necessary, repeated the process a third time. Finally, it sorted wagons at the top then worked wrong line to Bethesda Junction where it assumed its proper track, then worked forward to Menai Bridge yard for the wagons to be marshalled for onward movement.

Normally a Class 4 tank engine was diagrammed, although the Fowler 0-6-0s based at Bangor would be used on occasions. The working was generally arranged so that the smokebox was leading when climbing from the port. Prior to 1950, one of the Aspinall Lancashire & Yorkshire (L&Y) Railway-design Class 27 0-6-0 tender engines was preferred, as these engines were considered to be stronger than the LNWR equivalent.

There is no evidence to support reports that a Class 5 4-6-0 ventured down to the quay on one occasion. The traincrew working down to the port was required to open and close the gates. Brake vans were not worked down the branch but were left in the sidings at the top of the branch.

The locomotive and crew worked first to Menai Bridge yard and spent some time shunting there, before working through Bangor station, without stopping, to Penrhyn sidings signalbox. On arrival at Penrhyn sidings box and setting back into the sidings proper, the brake van was detached and parked. The locomotive, crew and guard would then work up to three round-trips between the port and the top of the incline. After working back to Menai Bridge, passing through Bangor without stopping, a brief spell of yard shunting would be undertaken before engine and traincrew would work back light engine to Bangor shed.

It was usual to find a Class 4MT 2-6-4T on the turn and a photograph exists of Fowler design No 42416 at the port, although this version of the tank was based only briefly at Bangor in the mid-1950s. If no tank engine were available, one of the 0-6-0 tender engines would deputise, but they were not popular with traincrews, particularly when it was wet.

The branch finally closed to traffic on 24 July 1964, the same day as the Penrhyn Railway, and the track was subsequently lifted. Part of the trackbed of the narrow gauge line is now a public walkway, though I have not personally walked it. Port Penrhyn is still a working port but also a rather snooty marina with boat chandlers alongside.

Bangor

The Bethesda branch lost its passenger services on 3 December 1951. Services had been on the decline since World War 2 and had become uneconomic during 1951. Competition came from Purple Motors of Bethesda and Crosville Motor Services Ltd, which operated at a 10-minute frequency between the two places. The bus services had the advantage of picking up at numerous points on the main road and setting down in the centre of Bangor town. Here seen in the section of the down platform, referred to as the 'Bethesda bay', was the penultimate train, worked by Webb 0-6-2T No 58903 hauling its single coach, which was adequate for the journey. The driver was Hugh Caulfield and fireman was Eric Lynn. By the date this photograph was taken motive power for the pull-push trains was more usually an Ivatt Class 2MT 2-6-2T but for sentimental reasons the Webb engine replaced the more modern power, not altogether with the approval of driver and fireman. *J. M. Dunn*

1914-18 Ordnance Survey map showing Bethesda Junction layout. *Crown Copyright*

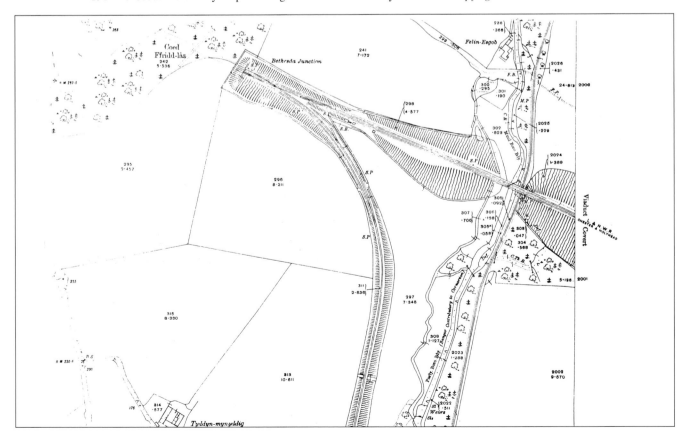

Bethesda Branch

Historical

In c1800/1 the first Lord Penrhyn, having just been ennobled, constructed a 6¼-mile horse tramway to 1ft 10¾in gauge from his slate quarry at Bethesda to the coast, for onward shipment.

In 1866 the LNWR proposed a branch from Bangor to Bethesda and opposed the scheme by the Bangor & Llanberis Direct Railway to construct a line to Bethesda off the LNWR projected route.

In the light of these schemes, Lord Penrhyn considered altering his tramway to a narrow gauge passenger-carrying line between the two places, or converting the tramway to the standard gauge, but both these proposals came to naught. The tramway, nevertheless, was modified and steam power introduced in 1877/8. The line became known as the 'Penrhyn Railway' and was freight only, with the exception of carrying workmen to the quarry.

Simultaneously, the slate trade had increased dramatically and the LNWR successfully sought Parliamentary Powers to build a standard gauge line.

The line as built was single track, 4¼ miles in length. It branched off the main line on the down side at the east end

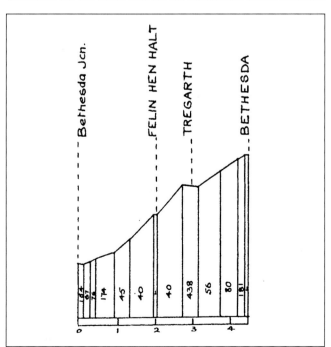

Bethesda Junction-Bethesda gradient profile.

of Bangor Tunnel, running south up the Ogwen valley on land wholly owned by Lord Penrhyn, who received £7,000 for the freehold at the time. It had several unusual conditions written into the conveyance so as not to obstruct the lord's view, as had happened at Kielder, where a viaduct had to be castellated so as not to offend that lordship's view!

Construction commenced at Felin Hên and Tregarth simultaneously on 3 September 1881. The line opened for passenger traffic on 1 July 1884 and for goods traffic the following year on 1 September 1885. The line had steep gradients, sharp curves, two viaducts and a tunnel. It passed over (once) and beneath (twice) the original Penrhyn Railway.

The line led an uneventful life and, due to increased competition from road transport, closed to passenger traffic from 3 December 1951. Freight lingered on, ceasing on 7 October 1963. The track was subsequently lifted and some structures removed although the Ogwen viaduct near Felin Hên still stands. The trackbed is now a footpath provided by Gwynedd Council.

Route Description

The line made a connection with the main line east of Bangor Tunnel, controlled from Bethesda Junction signalbox, where a double junction took off on the down side and immediately converged into a single line which then headed south, passing through well-wooded countryside on a rising gradient.

At 1½ miles the line crossed Afon Cegin on a stone viaduct which is still standing, then over the Penrhyn Railway, which ran more or less parallel to the east.

Felin Hên

At 1 mile 1,756yd came Felin Hên halt which served the villages of Pentir and Glasinfryn. Here the gradient levelled out briefly for the halt before resuming at 1 in 40 through a succession of curves of varying radii. A 400ft timber-construction platform with a simple shelter was located on the up side. At the time of opening there were signals here, controlled from an open frame on the platform, but these were removed just after the Grouping. Passengers accessed the platform by a flight of steps. Weekday traffic after World War 2 was mainly children to the Bethesda County School (latterly Ysgol Dyffryn Ogwen) travelling from and to Felin Hên halt and Tregarth. Passenger traffic to Bangor suffered at the hands of Crosville Motor Services and Purple Motors Ltd of Bethesda.

Bethesda Junction

The branch took off on the down side immediately after emerging from Bangor Tunnel. The junction was controlled from Bethesda Junction signalbox, a standard LNWR-design composite structure. The single-line staff token equipment however was located in Bangor No 1 signalbox. This view is looking towards Llandudno Junction and in the distance can be seen Llandegai Tunnel mouth. Note the small siding that ends in the embankment in front of the signalbox. This was sometimes used to dispose of ash and clinker from Bangor shed. It was the place where a runaway loaded coal wagon ended its days after escaping from Bethesda, following a rough shunt. It discharged its contents across the line and over the field beyond the track, to the delight of nearby residents who recovered most of the coal and disposed of it. *J. M. Dunn*

Bethesda Junction
Another view of Bethesda Junction shows Class 5 4-6-0 No 45028 passing with a down local from Chester to Bangor in 1954. Note the signals on either side of the track at the commencement of Cegin viaduct. Those on the up side protected, and at the time were controlled by, Penrhyn Siding box. *G. I. Davies*

Ogwen Viaduct
The Bethesda branch crossed over Ogwen viaduct shortly before reaching the halt at Felin Hên. This was a stone-built structure carrying the line over the River Ogwen. The viaduct still stands; the trackbed has been converted into a bridlepath but over the years the timber has grown and the viaduct can be seen only momentarily. This view is looking back towards Bethesda Junction. *Bill Rear collection*

Tregarth
Tregarth station was a staffed halt close to the centre of the village. The station was well patronised by the local residents who fought hard to retain the passenger service on the line when closure was announced. Here a Webb 0-6-2T pauses with a Bethesda-bound auto-train in 1949. *BRM*

After closure and removal of the track, bridge No 10 over the main road north of the station remained for many years before being removed in the 1970s.

Tregarth

The line continued east, running through a series of cuttings and underbridges before reaching Tregarth station, 2¾ miles from Bethesda Junction signalbox. Tregarth platform was on the down side, the rising gradient easing to 1 in 438 through the station. The buildings were of LNWR-design wooden modular construction.

Beyond the station the line swung southeast and resumed climbing at 1 in 56, running into a short 27yd tunnel followed by a bridge which carried the Penrhyn Railway track over the standard gauge line. Immediately after this the line entered Tregarth Tunnel, 279yd long. On emerging, the Penrhyn Railway recrossed the line and the gradient eased to 1 in 80. The standard gauge line then crossed the Afon Ogwen on a single 40ft span, 25ft above the river. At about 4¼ miles the rising gradient eased to 1 in 181 for about a hundred yards before levelling out for the run into Bethesda station, which was 527ft above sea level, 4¾ miles from Bethesda Junction and 5½ miles from Bangor station.

Bethesda

Bethesda station consisted of a single platform, 430ft long, constructed of stone. There was a run-round loop on the up side and a goods yard on the down. The single platform originally had a long canopy that was cut back during World War 2. On cessation of the passenger traffic, the platform line and run-round loop were lifted, although the station building, minus canopy, survived for many years.

The goods yard had a capacity of 121 wagons. The goods shed was a non-standard design, constructed of timber with a slate roof. Inside the shed were three cranes. A 5-ton hand-operated crane stood in the yard. There were privately owned coal wharves, cattle pens and a loading dock. There was a goods office and a weighing machine. Freight traffic was mainly coal and agricultural foodstuffs inward and some slate traffic outward.

There was no signalbox but a small lever frame mounted on the platform controlled signals. Points were worked from trackside ground frames. The single-line token equipment was located in the station office.

An LMS country lorry service was operated from Bethesda yard and after nationalisation the newly formed British Road Services briefly transferred vehicles from its Waenfawr depot to the station yard, under the control of the stationmaster.

Near Bethesda
Ivatt Class 2MT 2-6-2T No 41233 nears the end of the line with the daily freight from Menai Bridge yard one morning in 1952 after passenger services ceased running. This type of locomotive was the normal motive power in use on the line although engines up to the power classification 6 were authorised. Freight traffic continued until 1963. *G. I. Davies*

Bethesda

The station at Bethesda was a two-storey stone building, part of which included the stationmaster's house, and consisted of a single platform over which a canopy extended. There was a run-round facility off the platform road, but as pull-push trains were employed almost exclusively the loop was little used. Before 1939 the canopy was cut back giving protection for about a coach length. Here Ivatt 2-6-2T No 41223 stands at the head of its single coach. Driver Trefor Williams stands alongside with his guard. On cessation of passenger services the track was lifted from the passenger platform although the building stood for several years before demolition. *E. S. Russell*

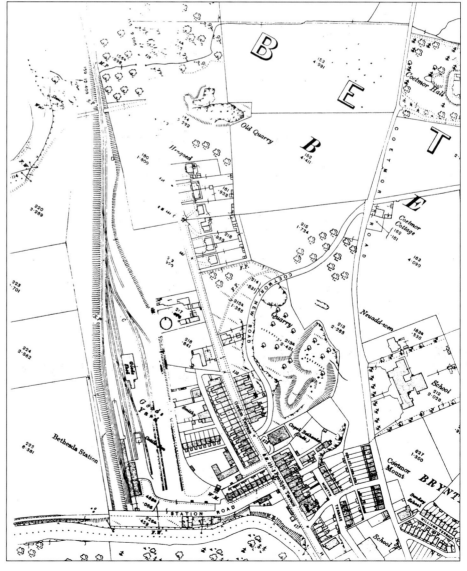

1914-18 Ordnance Survey map showing Bethesda station layout. *Crown Copyright*

BETHESDA BRANCH—Single Line. One class only.
Train Staff Stations—Bangor No. 1 and Bethesda.
A Passenger Train cannot cross another Passenger Train on this Branch.

Miles.	WEEK DAYS. Down Trains.	1	2	3	4	5	6	7	8	9	10	11	13	14
		Motor Train.		Motor Train.		Goods	Motor Train.	Motor Train.		Motor Train.		Motor Train.		Motor Train SO
		a.m.		a.m		a.m.	p.m.	p.m.		p.m.		p.m.		p.m.
...	BANGOR...dep	7 35	...	9 0	...	10 35	1 10	3 10	...	5 43	...	7 10	...	9 0
½	Bethesda J. pass	7 38	...	9 3	...	10 38	1 13	3 13	...	5 46	...	7 13	...	9 3
2¼	Felin Hen ...dep.	7 48	...	9 13	...	...	1 23	3 23	...	5 56	...	7 23	...	9 13
3½	Tregarth arr.	...	...	...	...	10 50	...	...	...	...	...	...	...	...
	Tregarth dep.	7 55	...	9 20	...	11 10	1 30	3 30	...	6 3	...	7 30	...	9 20
4⅞	BETHESDA arr	7 59	...	9 24	...	11 15	1 34	3 34	...	6 7	...	7 34	...	9 24

Miles.	WEEK DAYS. Up Trains.	15	16	17	18	19	20	21	22	23	24	25	26	27
		Motor Train.		Motor Train.		Goods	Motor Train.		Motor Train.	Motor Train.		Motor Train.		Motor Train. SO
		a.m.		a.m.		p.m.	p.m.		p.m.	p.m.		p.m.		p.m.
...	BETHESDA dep	8 5	...	9 35	...	12 10	1 50	++—Public Bills 2.17 p.m.	3 45	6 10	...	7 40	...	9 30
1⅜	Tregarth arr.	...	...	...	...	12 15	...		...	...	...	...	...	...
	Tregarth dep.	8 10	...	9 40	...	12 30	1 55		3 50	6 15	...	7 45	...	9 35
2⅝	Felin Hen ... „	8 17	...	9 47	...	...	2 2		3 57	6 22	...	7 52	...	9 42
4⅜	Bethesda J. pass	8 23	...	9 53	...	12 42	2 8		4 3	6 28	...	7 58	...	9 48
4⅞	BANGOR ...arr	8 26	...	9 56	...	12 45	2‡11		4 6	6 31	...	8 1	...	9 51

Extract from July 1919 LNWR timetable for the Bethesda branch.

BANGOR AND BETHESDA.
Week days only. One class only.

Bangor ...dep.	7 37	8 55	9 55	11 0	1 10	3 5	4 25	5 37	7 10	9 10	10 45	
Felin Hen	7 44	9 2	10 2	11 7	1 17	3 12	4 32	5 44	7 19	9 19	10 54	
Tregarth	7 50	9 8	10 8	11 13	1 23	3 18	4 38	5 50	7 25	9 25	10 58	
Bethesda ...arr.	7 55	9 13	10 13	11 18	1 28	3 23	4 43	5 55	7 30	9 30	11 5	
										Tues., Weds. and Sats. only. Runs until Sept 8th, only on Tuesdays.	Saturdays only.	
					SO	S						
Bethesda ...dep.	8 5	9 20	10 18	12 29	1 35	1 45	3 40	4 50	6 0	7 35	9 40	11 13
Tregarth	8 9	9 24	10 22	12 33	1 39	1 49	3 44	4 54	6 4	7 39	9 44	11 17
Felin Hen	8 14	9 29	10 27	12 38	1 44	1 54	3 49	4 59	6 9	7 44	9 49	11 22
Bangor ...arr.	8 23	9 38	10 36	12 47	1 53	2 4	3 53	5 8	6 18	7 53	9 58	11 31
											Tues. Weds. and Sats. only. Runs until Sept. 8th. only on Tuesdays.	Saturdays only.

Extract from July 1925 LMS timetable for the Bangor and Bethesda line.

Traffic

Originally the line was worked by an ordinary train, the locomotive running around the stock at Bethesda. From 1906, for three years, a steam railmotor was in use, which gives some indication of the low density of traffic.

In 1910 the LNWR introduced a two-coach pull-push unit to perform the service, powered by a 2-4-0T, and a similar unit operated on the Red Wharf Bay line in Anglesey. Two 2-4-0T '4ft 6in' engines, Nos 1000 and 1001, worked both the branches. The unit was withdrawn from the Bethesda line because of difficulties in maintaining a sufficient head of steam. The locomotive trailing axleboxes frequently ran hot.

LNWR-design '4ft 6in' Class 1P 2-4-2T engines then worked the branch but by 1941 these were replaced by 2-4-2T engines with larger driving wheels, which were in turn replaced by Webb-design Class 1F 0-6-2T auto-fitted tank engines. When the Ivatt 2-6-2T push-pull fitted engines arrived on the scene, they replaced the LNWR engines.

The final day of passenger services was worked by 0-6-2T No 58903 in the hands of driver Hugh Caulfield and fireman Eric Lynn.

Freight traffic continued until 1963.

The mainstay of the branch was its passenger traffic, the initial service being of six trips each way. By 1932 this had grown to 16 trains each way each weekday and 19 trains on a Saturday. There were even nine trains on a Sunday. All were push-pull operated, and operated between Bangor and Bethesda. Some workings ran through to Menai Bridge, Caernarvon and even Llanberis. Additionally, there were Saturday excursion trains from Bethesda to Llandudno or Rhyl during the summer season.

With the onset of World War 2 the service was drastically reduced, from which it never recovered. On Saturday 1 December 1951 the 5.53pm from Bangor was the last regular passenger train to work the branch although an occasional special made the trip up the branch from time to time.

From 1924 passenger trains worked from the Bethesda bay at Bangor station, a short-length platform set into the down-side passenger loop platform. It could accommodate a locomotive and a single 57ft coach. The locomotive was located at the Bethesda end and hauled the coach up hill, working bunker-first outward. After World War 2 two sets of men worked four return trips each.

Timings were relaxed, with 15 minutes allowed for the outward journey, and 16 for the return. Trains were allowed two minutes to run through Bangor Tunnel to Bethesda Junction, then six minutes to Felin Hên and four minutes to Tregarth. The gradients, curvature and foliage generally made the going tricky and it was not unusual for an engine to run out of sand before the end of its shift. Run-round time at Bethesda was short, usually about five minutes. Although Felin Hên was unstaffed and had been for many years, trains stopped here in either direction. Up direction freight trains stopped to pin down brakes. Tregarth was well placed close to the village and passenger trains were better patronised.

Immediately after World War 2 the first up train from Bethesda worked through to Menai Bridge with workers for Saunders Roe factory at Beaumaris. After discharging its load the train returned as empty stock to Bangor, where it stood for two minutes before working back up the branch to

Bethesda
An unusual mishap occurred on 6 August 1947. Following a climbing accident the railway was instructed to take a van to Bethesda to receive the coffin of the victim. It had been decided to put the van into a little-used siding. On coming out after loading, the engine became derailed on trap points which the shunter at Bethesda had forgotten to close. The engine and tender ran into soft ground and started to turn over. Fortunately, a telegraph pole prevented the engine and tender from completely rolling over and they came to rest at a precarious angle. This happened at 9.30am and it took until 4am the next morning to recover the engine and tender. The locomotive involved was an ex-LNWR 'Cauliflower', No 28513, seen here in its derailed state. *J. M. Dunn*

Bethesda. A similar arrangement took place in the afternoon. On the late turn, the 4.45pm from Bethesda stood at the down passenger loop platform at Bangor for 19 minutes. Once the train from London had cleared Menai Bridge, the motor train would follow it as empty stock as far as Menai Bridge and, having picked up the workmen, would depart at 5.30pm, working through to Bethesda. One minute was allowed for station duties at Bangor before continuing.

Freight traffic was rarely more than one train each way daily. Freight motive power to and from Bethesda was by LNWR 0-6-0 coal engines, although latterly Ivatt 2-6-2T or 2-6-0 tender engines undertook the duty.

The line was single throughout, with sidings at Tregarth but no passing loops, and was listed in the Sectional Appendix to the working timetables as being worked under the 'Train Staff and Ticket' system. The section was from Bangor No 1 box to Bethesda station; the staff shape was round and it was coloured red.

Incidents

Two known incidents are recorded. One on 6 August 1947 concerned an '18in' 0-6-0 goods engine which became derailed on catch points after propelling a hearse van into a little-used siding at Bethesda. The track gave way and the

engine came to rest leaning against a telegraph post. Llandudno Junction breakdown crane was called out to rescue the locomotive.

The second known incident concerned a wagon that broke a coupling after a rough shunt at Bethesda during operations. It ran away and covered the 4¼ miles in even time. The signalman at Bethesda Junction set the road for the trap siding and the wagon came to rest against an earth bank, propelling its load of small coal over the box, across the main line and over a retaining wall. The contents were gratefully scooped up by residents of the nearby Maes Geirchen estate.

There were other incidents, less spectacular. Occasionally a train would stall in section, usually on wet rails, and because of the gradient could not restart. Because of special instructions in force, it was necessary for the fireman to take the staff and walk down the line to Bethesda Junction, where he would hand the staff to the signalman. This enabled a banker to proceed on to the branch with the fireman in attendance and move cautiously up to the stalled train. After coupling up, the train would then proceed to Bethesda. After shunting was completed, the two locomotives would remain on the train and return coupled back to Bangor.

Menai Bridge

In the latter days of the Caernarfon line, after single-line working was instituted between Menai Bridge and Caernarfon, an LMS Class 5MT 4-6-0 moves slowly forward past the signalbox so that the signalman on duty can retrieve the train staff for the section from the fireman. Note that the up line from Caernarfon has been lifted by the platform ramp. The reporting number 1T59 indicates that the working was an excursion or special passenger train working within the London Midland Region. The locomotive appears to be in a run-down state but that might be due to a lack of cleaning. *Norman Kneale*

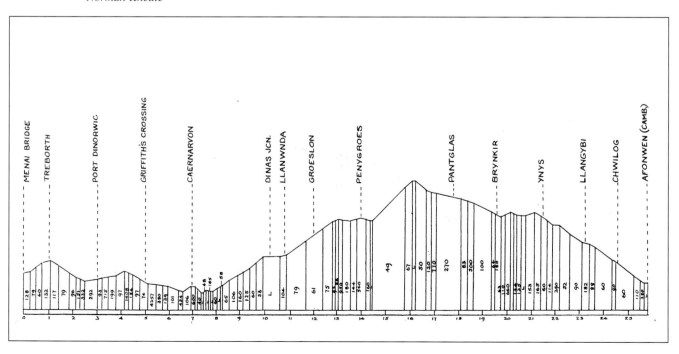

Menai Bridge-Afon Wen gradient profile.

Menai Bridge to Caernarfon and Branches

Historical

The first railway into Caernarfon was the Nantlle Railway, a 3ft 6in-gauge horse-drawn tramway which opened in 1828 to carry minerals, and subsequently passengers, from the Nantlle valley to the quayside at Caernarfon.

The first standard gauge railway to reach Caernarfon was the Bangor & Carnarvon Railway, incorporated on 20 May 1851. It was initially a single-track line constructed from Menai Bridge, where a connection was made with the Chester & Holyhead Railway, which leased the Bangor & Carnarvon line. The C&H was itself worked by the LNWR.

Whilst trains from Caernarfon could work directly on to the C&H up line, trains to Caernarfon had no direct access and were required to draw past the station at Menai Bridge and cross on to the up line, then set back past the junction before continuing. Following an accident in 1865, the junction was altered to provide a direct double junction. An additional platform was provided on the branch on the down side. Passengers accessed all platforms from the main building by subway.

Freight traffic commenced between Bangor and Port Dinorwic on 1 March 1852, with passenger traffic starting nine days later. The remaining section to Caernarfon was completed as a single line from Port Siding, about a mile north of Port Dinorwic. Caernarfon station opened on 1 July 1852. Stations were opened at Griffiths Crossing in 1854 and Treborth in 1855.

The Carnarvonshire Railway was incorporated by an Act of 29 July 1862, with powers to construct a line from the Bangor & Carnarvon Railway to Portmadoc. In the event, only the section of line from Afon Wen to Penygroes, on the Nantlle Railway, was built.

The Nantlle Railway section was part-abandoned when it was absorbed into the Carnarvonshire concern. Thomas Savin, the contractor, modified and realigned the Nantlle Railway trackbed to ease curves and gradients. Progress was sufficiently advanced by February 1866 that an engine ran between Afon Wen and Penygroes. The temporary northern terminus was established at Pant, about one and a half miles south of Caernarfon. The line was formally inspected in October 1866, but due to certain works being incomplete, official consent to open the line was withheld until 2 September 1867. Stations were provided at Pwllheli Road (later renamed Llanwnda), Groeslon, Penygroes and Brynkir. Chwilog station was opened in 1868 and the following year small stations were authorised for Pant Glâs and Llangybi. Ynys was opened in 1872. The Carnarvonshire Railway was transferred to the LNWR in March 1869. Dinas Junction station opened in September 1877.

Schemes were mooted to link Llanberis with the main line network; the final victor was the Carnarvon & Llanberis Railway. The royal assent was received and the ceremonial cutting of the first sod took place at Llanberis on 15 September 1864. The Caernarfon terminus was at Morfa, near Seiont Bridge. Financial difficulties were encountered from the start, and the line eventually came under the control of the LNWR, which completed the construction. The branch was inspected in June 1869 and opened on 1 July. The independent concern became vested in the LNWR in July 1870.

So it was that three lines came to terminate at different stations in Caernarfon. Proposals were authorised on 5 July 1865 to link the Bangor & Carnarvon Railway, the Carnarvon & Llanberis Railway and Carnarvonshire Railway under a scheme entitled the 'Carnarvon Town Line'. The Carnarvonshire line was extended to meet the Carnarvon & Llanberis line, the two lines then running parallel along the harbour before burrowing under Castle Square in Carnarvon Tunnel (163yd), climbing to meet the LNWR line at an end-on junction. The Carnarvon Town Line opened for freight traffic on 5 July 1870, whereupon orders were given in August 1870 for Morfa and Pant stations and the goods shed and turntable at Pant to be removed although through running for passenger traffic was not authorised until January 1871.

This track arrangement survived until 1894 when Caernarvon station was rebuilt. The crossover was removed from the entrance to Caernarvon Tunnel to the south end of the station and movements were controlled from No 2 signalbox. From there the Afon Wen and Llanberis lines worked as two single lines under Turf Square, into a tunnel beneath Castle Square, crossing the River Cadnant inside the tunnel, and emerging near the harbour just above sea level. Near the southern entrance of Caernarvon Tunnel a scissors crossover was located, controlled from Carnarvon No 3 Signalbox. Both lines then commenced climbing as far as Seiont Bridge, where they parted company.

The LNWR was under obligation to build a station below Segontium Terrace, near Caernarvon Tunnel. This would have had a single-island platform with offices at street level. Space was very tight and in return for a contribution towards the construction of Bridge Street, the corporation waived its claim to the station. The proposal to build a station at this point was in later years resurrected and considered four times.

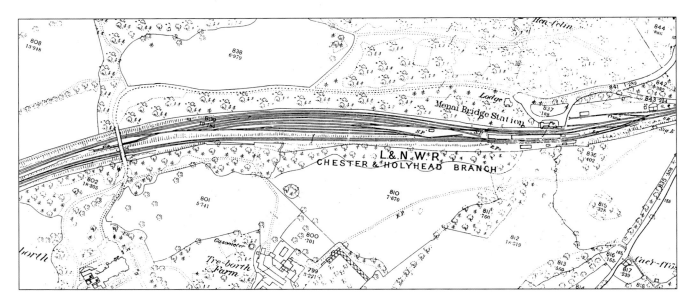

1914-18 Ordnance Survey map showing Menai Bridge station layout. *Crown Copyright*

In 1871 the Bangor & Carnarvon Railway was authorised to double its line from Menai Bridge, necessitating a second single-line tunnel to be bored parallel to the first line, south of Treborth.

In 1894 an up platform, a footbridge and additional sidings were installed at Caernarfon. A new booking hall was built on the gable end of the existing building into the station forecourt. Track modifications were implemented at various times.

The section from Caernarfon to Pant and Dinas is now the route of the narrow gauge Welsh Highland Railway, opened in 1999, which heads south up the Gwyrfai valley to Waunfawr and work has started to extend the line to Rhyd Ddu. It will ultimately reach Porthmadog.

The late J. M. Dunn had copies of confidential proposals which the author saw briefly in 1951 that indicate that when determination of the regional boundaries was being considered in 1947, two proposals were under discussion which would have affected the lines through Caernarfon. The first proposal was to transfer all lines in North Wales from the London Midland Region (Western Division) to the Western Region. The notes attached to the minute from the district engineer at Bangor indicated that the necessary costs incurred to provide adequate clearances at platforms and other structures in North Wales to accommodate the wider loading gauge of ex-GWR design locomotives would have been prohibitive. The district engineer recommended its rejection. An alternative proposal, dated December 1948, suggested that the line from Afon Wen to Caernarfon be transferred to the Western Region, with the latter station remaining in London Midland Region control. The Afon Wen line would come under Central Wales District (Oswestry) control. Portmadoc, Pwllheli and Penmaenpool men would be required to learn the road to Caernarfon and Bangor. The modifications necessary to platforms, lines, etc to accommodate the wider loading gauge were not considered unreasonable. Mr Dunn, on behalf of his staff, objected to the proposal, and it was not pursued further.

By 1955 the island platform building at Caernarfon was deteriorating badly. A decision was made to demolish the wooden structure and replace it with a single-storey brick building. At the same time the covering over the footbridge was removed. The old building had some protection from an all-over canopy, but the new building was devoid of such a luxury. When the line from Caernarfon to Afon Wen was closed in 1964, the island platform building and the up platform line were removed.

Most of the workings to Caernarfon after 1965 were undertaken by DMUs from Bangor or Llandudno. The line from Menai Bridge was singled and the intermediate stations were closed. Menai Bridge station was demolished. Caernarvon No 1 signalbox was taken out of use and the track layout simplified. Signals and points were controlled from No 2 signalbox.

Dismantling of the Afon Wen line commenced at Llanwnda and worked back to Afon Wen. Diesel locomotives based at Pwllheli were to be seen on the branch for the first time, albeit on demolition trains.

With the imminence of the Investiture of Prince Charles, scheduled for summer 1969, it was decided to store special traffic stock on the day of the Investiture on the former Afon Wen branch. so the track between Caernarfon and Llanwnda was left in situ, and taken up immediately after the Investiture.

On summer Saturdays between 1965 and 1968 locomotive-hauled trains worked into Caernarfon. From 1968 only one summer Saturday working was locomotive-hauled throughout when Class 40s were seen briefly at Caernarfon.

Latterly, freight trains worked into the station, usually hauled by Class 24 locomotives, but by 1968 all freight facilities had been withdrawn. Only the DMU reigned supreme.

Demolition of the Llanberis branch took place in 1965. The track was lifted right back up to Caernarvon No 2.

The passenger service stuttered on, a minimal train service between Bangor and Caernarfon sufficed and the trains which ran did not make connections. Closure notices were posted in the autumn of 1969 and the last passenger services ran on Saturday 3 January 1970.

Menai Bridge

Fairburn 2-6-4T No 42212 stands at the up branch platform at Menai Bridge on a Caernarfon to Bangor working. The engine was attached to Chester LM shed (6A) at the time and never was allocated to Bangor, so presumably it was on short-term loan. Behind it stands Ivatt Class 2MT No 41234, a resident of Bangor shed from 1956 to 1965, which was working the yard shunt. There was a small goods yard on the up side between the station and the Caernarfon road overbridge which handled local traffic. The roof of the goods shed is visible in the background. *Norman Kneale*

There was still one ironic twist to the saga of the branch. The fire in the Britannia bridge on 23 May 1970 caused logistical problems for the nascent Freightliner traffic between Holyhead and Ireland. On 16 June 1970 a decision was taken to utilise Caernarfon yard for Freightliner container traffic. The containers were offloaded from rail on to road lorries by mobile road cranes. Menai Bridge yard was reopened briefly for the Irish cattle traffic. Normally, two trains a day worked into Caernarfon yard, with Class 47 locomotives predominating. This arrangement persisted until January 1972, when the facility was withdrawn, despite the fact that the rail link to Holyhead was not restored until 30 January 1973.

On a positive note, part of the Carnarvonshire Railway between Dinas and Caernarfon has risen, phoenix-like, to become the trackbed for the Welsh Highland Railway, thus achieving the ultimate aims and ambitions of the old NWNGR to reach Caernarfon. The line now extends to Waunfawr, having been opened to traffic in August 2000, and at the time of writing, track-laying is taking place between there and Rhyd Ddu.

Route Description

Menai Bridge

The line to Caernarfon branched off the Chester to Holyhead main line at Menai Bridge, 1¼ miles from Bangor. When first opened the line was single, but increased traffic, the difficulty in operating the down line connection at the station, plus an accident, saw the

connection to Caernarfon remodelled and the line was doubled. The junction took off on the down side, controlled from No 1 signalbox. There were three platforms on the site. The main station building, which was very exotic and quite unlike anything else on the C&H, was on the up main line side.

An island platform which had a small canopy, and bench seats, lights and nameboards served the down main line and up trains from Caernarfon. Passengers boarding for Caernarfon had to cross to the third platform by a subway, which was always very gloomy and smelled of unmentionable indiscretions. The Caernarfon line had an open brick-built shed with little protection from the elements. When Menai Bridge station closed to traffic in 1964 everything was removed. Even the main station building was demolished, although it would have made a delightful home.

The Caernarfon line commenced climbing at the platform ramp on a gradient of 1 in 128 which stiffened almost immediately to 1 in 79. Between the Caernarfon line and the Holyhead main line was a concentration yard. Most freight trains from the branch started or terminated here. At one time there was a second signalbox which controlled movements in the yard. It closed in the 1930s.

The yard was busy at all times, with a shunting engine in attendance for most of the day and night. Some freight trains to and from Holyhead passed through without stopping but all other traffic called at the yard. Menai Bridge had had a small contingent of goods guards from early days, but these were absorbed into Bangor duties from about 1950.

Menai Bridge

The Stanier 2-6-2T engines were used for a variety of duties at Bangor, there being six members of the class at the time of this photograph in May 1949. Here No 124 (still with LMS numbering) pulls out of Menai Bridge yard onto the up main line, shunting freight stock. A gathering of yard staff sits basking in the sunshine in front of the main platform building. The engine had returned to Menai Bridge after working the early shunt turn at Caernarfon and was making up a train for the evening working to Mold Junction. *E. S. Russell*

Menai Bridge

The climb out of Menai Bridge to Treborth was steep and at times slippery because of the overhanging trees. Equally, the descent from the summit to the junction with the main line could be treacherous and drivers descended with extreme caution. The exchange sidings can be seen between the Caernarfon and Holyhead lines and are, on this occasion, somewhat empty. An unidentified Stanier 2-6-4T storms up the bank from a standing start at Menai Bridge, the white exhaust suggesting the fireman was on top of his job. *Norman Kneale*

Treborth

The first summit of the line was at this station. Here, devoid of trains, are the platforms with the main building on the down side. The stationmaster lived in the adjoining house and by the appearance of the garden had plenty of spare time. Not every train called here, although a condition in the acquisition of the land required that a minimum number of trains in each direction called here in perpetuity. Note the Hawkeye sign that survived until the station closed. Its yellow background was repainted maroon, as at most other stations on the branch that retained these station nameboards. Beyond the down platform a camping coach can just be seen. This was a feature for a couple of years in the 1950s but it was never very well patronised and was removed after a couple of seasons. *W. A. Camwell*

Vaynol Tunnel
Fairburn 2-6-4T No 42157 of Bangor shed storms out of the single bore with the 11.30am Bangor to Pwllheli on 4 October 1952. The line as built was single track but when the Bangor & Carnarvon Railway was acquired by the Chester & Holyhead it doubled the line to Caernarfon. This necessitated boring a second tunnel on the down side. The bore was tight and it was necessary to keep steam on until emerging, by which time speed was in the high 50s or even over 60mph. The locomotive came to Bangor in June 1950 and remained until 1956 when it was transferred away to Stoke. *Bill Rear*

Port Siding
The freight-only branch to Port Dinorwic harbour took off the Caernarfon to Bangor line on the up side via a trailing connection, controlled from Port Siding signalbox. When the line was singled in 1965 the freight branch was taken out of use and the signalbox demolished. The house remained until the 1990s when part of the trackbed was used for the Port Dinorwic bypass. Today there is no trace of the railway presence on this site, although a short distance towards Caernarfon the trackbed became a private access road. *F. W. Shuttleworth*

Climbing out of Menai Bridge towards Caernarfon was Davies Siding, halfway up the bank towards Treborth, which served the Vaynol estate. It was a tricky place to work. The track was lined with an avenue of trees that kept the sunlight off the tracks for most of the day and shed their leaves in the autumn. The siding was little used and was taken out of service before 1948.

Sanding all the way up the gradient on the climb out of Menai Bridge was the general order of the day. Heavily loaded freight trains to Caernarfon sometimes slipped to a stand and were obliged to set back to have another go.

Treborth

The first passenger station on the line was Treborth, just short of a mile from Menai Bridge and 2¼ miles from Bangor. The gradient eased at the station and changed direction. The first summit was at the station itself.

Treborth opened to traffic initially in 1855 but closed in 1858, only to reopen the following year. It was some way from Treborth village and had a quiet existence. A clause inserted in the conveyance of land to the Bangor & Carnarvon Railway stipulated that two trains had to call at the station.

The main building was on the down side and comprised the stationmaster's house and facilities. The building still stands and is now a delightful private house in a very quiet location.

The up-side platform was devoid of fittings, save for a small wooden waiting shed. Menai Bridge distant signal was on the up platform ramp at the Caernarfon end. Passengers crossed the line by an occupation crossing.

A small yard, rarely used, was installed on the down side behind the station building. At one time a camping coach was located in the siding but this was not successful and was removed after a couple of seasons.

Down trains departing Treborth encountered a descending slope of 1 in 117 for a quarter of a mile into a cutting which ended in the twin-bore Vaynol Tunnel, where the gradient increased to 1 in 79. The down bore was particularly tight and blow-backs were not unknown. Accordingly, drivers kept steam on until emerging, by which time the speed of passenger trains was over 60mph. Goods trains stopped to pin down brakes at Treborth station and their progress was very controlled.

On emerging, the line crossed over the main Caernarfon to Bangor road on a plate bridge and then went round a sharp right-hand curve, continuing to fall, albeit at a slightly less severe gradient, until Port Siding was reached.

Port Siding

Port Siding was 2½ miles from Bangor and the point for the line to Port Dinorwic harbour to diverge on the up side. The branch to the quayside was a freight-only line, details of which can be found elsewhere.

Access to the branch was controlled from an old Saxby & Farmer signalbox located on the down side at the point where the gradient changed from falling to rising. The signalbox was switched in to the long section from Menai Bridge to Caernarvon No 1 between the hours of 6am and 6pm. It was a tall structure, some 18ft 6in above ground level, to give signalmen a clear view of the line over a road bridge. Constructed of brick, it measured 14ft x 12ft. A staff cottage stood alongside.

Port Dinorwic

Port Dinorwic, 4½ miles from Bangor, opened to traffic on 10 March 1852. The original station on the up side was some 200yd north of the second station which was much bigger and which opened to traffic in 1874. The main building on the up side survives to this day in private ownership. Its design was optimistic in view of the traffic but it failed to justify its size. By contrast, the down platform had a very basic shelter, open to the elements. Passengers crossed the line by a subway.

Port Dinorwic
The main building was on the up side and was a grand if depressing structure, constructed of yellow brick. The premises were too large for the volume of traffic that passed through the station. By contrast the down side shelter was a rudimentary affair open to the platform edge and likened by some to a cattle shelter! Here BR Standard Class 4MT 2-6-4T No 80094 pauses on its journey to Caernarfon and Pwllheli. A block of eight of these Standard tanks was transferred to Bangor shed in June 1956, being exchanged for a mix of Fowler, Stanier and Fairburn tank engines of the same power and wheel arrangement. For some the stay was brief, merely a few months, but others remained for a couple of years before being transferred away, in some cases to Three Bridges or Dundee. This individual engine remained at Bangor until October 1959, when it moved to Birkenhead. *BRM*

Felin Heli
The Caernarfon to Bangor line skirted the Menai Strait for most of the journey as far as Port Dinorwic, where it cut inland. The line reached a secondary summit between Griffiths Crossing and Port Dinorwic and trains coasted down the grade for about a mile. Halfway down the bank the line crossed a minor road on the level on the outskirts of Port Dinorwic at the area known locally as Felin Heli. At the crossing, which was under the control of a lady crossing keeper, a footbridge spanned the line which was a good viewing and photographic spot. Here Fairburn 2-6-4T No 42075 heads towards Bangor with a Saturdays Only working from Pwllheli in the summer of 1963. *Bill Rear*

A small yard was located on the up side, just before the passenger platform, controlled from another Saxby & Farmer signalbox, also on the up side. The box was built of the same yellow brick as the station building. It was switched in as required.

Beyond the station the line crossed over the Caernarfon to Bangor road on a plate bridge, since removed, and continued to climb for the next mile, keeping company with the road for half a mile. At Felin Heli a minor road level crossing and passenger footbridge crossed the tracks. The road then deviated inland, the railway keeping to the coastline. Just beyond Milepost 4, the second summit of the line was reached and the gradient descended at 1 in 74 to the next station. Parts of the trackbed have been removed for road widening purposes; what remains of the trackbed as far as Caernarfon is now a footpath and cycle route, known as Lôn Lâs Menai.

Griffiths Crossing

This station was 6½ miles from Bangor. It opened to traffic in 1854 but patronage was sparse. It had a brief moment of glory in 1911 when King George V and Queen Mary alighted there for the Investiture of the then Prince of Wales. In 1969 a temporary platform was erected slightly further west by the Ferodo factory for Prince Charles' Investiture. Griffiths Crossing closed to all traffic on 5 July 1937 and the platforms were removed almost immediately,

although the former stationmaster's house remained as a crossing keeper's cottage. The building still stands today, much modified and enlarged, functioning as a bed & breakfast establishment.

Built of local stone, the design of the station was unusual. The platforms were 320ft long, also of stone construction. On the down platform a single-storey building contained a booking office and a general waiting room. The up platform contained a small building partially open to the elements. There was a level crossing at the Bangor end, controlled from a small lever frame. Passengers crossed the tracks on the level and accessed the booking office through a wicket gate.

At one time Griffiths Crossing was a popular destination for Sunday School trips from Caernarfon and special trains were chartered in LNWR days for the purpose. In the run-up to World War 1, Territorial Army regiments used fields close to the station for their training camps and travelled by train to the station from different parts of the country.

A small goods siding was behind the down platform, equipped with a loading platform and pens for cattle traffic. This was removed on closure.

At one time there was another siding off the up line that led into Parkia brickworks. This fell out of use just before World War 2. After a period of abandonment it was requisitioned and brought back into use, serving an underground petroleum store, and a second siding was

Near Griffiths Crossing
In the dying days of the Caernarfon to Bangor line, passenger traffic was left to DMUs working a shuttle between the two towns. On Saturdays in the summer season trains from further afield travelled to Caernarfon, the then terminus, carrying passengers for the Butlin's camp at Pwllheli. One of the locomotive-hauled workings started at Warrington and was worked by Class 40 locomotives. Here No D370 hauls the return working to Warrington, reporting number 1T58, near Griffiths Crossing halt and close to the summit of the section. The line had by this time been singled and the down line was out of use, shortly to be lifted. A platelayer's hut stands disused, with ivy growing on the roof. *Bill Rear*

Griffiths Crossing
The station, looking towards Caernarfon, was poorly patronised, mainly due to the fact that there was no community nearby. Instead it was located at a point where the Caernarfon to Bangor road was crossed by an unclassified road which led from the village of Bethel to the coast. The single-storey buildings on the 320ft-long platforms were of local stone, the structure on the up platform being merely a rudimentary shelter. The level crossing gates were hand operated, the stationmaster living in a railway cottage at the crossroads which passed into private hands before World War 2. The station closed on 5 July 1937, the platforms and the shelter being demolished immediately. It would seem that there had been some optimism by someone with the installation of a chocolate vending machine by the platform entrance. In the distance can be seen the chimneys of the closed Parkia brickworks. *Bill Rear collection*

Griffiths Crossing
The former stationmaster's house still stood after the station was closed in 1937 and indeed stands to this day. Although much modified and enlarged, the original structure can be readily identified. A Metro-Cammell Class 101 two-coach unit heads for Caernarfon with the 19.20 Bangor to Caernarfon working on 13 April 1966. *A. Wyn Hobson*

Griffiths Crossing
The Investiture of Prince Charles as Prince of Wales in 1969 required the royal party to disembark from the royal train some distance from Caernarfon town. A temporary platform was erected at the Ferodo works about two miles from the town centre. Here workmen can be seen erecting the platform prior to the event. It was demolished soon afterwards. *Norman Kneale*

Waterloo Port

Fairburn 2-6-4T No 42259 with a six-coach set coasts down the grade and, where the track levels out, passes over Waterloo Port occupation crossing, about a mile from the station at Caernarfon. It was the practice to shut off steam before the crossing signals and whistle up to announce one's forthcoming arrival. An unofficial warning was given of the location by 'roaring rails'. These engines were the author's favourite and this particular engine was the first he ever drove (albeit unofficially) and accordingly it has a permanent place in his list of favourite engines. The working on this occasion was the 5.39pm Bangor to Afon Wen and Pwllheli in the summer of 1952. *Bill Rear*

installed. After the war the site became a precast concrete works for Dow Mac, which made, amongst other items, concrete sleepers. The site was served by a minor road that crossed the tracks over an ungated but supervised level crossing. It was the scene of an accident in about 1950 when a lorry collided with the 4.4pm Bangor to Pwllheli passenger working, the driver of the lorry being killed.

Caernarfon

The station opened to traffic from 1 July 1852. It was the terminus of the line from Bangor (8½ miles away) and had a single platform face, which was worked bi-directionally. Sidings ran the length of the site and were used for the storage of stock as well as for goods traffic. A goods warehouse and an engine shed were built at the same time but their exact positions are uncertain.

Caernarfon station was the largest of all the North Wales branch line stations. It was a long station, equalled in length only by Afon Wen and Denbigh.

With the opening of the Carnarvon Town Line on 5 July 1870, the station was enlarged. Bay platforms were provided at either end of the main platform. The goods shed, which formerly had been opposite the main platform, was demolished and a new building constructed on a different site in the yard. A scissors crossover was installed midway along the main platform line. A new locomotive shed with a 42ft turntable was provided. Stables for eight horses, together with a feed and harness store, were provided in a small yard accessed off the main station yard, close to the now deconsecrated Christ Church, which after years of neglect has been tastefully renovated as a children's fun centre.

Further developments took place in 1894 when an island platform was constructed together with an up loop and additional freight sidings. The platform faces on the island platform were designated 'local platform line' and 'Up platform line'. Parallel to the up line was the designated up and down goods loop line. The scissors crossovers were removed from near the northern portal of Carnarvon Tunnel and the centre road of the up and down platform road was replaced by a new scissors crossover at the commencement of the two single lines to Llanberis and Afon Wen, in front of No 2 box. The main station building was enlarged and a new booking hall and office were provided. An extensive all-over canopy offered protection from the elements on both the up and down platform, extending from over part of the Bangor bay to No 2 signalbox, and over part of Llanberis bay. Outside the building another canopy was provided, extending from the left luggage office across the front of the new ticket hall up to the ticket barrier. It is

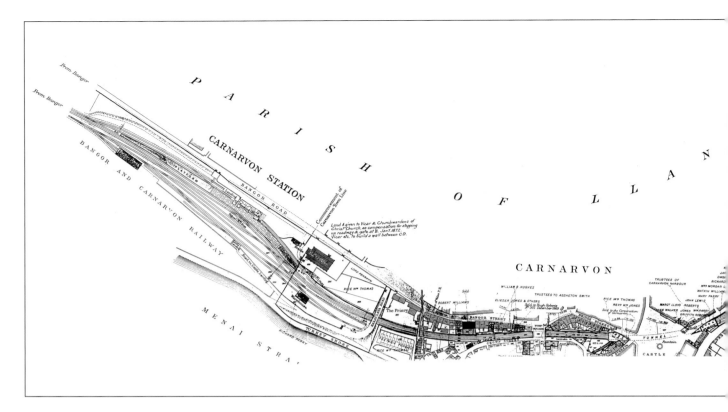

Caernarfon station prior to 1900. *Crown Copyright*

Caernarfon
Ivatt Class 2MT 2-6-0 No 46424 of Rhyl shed, working the 'Radio Land Cruise' from Rhyl to Denbigh, Corwen, Barmouth and Afon Wen, picks up speed after a water stop at the station. In the foreground is the 42ft turntable pit which, though the table was intact, was devoid of track and out of use. The water tank was the sole survivor of the shed that once stood here. No 1 box in its shabby condition faced the sea, the paint peeling off and its remaining paintwork bleached by constant battering from wind and spray off the Menai Strait. *Bill Rear*

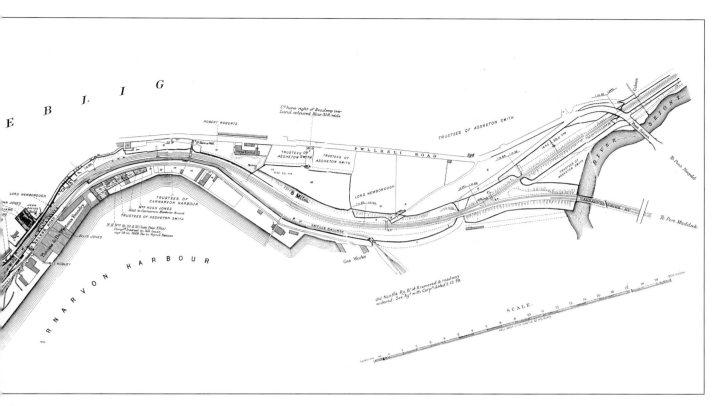

Caernarfon

This most unusual photograph was taken by the late Flt Lt A. E. Rimmer from his aeroplane in the spring of 1942. It shows the extent of the station at Caernarfon. Landmarks will be readily identified. In the foreground can be seen Caernarfon No 1 Signal box (the Rat Hole) and the 42ft diameter hand operated turntable, in front of which is the water tank that stood near the site of the former locomotive shed. The tracks on the right hand side descended to the coal yard and sidings, agricultural store and extended into the petroleum store on the upper right hand edge of the picture. The long Up and Down platform adjoined the station building and was paralleled by the shorter island platform. Note the locomotive standing at the water tank on at the Bangor end of the island platform. The goods sidings alongside were surprisingly empty of wagons. Normally they were full. Three cattle wagons stood at the dock. Beyond them was the goods shed. The lines to Llanberis and Afon Wen passed in front of the Crosville Motor Services garage before passing under Balaclava Road bridge. In the bay platform two coaches stood at the Excursion platform line. Note to Christ Church, now a Children's Fun centre, in front of which were the stables, then still in use. In the upper background can be seen the old Pavilion, built for the 1910 National Eisteddfod and subsequently under-used, being demolished in the 1970s. Today, local government offices stand on the site. Caernarfon station closed in 1970 and after a period of disuse, was demolished and replaced by a Safeway supermarket. In the late 1990s, a small mural of railway scenes formerly on the site was displayed near the checkouts. The Crosville Motor Services garage was also demolished in the early 1990s and a Kwik-Save supermarket not occupies the site.

The late A. E. Rimmer, Welsh Highland Heritage collection

Caernarfon

There was plenty of freight handled at Caernarfon right up until the traffic was extinguished in the mid-1960s. Here Fairburn 2-6-4T No 42283 draws a raft of wagons out of the upper yard whilst making up the evening working to Mold Junction. This locomotive had two spells at Bangor, the first in 1962 when it arrived from Shoeburyness and remained for the summer. It next returned in 1964 and worked in the district for about a year. It went into Cowlairs works for overhaul prior to returning to Bangor and, to the great delight of Bangor men, had the word 'Bangor' painted on the front bufferbeam in true Cowlairs fashion. Note the variety of wagons being shunted. In the background can be seen the tanks for the Esso petroleum store, now removed, and the spire of Christ Church, now deconsecrated but restored and functioning as a children's play centre. *Norman Kneale*

believed that the second freight yard opened about this time. This line descended to Victoria Dock and served a coal siding, a covered agricultural store and, latterly, a petroleum store. From the turn of the century the nightly mineral train to Springs Branch, Wigan, was assembled and started from here. This yard remained in use until after the official station closure in 1970 but was demolished and the site cleared only towards the end of the 1970s.

Two new signal cabins were constructed at either end of the station site in 1894.

Caernarvon No 1 cabin was an all-wood construction with 68 levers located on the down side, at the northern end of the station. It was a big, ugly LNWR wooden structure, constructed against an embankment which backed on to private properties on North Road. It was a gloomy,

draughty box and in its later days very unpopular. It was always a problem to get permanent staff to work there. The relief men in the district landed themselves with the working on a regular basis. There were two shifts. The early turn opened up about 4.30am, a porter signalman covered the midday gap, and the second shift closed up at about 10.30pm. In times of shortage or sickness, the signalmen had to work overtime to cover for absent colleagues.

The reason for the reluctance to take on the post as a permanency was the rats.

Now, most railways had a rat problem, so this was nothing new. But the rats in No 1 box were something else. They were huge; they were massive. As Geoff Smethurst, one of the relief signalmen, said: 'They were bloody ginormous.' They were as big as a normal-sized cat.

Caernarfon

In the last years of the station's life, steam gave way to diesel locomotives on the remains of the Bangor to Afon Wen line, although most of the passenger work was in the hands of DMUs. On summer Saturdays, however, through workings from Manchester or Warrington with passengers for Butlin's camp at Pwllheli had locomotive-hauled stock which terminated at the town. Here No D379 stands at the former local platform with the return working to Warrington. Note the water tank on the island platform, disconnected but still standing, and the gas lamps on the platform with the totems still in place. The former yard inspector's hut is abandoned on the edge of the yard. The Esso tank farm stands clean and pristine in the lower yard. These tanks would eventually disappear in the 1980s. *Bill Rear*

Caernarfon

Standard Class 4MT 4-6-0 No 75027, nominally allocated to Wrexham Croes Newydd shed, stands at the up & down platform with the 7.40am Pwllheli to Manchester Exchange in August 1964. This was a regular service train during the week which terminated at Bangor, but on Saturdays it worked through. This engine appears to have been commandeered, as former Western Region locomotives rarely strayed off their own diagrams. Note the barrow loaded with goods on the platform. A considerable amount of parcels and smalls traffic was conveyed in the guard's vans of passenger trains — this was a small consignment! The station is still clean and tidy and, although closure of the line beyond Caernarfon was imminent, the staff still took pride in their workplace. On the three lamp posts in the foreground six half-flanged totems bearing the station name abound, today worth a fortune at a railwayana auction. *Norman Kneale*

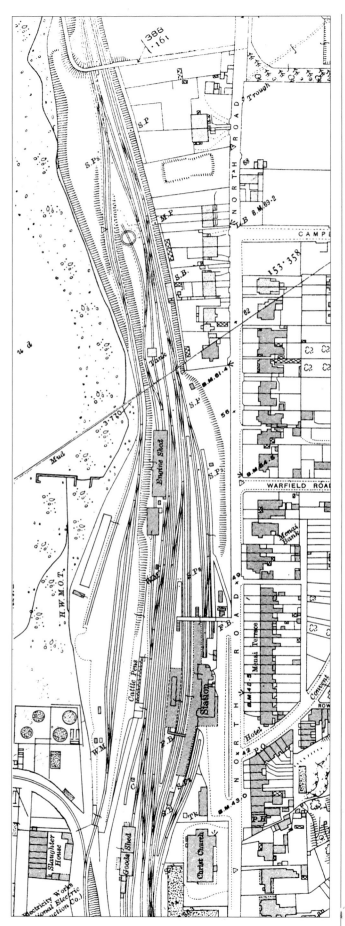

1914-18 Ordnance Survey map showing Caernarfon station layout. *Crown Copyright*

Moreover, they were fearless and downright cheeky. I have been inside the box when they sauntered across the floor of the cabin and casually munched any crumbs that might have fallen. They were impervious to sudden noise, and they gave the rat equivalent of two fingers to anyone who might try to intimidate them.

They lived somewhere in the interlocking room under the frame, and although their nests could not be seen, one was conscious of beady eyes watching whenever anyone went in there. In summer months it was necessary for signalmen to adjust the tensioners when heat slackened the wires. On more than one occasion a fireman on the yard shunt was asked to accompany a timid signalman into 'the pit', as it was called; 6ft 6in firemen had been known to refuse. The uninitiated, curious railwaymen would venture to see for themselves. They never went back a second time. Despite the best efforts of the LM vermin control, they could not be got rid of. It seemed the rats had a particular appetite for the grease that was used to lubricate the slides and pulleys and one could hear them muttering the rat equivalent of 'yum, yum' as lubrication time came round.

Of course there were rat drives. One of the gangers had a Jack Russell terrier, which went berserk when introduced to the locking room. It made regular visits after being 'requested' (perhaps that should be pleaded for) by the stationmaster.

On such occasions the impending visit was advertised and men came from near and far to witness the event. The chosen day was usually a Sunday when the box was closed. It was timed to coincide with the eviction of members from the Crosville Sports & Social Club, when a motley crowd of 10 or 15 Crosville staff shuffled along the up and down platform and across the tracks of the Bangor bay to the box. The dog was already getting excited by the gathering crowd and by the time the locking frame door was reached its enthusiasm knew no bounds. It growled and snarled and dribbled in high expectations of some sport.

The door was opened, the dog thrown in and the door slammed shut. Yelps and barks were heard and then from between the rodding came the rats, scores of them, all looking back over their shoulders at the gathered crowd and cursing humanity for disturbing their Sunday afternoon siesta.

After about 10 minutes the door was opened and a very pleased-looking dog emerged, seeking praise, which he got. The braver members of the gathering went inside and

Caernarfon

Until about 1950 motor trains or pull-push working extended to Caernarfon, but these were deemed unsatisfactory for some reason and never appeared in the timetables after 1951. Most workings were short journeys between Bangor and Caernarfon but one or two, particularly before and during the war, were extensions off Llandudno Junction to Bangor, or Bethesda to Bangor workings, performing a short working, filling in when the units would otherwise be standing at Bangor. Here in May 1947 Webb Class 1F 0-6-2T No 27603, which was normally working on the Bethesda branch, pulls away from Caernarfon with two coaches, one of which was a motor driving trailer. Note the old-style running-in board with black letters on a yellow background on the end of the 'up & down platform', and the sheeted wagons stored in the 'King Edward' or excursion bay platform. These wagons could well have contained bombs from Glynrhonwy complex at Llanberis which at this time were being removed from that site for disposal. *Bill Rear collection*

Caernarfon

Latterly it was the practice to take empty cattle trucks from Holyhead to Caernarfon for washing out. These were stored in the upper yard and at times there would be a hundred or so being cleaned. The cleaning was done on the far siding, adjoining the cattle dock, and the contents of the wagons would be dumped in the pens, and sold off to farmers who cleared the pens. It was not unknown for a stack of 20 tons to be available. It was necessary to move the wagons around and cleaned cattle wagons were stored elsewhere in the upper yard, to be replaced by unclean ones. In 1966 a Class 24 diesel locomotive was on goods yard shunt at Caernarfon for about six hours each day. Here No D5073 shunts a raft of wagons about the yard. *Bill Rear*

Caernarfon
The up & down platform at Caernarfon was the most frequently used face by through trains. It was protected by an all-over canopy for most of its length. At the time that this picture was taken the footbridge cover was still in place and it is believed that this photograph was one of a series which showed the station platform before alterations. Note the abundance of enamel signs — a collector's dream, today worth a lot of money. Note also the seats with the station name on the back rest. The station was still lit by gas lamps and some examples are visible hanging from the roof. Beyond the suspended clock can be seen the ticket collector's office. The bay window of the booking hall extends into the platform area. In the distance can be seen Caernarvon No 2 signalbox on the platform. *BRM*

Caernarfon
The original island platform was erected in 1894 when the station was enlarged. The building was a standard LNWR modular single-storey wooden structure, typical of many stations elsewhere on the LNWR system. It was fitted with an all-over canopy extending to the platform edge. By 1950 the building was suffering from neglect during the war years, and the timber was rotting in part. It was decided to replace the wooden building with a modern single-storey brick structure and this was done in 1955-6. The overall canopy was removed, as was the cover over the footbridge. This is another of the photographs taken to show the station platforms before alterations. The platform face shown here was known as the 'local' platform and for some unknown reason was little used until after the line to Bangor was singled in 1965. *BRM*

Caernarfon

A full-length canopy extended over the front of the booking hall and over the parcels and left luggage offices. The two-storey brick building was part of the extension to the station undertaken in 1894. After the renovation in the mid-1950s this canopy was removed, depriving the public of some shelter, and the front of the building was given a red cement covering which made it look dreadful. Here, in 1950, the only change since 1894 had been the erection of white-painted rail barriers to prevent cars or vans with poor brakes from crashing into the building, which happened on several occasions in wartime when the blackout was strictly enforced. *BRM*

Caernarfon

The island platform is seen here after the replacement of the wooden LNWR building. Although the brick structure is functional and probably sufficed for the declining number of passengers travelling by rail, the platform had become a draughty place to wait for a train, despite the waiting rooms. The all-over canopy had given adequate protection in bad weather but now the passengers were exposed to the full force of spray and wind blowing off the Menai Strait. The main up & down platform was little changed and some shelter was to be had under its cover. Note the mail van on the platform unloading mailbags into the DMU. This became the normal practice in the late 1950s until the line closed in 1970. *BRM*

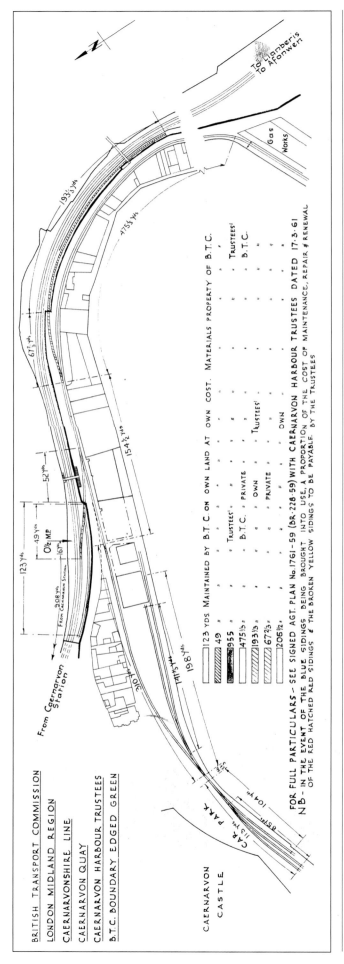

CAERNARVON CASTLE

FOR FULL PARTICULARS - SEE SIGNED AGT. PLAN No.1761-59 (BR-228-59) WITH CAERNARVON HARBOUR TRUSTEES DATED 17-3-61

NB- IN THE EVENT OF THE BLUE SIDINGS BEING BROUGHT INTO USE, A PROPORTION OF THE COST OF MAINTENANCE, REPAIR & RENEWAL OF THE RED HATCHED RED SIDINGS & THE BROKEN YELLOW SIDINGS TO BE PAYABLE BY THE TRUSTEES

a head count began. On one occasion we counted six deceased and a couple of injured ones which were disposed of with a hefty boot. The corpses were laid out and on one occasion someone even took a photograph of the victims. The dog was praised and given chocolate pieces as a reward. The assembled gathering muttered comments, and gradually dispersed, leaving the victims to be disposed of by the permanent way gang. It was to no avail, though. The next day the early turn signalman would report that the enemy was back and looking for revenge.

The 'authorities' did try other methods from time to time. They claimed to put poison down, but probably the rats thrived on this and seemed to grow even bigger and bolder.

In due course the arrangement at Caernarfon was modified, and points and signals linked up to No 2 box. There was no question about recovery of anything at No 1 but the frame. The timber was rotten, distorted and good for nothing but a bonfire. Burly men from the Signalling Department who knew no fear went into the locking room and, impervious to the rats, dismantled everything that needed to be recovered, and removed it. The millwright's department from Crewe works came and removed anything else salvageable. The rats must have thought that they were at last going to be left in peace, and remained until paraffin was splashed around everywhere, when the assembled crowd watched in fascinated silence as a match was put to the building, which roared into flames. From inside the locking room, from every gap in the woodwork, came hundreds of rats, all big and brown and slinky. They scurried down the track pursued by a couple of dogs who didn't know what to do with them. It was a fitting end to a persistent problem that had troubled signalmen for 20 years. No one wept for No 1 box. Some of the rats allegedly invaded a nearby hotel, which hated its 'visitors'!

No 2 cabin was constructed on the platform at the opposite end of the site, between the Llanberis bay platform road and the up and down platform. It was of composite construction, had 51 levers and contained single-line Webb & Thompson long staff token equipment for the sections to Pontrhythallt on the Llanberis branch, coloured blue, and to Dinas Junction on the Afon Wen line, coloured red.

An LNWR standard covered footbridge of wooden construction linking the platforms was installed when the island platform was built. This contained a general waiting room, a ladies' waiting room with a toilet, and a urinal. A canopy offered protection on both faces and extended to meet the footbridge.

In the goods yard a wooden extension and office were provided for the shed which were designated as 'temporary' but which lasted for 70 years and were removed only when the line closed to all traffic. Cattle pens were installed on the 'back road' and animals could be removed from the pens along a private path. Road access to the main goods warehouse was off Balaclava Road.

For the 1911 Investiture a temporary island platform was built in the goods yard to cater for trains from Afon Wen terminating at Caernarfon. A second bay platform was provided at the Bangor end, parallel to the Bangor bay. It was designated the 'excursion platform' and was rarely

Caernarvon harbour track plan, 1961.

Caernarfon

The LNWR had in the past named passenger engines after the various counties through which its lines passed, and this was extended in the 1930s by the LMS to naming express passenger engines of the 'Patriot' class after various towns on the North Wales coast. In February 1939 the engine No 5515 was named *Caernarvon* at a small ceremony at the station. The engine was based at Preston (10B) shed at the time and made a once-only journey to Caernarfon for the purpose. It was, as far as anyone can tell, never seen in the town again. Here the engine stands in the Bangor bay at the north end of the up & down platform with a group of staff. For the ceremony the engine moved to the up & down platform and the town's mayor performed the ceremony. An unknown official photographer took three views of the occasion, of which this is one. The photographs were given to the author by Miss Hall, at one time a booking clerk employed at the station and whose father was the stationmaster, living in the station house. *Bill Rear collection*

Caernarfon

By 1966 things had changed at Caernarfon. The Llanberis line had been lifted and the Afon Wen line was out of use and lifted from Llanwnda. No 1 signalbox at the north end of the station had been demolished and all signalling movements were controlled from No 2 box, seen here. There was still some freight traffic, and LMS Class 5 No 44875 of Chester shed propels a brake van back to the headshunt by the goods shed. The date of the photograph is 12 November 1966 and freight traffic would linger on at Caernarfon for only a few months more. *A. Wyn Hobson*

Caernarfon
This 1964 view of the goods shed at Caernarfon was taken from the up & down platform, looking towards Afon Wen. The wooden extension to the goods shed still stands but this would be removed in the upheaval that followed the simplification of the track layout when the Afon Wen line closed in December the same year. Note the two two-arm bracket signals: the left-hand arm on each signal is for the Llanberis line, still open at the time of the photograph, whilst the right-hand arm is for the Afon Wen line. A scissors crossover beyond the signalbox gave access from either line, both platform roads being bi-directional. *G. H. Platt*

Caernarfon
Fairburn 2-6-4T No 42076 was allocated to Bangor (6H) shed from June 1962 until January 1964, when it was transferred away to Trafford Park. Here it pauses at the up & down platform with a four-coach working to Afon Wen in the summer of 1963. Note the Prince of Wales' feathers on the gable end of the stationmaster's house, a feature that was often missed because the canopy concealed the upper storeys of the main building. Almost invisible, holding the Webb & Thompson long train staff for the single-line section to Dinas, is signalman Wil Rees, who was on duty in No 2 box. *Bill Rear*

Caernarfon

Caernarfon station and the line from Menai Bridge closed to all traffic from 4 January 1970 and for a while the line lay abandoned. Contracts for demolition were advertised but before this could commence the fire on the Britannia tubular bridge over the Menai Strait occurred and the decision was taken to reopen the Caernarfon line to Freightliner traffic. Two mobile cranes were installed in the former goods yard and two Freightliner trains each day worked into the station. The containers were transferred to lorries which then took them to Holyhead for onward transportation. Here Class 47 No D1818, working the 4G80 Caernarfon yard to Bescot yard, positions the wagons for the crane to load the containers on 1 January 1971. *A. Wyn Hobson*

Caernarfon

Until 1947, drivers of trains approaching Caernarfon from the south (Llanberis or Afon Wen) encountered this impressive array of signals. The gantry had been installed by the LNWR in 1904 but the posts were in need of renewal and in 1948 the signals were replaced by upper quadrant posts with indicator boxes further away from the station throat. From left to right the signals indicated Afon Wen line to up goods loop; Afon Wen line to up platform; Afon Wen line to local platform; Afon Wen line to up & down platform; Llanberis line to up goods loop; Llanberis line to up platform; Llanberis line to local platform; Llanberis line to up & down platform; Llanberis line to Llanberis bay. This view was taken about 1938. *Bill Rear collection*

Caernarfon

Fairburn 2-6-4T No 2258 pulls away from the up & down platform with a local to Afon Wen. This engine arrived at Bangor from Crewe North on 18 January 1947, along with three others which were virtually new. This engine had the 1946-style block lettering on the tank sides, as did No 2259 that came in the same batch, whilst Nos 2260 and 2261 had the old prewar shaded lettering. These engines were very popular and gave little trouble apart from their habit of the exhaust steam injector blowing back whenever the driver shut off the regulator. Their stay at Bangor was brief. By 1954 they had been transferred away to Greenock in exchange for Fowler 2-6-4T engines. *Bill Rear collection*

used. It was where stock was stored or carriages were washed down. A second wooden footbridge was erected, linking all platforms including the temporary one in the goods yard. The temporary platform was removed immediately after the 1911 Investiture but the footbridge remained until about the time of the Grouping in 1923.

The locomotive shed staff complement in July 1930 included 17 drivers, 12 passed firemen, five firemen, and 11 passed cleaners. The shed closed for operational use in September 1931. The work and some of the staff were transferred to Bangor.

When the station was being modified in 1956, the island platform building was demolished. The canopies on the up and down platform were cut back, and the one outside the main building in the station yard was removed completely. A modern brick goods office replaced the rickety wooden office. Other minor modifications were made over the following years.

When the Afon Wen, Llanberis and Nantlle lines were closed to all traffic, the Nantlle and Llanberis branches were lifted almost immediately. The line to Menai Bridge was singled, and No 1 signalbox was taken out of use, with all necessary functions from that box being transferred to No 2 cabin. The up passenger platform was taken out of use and the track lifted. The Bangor bay platform road was also lifted and the connections from the upper and lower goods yards were modified.

The line between Caernarvon No 2 signalbox and Llanwnda was used to store trains working to the Investiture of Prince Charles in 1969. After the event, the track was uplifted back to Caernarvon No 2 box.

Passenger trains then used the up and down platform, although occasionally the local platform was used.

On departing Caernarfon station, the Afon Wen and Llanberis lines took a parallel course, descending at 1 in 47 under Turf Square and into Carnarfon Tunnel, emerging at the harbour level. Here, at one time, sidings were located, some leading back in front of the castle where once there were extensive slate wharves.

Until 1960 these sidings were listed as being of 'strategic necessity'. The Ministry of Defence was responsible for the track and general maintenance of the harbour. In June 1958 the MoD funded the re-laying of track and the resurfacing of the area. It hired an engine from Bangor shed to run along all the harbour lines, depressing the tarmac between the rails before it had time to set. A photograph was taken of that exercise which shows BR 2-6-0 No 78057 standing near the Eagle Tower of the castle. Never afterwards did a locomotive venture this far along the harbour. When the harbour was declassified the tracks were either lifted or covered over. The area is now used solely as a car park.

Another siding ran parallel to the Afon Wen line on St Helen's Road and served various commercial stores.

Caernarfon Harbour

In 1958 the Ministry of Defence via the Caernarvon harbour trustees ordered that the surface of Caernarfon harbour be relaid with tarmac. The harbour was deemed to be a port of strategic importance in times of emergency. Accordingly, the surface was relaid flush with the rail-head. To ensure that the tracks were able to accept railway traffic it was necessary to depress the flangeways before the tarmac had time to harden. BR Standard Class 2MT 2-6-0 No 78057 was hired from Bangor shed on Tuesday 17 June 1958 and proceeded to travel over all the harbour lines. It is seen here undertaking this task in front of the Eagle Tower, with the Aber swing bridge in the background. It is doubtful if an engine ever ventured forth this far before or after. Note the 1948 Morris 10 standing in an empty car park. *A. A. Lambert*

Caernarfon Harbour

By 1958 most of the passenger traffic between Bangor, Caernarfon and Afon Wen was in the hands of DMUs although some trips remained steam hauled until the end. Here a Derby 'Lightweight' DMU emerges from Caernarvon Tunnel with the 12.20pm Bangor to Afon Wen and Pwllheli. Note the wagon and van on the harbour lines and the small wagon turntable. These vehicles would have been shunted off the daily trip working to the gate on St Helen's Road and then pulled by horse or pushed by tractor to their required destination. Today this area of land is the car park for the Welsh Highland Railway, although plans are afoot to extend the narrow gauge station into it. *Bill Rear*

Caernarfon Harbour

In 1969 the forthcoming Investiture of Prince Charles as Prince of Wales at Caernarfon Castle required storage space for trains which exceeded the capacity available in the station yard. Accordingly, it was decided to store DMUs and locomotive-hauled trains on the former line to Afon Wen. In early June 1969 an engineer's inspection train made its way to the end of the line near Llanwnda station, and is seen here emerging from Caernarvon Tunnel with the district engineer's saloon. Motive power was an unrecorded Class 47. Note the banner suspended from the side of Queen Eleanor's Gate where the Queen would present Prince Charles to the people after the ceremony. *Bill Rear*

Caernarfon
In 1952 Fairburn 2-6-4T No 42157 ambles down the bank near Seiont Bridge with the daily return freight working from Llanberis. Beyond the brake van is the site of Caernarvon No 3 signalbox that was removed in 1904. Today, the Llanberis line is the site of the run-round loop for the Welsh Highland Railway. Note, too, the road vehicles on St Helen's Road. The leading van would probably be branded as racist in today's politically correct climate. It was, however, a trading name for the food wholesalers Morris & Jones who had their depot just round the corner. *Bill Rear*

Caernarfon
Seventeen years after the previous picture was taken, the engineer's inspection train passes the site where today passengers board the Welsh Highland Railway train to Waunfawr. Contrast this view with the previous picture and the subsequent view taken in March 2002 showing the narrow gauge line. *Bill Rear*

Caernarfon

On Saturday 30 March 2002 Welsh Highland Railway Garratt No 138 *Millennium* pulls into Caernarfon station with the 11.10am from Waunfawr, prior to running round the train. This was the closest viewpoint I could get to complete the trilogy of views taken over a 50-year span. The contrast with the other two views is very marked. The track and ballast is once more clean and although there never was a station on this site before, the loading of a train from the south was similar to the loadings off the Afon Wen branch in the 1950s. St Helen's Road does not seem much busier either.
Bill Rear

Caernarfon Seiont Bridge

Near Seiont Bridge the line to Afon Wen parted company with the line to Llanberis. The Afon Wen line continued to climb, passing over Afon Seiont Bridge. Here a Butlin's special hauled by two 2-6-4Ts blasts its way towards Dinas with a 10-coach Saturdays Only working from Huddersfield in the summer of 1952. This point was one mile from Caernarfon station and it is possible that the site of the Llanberis line might in future become a carriage storage position for the new narrow gauge line. Note the dazzling brightness of the permanent way ganger's hut and the white-painted railings over the road bridge. The permanent way gang on this section took great pride in its length of track. *Bill Rear*

Dinas

Fairburn 2-6-4T No 42156 and Fowler 2-6-4T No 42416 pull away from the up loop at Dinas and on to the single line, after waiting in the station to cross a down train. This was a Saturdays Only Butlin's special from Penychain to Manchester Exchange in July 1952. The line branching off to the left leads into the goods yard, which at this time had been taken out of service but was used to store crippled wagons awaiting workshops. The line behind the camera was the headshunt. The leading locomotive is at the commencement of a falling gradient of 1 in 53 and steam was necessary only to get the train on the move. From this point on it would be braking most of the way to Caernarfon harbour. Today, narrow gauge engines experience the same gradients as their predecessors. *Bill Rear*

Once clear of the tunnel, the main lines started to climb as far as Seiont Bridge where they diverged. The Llanberis line descended towards Seiont brickworks, whilst the Afon Wen line crossed Afon Seiont and continued climbing at varying grades to Dinas Junction. This part of the trackbed is now the route of the Welsh Highland Railway. At the approach to Dinas the line levelled out.

Dinas Junction

This station came into being in 1877 on the construction of the North Wales Narrow Gauge Railways (NWNGR), and was built to serve as an exchange and tranship point for passengers and freight to and from the North Wales Narrow Gauge line.

Dinas Junction was 3¼ miles from Caernarfon. The NWNGR station building was a stone-built structure.

As originally built there was a single platform on the up side and a small tranship yard, but this was inadequate for the developing traffic and a passing loop was put in with a cross-platform facility with the NWNGR. The passing loop was extended in 1893 and again in 1947.

There was a standard LNWR-design composite structure signalbox with a Webb-type frame, which survived until the line closed. The station was a staff token point and the signalbox was in the centre of the up platform. The up loop line was signalled for up and down working.

The goods yard was at the Caernarfon end, access being controlled from the signalbox. The yard included a transship siding, a shed and storage sidings. There was also a tippler facility to enable stone off the narrow gauge to be discharged into standard gauge wagons. It was originally installed for Dudley Park quarry of Waenfawr which processed granite but was rarely used.

A hut on the up platform served as a waiting shelter. On the down side the Welsh Highland Railway station building shared its booking office with the LMS. Another wooden hut served as a waiting shelter. When the WHR stopped running in 1937 its building was leased to the LMS and the station name was changed to 'Dinas'.

The station closed to all traffic on 10 September 1951. The signalbox remained in use until the line closed in 1964.

Trains entering the loop were restricted to 10mph but down trains sometimes exceeded that restriction, having a straight path through the station. I have an abiding memory of working the 4.35am Afon Wen mail, exchanging the staff for the key token in blinding snow, the signalman holding

Dinas

A tranquil scene in the summer of 1951 as Stanier 2-6-4T No 42460 approaches Dinas station with the return Nantlle goods. The train would have been brought to a stand at the home signal before entering the loop, the signalman collecting the train staff in front of the box steps. Note the Welsh Highland Railway office, at this time on lease to the London Midland Region, where it served as a booking office. Down-direction passengers waited in the building until their train arrived; up-direction passengers had to climb up the footpath and cross over the tracks where a small wooden (unheated) waiting shed served to give some protection. Traffic was poor as a frequent bus service operated on the main road. Today the WHR building has been renovated and recently won a heritage architecture award. *Bill Rear*

the hoop aloft with his left hand, the scene illuminated by the flickering lights of a platform oil lamp and a hand lamp. To release the hoop and almost simultaneously grasp the long staff, to prevent a late-running train from losing speed, took both skill and courage. Many an inexperienced fireman lost his nerve and released the staff prematurely, leaving the poor signalman to ferret about in the dark to try and find the staff, mindful that he had to get back to his cabin to bell 'train entering section' to Groeslon and to clear the section back to Caernarvon No 2.

Trains returning to Caernarfon in the up direction were less likely to transgress. They were brought almost to a stand at the home signal before being allowed into the loop, and the token exchange could be carried out in a civilised manner. At times it was necessary for trains to be held in the loop whilst awaiting an approaching train to clear the section. The signal cabin would echo to the sound of footplate crews chattering with the signalman, a pleasant distraction from the normally lonely life of that worthy.

In the golden era of steam during the 1950s and early 1960s, on summer Saturdays the line was a hive of activity. The special workings to Butlin's camp were slotted amongst the regular service trains, and from 9am until 4pm

trains stood at every crossing point awaiting a path. Heads popped out of coach windows; puzzled faces enquired: 'why the stop in the middle of nowhere?'. At Dinas the signalman would retrieve the staff and scurry back to his cabin, followed by the fireman who was required to 'sign the book' in compliance with Rule 55 because the train was due to stand for longer than two minutes. Eventually a whistle would be heard as an up train called for the home signal to be raised. The signalman descended to the platform and held up the staff, exchanging it for the hoop containing the key token as the train crawled through the loop. On collecting the staff, the driver popped his whistle and two engines would bark into life, albeit briefly, before shutting off and coasting out of sight down the bank towards Caernarfon.

The signalman, meanwhile, had scurried back into the cabin and, after belling '2' ('train entering section') to Caernarfon No 2, inserted the key token into the instrument and belled to Groeslon that the up train had cleared his section and then called up 'Is line clear?' almost immediately. Having got the OK, he would release the key token, replace it into the hoop pouch and hand it to the fireman who would dash back to his locomotive. After a

Llanwnda
Originally named 'Pwllheli Road', this station was renamed when the North Wales Narrow Gauge Railways commenced operations in 1877. The station consisted of a single-storey brick-built structure on the platform, which was on the up side. From the footplate it was a difficult station to work as the curve meant that the fireman had to get off the footplate to see the guard's signal. The distant signal at the platform ramp was the up distant for Dinas. After the line closed and the track was lifted, the building survived for a few years in derelict condition but ultimately it was demolished to make way for road improvements. *Bill Rear collection*

'pop' on the whistle, the starter signal arm would be raised and with another 'toot' the two engines would move off. The train would labour up the bank towards Groeslon, where the procedure would be repeated, and so on up the line.

Dinas had a brief moment of glory when, on 9 August 1963, HM The Queen boarded the Royal Train at Dinas, on her way to Criccieth. The 'tarting up' of the station included tidying up the growth on the platform and the laying of a 6ft strip of tarmac. There was no formal ceremony as her visit to Plas Dinas, family home of her then brother-in-law, Anthony Armstrong Jones, Earl of Snowdon, had been private.

With the reopening of the Welsh Highland Railway in 1997 between Caernarfon and Dinas, the original NWNGR station building was restored by volunteers to its near-original condition and won the Ian Allan National Railway Heritage Award for 2000 for the work. A commemorative plaque and a cheque (for £1,000) was presented at the station in May 2001.

On resuming single-line working, the line continued on the level for about 200yd before climbing at 1 in 79. Between Dinas and Llanwnda was Glanrhyd Crossing, where a minor road crossed the line. The gates were normally across the line; a lady crossing keeper lived in the

railway owned house and attended as required.

Llanwnda

Llanwnda station was one of the Carnarvonshire Railway's original stopping points. In early days it was called 'Pwllheli Road'. It was 12¼ miles from Bangor but was never a block or token exchange point. The name was changed to Llanwnda when Dinas Junction station opened to traffic and remained open until services were withdrawn in December 1964. The main Caernarfon to Pwllheli road crossed the line via an overbridge at the Dinas end.

The station building was a single-storey red brick structure. There were two wooden huts on either side of the main building. The one at the Caernarfon end served as a ladies' waiting room; the other was a goods shed. There was one siding on the up side that served as a coal siding, although from time to time it was used for other occasional traffic.

The goods yard was served by down direction trains only, usually the Nantlle goods. A wagon of coal would be dropped off on the outward journey and the empty uplifted two days later. Llanwnda yard could hold up to five wagons but it was very rare to find more than one at any one time. The siding was controlled from a small two-lever ground

Groeslon
Stanier 2-6-4T No 42601 stands at the down platform with an afternoon working from Bangor to Afon Wen and Pwllheli on Saturday 27 July 1963. Note the portable steps, handy for the low platforms which were a relic from the Carnarvonshire Railway days and which were never remedied. The station building survived after the closure of the line but was demolished in the 1980s. Only the goods yard on the down side at the Penygroes end survives as a coal merchant's yard and an unofficial dump for old cars. *Bill Rear collection*

frame unlocked by the train staff. The local coal merchant usually received his consignment on a Monday, when it would be emptied and worked away.

Not every passenger train stopped at the station. It was not unusual to have no passengers getting on or off. One of Bangor's drivers was moved to comment that the station was like a 'bloody Hornby station — no signs of life!'. The only regular traffic until the mid-1950s was newspapers dropped off the first train of the day.

The stationmaster did not live on the station but had accommodation a short distance away. One stationmaster was reputed to be a 'character'. Scurrilous rumour has it that he was a defrocked minister who had been found his position on the railway by a well-placed relative. It was muttered darkly that he had been caught in a compromising situation in a chapel doing sinful things with a lady organist and had been forced to flee from both cuckolded husband and incensed authority. Whether there is any truth in the tale is anybody's guess.

It is also alleged that one Christmas the local coal merchant was surprised to receive a consignment of two coal wagons instead of his usual one. Close examination of the labels indicated that one wagon was correctly designated, but the other was bound for Llanwrda on the Central Wales line. A conspiracy evolved between the merchant and the stationmaster. The one wagon was unloaded in double quick time, the incriminating label conveniently lost and the wagon uplifted on the next day's working. The Dinas signalman, the driver and the guard of the Afon Wen goods were also in on the plot and obliged with an irregular stop to uplift. The contents of the wagon were duly sold off on the coal merchant's round and the proceeds of the heist shared out between the criminal parties. The railway's representative on the spot disposed of his share of the takings in liquid form and was apparently legless for three days!

Llanwnda station was on a curve and the platform was short and low. The guard could not be seen from the footplate and the 'right away' had to be relayed via the station staff. The station was at the commencement of a 1 in 79 climb and starting off towards Groeslon was tricky. Experienced drivers applied sand to the rails when stopping, and most had no difficulty restarting. The inexperienced found out the hard way.

The up distant for Dinas was at the ramp at the Dinas end, and trains would coast away from the station to Dinas, whistling up for Glanrhyd Crossing on the way.

The station building and road overbridge were demolished in the 1970s; the trackbed was made into a one-way private road, starting at the station site, for contractors' lorries accessing gravel workings near Pant Glâs during a construction contract. Once the contract came to an end the trackbed became a long-distance cycleway and footpath. In 2000 the site was further transformed by the creation of a new road to bypass Groeslon, Penygroes and Llanllyfni. A roundabout was constructed where the station building once stood. Parts of the trackbed are still traceable from the new road but other parts of it have disappeared.

On leaving Llanwnda, it was a hard slog all the way to Groeslon. At a mile out of Llanwnda the gradient stiffened to 1 in 61 and this was maintained through to Groeslon.

Groeslon

This was one of the original stations on the Carnarvonshire Railway, opening in 1866. The track at this point was on the formation of the earlier Nantlle Tramway. It became a token exchange station following the installation of a crossing loop here in 1911.

The station was 13½ miles from Bangor, still on a rising gradient. At the Dinas end a road crossed over the tracks, protected by hand-operated level crossing gates and locked from the 18-lever open frame on the down platform which also controlled the loop points and the associated signals.

Traffic from the station was always healthy, the station being conveniently located at a crossroads in the centre of the village with several small hamlets close by.

The station consisted of two platforms, the main building on the down platform being a single-storey structure built of red brick with a slate roof, similar in architectural design to Llanwnda. The single-line token instruments were located in the station office, which also doubled up as a booking office. A general waiting room occupied the centre part of the building and there was a small porters' room that doubled as a lamp room. There was a second wooden building designated as a goods shed alongside at the Penygroes end.

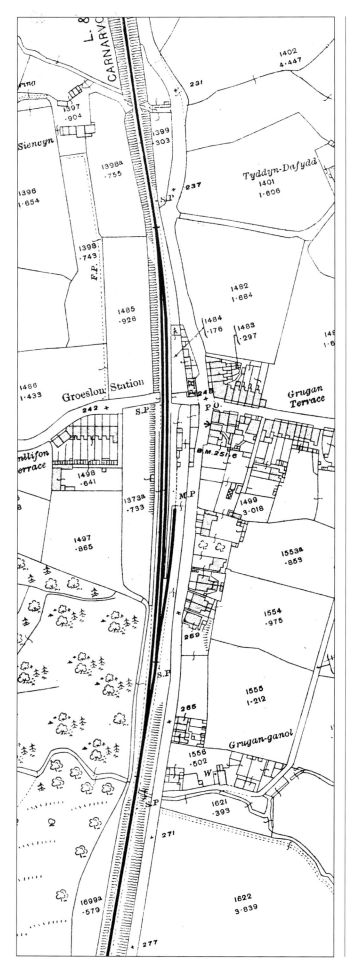

The up platform was in part stone built, a wooden extension being added later. It was less well equipped as the only protection provided was a small wooden hut. Both platforms were low and station staff had to be in attendance with portable steps. There was no footbridge; passengers crossed the line over the level crossing.

The next section of single line was to Penygroes. Here the large Webb & Thompson train staff, coloured red, was in use.

About a mile from Groeslon was Tudor siding on the down side. It was a trailing connection, access controlled by the train staff. Freight trains heading for Nantlle or Afon Wen were booked to call here. The private siding was little used after 1956 but remained available until the line closed to traffic.

Penygroes

This was the largest intermediate station on the Afon Wen line and was also the junction for Nantlle. It was 15½ miles from Bangor. Formal opening of the station was 2 September 1867, although the track had been laid some time earlier. It was one of the original stations to open on the Carnarvonshire Railway which incorporated parts of the Nantlle Tramway.

The line doubled at the approach to the station. Clynnog Road crossed the tracks over the station. The cast iron beams supporting the road were stamped 'De Winton Foundry' and the supporting walls and abutments were faced in local stone. The bridge was removed in 2000 during bypass works, replaced by a modern, ugly precast concrete structure.

The down line was signalled for two-way working. The main two-storey station building built of red brick with a local slate roof was on the down side. The stationmaster's house was integral. A small canopy extended over the central part of the building on the platform side. An open footbridge spanned the tracks. Off the end of the down platform was a barrow crossing and a 33-lever standard LNWR-design signal cabin. The single-line token equipment for both directions was located in the cabin, as was the Nantlle branch train staff.

The up platform had an open, stone shelter. Both platforms were built of stone with concrete edging slabs.

The track was lifted after the line closed in 1964 but the platforms and main station building, together with part of the embankment towards Nantlle, remained for many years. The trackbed from Llanwnda to Grianog quarry near Pant Glâs was converted in the 1970s into a private roadway for loaded MacAlpine lorries to travel unhindered from the quarry at Grianrhyd to their construction site. After this traffic had ceased, the trackbed through the station was converted into a cycle and footpath, now known as Lôn Eifionydd.

On leaving Penygroes the line south climbed for about 200yd at 1 in 540 before changing to 1 in 160, then fell for 100yd and levelled out for 50yd before the gruelling 1 in 49 climb commenced. This continued for over a mile to the summit at Grianrhyd, 480ft above sea level, where the line levelled out briefly before commencing to descend at

1914-18 Ordnance Survey map showing Groeslon station layout. *Crown Copyright*

Near Penygroes

The 'Welsh Chieftain' was the updated version of the 'North Wales Land Cruise' trains that started their seasonal circular tour in 1951. By the date of this photograph (July 1960) the tours had undergone some modification, this working starting from Rhyl and travelling first along the North Wales coast. These Class 4MT 4-6-0s had replaced the smaller Ivatt Class 2MT 2-6-0 engines that worked the circuit for several years. The retitling was only a partial success: the train ran at less than 100% loadings despite the use of more modern coaches in the formation, and even the inclusion of the former 'Devon Belle' observation coach at the rear (for a supplementary fare) could not bring back the holidaymakers. Here No 75054, based at Rhyl for the season, passes underneath a minor road bridge approaching Penygroes. The observation coach can just be seen rounding the curve. *Bill Rear collection*

Penygroes

Stanier 2-6-2T No 40116 draws into Penygroes with the up 'Welshman' from Portmadoc and Pwllheli to Euston on 30 August 1961. These locomotives were hardly up to the job of hauling six Mk I coaches over Pant Glâs and the job was always a struggle for the fireman with these poor steaming engines. This was the penultimate season for this particular engine; it was withdrawn from Bangor on 24 November 1962. Note the gardens laid out on the platform. Penygroes regularly won the 'Best Garden' competition for the district. A Stanier 2-6-4T waits at the up platform for the passenger train to pass before resuming shunting in the up-side yard. *T. J. Edgington*

Penygroes

Stanier 2-6-4T No 42585 pulls into Penygroes with a down working to Afon Wen. The fireman collects the hoop containing the key token for the section to Brynkir, his left hand containing the long train staff for the section from Groeslon. The engine had a brief stay of six months at Bangor, having transferred from Willesden in March 1961. It returned to Willesden in September. Several passengers wait for the train to stop. The number boarding was average for a Wednesday. In the up platform the return Nantlle goods waits for the token. The passenger working was presumably the 11.26am from Bangor to Pwllheli. *T. J. Edgington*

1 in 50 for ¾ mile. Another series of gradient changes ensued, including an uphill stretch of 1 in 770, before the descent continued at 1 in 270. Halfway down this length came Pant Glâs.

Pant Glâs

Pant Glâs station was 19¼ miles from Bangor and 3¾ miles from Penygroes. It was authorised in December 1869 after the Carnarvonshire Railway line had opened. The station was some distance from the village.

At one time there was a short siding on the down side but it was rarely used and was removed just after World War 2.

Between the station building and a wooden lamp room was an open four-lever frame controlling the protecting signals that were interlocked with the hand-operated level crossing which preceded the station. The 220ft-long platform was on the down side. The station building was constructed of local dressed stone; the platform was constructed mainly of stone infill, the platform edge being timber.

Freight traffic was withdrawn in 1955 and the station closed to all traffic in January 1957. The station building was demolished some time after although the former lamp room was retained for the staff on duty who manned the level crossing gates.

Pant Glâs was the butt of local humour and, on closure, a delightful poem appeared in the *Caernarvon & Denbigh Herald* in January 1957, reproduced below. The author is unknown.

'If you've travelled down from Bangor,
more in sorrow than in anger,
To Pwllheli in a British Railways train,
Or to Bangor from the latter,
(for direction does not matter)
And are doomed to do the journey yet again,
If you've tarried at Caernarvon
in a train you slowly starved on,
If you've sat while boys beside you grow to men,
And before you reach Llanwnda,

Pant Glâs
Ivatt 2-6-2T No 41239 of Bangor shed pilots Llandudno Junction Stanier Class 3MT 2-6-2T No 40083 with a summer Saturday Butlin's special from Warrington in July 1952. It is seen here approaching Pant Glâs level crossing. The demand on power was such that engines were borrowed on a regular basis. This train was listed in the working timetable as 'Conditional' and ran regularly only in the peak six weeks of summer. Tank engines hauling Butlin's trains generally worked bunker to bunker in order that the leading engine was smokebox first whatever direction the train was travelling. When this conditional train ran it was often the case that the traincrew of the pilot engine was working its third trip of the day over the branch. *Bill Rear*

have indeed began to wonder,
If you'd live to see the lights of Afon Wen.

If you've started to rejoice
at the sight of Penygroes,
Then remembered all the stations yet ahead.
If you've thought, when tired of staring
at the wrist-watch you are wearing,
That you should have bought a calendar instead.
If you've nursed a babe that's crying
all the way to Pen-y-Chain,
And it seemed that Butlin's Camp you'd never pass,
Here's a spot of news to brave you
for the journeys still to face you
Henceforth you won't be stopping at Pant Glâs.

For there, despite the mutters
of the residents, the shutters
At the station now are up, for good and all
And you'll pass Pant Glâs in future

(which I hope is going to suit yer)
Without stopping, at a canter or a crawl,
So the train should save a minute,
on the trip and when you're in it,
That is something, though a florin off the fare
Would do more to make you happy,
till an enterprising chappie
Puts the first "Pwllhelicopter" in the air.'

On leaving Pant Glâs the line continued to fall at 1 in 270, stiffening after 600yd to 1 in 83, then after a quarter of a mile easing to 1 in 500, then stiffening again to 1 in 100 and later to 1 in 64. The line crossed a river as it approached Brynkir station. In 1937 a flash flood washed away a small bridge, necessitating the line being run in two sections, connected by a bus service. The engineers effected temporary repairs within a few days, although the temporary structure had a severe weight restriction imposed, and trains were hauled by ex-LNWR Class 1F 0-6-2T engines hauling short-formation stock until the

Brynkir
The main station building at Brynkir was on the down side and was constructed of local brick. The platforms were low and portable steps were available, as can be seen on the left of the photograph. Behind the steps was an open-lever frame which controlled the passing loop points and signals. Note the long-burning oil lamps, one to illuminate the lever frame, the other on the front of the building. The booking office door is open, displaying a fare board and stating that a cheap day return to Chester would cost 18s 9d (94p in today's money). The platform and building were demolished after the line closed, although the former stationmaster's house still stands. The trackbed through the station is now part of Lôn Eifionydd, a bridle and cycle path. *BRM*

Brynkir
BR Standard Class 4MT 2-6-4T No 80090 of Bangor pulls into Brynkir with a down train for Afon Wen in the summer of 1958. These Standard engines, which replaced a mix of Fowler, Fairburn and Stanier tanks of the same wheel arrangement, had a short stay at 6H shed. They in turn were transferred away, to be replaced by Stanier and Fairburn types. The porter is emerging from the booking hall with the train staff for the section to Llangybi. Beyond him is the open-lever frame and beyond that the ladies' waiting room. *W. A. Camwell*

Ynys

Just before Ynys station, heading south, the line crossed over an unclassified and ungated road. In 1948 the driver of a Commer van tried to beat the train to the crossing, but we were quicker, and he was struck a glancing blow, denting his van and pride. He was carrying groceries and in that time of rationing, whilst waiting for recovery, his stock was looted! Out of shot but stopped we also awaited the law, and whilst so doing, managed to get this view. Ynys station platform is just visible on the right-hand side beyond the cast-iron crossing warning notices which the van driver claimed he did not see. *Bill Rear*

permanent bridge was completed. That bridge stands to this day, though unused. On approaching Brynkir the gradient eased to 1 in 168.

Brynkir

Brynkir was 21 miles from Bangor. The station opened to traffic on 2 September 1867. A crossing loop was provided from the start. This was extended in 1893, and again in 1947. The station was in the centre of the village and was always busy. It handled a large quantity of livestock traffic. The local auctioneer had a livestock market adjoining the station which survived the line's closure, only to be a victim of the 2001 foot-and-mouth epidemic that hit North Wales. The market site has now been sold.

The main platform was on the down side and on it was a wooden goods shed. Adjoining this was an open LNWR-pattern frame mounted on a plinth which controlled the loop and siding points and signals. The frame also controlled access to the goods yard that was part located south of the platforms and which had a headshunt that extended back across the station access to another headshunt. The main station building was a brick-built single-storey structure that contained a booking office and a general waiting room. Passengers crossed the line at the southern end of the platforms on a barrow crossing.

At the northern end, just off the platform, was a cylindrical water tank mounted on pillars which supplied columns on both platforms. It was still in situ in January 2002.

Brynkir was a token exchange station and the next section of single line, to Llangybi, was controlled by Webb & Thompson large train staff, coloured red. The instruments were located in the station office. The stationmaster had a two-storey house at the entrance to the station yard, now in private hands.

The goods yard consisted of two trailing sidings off the yard headshunt. No 1 siding ran alongside cattle pens. For several summer seasons a camping coach was located here.

On leaving the station, heading towards Afon Wen, the single line resumed its descent at 1 in 63. There was a brief change of gradient for 200yd before it continued its descent at 1 in 125. At 20¾ miles it changed again, climbing at 1 in 153 for ½ mile before returning to a descending gradient which persisted until Afon Wen was reached.

Ynys

Before the station was a short siding on the down side. The siding was locked by the train staff and serviced by up direction trains. It was preceded by an unprotected

crossing, the scene of a collision between a van and an Afon Wen-bound train in 1948.

Ynys station was 23 miles from Bangor and was on the single-line section from Brynkir to Llangybi. It opened to traffic in July 1872.

The station was a single-storey structure on the up side platform. Between the booking office and the stationmaster's house was a small six-lever frame that controlled signals and locked a pair of level crossing gates which were south of the platform. These were normally against the railway and protected a minor road.

The station house was at the southern end of the platform and survives to this day in private hands.

On leaving the station the line continued to fall at 1 in 60, then fell at varying degrees of inclination to Llangybi.

Llangybi

Llangybi station was 24¾ miles from Bangor. The station was authorised in December 1869 and was initially a simple halt with a platform on the down side and a siding on the up, which was taken out in 1938. The line was on a falling gradient towards Afon Wen, at 1 in 162. A crossing loop with another platform was installed in 1914/15 when the station became a staff section. Because the site is somewhat isolated, two pairs of cottages were provided for the staff. An unclassified minor road crossed the track at the Afon Wen end, protected by hand-operated level crossing gates.

When the passing loop was extended in the winter of 1946-7 the platforms were also increased in length. Passengers crossed the line to the down platform by a

barrow crossing. The down starter was mounted at the top of the ramp protecting the crossing.

Facilities provided were basic. The down platform had a nameboard, a couple of long-burning oil lamps but nothing else. The main buildings were on the up-side platform and consisted of a wooden LNWR-design hut that served as a ladies' waiting room. Off the platform was a stone-built single-storey building that served as a booking and parcels office, and a wooden lamp room. A standard LNWR signal hut measuring 12ft 0in x 12ft 0in but only 8ft 6in above ground level containing a 15-lever frame, which controlled the loop points, crossing gate lock and signals, was at the south end of the up platform. The single-line token equipment instruments and the circuit telephone were kept in the station office. After closure the station site was cleared and the staff cottages sold off into private hands.

On leaving the station limits the gradient continued to fall towards Afon Wen at 1 in 162, stiffening to 1 in 60 almost to Afon Wen.

Chwilog

Chwilog station was 26 miles from Bangor. The station opened on 2 September 1867 and was larger than either Llangybi, Brynkir or Groeslon. It was centrally located in the village. The main Llanystumdwy to Four Crosses road traversed the line over a hand-operated level crossing at the southern end of the station.

Chwilog was a token exchange station but with no provision for passenger trains to cross. The single passenger platform on the up side contained the station

Llangybi

The station here served a few houses but little else. It was merely a convenient point where a crossing loop enabled trains to cross on the long section between Brynkir and Chwilog. The main buildings were on the up platform and comprised a single-storey stone structure which housed the station office, booking hall and general waiting room. A signalbox stood at the Chwilog end of the loop, seen here with the station name over the box door. The single-line token equipment was in the station office. The down platform was devoid of shelter and it was the custom for passengers travelling to Chwilog, or Afon Wen and beyond, to wait until the train was in the platform before crossing the tracks on the barrow crossing. The old gentleman climbing the ramp had a particularly irritating habit of waiting until the train was ready for departure before he would stagger across the barrow crossing and take his time, inevitably causing delay. *J. Spencer Gilks*

Chwilog

In the final years of the branch, the 'Welshman' (Portmadoc and Pwllheli to Euston) was hauled by BR Standard Class 3MT 2-6-2T of the '82xxx' class. With the demise of the Stanier Class 3 tanks, their place at Bangor was taken by three of that class cascaded from Machynlleth shed, where they had been replaced by Class 4MT 2-6-4Ts of the '80xxx' class. Here, ready to depart for Caernarfon and beyond, is No 82032 with four Mk I coaches. The fireman looks along the platform, holding the hoop with the key token for the section to Llangybi and waiting for the green flag, whilst on the platform the porter signalman, holding the train staff from Afon Wen, waits to relay the guard's signal. The date is July 1963. *J. W. T. House*

Chwilog

On Saturday mornings in the summer season, a procession of trains made its way over the Afon Wen line from Bangor to Penychain or Pwllheli for the return Butlin's specials to points east. Here, on an empty stock, drawing away from Chwilog, is Ivatt Class 2MT 2-6-2T No 41200 piloting an unknown Class 5 4-6-0. The train has crossed over the main road from Llanystumdwy to Four Crosses and is passing the siding that was formerly a cattle dock and used to load milk churns. The gradient is falling towards Afon Wen, about three minutes away, and apart from a whiff of steam to get the train in motion, train crews coasted all the way to the junction with the Western Region line. *J. W. T. House*

building. Two sets of sidings were located within the station limits, both on the down side. The first group, which was east of the platform, was a pair of lines ending in stops. The outer, longer siding was used as a coal siding and by the Eifionydd Farmers' Association, which had a small goods shed attached. A second, smaller shed served as a general goods store for other traffic. The sidings were in an enclosed yard with a weigh machine and an office near the gated entrance. The second siding was beyond the level crossing and was used to load churns of milk into vans for Hanson's Dairies in Liverpool. This siding also had cattle pens alongside and a weighing shed.

On departing Chwilog the line continued to fall at 1 in 60 for about a mile. As it approached Afon Wen it crossed over the Portmadoc to Pwllheli road on a plate bridge on a sweeping descending curve, to meet and make a connection with the GWR's Cambrian Coast up line for the run in to the station at Afon Wen, which was on the level. The connection marked the end of the LNWR line. On 1 January 1963 the Cambrian Coast line was transferred to the London Midland Region.

Afon Wen

Afon Wen station was 27¼ miles from Bangor. The LNWR had running powers through the station. Passenger trains from the Bangor line mostly used the up-side passenger loop line, although other platform faces were also used. The single-line equipment for the LM line was located in the signalbox which stood on the down side at the Pwllheli end of the platform.

1954 North Wales Land Cruise.

Afon Wen

The land cruise trains of the early to mid-1950s were booked to take water at Afon Wen before commencing the climb over Pant Glâs. Ten minutes were allowed which usually gave the footplate crew a chance to get a cup of tea (or something stronger). The Class 2 engines were drafted in for the summer and, at the time of the photograph, moved back to the home shed in September. Here No 46428 still wears its 10A (Springs Branch) shed plate on the smokebox door, which dates the photograph to the summer of 1954. It arrived on 5 June 1954 and returned to 10A on 2 October of the same year and never came back. Note the coaching stock carried carriage boards.
Bill Rear collection

Afon Wen

In the last week of service for the 1952 season Ivatt Class 2MT 2-6-0 No 46430 pulls away from the up loop platform with the 'North Wales Radio Land Cruise' on the penultimate leg of its journey, heading towards Caernarfon. This was probably the Llandudno train, from the make-up of the stock, the first coach being an ex-LNWR coach. The locomotive remained at Rhyl until October when it was transferred away to Preston. *C. H. A. Townley, courtesy J. A. Peden*

Although there was no goods yard at Afon Wen, there were exchange sidings on the up and down sides at the Criccieth end. The Western Region sorted all the freight stock. Incoming freight trains from Menai Bridge worked into the sidings on the Criccieth end of the station. The locomotive would then run round its train and detach the brake van, moving to the machine sidings off the GWR main line east of the platforms on the down side. The locomotive would pick up any stock for the LM line, reattach the brake van and await departure time.

Passenger facilities at Afon Wen were concentrated on the up side. The main building was a two-storey structure which included a booking hall and an office, a general waiting room, a ladies' waiting room with a toilet, a porters' room, a coal store and urinals.

There was a separate refreshment room which did little trade apart from railwaymen. A formidable lady attended, and it was rumoured she would harangue railway staff who refused or criticised her beer. It was where I was put off beer for good! Anyone who entered the building did so at their peril. For the more delicate footplate staff it was deemed prudent to remain on the footplate. On my first visit to Afon Wen, working the afternoon goods from Menai Bridge, I went with my mate into the bar. A pint of foul-looking and even worse-smelling brew was slammed down before me. Being innocent and not wishing to appear 'chicken' I sipped my drink whilst my mate looked on with an evil leer on his face. Somehow I got through the pint but, boy, was I ill on the return trip. I remember very little of the journey which took several hours. My main recollection is of being violently sick, and having to wash

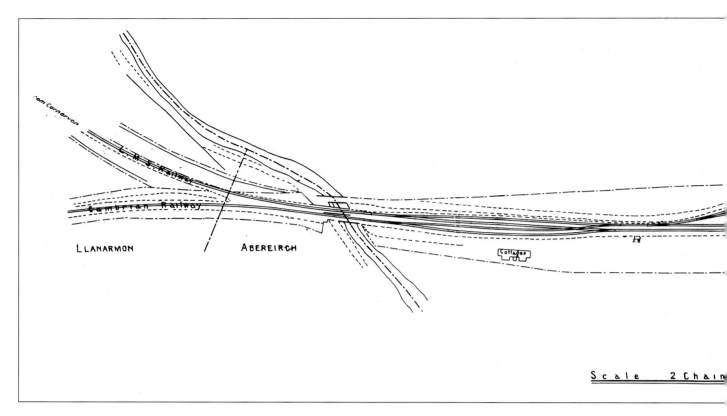

Afon Wen

The main station building at Afon Wen was on the up side, which had two platform faces. The Western Region normally used Platforms 1 (Down line) and 2 (Up line), whilst the London Midland Region usually used Platform 3 which was the up passenger loop platform. There was also an up goods loop that ran parallel to the up passenger loop. All lines through the station were bi-directional, although trains terminating at Afon Wen tended to run into Platform 3. Here a Stanier 2-6-4T is running round its stock parked at Platform 3, passing through the up line to the crossover. It will then set back onto its train. *G. H. Platt*

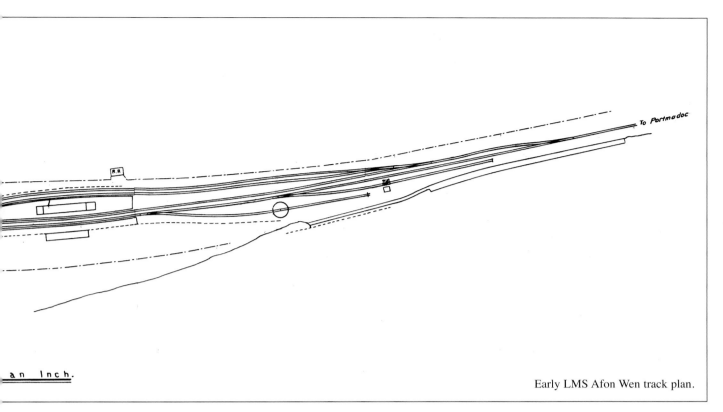

an Inch.

Early LMS Afon Wen track plan.

Afon Wen
The up passenger loop platform was difficult to photograph as it was in shade in sunlight and gloomy at other times. It was used mostly by London Midland Region trains from Bangor which terminated here. The left-hand line was designated the up goods loop and was sometimes used to run round stock in No 3 platform. The white concrete slab covered an inspection pit for rainwater draining off the station roof. It was also a marker for engines to clean out their fire. Goods trains from Pwllheli or Caernarfon passed through the station to the exchange sidings beyond the platforms. The stationmaster's house is the white-painted bungalow in the middle distance and is the only structure left standing today, albeit in private ownership, following the closure and demolition of the station and removal of most tracks.
Bill Rear collection

179

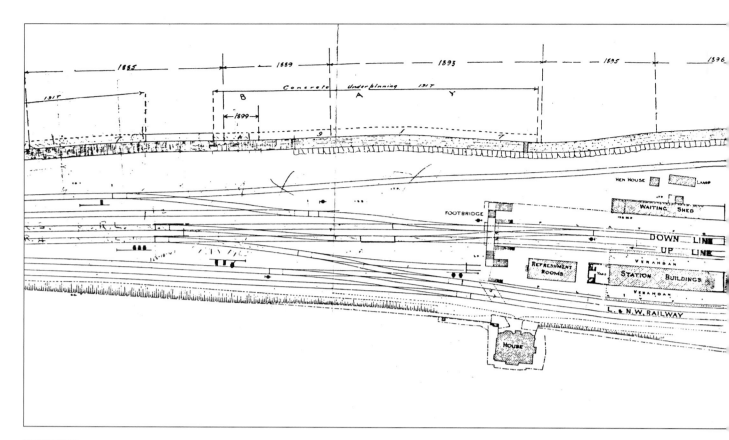

Afon Wen

This was the Criccieth end of the platforms, seen from the down-side Platform 1, taken in 1960. Whilst there is no record of the exact date, it is known that the day was a Saturday by the positioning of the trains. In Platform 3 stands a 2-6-4T from Bangor. The working is not known but from its position on the platform it must have been at least eight coaches in length. In the up side machine sidings stands another LM train with 10 coaches, presumably waiting for a path through the station and back up to Caernarfon. In the exchange sidings stands more coaching stock, probably also waiting to be moved back to Bangor. The corner of the infamous refreshment room is just visible, with some clients about to enter. *G. H. Platt*

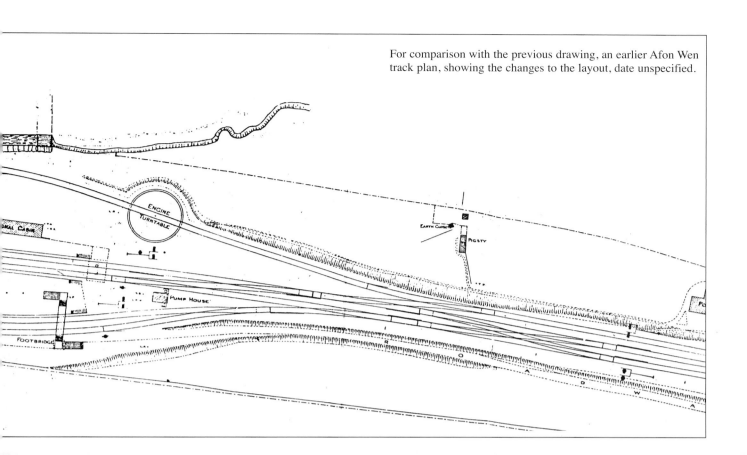

For comparison with the previous drawing, an earlier Afon Wen track plan, showing the changes to the layout, date unspecified.

Afon Wen
A view of the approach to Afon Wen station from the Criccieth end, looking towards Pwllheli. This photograph was taken in the winter of 1964, a week after services to Caernarfon had ceased. The buffer stops in the foreground were in front of the machine siding. A second siding extended further back and both sidings were used to store stock awaiting transfer from the Western Region onto London Midland metals. *Bill Rear*

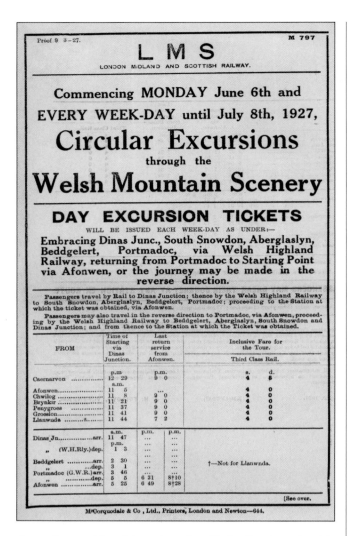

LMS 1927 Circular Excursions through the Welsh Mountain Scenery.

Extract from summer 1955 BR freight timetable for the Menai Bridge to Afonwen line, weekdays.

Train Working

The earliest train services were worked by the LNWR for the C&HR, which in turn had agreed to work the Bangor & Carnarvon Railway. The first recorded slate train ran on 10 March 1852. Passenger trains to and from Caernarfon commenced on 1 July the same year; the line finally opened to freight traffic from 10 August. By 1853 there were four trains each way on weekdays, with two on Sundays. Mails were carried from 1 October 1854. By 1860 these had increased to six weekday trains and three on Sundays each way. The working timetables for August 1862 show a service of seven passenger trains each way, Monday to Saturday, mostly worked by Caernarfon engines and men, and three trains each way on Sundays.

South of Caernarfon, the Nantlle Tramway operated four passenger trains each way daily in 1852, using eight horses, whilst a further four horses worked a Portmadoc to Penygroes omnibus. By February 1866 an engine was reportedly running between Afon Wen and Penygroes. On 6 September of the same year an excursion train was run from Portmadoc to Caernarfon whilst still awaiting Board of Trade Inspection. Alas, there was a derailment at Brynkir, in which six people were killed, but the coroner found the railway company not to be to blame. The line was formally inspected the following month and opened to traffic on 2 September 1867 between Pant (Carnarvon) and Afon Wen. Paradoxically, the Cambrian Railways had completed its line only as far as Harlech and so, until 10 October of the same year, the Carnarvonshire Railway extended its services over Cambrian Railways metals to Penrhyndeudraeth. Cambrian Railways engines were used until the Carnarvonshire accepted delivery of its own engines.

From 25 July 1867 reciprocal running powers were agreed with the Cambrian between Carnarvon, Portmadoc and Pwllheli, which were never revoked when the LNWR took over control in 1868. These running powers remained available but dormant after the Great Western Railway took over the Cambrian Railways in 1922 and remained in place into British Railways days, continuing until the line between Afon Wen and Caernarfon closed in 1964.

There was steady growth in passenger numbers travelling, with freight traffic also developing steadily. Until 1928 an interesting daily working was the provision of a yard shunter at Dinas Junction.

Services over the Afon Wen line on weekdays were fairly static, and traffic between the wars declined in the recession following the 1926 General Strike. The winter period from late September to April saw on average 11 trains each way over the line on weekdays, with another 11 trains between Bangor and Caernarfon, some of these extending to Llanberis. On Saturdays this increased to 16 trains to Afon Wen and nine between Bangor and Caernarfon or

down the outside of the cab and swill the floorboards with the slaking pipe. By the time I had disposed of the engine and cycled back home I was somewhat recovered but several pounds lighter and I was off my food for days after that. From then on I resisted all efforts to entice me into the Afon Wen refreshment room. The lady remained in residence for several years but ultimately she retired and, with no one to replace her, the building was boarded up and demolished with the rest of the station buildings after closure.

Two footbridges connected the station. The first, at the Pwllheli end, connected the up island platform with the outside world via a dirt road that led to the centre of Afonwen village. The second footbridge connected the up and down platforms. Both were open structures and since protection from the elements was non-existent, passengers wanting to get to the down side experienced the full fury of winter weather off Cardigan Bay. On the down side was a rudimentary wooden shelter, open to the platform edge, and the wooden signal cabin. It was commonplace for footplate crews on the GWR engines that operated on the coast line to become soaked with sea spray. I remember travelling from Dovey Junction to Pwllheli in the cab of a 'Dukedog' in the winter of 1954, being soaked through by Fairbourne. The crossing of Barmouth viaduct was nasty and I was surprised that the fire hadn't gone out, such was the ferocity of the wind and spray. The rest of the trip was extremely miserable and I had even more respect for the traincrews of Machynlleth, Portmadoc and Pwllheli after that!

MENAI BRIDGE TO AFONWEN

DOWN

							H	H			H	G	H	K		H	K	K	G	G	K
							12.1 am from Mold Jn.	12.23 am from Mold Jn.			5.5 am LE from Bangor								2.15 pm LE from Bangor	EBV	
							59	59			9		9	12	13	13	15	14	16	15	
Mileage							MSX	SO		MO				SX	MW FO	SX	SO	SX	SX	SX Q	SX Q
M	C	M	C				am	am		am	am	am		am	am	am	am	am	am	PM	PM	PM
0	0			MENAI BRIDGE	.. .. dep		3 45	4 50	..	..	4 10	5 11	..	..	6 25	am	..	7 30	8 30	10 50	11 50	2 20	2 30	3 5	..
0	77			Treborth			..	..															
2	37			Port Siding	.. ..		..	..											11 5			2 40		
3	22			Port Dinorwic	.. .. arr		..	..															
7	2	0	0	CAERNARVON	.. .. dep / arr		4 5	5 10	..	..	4 30	5 25	..	..	6 45		..	7 50	8 50	..	12 10	2 40	..	3 31	..
		1	26	Seiont Siding	.. .. dep		..	..					..	5 28	GL 8 5			GL 8 16	..		GL 12 53			GL 3 40	..
5	59			Pontrhythallt	.. .. arr / dep		..	..							8 25										
6	62			Cwm-y-glo	.. arr / dep		..	..							8 55 / 9 0									4 0	..
8	23			Glynrhonwy Siding	..		..	..					To shunt		9 25										
8	75			LLANBERIS			..	..							9 50 / 9 55									4 25 / 4 30	
7	43			Quay Siding	.. .. .. arr		..										8 20 / 8 30	..		12 57					
10	34			Dinas	.. .. arr / dep		..	..									8X45	..		1 5 / 1X18					
10	76			Llanwnda	.. arr / dep							5 43				Glynrhonwy Siding arr. 9.35 am	8 54 / 8 58			1 38 / R					
12	6			Groeslon	.. arr / dep												9 8 / 9 15			1 48					
14	3			Penygroes	.. .. arr / dep							5 51					9 25 / 9 33			1 55 / 2X3					
17	62	0	0	Nantlle	.. .. dep / arr							5 59				10 18 / 10 33				2 41					
19	51	1	36	Pant Glas Brynkir	.. .. arr / dep							6*X19 / 7* 0								3X0 / 3 9					
21	48			Ynys																					
23	26			Llangybi	.. .. arr / dep							7 12													
24	51			Chwilog	.. .. arr / dep							7 19						Glynrhonwy Siding arr. 4.10 pm		3 20 / 3 26					
25	61			AFONWEN	.. .. arr							7 25								3 36 / 3 41					

Llanberis. On Sundays there were six trains each way between Bangor and Caernarfon.

As the country climbed out of the recession the services increased, and the period from 2 July to 24 September 1939 saw 11 weekday trains between Bangor and Afon Wen, 18 on Saturdays and two on Sundays, with 11 between Bangor and Caernarfon or Llanberis weekdays and nine on Sundays between Bangor and Caernarfon, one of which was extended to Llanberis.

Emergency services were introduced on 11 September 1939 with the outbreak of World War 2, and three trains each way between Bangor and Afon Wen sufficed, with two additional trains between Bangor and Caernarfon SX, five on Saturdays and two on Sundays.

This improved by 1 January 1940, when six trains ran to Afon Wen and return on weekdays, and eight on Saturdays. In addition, three trains ran to Caernarfon SX and four on Saturdays. There were no Sunday trains.

Billy Butlin had selected a site for a holiday camp between Afon Wen and Abererch and by 1938 construction work had commenced. In 1939 the camp was requisitioned to serve as a naval training centre, named HMS *Glendower*. The training centre became operational some time in 1942. The Passenger working timetable from 4 October 1943 listed unadvertised specials that ran daily Tuesdays to Saturdays (reporting number 678), departing Afon Wen at 6.15am, to convey naval personnel to Crewe and beyond. Drafts of naval servicemen attended courses and travelled by train during the week on ordinary passenger trains. On Sunday night/Monday morning unadvertised naval special trains ran to and from destinations as far afield as Thurso

via Inverness, Carlisle and Crewe. The return special working (reporting number 67) departed Crewe at 4.30am. Locomotives were changed at Bangor, departing at 6.55am and reaching Afon Wen at 8.32am. This unadvertised working continued until the end of the war. It was shown in the Passenger working timetable for 1 October 1945. After hostilities ceased the camp was decommissioned and when the construction work was completed it became a Butlin's holiday camp, coming into use for the 1947 summer season. As a consequence of experiences and problems encountered with the naval special workings, when trains of 10 coaches were the norm, it became necessary to extend the passing loops on the single-line section and this work was put in hand. The Great Western Railway was somewhat slow on the uptake but by late 1946 had commenced doubling the former single line of track between Afon Wen and Penychain, completing the work in time for the camp's reopening.

Also commencing in September 1943 was a Monday to Saturday milk special working, designated 'parcels' traffic and running under Class C lamps, that ran every evening from Chwilog to Broad Green to convey milk to Hanson's Dairies, Liverpool. The duty was worked throughout by Bangor men, who lodged overnight at Edge Hill. The return milk empties working was combined with an ordinary passenger train to Bangor, where the traincrews changed. The fresh crew took the locomotive and the milk empties forward to Afon Wen, and after running around the stock, worked it back to Chwilog, where the vans were shunted into the siding. The locomotive then returned light engine to Bangor. At one time, five six-wheeled vans comprised

D78 WEEKDAYS BANGOR TO AFONWEN

DOWN

Mileage M	C	Station		No.	B	B	G	C	G	G	G	C	C	B	C	B	A
						To Pwllheli	LE	6.5 am ECS Llandudno Jn. to Penychain	LE	Two LE	LE to Portmadoc	6.58 am ECS Holyhead to Penychain	7.50 am ECS Llandudno Jn. to Penychain		ECS to Penychain	9.0 am from Llandudno Jn.	7.40 am from Manchester
																	313
								SO	SO	SO	SX	SO	SO Q		SO Q	SX	SO
					am	am	am	am	am	am	am	am	am	am	am	am	am
0	0	BANGOR	dep	1	4 35	5 30	6‖ 5	6AE32	7‖18	7‖25	7‖36	7L50	8L15	9 0	9†15	9 40	10 46
1	32	Menai Bridge	arr	2		5 34				7*29				9 4		9 44	
			dep	3	4 38	5 35	6 9	6 37	7 22	7*31	7 41	7 54	8 20	9 5	9 20	9 45	10 49
2	22	Treborth		4	Mails									9 8			
4	41	Port Dinorwic		5		5 41	..	..	..	..	..	..	..	9a13	..	9 51	..
8	37	CAERNARVON	arr	6	4 48	5 49	6‖23	6W50	7*36	7W49	8W0	8W9	8W35	9 21	9W35	9 59	11 0
			dep	7	4 52	5 58		6W55	7*42	7W59	8W5	8W18	8W45	9 26	9W40	..	..
11	55	Dinas	arr	8									8X*56		9X49		
			dep	9	5 1	6 7		7 5	7 49	8 9	8 14	8 28	9* 1	9 35	9*54	..	
12	28	Llanwnda		10										9 38			
13	38	Groeslon	arr	11	5 6	6 12		7X*10	..	..	..	..	..	9X41	..	..	
			dep	12	5 7	6 14		7*15	7 53	8 14	8 18	8 33	9 6	9 43	9 59		
15	34	Penygroes	arr	13	5 12	6 19		..	..	..	8X*23	8X*37	..	9X48	10X3	..	
			dep	14	5 13	6 21		7 20	7 58	8 23	8*43	8*52	9 10	9 50	10* 8	..	
19	12	Pant Glas		15	..	6 30	..	..	..	..	..	..	..	9 59	..	..	
21	0	Brynkir	arr	16	5 23	6 33					8X*55		9X*21	10 2	10X18		
			dep	17	5 24	6 36	..	7 34	8 10	8X35	9*11	9 5	9*28	10 3	10*25	..	
22	75	Ynys		18		6a40								10a 7			
24	36	Llangybi	arr	19	..	6X43	..	..	8X*18	..	..	..	..	10X10	10X33	..	
			dep	20	5 30	6 48		7 44	8*24	8 43	9 19	9X14	9 36	10‡13	10*37		
25	60	Chwilog		21	5c36	6a52	..	7 47	8 27	8 46	9 22	9 17	9 39	10a17	10 40	..	..
27	14	AFONWEN	arr	22	5 39	6 55		7†50	8‖30	8‖49	9‖25	9†20	9†42	10 20	10†43		
		Notes					To work 6.50 am to Llandudno	Until 10th September inclusive	To work 11.12 am from Afonwen, 18th, 25th June and 10.45 am from Afonwen commencing 2nd July	To work 10.1 am to Manchester and to Portmadoc	From 11th July to 9th September inclusive	Until 10th September inclusive	To work 11.25 am Q Penychain to Warrington	‡ 10.11 am	To work 12.5 pm Q Penychain to Manchester		Is 10.10 am from Llandudno Jn. until 25thJ une inclusive and commencing 3rd September

WEEKDAYS AFONWEN TO BANGOR

UP

Mileage M	C	Station		No.	B	B	B	B	A	A	B	A	A	C	A	B	A	B
					To Llandudno	To Bangor SX To Manchester SO		To Llandudno Jn.	8.45 am Penychain to Stoke-on-Trent	To Manchester	To Chester	9.40 am Penychain to Manchester	9.55 am Portmadoc to Euston	ECS	To Liverpool		10.50 am Penychain to Liverpool	To Manchester
						494			164	206		138	100		454		142	90
							SX	SO	SO	SO	SX	SO	SO	SO	SO	SX	SO	SO
					am	am	am	am	am	am	am	am	am	am	am	am	am	am
0	0	AFONWEN	dep	1	..	6 37	8 5	8 10	9 2	..	..	10 1	10 25	..	10 45	10 50	11 3	11 12
1	34	Chwilog		2		6a42	8 9	8c16	9 7			10 6	10a30		10c51	10c56	11 8	11c18
2	58	Llangybi	arr	3	..	..	8 14	8X22	9X*12	..	..	..	..	..	10 56	11 1	..	..
			dep	4		6X47	8 15	8 23	9*16			10X11	10 35		10 57	11 2	11 13	11 23
4	19	Ynys		5	..	..	8 19	8 28	..	..	..	..	..	..	..	11 6	..	11 28
6	14	Brynkir	arr	6		6X54	8 23	8X33					10 42	..	11 4	11 10		11 33
			dep	7	..	6 55	8 24	8 36	9X24		..	10 19	10 43		11 5	11 11	11 20	11 34
8	2	Pant Glas		8			8 28	8 41								11 15		11 39
11	60	Penygroes	arr	9	..	7 5	8X36	8X49	..	Until 27th August inclusive	..	..	10 53	After working 10.10 am from Llandudno Jn.	11 16	11 23	11 31	11X47
			dep	10		7 6	8 37	8 50	9 35			10 29	10 54		11 17	11 24		11 48
13	56	Groeslon	arr	11	..	7X10	8 41	8 54	9X*39		..	..	10 58		11 21	11 28	..	11X52
			dep	12		7 11	8 42	8 55	9*44			10 33	10 59		11 22	11 29	11X35	11 53
14	66	Llanwnda		13	..	7 14	8 45	8 58	..		..	..	..	..	11 25	11 32	..	11 56
15	39	Dinas	arr	14													11X*40	11X*59
			dep	15	..	7 16	8X47	9X 0	9 50	..	..	10 37	11 3	..	11X27	11 34	11*46	12* 5
18	57	CAERNARVON	arr	16		7 24	8 55	9 8	9 58			10 45	11 11		11 35	11 42	11 54	12 13
			dep	17	6 50	7 27	8 58	9 12	10 7	10 15	10 20	10 55	11 16	11†25	11 40	11 45	12 3	12 18
22	53	Port Dinorwic		18	6 58	7 35	9 6	9 20	Not advertised	10 23	10 28				11 48	11 53	Not advertised	
24	72	Treborth		19	..	..	..	..		..	..	..	..	..	..	..		..
25	62	Menai Bridge	arr	20	7 6	7 43	9 14	9 28			10 35		11 28			12 1		
			dep	21	7 7	7 44	9 16	9 29	10 18	10 31	10 36	11 10	11 29	11 39	12 0	12 2	12 14	12 29
27	14	BANGOR	arr	22	7 11	7 48	9 20	9 33	10L22	10 35	10 40	11L14	11 33	11†43	12 5	12 6	12AE19	12 32
		Notes				Terminates at Bangor on Saturdays 18th, 25th June and 17th September		On 18th, 25th June, 10th and 17th September runs to Liverpool and is Rep. No. 490	Until 10th September inclusive			Not advertised		Runs 18th, 25th June and 17th September only	Terminates at Llandudno Jn. 18th, 25th June 17th September		Until 10th September inclusive	

BANGOR TO AFONWEN — WEEKDAYS — D79

	A	A	B	B	A	B	A	B	G		A	B	B	A	B	B	C	B	B
	8.5 am Manchester to Penychain	6.15 am Manchester to Penychain	6.25 am Liverpool to Pwllheli	To Pwllheli	10.35 am Warrington to Penychain	11.35 am from Llandudno Jn.	9.35 am Liverpool to Penychain	To Pwllheli	LE		1.30 pm Llandudno Jn to Penychain	To Pwllheli	11.15 am Euston to Portmadoc	To Pwllheli	6.42 pm from Llandudno Jn.	ECS			8.35 pm from Llandudno Jn.
	311	325			355		399				467			89					
	SO	SO	SX	SO	SO	SX	SO	SO	SO		SO	SX	SO			SX	FO	SO	
1	am 10L58	am 11L8	am 11 23	am 11 23	PM 12L15	PM 12 20	PM 12L31	PM 12 45	PM 1∥16	..	PM 2 10	PM 2 52	PM 3 15	PM 4 40	PM 5 39	PM 7 5	PM 7†15	PM 7 20	PM 9 10
2			11 27	11 27		12 24		12 49			2 56	2 56	3 19	4 44	5 43				
3	11 2	11 12	11 28	11 28	12 19	12 25	12 35	12 50	1 20	..	2 13	2 57	3 20	4 45	5 44	7 8	7 19	7 23	9 13
4			11 31	11 31							3 0		3 23						
5			11a36	11a36					12 56			3a 5	3a28	4 51	5 50	7 14		7 29	9 19
6	11 13	11 23½	11 44	11 44	12 32	12 36	12 48	1 4	1∥35	....	2 26	3 13	3 36	4 59	5 58	7 22	7†32	7 37	9 27
7	11 15	11 36	11 49	11 55	12 38	12 42	12 55	1 7		..	2 32	3 17	3 42	5 3	6 2	7 28		7 40	..
8	11X*24		11X*58															7X49	..
9	11*28	11X45	12* 4	12X*4	12 47	12 51		1 4	1 18		2 41	3 26	3 51	5X12	6X11	7 37		7*52	
10			12 7	12 7		12 54			1 21			3 29	3 54		6 14	7 40		7 55	
11	11X*32	11X*50	12 10	12X10		12 57			1 24		2 46	3 32	3 57	5 17	6X17	7X43		7 58	
12	11*36	11*57	12 12	12 12	12 51	12 58	1 9	1 26			3 33	3 58	4 3	5 18	6 18	7 47		7 59	
13	11X*42		12 17	12 17	12X*56	1X 3	1*14	1 29		2X51	3 38	4 3	5X23	6 23	7 52		8 4	
14	11*49	12 1	12 18	12∥23	1* 1	1 6	1*19	1 31		2 56	3 48	4 5	5 24	6 33	8 2		8 5	
15			12 26	12∥31		1 15		1 40			3 49	4 13		6 33	8 2		8 14	
16			12 29	12X*34		1 18		1 43		3X 6	3 52	4X16	5X34	6 36	8 6		8X17	
17	12X0	12X11	12 30	12∥37	1 12	1 19	1 29	1 44		3 7	3 53	4 18	5 36	6 37	8 18		8 18	
18			12a34	12∥41		1a23		1a48			3 57	4 22		6a41	8a10		8 22	
19		12X20	12 37	12∥44		1 26		1X51			4X 0	4X25		6 44	8X13		8X25	
20	12 6	12*30	12 38	12∥45	1X20	1 28	1X37	1 53		3 14	4 2	4 27	5 43	6 45	8 16		8 26	
21	12 11	12a42	12 42	12∥49	1 23	1a32	1 40	1a57		3 17	4a 6	4a31	5a47	6a49	8a20		8a30	
22	12 14	12 38	12 45	12 52	1 26	1 35	1 43	2 0		3 20	4 9	4 34	5 50	6 52	8 23		8 33	

Notes (Bangor to Afonwen):
- Until 3rd September inclusive. Not advertised.
- Until 10th September inclusive.
- ½ As SX.
- Until 10th September inclusive.
- To work 2.0 pm to Liverpool. From 2nd July to 10th September inclusive.
- Until 27th August inclusive. Not Advertised from Bangor.
- Starts from Bangor and terminates at Afonwen SX until 8th July inclusive and commencing 12th September.
- To work 10.15 am SO to Manchester.
- Until 24th August inclusive.

AFONWEN TO BANGOR — WEEKDAYS

	A	A	B	A	B	C	B	C	B	B	C	B	B	B	B	B	B	B	G
	11.0 am Portmadoc to Euston	11.25 am Penychain to Warrington	12.5 pm Penychain to Manchester	To Liverpool	12.37 pm ECS Penychain to Holyhead	1.45 pm from Pwllheli	2.20 pm ECS Penychain to Holyhead	3.30 pm from Pwllheli	3.30 pm from Pwllheli	4.0 pm ECS Penychain to Llandudno Jn.	4.35 pm from Pwllheli		7.40 pm from Pwllheli	7.40 pm from Pwllheli					LE
	100	318		144	252														
	SX	SO	SX	SO	SO	SO		SO	SX	SO	SO	SX	SO		SX	SO	SX	SO	
1	am 11 25	am 11 40	PM ..	PM 12 19	PM ..	PM 1† 5	PM 2 7	PM 2†40	PM 3 48	PM 3 50	PM 4†15	PM 5 14	PM 5 14	PM 7 5	PM 8 5	PM 8 13	PM 8 35	PM 8 45	PM ..
2	11a30	11 45		12 24		1 10	2a12	2 45	3c54	3c56	4 20	5a19	5a19	7a10	8a10	8a18	8a40	8a50	
3					1X15	2 17		3X59	4 1	4X*26	5 24	5 24	7 15	8X15	8X23		
4	11 35	11 50	12X28		1*55	2 18	2 49	4 4	4 5	4*29	5 25	5 25	7 16	8 17	8 26	8 45	8 55
5					2 22		4 8	4 9	5 29	5 29	7 21	8 21	8 30		
6	11 42	11X*59			2 4	2 26	3X*0	4 12	4X13	5X33	5X33	7 25	8 25	8 34	8 52	9 2
7	11 43	12*12	12 36		2 27	3* 9	4 14	4 17	4 38	5 37	5 37	7 26	8 26	8 35	8 53	9 3
8					2 31	4 19	4 21	5 41	5 41	7 31	8 30	8 39		
9	11 53		12X*45		2X39	4 26	4 29	5 49	5 49	7 40	8 38	8 47	9 3	9 13
10	11 54	12X22	12*59	2 14	2 40	3 20	4 27	4 30	4 48	5 52	5 52	7 41	8 39	8 48	9 4	9 14
11	11 58		1X*4		2X44	4 31	4 34	5 56	5 56	7X45	8 43	8 52	9 8	9 18
12	11 59	12X26	1*10	2 19	2Y45	3 25	4 32	4 35	4 53	5 58	5 58	7 46	8 44	8 53	9 9	9 19
13				2Y48	4 35	4 38	6 1	7 49		
14			1X*15		4X*57	6X*3	6X*3		
15	12X3	12 29	1*20	2 22	2Y50	3 29	4 37	4 40	5*13	6*13	6*13	7 51	8 48	8 57	9 13	9 23
16	12 11	12 37	1 28	2W30	2Y58	3*38	4 45	4 48	5W21	6 21	6 21	7 59	8 56	9 5	9 21	9 31
17	12 16	12 42	12 43	1 32	2 0	2W42	3 5	4* 5	4 50	4 52	5W30	6 25	6 25	8 5	9 1	9 10	9 25	9 35	9∥47
18			12 51		2 8	3 13	4 50	5 0	6 33	6 33		
19			12 57			5 5	5 7		
20	12 28		1 2	2 16	3 21	5 7	5 10	6 41	6 41	8 16		After working 8.35 pm from Llandudno Jn.
21	12 29	12 54	1 3	1 47	2 17	2 54	3 22	4 20	5 8	5 11	5 43	6 42	6 42	8 17	9 13	9 22	9 37	9 47	10 2
22	12 33	12L58	1 7	1L50	2 21	2L58	3 26	4A E24	5 12	5 15	5L47	6 46	6 46	8 21	9 16	9 25	9 40	9 50	10∥ 7

Notes (Afonwen to Bangor):
- From 11th July to 9th September inclusive.
- From 2nd July to 10th September inclusive.
- Until 3rd September inclusive.
- Y—2 mins later SO WTT only.
- Until 10th September inclusive.
- Mails.
- After working 8.35 pm from Llandudno Jn.

Extract from summer 1955 BR passenger timetable for the Bangor to Afon Wen line.

Afon Wen
On a summer Saturday in 1960 Standard Class 4MT 4-6-0 No 75026, nominally attached to Machynlleth shed but outstationed at Pwllheli, stands at the up platform at Afon Wen with the 11.10am SO Pwllheli to Birmingham via Ruabon. Across the platform Bangor shed Class 4MT 2-6-4T No 42601 pauses with the 8.5am SO Manchester Exchange to Penychain. For some unknown reason the Manchester train was reduced to six coaches and a single 2-6-4T was used. Normally this would have been a 10-coach working and two tank engines would have been required. The fireman was unable to explain the reason, but the driver, Moi Edwards of Bangor, blamed it on control! *Bill Rear*

the train from Chwilog with a similar load coming from Gaerwen on Anglesey being attached at Bangor, from where both sets were worked forward. By May 1949 the traffic was lost to road tankers.

From 1948 to 1963 the line experienced seasonal fluctuations. Nationalisation saw London Midland Region locomotives working through to Pwllheli on a regular basis, eliminating the need for the Western Region to provide power. From 1948 Bangor engines and men worked to and from Portmadoc on the 'Welshman' workings, but due to weight restrictions Stanier Class 3 2-6-2Ts were the largest motive power allowed between Afon Wen and Portmadoc. In 1948 the down 'Welshman' stock was worked through from Bangor to Portmadoc, but this was not repeated in following years, being cut back to Afon Wen and the stock worked forward by Portmadoc. The morning 'Up' working remained a Bangor turn through from Portmadoc to Bangor until the line closed.

With the introduction of diesel multiple-units from 1957, a basic winter service of eight trains each way to Afon Wen, of which seven worked through to Pwllheli, together with three trips between Bangor and Caernarfon and return, prevailed. The summer season saw increases in traffic during the week, and in the holiday season land cruise excursion trains worked over the line. Subsequently some additional land cruise trains worked in the reverse direction, with as many as four trains daily at the peak.

From summer 1958 11 trains ran daily, Monday to Friday, each way, with three workings to Caernarfon. On Saturdays, however, there were 17 workings from Bangor to Penychain or Pwllheli and return, excluding light engine workings, and an additional three workings to and from Caernarfon.

Picture the scene. On peak Saturdays every passing loop along the line was occupied, trains frequently being held up awaiting the train staff, and it was not uncommon for trains running late into Bangor to be held there for nearly an hour, awaiting a change of locomotive. Most trains over the Afon Wen line were double-headed by various permutations of tank engines. The double track to Caernarfon created a false sense of optimism as the eight miles were run off in what seemed record times, usually about 15 minutes. Most trains took water at Caernarfon. Another double-headed working from Afon Wen laboriously climbed the 1 in 40 gradient from the harbour through Caernarvon Tunnel up to No 2 signalbox. The signalman would dash down the steps and into the six-foot to take the staff off the up train, then hurry back to his box and replace the token in the machine and, amid a flurry of bell signals, would withdraw it again and hand it to the driver of the down train, who would toot to draw attention to the second driver, then open the regulator briefly. Having got the train on the move they would coast down the 1 in 40 and pass through Carnarvon Tunnel to the harbour, where the twin exhausts would blast forth as both drivers opened the regulators to commence the climb to Dinas. The gradient was almost as severe, and the 3½ miles would be an unremitting slog for both firemen, with 10 heavily laden corridor coaches. At Dinas the train would draw to a halt, and the train staff would be handed over to the signalman, who would dash up to the box and insert it in the instrument, with a flurry of bells from Caernarvon No 2 box, before withdrawing the staff again for an up train that was bearing down from Groeslon. The rule book demanded that the home signal was kept at danger, and as an up train passed through Llanwnda it would whistle up for the Dinas home. This was repeated at Groeslon, Penygroes, Brynkir and Llangybi, and however smartly the tokens were exchanged, however hard the drivers worked their engines and firemen, it was as much as one could do to keep to running time, never mind making up lost time.

Leaving Chwilog, it was the practice to release the brakes and apply light steam to get the train moving, and then coast down to Afon Wen, braking steadily all the way, for it was a certainty that your train would be held at the junction with the Pwllheli line, awaiting a platform road. Eventually the arm would come 'off' and the last half mile to Afon Wen would be covered in a minute or so. Most Butlin's trains were 10 coaches in length, but 11-coach trains were not altogether unknown.

At Afon Wen, once at rest, the fireman on the train engine would nip down and uncouple the stock whilst the driver would change the headlamps for the light engine movement beyond the crossover. There would be a quick change of lamps on both engines and a toot on the whistle, and another 'pop' to acknowledge the signalman's response of giving the road, and then they would set back, through the down main line until the crossover was clear, change the lamps once more, and toot up the signalman. Having got the road, the train engine opened up and set back on to the stock. The pilot engine fireman then changed the headcode whilst the train engine fireman coupled up and removed his lamp; it was then time to be 'off'. The movement was straightforward, but if the three platform faces were occupied it became necessary to run round using the up side goods loop, and frequently a wait was necessary until the signalman could permit the move to continue.

The track to Penychain was double-line, and only five minutes were allowed from Afon Wen. The empty stock would then either be worked forward to Pwllheli East and stabled, or worked back to Afon Wen, where it was parked for a short while beyond the platform on the Criccieth side until the path for the return working became available. Frequently, it was necessary to move the locomotives to the ashpit road, to take on water from the tanks on the down side, and to clean the fire. There could be as many as four engines standing on the ashpit road, with an LM Region inspector on duty to sort things out. It was not unusual to part company with one's pilot or train engine and couple up to another locomotive for the return working up the line. Some stock stopped at Pwllheli East for the week, and locomotives thus released worked back light engine to Bangor as quickly as possible, whilst others would be utilised to pilot trains to Caernarfon, Bangor or Llandudno Junction. It was not uncommon to see 10 locomotives at

Afon Wen at about midday on busy Saturdays. The regular Western Region staff were assisted by LM Region traffic inspectors, who generally kept a low profile, acknowledging that the local men knew best and should be left to it.

It was not always so, though, and on occasions a Western Region 'know-all' arrived and proceeded to shout his mouth off, displaying his ignorance to the uninterested and unimpressed multitudes by his performance. It was on such an occasion that a visiting 'brains trust' allocated a Class 5 4-6-0 as the train engine, tender-first, piloted by another Class 5 4-6-0, with smokebox leading. Despite the protestations that the locomotive positions should be reversed he ignored all advice and despatched the train to Warrington. At Caernarfon, the pilot engine detached as per instructions to reattach itself on the front of a Penychain-bound working, whilst the 6H (Bangor) men on the train engine proceeded alone tender-first to Bangor, where they handed over to Chester men, who worked the train (tender-first) all the way to Chester. Their comments were voiced to every official who dared show his face, but there was neither the time nor facility to rectify the situation, and so they worked from block post to block post, cursing volubly every inch of the way. It might have been less irritating had the weather been fine, but it was a gusty day with driving rain, and coal dust swirled around the cab to add to the general discomfort. The Warrington men who relieved our heroes at Chester were equally impressed with the inspector's abilities, and just as vocal in their praises, called his parentage into question!

This was an exceptional case, but the 'brains trust' was just as likely to mess things up in other ways. One such gentleman in July 1954 was anxious about the build-up of motive power hanging around the ashpit road at Afon Wen one Saturday afternoon, and, misreading his power requirements, despatched several 2-6-4T locomotives back to Bangor 'light engine'. It so happened that an additional train comprising four coaches had been added to the Supplementary Notice of Special Trains at very short notice and was running that day from Llandudno Junction to Penychain. It was then booked to work back ECS to Afon Wen, where it was scheduled to attach an additional six coaches which were standing temporarily in the machine siding, using one of the spare 2-6-4Ts off the ashpit road as pilot. The pair were booked to disappear over Pant Glâs summit working the stock to Menai Bridge, where the empty coaches would be worked forward to Holyhead by a Holyhead Class 5 that came LE off Bangor shed for the purpose. A 2-6-4T had been booked to pilot the ECS from Afon Wen to Menai Bridge, where they would come off the train and return LE to Bangor shed. The 'brains trust' found to his horror that he had dismissed the pilot locomotive and the sole motive power available to work the ECS was the Ivatt Class 2MT 2-6-2T, which was clearly under-powered and outclassed although the driver in question was quite willing to 'have a go'. After a flurry of telephone calls, the ECS stock had to be parked in the up-side sidings at the Criccieth end of Afon Wen station to await a locomotive that was despatched from Bangor to assist the 2-6-2T. A driver and fireman made their third trip of the day to Afon Wen. The inspector was never allowed to forget it, and he was never seen at Afon Wen again!

The introduction of DMUs to the line saw their limited use at first, with only two such units working through to Afon Wen or Pwllheli. This traffic was largely in the hands of Derby 'Lightweight' units, ultimately to be replaced by Metropolitan-Cammell two-car units which handled the requirements of the line satisfactorily, but most of the passenger services remained in the hands of 2-6-4T locomotives. By the winter period of 1959 this had changed, when all but the second passenger train of the day was handled by DMUs. The 1960 summer season saw reversion to steam-hauled trains for most workings and this pattern persisted until late September 1963, with only one DMU working through to Afon Wen daily. The 1964 summer season, the final one for the line as it happened, repeated this pattern with only the last three trains of the day being worked by DMUs. The final months of the branch saw all the passenger services worked by DMUs with the exception of the 05.20 from Bangor to Pwllheli and the 07.45 return working which were hauled by 2-6-4T engines. The reason was that there was still some mail and parcels traffic handled and a van was worked forward off the 02.10 from Crewe to Pwllheli.

There were other incidents. On 28 August 1956 locomotive No 42157 off the 4.50am Bangor to Afon Wen ran through point No 49 against signals just as the 6.21am to Portmadoc was starting. Both engines came to an abrupt halt and no collision occurred, but the engines were only 10yd apart when both came to rest. At the subsequent enquiry the Bangor driver was held responsible, although

there was some doubt amongst Bangor men about the orientation of the signal adjudged to be at danger.

Freight Traffic

Freight working on the Afon Wen branch was developed from the outset. Dressed slate formed the bulk of the traffic carried out of the area, balanced by coal, agricultural stock and general merchandise traffic carried in. There was some freight interchange at Afon Wen, but this was limited to whatever traffic could be directed over the line by the LNWR/LMS agents.

In LNWR days all the freight traffic was worked into Caernarvon where it was sorted and remarshalled for working forward. After Caernarfon shed closed, Menai Bridge yard undertook most of the sorting for main line traffic heading to Mold Junction or Holyhead. Caernarfon yard was the concentration point for the branches and traffic remained heavy until the facility was strangled under the implementation of the Beeching proposals. Most important was the loss of slate traffic from Llanberis and Nantlle. The loaded mineral wagons off the branches had been sorted and marshalled at Caernarfon daily, and until 1926 worked to Springs Branch every evening at 10pm. After the General Strike the job was cut back to Mold Junction. The usual motive power until 1926 was an ex-LNWR Class G2 0-8-0 locomotive from Springs Branch, which was regularly worked up to its load limit. The train was assembled in the coal yard by the freight shunt locomotive on duty, which worked in the lower yard from 4pm until departure time. The Springs Branch mineral train started from the coal yard and the freight shunt locomotive assisted uncoupled, shoving up the sharp climb to the main line before stopping inside the yard limits and running back into the shed road, where the crew then disposed of the engine and signed off. The decline in mineral traffic following the General Strike saw the traffic diminish and the power requirement was reduced. Two Fowler 0-6-0 Class 4F engines were drafted in to Caernarfon shed for the purpose and became the top job for the shed. Moreover, it was a lodging turn and lucrative. The men booked off at Mold Junction. When Caernarfon shed closed, the work passed to Bangor and ceased to be a lodging turn. The mineral train to Mold Junction persisted throughout World War 2 and lasted until the late 1950s.

There was also considerable inward coal traffic, and some livestock and agricultural feedstuffs. Outward there was a significant tonnage of smalls (eg small parcels and newspapers) and livestock traffic, particularly in the autumn when several specials would be chartered from Brynkir and Chwilog markets. In the 1930s there were three booked freight workings each way over the Afon Wen line every day, Sundays excepted. There was also the daily mineral train to and from Nantlle and two paths to Llanberis for Class K freight trains. The afternoon working was marked 'Conditional' but frequently ran.

A freight train shunting book for August 1936 in Gwynedd archives gives some idea of the density of the traffic at Caernarfon. It was common to find four or five locomotives shunting the yards and making up freight trains at the same time.

Caernarfon to Llanberis

Various proposals were made to link Llanberis with the outside world in the 1860s, two to Caernarfon and a third to Bangor.

In June 1869 the Carnarvon & Llanberis Railway was inspected and opened between Morfa (Caernarvon) and Llanberis on 1 July. The LNWR worked the line from the start. The inaugural service consisted of five trains daily. Because the Carnarvonshire Railway and Carnarvon & Llanberis Railway lines were not physically connected with the LNWR, it was necessary to work the stock for the Llanberis line over the Cambrian Railways' and Carnarvonshire Railway's lines via Afon Wen.

Route Description

From Caernarfon, the line followed a parallel course to the Carnarvonshire Railway for the first mile. At Seiont Bridge the two lines parted company. The Llanberis Railway line descended at 1 in 340 before levelling out to pass under the Caernarfon-Pwllheli road then followed the Seiont river for about a mile, passing Peblig Mill on the down side, two miles from Caernarfon station. Then the line commenced climbing steeply for the next six miles until it eased beyond Pontrhythallt.

Pontrûg

Pontrûg station was 3¼ miles from Caernarfon. Apart from a short platform on the up side and a station house a short distance away, there was nothing else at the site. The station closed in 1917 as a wartime measure, reopening after the conflict ceased. It saw little traffic and there was no provision for freight other than small parcels.

The station closed to all traffic on 22 September 1930, when regular passenger services were suspended. The platform was removed before World War 2 but the station house still survives, much modified and in private hands.

The line continued to climb towards Pontrhythallt for a mile before easing slightly. At 5½ miles the gradient eased to 1 in 358 at Pontrhythallt.

Pontrhythallt

The approach to the station went under a minor road bridge and over the River Rhythallt before running into the station. The platform was on the up side. The main building was a two-storey structure and housed the usual facilities, in an idyllic location. The station was also a staff token station; the instruments were in the station office. The stationmaster lived in part of the main building. A small yard with three

sidings was on the up side beyond the platform and comprised a loop off which the sidings ran. Two two-lever ground frames locked by the train staff protected both entrances to the loop. Signals were controlled from an eight-lever open ground frame mounted on the platform. There was no separate goods shed.

The station site was sold immediately on closure and sympathetically developed. Today it is a delightful private residence, fairytale-like in its location, and has lost none of the charm and character that it possessed in its operational days.

The line continued almost on the level for another mile until Cwm y Glo was reached.

Cwm y Glo

The line passed underneath the Caernarfon to Llanberis road immediately prior to running into the station. The single short-length low-height platform and main building were on the down side. The station building was similar in design to Pontrhythallt but nowhere near as attractive. Beyond the platform was a small goods yard with two sidings and a goods shed.

The road bridge and station buildings were demolished in the 1980s to make way for a bypass road around the village.

An incident occurred that has been the subject of a recent book. The Dinorwic quarry at Llanberis imported nitro-glycerine explosives from Hamburg for blasting purposes. Ships carrying the explosives were not permitted into

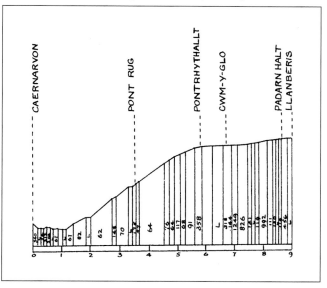

Caernarvon-Llanberis gradient profile.

Pontrûg
Stanier Class 5MT 4-6-0 No 45277 snakes round the reverse curve approaching the site of Pontrûg station with a demolition train of sleepers from the railhead south of Cwm y Glo. The engine was based at Llandudno Junction, which worked these trains in the dying days of the line. The trackbed at this point is still discernible but the shrubs have encroached the riverbank and the river can no longer be seen from the trackbed. The line passed underneath the Caernarfon to Llanberis road at this point. *Bill Rear*

Pontrhythallt
The station was in a very picturesque setting. Trains from Caernarfon ran over a river bridge into Pontrhythallt. The original platform was short, but when longer coaches were introduced by the LMS it had been necessary to lengthen it over the river, although the abutment extensions had been installed when the line was built. Here the melancholy task of dismantling the line is under way and Stanier Class 5MT 4-6-0 No 45277 stands at the platform awaiting departure time. *Bill Rear*

Pontrhythallt
Another demolition train, another locomotive: Llandudno Junction's BR Standard Class 4MT 4-6-0 No 75009 stands on the river bridge shunting wagons. The lifting of the track is just beyond the station and a mobile crane can be seen lifting rail past the loop point in the distance. The lifting continued apace and by the following week the track had been removed and Pontrhythallt station changed hands into private ownership. The river bridge was left intact and the new owners developed the site sympathetically, making it into a beautiful residence in secluded grounds. They planted trees alongside the boundary fence and today the whole site is enclosed by mature conifers. *Bill Rear*

Pontrhythallt
Standard Class 4MT 4-6-0 No 75009 stands in the yard loop at Pontrhythallt waiting to propel an empty bolster wagon a short way along the line to the railhead, just out of sight round the corner. Faintly visible in the distance, Snowdon dominates the landscape. When the line was operational it was a magnificent sight to see the mountain coming into view, especially on clear days. *Norman Kneale*

Cwm y Glo
The stations at Pontrhythallt, Cwm y Glo and Llanberis were of a similar design, although that at Llanberis was larger. Here the exterior of Cwm y Glo stands, still occupied but soon to be demolished. Beyond the station is the goods shed, which was rarely used to capacity — that, too, was swept away for road improvements. *Bill Rear collection*

Near Cwm y Glo
About half a mile from Cwm y Glo station the line came close to Llyn Padarn. It first passed by a rocky outcrop where the 1904 quarrymen's strike at the nearby slate quarries was convened. The main road from Caernarfon to Llanberis briefly ran alongside before climbing and crossing over the line which burrowed into another rocky outcrop known as Llanberis Tunnel. Here the morning excursion from Rhyl, hauled by Stanier 2-6-4T No 42460, is seen approaching the tunnel on the final leg of the journey to Llanberis in July 1952. Today, this section of the trackbed is part of the main road. *Bill Rear*

Llanberis Causeway
On emerging from Llanberis Tunnel the line passed over a causeway cutting off a corner of Llyn Padarn. In the distance Snowdon can be seen, hazy in the afternoon sunlight. Passengers from Rhyl who travelled out on this excursion train will have had time to ascend the mountain by the railway and have a cup of tea before the return departure. Here Stanier 2-6-4T No 42617 approaches the tunnel. *Bill Rear*

Caernarfon harbour and had to stand off shore in Caernarfon Bay. The product was off-loaded into small boats and conveyed to the harbourmaster's office, where it was stored — very casually — until it was required at the quarry. The glass containers were loaded on a horse-drawn cart which proceeded along the road, which was, by all accounts, unmade, all the way to Llanberis.

About a week before the line opened, a cart-load of explosives was passing the station road when the consignment exploded. The horse and driver were never found but bits of the cart were recovered almost half a mile distant. A huge hole was blown in the road and the depression can still be traced to this day.

On leaving Cwm y Glo the line resumed climbing, albeit at a gentle rate. Half a mile from the station the line passed under a rocky outcrop into a short unlined tunnel, emerging on a causeway that crossed a corner of Llyn Padarn, with one of the most beautiful views in the British Isles.

After the causeway the line passed through a rocky cutting and came to Glynrhonwy where sidings for quarry workings once existed. This complex was disused from about 1914. In 1940 it was requisitioned for defence purposes. A Royal Air Force camp was established and a government ordnance factory was built into the old quarry workings to assemble bombs. The components were brought in and the finished products removed by rail. Normally, two trains a day sufficed. The traffic ceased by 1945. For a while the sidings were used to store coaches. Today this area is a small industrial estate.

Llanberis Causeway
The usual arrangement was for the engine and observation car of the Rhyl excursion, having discharged their passengers, to return to Caernarfon in order to effect a crew change. In mid-afternoon the locomotive and coach returned to Llanberis. Here Stanier 2-6-4T No 42617 ambles across the causeway with the observation coach in tow, heading for Llanberis. On the other side of the lake was the trackbed of the 4ft 0½in Padarn Railway, although no train was running on that line at the time of this photograph, which was taken in early September 1952. Today the former Padarn Railway is the route of the Llanberis Lake Railway. *Bill Rear*

Llanberis Causeway
Before the advent of the 'Snowdonian', the observation excursion train from Rhyl, services on the Llanberis branch were very much a local concern. Coaches were invariably six-wheel stock and motive power was an LNWR Webb-design 2-4-2T. Until about 1917 the engine was based at Llanberis but in that year the shed closed and the work and men transferred to Caernarfon depot. An unidentified 2-4-2T with 5ft 6in diameter wheels (probably No 620) heads a train of six-wheel coaches over the causeway and towards the approaching Llanberis Tunnel on its journey to Caernarfon. The date is before World War 1 but the photographer is unknown. *Bill Rear collection*

Padarn Lake Halt

About 8 miles from Caernarfon was Padarn Lake halt — a short wooden platform on the up side with a wooden booking hut that faced the lake. It was built in 1936 to cater for excursion and local traffic, being located near the centre of Llanberis, within 100yd of the main street. It never reopened after World War 2 but remained standing until at least 1956.

Llanberis

Llanberis station was located on the edge of the village and opened on 1 July 1869. It was convenient for the Dinorwic quarries and the Snowdon Mountain Railway. The complex consisted of a single platform on the up side, with its main station building being similar in design to those at Pontrhythallt and Cwm y Glo, but bigger. The main platform had a narrow 'ticket platform' extension erected by the LNWR, where passenger trains paused so that collection could be made. There existed a run-round loop and three sidings, one of which passed through the stone-built goods shed. One line extended to a 42ft turntable that was reputed to have come from Betws y Coed. Another line off the turntable was used by local coal merchants who unloaded their wagons and stocked the coal alongside. There was a carriage landing off the main passenger platform that was used to park a camping coach.

Llanberis old station is now a gift shop and café. The platform awnings can still be seen, facing the new bypass and Llyn Padarn.

When the Llanberis line was first opened to traffic, a small single-road engine shed was built. Most of the branch trains were worked by Llanberis men using engines out-stationed from Caernarfon shed. For many years a Webb 2-4-2T, No 620, was resident. The shed closed some time after July 1915, when the seven shed staff were transferred to Caernarfon.

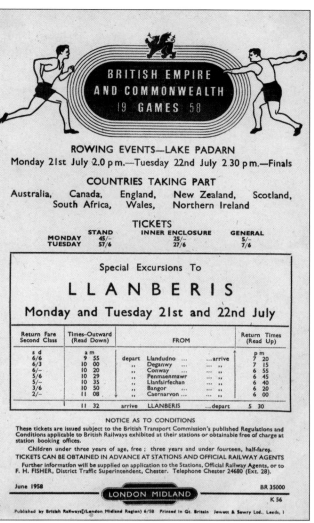

British Empire and Commonwealth Games 1958.

Llanberis

An early view of Llanberis taken about 1910 from the footbridge that crossed over the tracks, showing the layout at the station at the time. The station layout itself changed very little until about 1956 when the sidings that extended beyond the platform road and adjacent tracks containing coaches were cut back by a couple of panels. The single-road locomotive shed is visible alongside. The left-hand track served as a coal siding and wagons can be seen being unloaded. This line extended back to the turntable. *Bill Rear collection*

Llanberis

This unusual picture, taken on 5 July 1960, shows a Stanier Class 8F 2-8-0 on the left. It was rare to find this class of engine on the Llanberis branch, as freight workings were in the hands of Bangor engines and they never had an '8F' based there. The photograph was taken in the morning, so possibly the 2-8-0 had been hijacked from Llandudno Junction shed, where it was based at the time. Another curiosity is the composition of the 'Snowdonian' which was normally six vehicles and the observation coach (seven vehicles in all), yet this train is composed of only four vehicles. Possibly the observation coach has been parked in one of the sidings in the distance. The '8F' is No 48667 and the 2-6-4T is No 42567. *J. A. Peden*

Llanberis

The platform at Llanberis was on the up side and could accommodate four coaches, a throwback to when the line opened and five or six six-wheel coaches constituted the normal train length. Note the ornate cast-iron canopy supports. These were incorporated into the station building extension when the station closed and passed into private hands. The building is now a gift shop and a café. A camping coach is just visible in the former carriage landing platform. Beyond it is the stone-built goods shed. On the extreme left of the picture can be seen the water tower. At one time this was built into the locomotive shed structure, but when the shed was demolished in 1938 the water tank was left standing. The water tank was used occasionally until it was demolished in 1963 when the site was cleared. *Bill Rear collection*

Llanberis

Fowler 2-6-4Ts were not normally seen at Llanberis, but this occasion was different. No 42366 stands by the starter alongside the ticket platform with the Stephenson Locomotive Society Caernarvonshire Rail Tour on 5 May 1957. These open-cab locomotives were not unknown at Bangor but they rarely appeared on the Llanberis branch. For a while in 1954-6 Bangor had a batch of the later version with enclosed cabs, and the author recorded No 42416 on more than one occasion on the Rhyl to Llanberis excursion workings. In the summer season a camping coach would be placed on the short length of track where the upturned sleeper acts as a stop, but it did not usually appear until mid-June. *Brian Hilton/ Bill Rear collection*

Llanberis

Another Stephenson Locomotive Society Caernarvonshire Rail Tour visited Llanberis in October 1963. Here Ivatt 2-6-2MTs Nos 41200 and 41324 pull into Llanberis with what was probably the last passenger train to call at the station. After a break the tour then retraced its steps to Caernarfon and then went on to work over the Nantlle branch. Note the small ground frame on the platform, which controlled signals only. Points were worked from two-lever ground frames locked by the train staff. No 41200 was the last engine to work off Bangor shed when it closed to all traffic in 1965. *Brian Cowlishaw*

Train Working

The Llanberis branch, as built, saw an upsurge in tourist traffic after the Snowdon Mountain Railway commenced operations in 1897. The LNWR took full advantage of the increased traffic by attaching an observation coach to certain seasonal workings from Llandudno until the outbreak of World War 1. This was restored in time for the summer season of 1920 and was then a regular feature every summer until the outbreak of World War 2. The out of season traffic declined due to competition from buses. Various experiments were tried to encourage trade including the use of 'motor' trains, but the half-mile walk from Caernarfon station into the town centre proved an obstacle. Regular passenger trains stopped running on 22 September 1930, although goods traffic continued much as before.

In LMS days there was much local excursion traffic from Llanberis running to and from Caernarfon, Llandudno, Rhyl and Prestatyn as well as advertised cheap day excursions to Liverpool and Manchester. These proved very popular but this traffic ceased with the outbreak of World War 2.

From 1946 summer excursions were run to Llanberis, initially from Llandudno but starting from Rhyl after 1950.

The observation car was restored to this service from 1948 and then ran every summer season until 1962, commencing about mid-June and working weekdays until mid-September. The engine and coach returned to Caernarfon at about midday for servicing and crew change, working back to Llanberis in the middle of the afternoon. On return the engine attached the observation coach to the rear of the train before running round the stock and taking its place at the head of the train for the journey back to Rhyl in the early evening. The train achieved the status of becoming 'named' in the late 1950s, and was advertised in the publicity brochures as the 'Snowdonian'. The locomotive never carried a headboard, but the coaches carried the nameboards under the roof.

Extract from July 1925 LMS timetable for the Carnarvon and Llanberis line.

CARNARVON AND LLANBERIS (FOR SNOWDON.

Week days only. — **One class only.**

					S											SO		
Carnarvon .... dep.	6 45	...	7 43	...	9 30	11 13	...	12 45	2 30	3 35	4 35	...	6 15	...	8 25	...	10 0	
Pont Rug	6 50				9 40			12 50	2 41		4 40		6 20		8 30		10 11	
Peatruythallt	7 3		8 1		9 48	11 25	...	1 3	2 48		4 53		6 33		8 43		10 18	
Cwm-y-Glo	7 8		8 6		9 53			1 8	2 53		4 58		6 38		8 48		10 25	
Llanberis .... arr. (For Snowdon)	7 15	...	8 13	...	10 0	11 33	...	1 15	3 0	3 53	5 5	...	6 45	...	8 55	...	10 32	

											S		SO	S	S	SO	SO	
Llanberis (For Snowdon) .... dep.	7 18	...	8 15	...	10 45	1 25	3 5	...	3 57	5 10	6 50	...	6 55	7 30	9 0	9 5	10 38	
Cwm-y-Glo	7 22		8 20		10 49	1 29	3 9	...	4 1		6 54		6 59	7 34	9 6	9 11	10 43	
Pontrhythallt	7 27		8 25		10 54	1 34	3 14	...	4 6	5 16	6 59		7 4	7 39	9 13	9 17	10 49	
Pont Rug	7 33		8 31		11 0	1 40	3 20	...	4 12		7 5		7 10	7 45	9 21	9 26	10 58	
Carnarvon .... arr.	7 43	...	8 41	...	11 10	1 50	3 30	...	4 22	5 30	7 15	...	7 20	7 55	9 31	9 37	11 9	

S—Saturdays excepted.

SO—Saturdays only.

After World War 2 there was some limited local excursion traffic, usually for chapels and Sunday schools. One popular trip was the annual 'Crowning of the Railway Queen' at Belle Vue, Manchester, and special trains were run from Nantlle and Llanberis. Return departure from Manchester was usually about 10pm. Arrival back at Llanberis was in the small hours. Passengers were picked up at Cwm y Glo and Pontrhythallt on the outward journey and it was necessary to set down these passengers on return. This meant staffing the halts out of hours and ensuring that lighting and portable steps were on hand. These excursions were always well patronised and the trains usually consisted of four non-corridor coaches from each starting point. The two sets combined at Caernarfon and were worked forward to Bangor, where the tank engines came off, to be replaced by one of Bangor's Class 5MT 4-6-0s for the rest of the journey to Manchester. On the return journey the situation was reversed.

In the August of 1961, and for three successive Sundays, an experimental working was tried. A six-coach DMU was run from Llandudno to Llanberis, calling at Caernarfon. Due to a lack of advertising the services were poorly patronised and never repeated.

Towards the end of the line's days, the Railway Correspondence & Travel Society (RCTS) organised a special to tour the branch. Two Ivatt Class 2MT 2-6-2T engines headed a 10-coach train that traversed the Llanberis branch and then the Nantlle branch.

Freight traffic was the mainstay of the line and was sufficiently stable to ensure that the line remained open during the Depression and experienced a renaissance as the country emerged from the dark days of the 1930s.

The goods traffic continued unchanged during World War 2, supplemented by the special workings to and from Glynrhonwy.

The line remained open for goods and excursion traffic, which continued until 7 September 1964. After closure the line was dismantled back to Caernarfon No 2 signalbox; the materials were conveyed away by steam-hauled trains.

An incident occurred during World War 2 which was hushed up, but which could have had serious consequences. A consignment of bombs was booked to work away from Glynrhonwy on a special afternoon working with a Bangor Stanier 2-6-0, carrying Bangor traincrew and a Mold Junction guard. The bombs were stacked in open shock-wagons and a brake van was attached. The train stopped at Pontrhythallt and some wagon brakes were pinned down for the descent to Caernarfon. After getting the staff they moved off. By Pontrûg the driver became aware that the train was out of control and was running away despite having the tender handbrake screwed down. The short climb at Seiont brickworks served to check the speed somewhat but the momentum was such that the climb through Caernarfon Tunnel was spectacular. Fortunately, as was the practice with these trains, they were given a clear road into the goods yard where they were booked to stop for wagon examination. They thundered into the yard and eventually stopped by No 1 box. The driver immediately got down and went to the brake van where he found the guard fast asleep and the van brake blocks stone cold. The brake blocks on the engine and tender were worn thin and too dangerous to move, so the driver failed the engine and awaited a replacement. At the subsequent internal enquiry the guard tried to claim that he had been braking but the driver's and wagon examiner's evidence was too strong and he was dismissed. Had the train derailed there was the likelihood of an explosion which would have been catastrophic. It was estimated that the speed at the entrance to Caernarfon Tunnel was in excess of 40mph.

After the war the Glynrhonwy quarry pit was used to dispose of surplus bombs and explosives, and the traffic flow was reversed. By 1949 this traffic had ceased.

The last train to run was on 7 September 1964 when a Stanier 2-6-4T, No 42489, hauling a solitary van sandwiched between two brake vans, ran over the line and back.

Five months later the demolition of the line commenced, and for a while steam trundled up the branch propelling empty wagons to the railhead and removing loaded ones back to Caernarfon yard. Llandudno Junction men worked ex-LMS Class 5MT 4-6-0s, as seen on the back cover of this volume, although sometimes a BR Standard Class 4MT 4-6-0 was used. The demolition train job was attached to the daily diagram of the Caernarfon trip and shunt engine notices of 1964. Gradually, as lifting progressed, the journeys became shorter. Once Llanberis station yard had been lifted, the locomotive worked to Pontrhythallt, pulling empty wagons which were then uncoupled. The locomotive then worked light engine to the railhead where it collected the full wagons and took them back to Pontrhythallt, pulling them into the goods loop before the station. It then uncoupled and ran on to the empty wagons, which it propelled to the railhead before running back light engine to Pontrhythallt. After a brew in the station office, the brake van was attached to the rear and they worked back to Caernarfon.

Once Pontrhythallt had been lifted, the locomotive worked light engine from Caernarfon and uplifted the loaded wagons, running them back to Caernarfon yard, then propelled empty wagons to the railhead before returning light engine to Caernarfon.

Port Siding Branch

The Bangor & Carnarvon Railway opened its line to Port Dinorwic on 10 March 1852. The original station was poorly placed for the transhipping of slates and there was inadequate space for the task of loading the wagons at the station. Moreover, the slate was delivered to the quayside at a lower level than the railway, which necessitated hauling it back up to the station from the quayside at Port Dinorwic.

Despite the fact that by the mid-19th century most of the quarry's output was worked away by sea, there was a growing demand to transport roofing slate to expanding towns and cities at inland destinations and it became necessary to arrange distribution using the railway. In early 1856 it was proposed to construct a freight-only branch line off the Bangor & Carnarvon line to run to the quayside at Port Dinorwic. The line was constructed and came into use later the same year.

The connection with the main line was effected at a point about a mile east of Port Dinorwic, where Port Siding signalbox controlled the junction. The box was a tall cabin, 14ft x 12ft and 18ft 6in above rail level, the height being necessary to give the signalmen visibility over a minor road bridge over the line. It was on the down side of the Bangor & Carnarvon line.

The branch junction faced Bangor. There was no direct connection from the down line but a trailing connection with a headshunt was made off the up line. Trains working

Port Siding Signalbox
Bangor had an allocation of four ex-L&Y Aspinall Class 27 0-6-0 engines, mainly used for shunting at Bangor, Caernarfon or Menai Bridge yards. However, one daily duty was the Port Siding trip, which worked out of Menai Bridge yard to Port Dinorwic harbour, where it shunted or tripped wagons up the line from the quay to the refuge sidings at the top. Here No 52407 stands in the headshunt whilst the returning Llanberis goods uplifts some loaded wagons for Menai Bridge yard to lessen the load of the returning Port Siding trip. Note the brake van on the main line. The signalman stands on the steps of the signalbox whilst the goods guard points out something in the adjoining field. *Bill Rear*

Port Siding Signalbox
The signalbox stood on the down side of the Bangor to Caernarfon line, in the shadow of the Deiniolen road which obscured a clear view of the tracks from Treborth. The box was accordingly built to enable the signalman to sight movement over the road. The cottage in the foreground was at one time the residence of the signalman but became unused in the mid-1950s and was sold into private ownership. When the Felin Heli bypass was built, the cottage and signalbox were demolished and a three-lane road now occupies the site. *Bill Rear*

to the port had to set back over a crossover before they could access the branch. Once a port train was enclosed, main line traffic could proceed uninterrupted. The branch was worked by the 'One Engine in Steam' rule, the Sectional Appendix to the working timetables stating that the branch was designated 'No Block'.

To facilitate wagon storage, two sidings were installed at the upper level. It was the practice for trains which were delivering empty wagons to the quayside and collecting loaded mineral wagons to park the brake van at the top level in one of the sidings.

The branch line descended on a severe gradient as single track for the first quarter-mile towards the harbour, passing below the Bangor to Caernarfon road, which consisted of seven stone skew arches, known locally as Cross Bridge (which still stands on the A487). About halfway down the gradient the line formed a loop for 200yd before reverting to a single line to the bottom of the gradient where it levelled out at the quayside.

The narrow gauge incline line from Penscoins emerged from a short tunnel; the descending loaded wagons passed over a weighbridge and an office on the left of the standard gauge tracks which the narrow gauge line then crossed and kept the standard gauge line company along the quayside. The standard gauge line then doubled and followed the quayside for several hundred yards before singling, ending in a coal yard. The narrow gauge line kept it company all the way into the coal yard. Probably coal for the quarry was transhipped here, too.

It would seem that the track layout for both narrow and standard gauge lines on the quayside remained unchanged throughout the years until rail traffic ceased in 1963.

Slate was unloaded from the narrow gauge wagons and stacked on the quayside according to size. The empty wagons were then returned to the foot of the incline in front of the weighbridge office to await hauling up to Penscoins and the subsequent return to the quarry at Llanberis on the back of the transporter wagons.

Bangor men worked a daily duty, usually with an ex-Lancashire & Yorkshire Railway Class A 0-6-0 light engine off the shed to Menai Bridge yard. There they would make up the train of empties and proceed to Treborth, where they would stop to pin down brakes. At

Port Siding they would stop clear of the crossover, propel the train back over the crossover on to the up line then draw forward on to the branch. The brake van was parked at the top in one of the two storage sidings. The engine would propel the wagons down the branch onto one of the vacant roads. Usually a raft of wagons was left overnight at the quayside for loading. When a consignment of eight wagons was ready, the wagons would be taken to the top of the branch. The engine would then descend to the quayside and repeat the operation. Usually three trips up and down the branch constituted the shift and after the last trip up to the top was made the train was made up, the signalman would be informed and he would bell up Menai Bridge signalbox to release the train, which would proceed to Menai Bridge yard where the wagons would be parked, to be uplifted by the evening mineral train to Mold Junction yard. Sometimes the returning Nantlle or Llanberis goods trains would uplift some loaded wagons, leaving the Port Siding locomotive to have a reduced load back to Menai Bridge.

Unlike the Port Penrhyn duty, the Port Siding locomotive was almost always a tender engine; rarely, if ever, was a tank engine used. No engine above Power Classification 3 was permitted to travel down to the Port.

One duty sufficed Monday to Friday all year round, and engine and traincrew would complete their shift in about eight hours. The turn was classified as 'office hours', the crew booking on about 9am and finishing mid-afternoon, if they were lucky! Sometimes, if there was a build-up or a shortage of wagons in the port, a conditional path would be invoked and an afternoon trip would be made.

One similarity between the Port Siding branch and the Port Penrhyn line in the working of their branches was that both quarries had their own narrow gauge locomotives on the quayside to shunt their own wagons.

The area around the signalbox was reputed to be haunted by a ghost which was alleged to be that of a woman in her late thirties who had committed suicide by walking into the path of the Afon Wen mail shortly after World War 2. She apparently walked from alongside the signalbox, which would have been switched out at the time. The accident certainly happened but the allegations of haunting were somewhat vague until one night, Merfyn

Port Dinorwic Quay

Until the early 1960s slate was brought down to the quayside from the Dinorwic quarries at Llanberis in narrow gauge trucks. They were stored on lines on the quayside and the slates were unloaded and stacked according to size, to be loaded into the quarry's own ships or to be carried away in standard gauge wagons. The quarry had a narrow gauge steam locomotive on duty for its wagon shunting, whilst the standard gauge engines positioned wagons according to requirements of the yard master, tripping them up to the sidings at Port Siding signalbox. Here, Aspinall Class 27 0-6-0 No 52230 pulls a long raft of wagons forward whilst the Dinorwic quarry engine — No 1 — stands alongside. The date is August 1954. *H. C. Casserley*

Port Dinorwic Quay

This view was taken about 1880, showing the harbour at its zenith. The sailing ships carried roofing slate to all parts of the world. Some of the boats used belonged to the quarry owners and behind the camera was a dry dock where sailing, and later steam, ships could receive a thorough overhaul. There was even a boiler shop here, where Snowdon Mountain Railway boilers were overhauled. Note the stacks of slates in the foreground. On the left of the picture can be seen narrow gauge wagons alongside standard gauge three-plank wagons. *National Library of Wales*

Hughes, a locomotive cleaner from Bangor shed, returning to his home in Deiniolen after finishing at 10pm, saw something which affected his mind. He was discovered the following morning gibbering incomprehensibly and was taken to hospital and eventually to a psychiatric hospital for treatment. He never recovered and never worked again. He stated he had seen a headless woman on the tracks where the road crossed over the line and he repeated this statement to me years later. Whatever he saw certainly made an impression on him. He learned that I had visited Port Siding signalbox when it closed and 'recovered' the box booking book, which I still have, and made a point of contacting me to warn me of the evil nature of the place.

The signalbox has long since been demolished and the trackbed at this point is now the Felin Heli bypass.

18

Nantlle

The origin of the Nantlle Railway was a horse-drawn narrow gauge mineral line that opened for traffic in 1828 running from the slate quarries in the Nantlle valley to the quayside at Caernarfon. Subsequently, a regular service of passenger journeys was operated.

The Nantlle Tramway was absorbed into the Carnarvonshire Railway on 25 July 1867. The contractor, Thomas Savin, modified, realigned and eased gradients and curves over part of the trackbed.

A temporary northern terminus was built at Pant, about 1½ miles from Caernarfon town centre. This had the usual facilities including a run-round loop, a turntable, an engine shed and sidings. Passengers and freight were conveyed by horse-drawn coach or wagon to the Bangor & Carnarvon Railway station in Caernarfon town centre until the lines were linked up by the LNWR, when all traces of Pant station were removed.

Parts of the course of the Nantlle Tramway are discernible around Bontnewydd including some earthworks and a level crossing, and an old tunnel near Seiont Bridge, Caernarfon, can be located without too much difficulty. At Penygroes a street bears the name Tram Lane.

Route Description

The standard gauge line was sufficiently short in length to be controlled from Penygroes and the line was worked

Nantlle
The photographer John Thomas toured North Wales in the last quarter of the 19th century taking views of the rural and industrial landscape of Wales. He visited Talysarn in the Nantlle valley and took this view of the LNWR station there. It contains many interesting features worthy of note. The locomotive appears to be a 2-4-0T standing at the head of a rake of four-wheel coaches. The engine is standing on a small turntable that was removed before 1900. In the distance is a signal cabin at the throat of the station. Note, too, the narrow gauge wagons on the tranship siding ramp. These wagons of slate were brought to the station by hired-in horses from the Dorothea quarry and the course of the tramway passed through the gate on the extreme right of the station and then along a private road. Apart from the removal of the turntable and signalbox, this site was virtually unchanged until the standard gauge line ceased operating in the 1960s.
National Library of Wales

202

PENYGROES AND NANTLLE. One Class only.

Week days only.

							S										SO		SO	
Penygroes ....dep.	7 40	...	8 25	...	10 5	...	11 45	1 20	...	2 55	...	...	4 42	...	5 55	...	6 25	...	7 55	...	8 0 ... 10 25 ...
Nantlle...........arr.	7 45	.	8 30	.	10 10	.	11 50	1 25	.	3 0	.	.	4 47	.	6 0	.	6 30	.	7 40	.	8 5 . 10 28 .

								S		SO										
Nantlle...........dep.	7 25	...	...	8 10	...	9 40	...	11 25 12 0	...	1 7	...	2 35	...	4 25	...	5 35	6 5	...	7 25	...	8 20 ...
Penygroes ....arr.	7 30	.	.	8 15	.	9 45	.	11 30 12 5	.	1 12	.	2 40	.	4 30	.	5 40	6 10	.	7 30	.	8 25 .

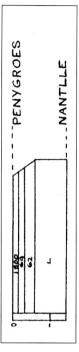

Extract from July 1925 LMS timetable for the Penygroes and Nantlle line.

Penygroes-Nantlle gradient profile.

Nantlle

Fowler Class 4F 0-6-0 No 44445 stands alongside the tranship sidings at Nantlle. Note the narrow gauge wagons alongside. It was common practice to transfer slates direct from the narrow gauge trucks into the standard gauge wagons, unlike the procedure at Port Dinorwic where slates were offloaded from the narrow gauge onto the quayside, where they were stacked according to size, then reloaded into standard gauge wagons as directed by the slate merchants. Note the rudimentary pointwork on the narrow gauge. Wagons were double flanged and a derailment was not uncommon. When it happened, the offending vehicle was usually dragged back onto the tracks at the nearest point.
W. A. Camwell

under the 'One Engine in Steam' procedure. When passenger trains were operated the train staff was square in shape and coloured white. It was controlled by the Penygroes signalman. My recollection of it is of a short length of shunter's pole, with a brass plate stamped 'Penygroes—Nantlle' at one end; it had a hole at the other end with a padlock key hanging from a piece of twine with which to unlock the crossing gates that protected an unclassified road near Penygroes.

The course of the line was single, on a rising gradient that started gently but finished on a 1 in 62 climb, levelling out at the terminus.

The station was entitled 'Nantlle', but in fact was in the village of Talysarn. The Dorothea quarries dominated the area and were the reason for the tramway and branch line being built in the first place. Today the quarries are better known as a deep diving area and notorious for fatal accidents, there being four in the first few months of 2002. At one time Nantlle station boasted a turntable and a signalbox, but both had been removed by the turn of the 20th century.

Slate from the quarries was taken by horse-drawn wagons to the tranship sidings in the station yard. The

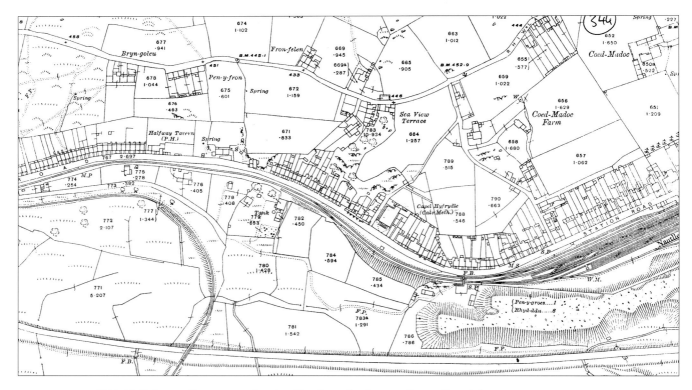

1914-18 Ordnance Survey map showing Nantlle station layout. *Crown Copyright*

tramway ran through the main street of Talysarn and was on private land which was the property of the British Transport Commission — as stated by small maroon enamel plaques mounted on posts. The quarry did not own any horses itself, but hired them in from local farmers on a daily rate. As many as six horses might be in use on any day. Each horse could pull two or three double-flanged wagons from the quarry and make several trips in the course of a shift. Dressed slates would be transferred direct into five-plank standard gauge wagons which would be removed by the daily (latterly alternate days) mineral working to Caernarfon yard. Sometimes slate would be stacked on the tranship wharf to be loaded later, depending on demand. Slate agents occupied small wooden huts at the end of the tranship wharf and generally supervised the loading. After the closure of the branch to passenger traffic, a single daily goods working sufficed and a Bangor-based locomotive — usually a Fowler Class 4F 0-6-0 — would bring in empty wagons, shunt the yard and rearrange wagons around the wharf, before making up a load for the return journey. The former passenger station building survives to this day as a community centre, whilst the greater part of the trackbed between Penygroes and Nantlle station has been incorporated into a replacement road.

Initial passenger services were handled by LNWR '17in Coal Engines' working trains of four- and six-wheel coaches. In between passenger services the engine would shunt or work slip trips with mineral wagons to Penygroes sidings where they would be uplifted by an Afon Wen to Caernarfon freight working.

Passenger services had always been poorly patronised due to the need to change trains at Penygroes. The journey was short in duration, only five minutes being allowed. Only the first down and last up trains worked from and to Caernarvon. A more suitable alternative was introduced in the form of motor or pull-and-push trains, and these came

into use from the early days of the 20th century. When steam railcars were introduced on the Dyserth branch in 1907 similar units were tried on the Nantlle branch, but were unsatisfactory mainly because of the need for a locomotive to shunt the freight yard, for which the steam railcar proved useless.

During World War 1 the LNWR experimented with a petrol-electric railcar on the Nantlle branch but it was not a success. The single-coach unit was not capable of pulling more than its own weight and was unable to shunt wagons, as was done with a locomotive working passenger services. The roof-mounted radiators of the unit were prone to freezing up in cold weather. Its duration on the Nantlle branch is unknown, but is believed to be less than a year, when the passenger service reverted to locomotive-hauled pull-push units. It was reported as having worked on the Bethesda and Llanberis branches with no more success.

Passenger traffic receipts were sufficiently poor to justify closing the line to passenger traffic from 1 January 1917 as an economy measure. It was subsequently restored on 5 May 1919. Nevertheless, buses were found to be more convenient and regular passenger traffic ceased on 8 August 1932, although occasional excursion trains continued to run until the outbreak of World War 2. Passenger trains rarely ran to and from Nantlle again, apart from the occasional private charter train run towards the end of the line's days.

Despite the Depression the traffic survived and the train ran daily until the winter of 1956 when the working was cut back to three days a week. It was largely the railwaymen's strike action in the previous summer that decimated the mineral traffic.

There was always some inward traffic, mainly coal and general stores, but generally one freight trip each way sufficed until 1957 when the daily trip was cut back to alternate days and eventually closed on 2 December 1963.

Menai Bridge, Gaerwen to Amlwch

Historical

The first proposal for a railway on Anglesey received royal assent on 9 June 1812 'for Making and Maintaining a Railway, from Penrhynmawr, in the Parish of Llanfihangel Esceifiog, to Redwharf, in the Parish of Llanbedrgoch, in the County of Anglesey; and also a Dock in the Parish of Llanbedrgoch aforesaid'. The Act was couched in the usual terminology of the day and specified that the line was proposed for the conveyance of coal, lime, limestone and other products. Motive power was not specified but at this early date can be assumed to be horse worked. The project came to naught.

The Anglesey Central Railway (ACR) was promoted as a result of a suggestion put forward by William Dew, an estate agent of Llangefni, at a meeting held on 5 July 1858. It, too, failed to get local support.

Eventually the company was incorporated by an Act of Parliament and received royal assent on 13 July 1863. This authorised the construction of a line from Gaerwen station on the Chester & Holyhead Railway, to the port of Amlwch on the north coast of the island. A further Act of 13 May 1864 authorised a deviation of three miles at Gaerwen, the work to be completed within five years.

The usual ceremony of cutting the first sod was performed by the wife of the deputy chairman in a field off the line of the track near Llangefni on 11 September 1863.

Menai Bridge
Engines working Amlwch branch trains normally worked out of Bangor bunker-first, as required by local operating instructions, although it was not a traffic requirement, more a preference of traincrews. Here Ivatt Class 2MT 2-6-2T No 41221 pauses at the down main platform at Menai Bridge with the 12.40pm Bangor to Amlwch working on 10 May 1949. *E. S. Russell*

Britannia Bridge
In LNWR days the normal stock used on passenger trains on the branch was six-wheeled vehicles in made-up sets of five vehicles. Motive power was invariably 2-4-2T engines with 5ft 6in diameter wheels. Here No 853, which was allocated to Bangor but out-stationed at Amlwch, emerges from the Britannia tubular bridge on 18 July 1921, heading for Bangor. Note the stone lions guarding the tunnel and the small hut between the tracks, with an attendant on duty at all times in case of an accident in the tubes. The lions are now obscured beneath the road deck, visible only from the railway. *L. J. Thompson*

By October 1864 the line was almost completed as far as Llangefni, at which point the LNWR engineer was authorised to form the junction with the main line at Gaerwen, at the Anglesey Central Railway's expense. The LNWR approved 'temporary arrangements at Gaerwen station', and provided some stock.

The first part of the single line was opened for freight traffic to a temporary station at Llangefni on 16 December 1864. The line was inspected in February 1865 and on 8 March 1865 was passed as suitable for passenger traffic. A service of trains commenced four days later.

Money ran short and it became necessary to raise more capital before further work was undertaken. On 26 January 1866 Captain Rich returned to inspect a further 3½ miles of line to Llanerchymedd. On the same date the temporary station at Llangefni was replaced by the permanent one, half a mile further on, and sidings were installed at both places.

An intermediate station between Llangefni and Llanerchymedd, at Llangwyllog, was listed by the following April.

The final 6¾ miles of single track line to Amlwch, with sidings and one intermediate station at Rhosgoch, was finally opened to passenger traffic throughout on 3 June 1867.

The LNWR took possession of the line on 1 July 1876. Its report indicated that the track needed replacement almost throughout and the stations were in a dirty state.

Developments by the new owners included the provision of a loop line and station building improvements at Llangefni in 1877, and the provision of a refuge siding at Llanerchymedd. A locomotive shed and additional sidings were installed at Amlwch during the following year. In 1882 new station buildings were provided at Holland Arms, Llangwyllog and Rhosgoch, whilst a new waiting shed, waiting room and lamp room, together with an extension to the platform, were provided at Amlwch at some time during the period 1883/4.

The platforms at Llangefni were extended in 1887 and at Holland Arms, Llangwyllog and Rhosgoch in 1890. In

1914 Llangwyllog received a new passing loop and an up platform.

The decline in traffic, particularly after World War 1, saw the LMS close Amlwch shed on 14 September 1931, the work transferring to Bangor. The shed building was demolished some time before 1939.

In October 1952 developments by the Associated Octel Co Ltd at Amlwch Port saw a new short private standard gauge light railway constructed and commissioned from its works which connected to the Anglesey Central Railway, approximately level with the site of the steam shed in Amlwch.

Another private siding was constructed in 1976, forming a trailing connection with the line between Rhosgoch and Amlwch, to serve an oil tank farm for the Shell company. This facility was short-lived and the site was cleared after a comparatively brief life. The rail connection was maintained and, although out of use, is still in place.

Description of the Line

Gaerwen to Amlwch

The line is 17¾ miles in length from the junction at Gaerwen and is single track throughout. Despite the illusion that Anglesey is flat, the line has several gradients of varying degrees of severity over its length. Initially the line was worked with train staff and ticket, replaced by the electric train staff which was brought into use on the line on 28 January 1894.

At first the sections remained the same, but despite greater flexibility than formerly, passenger trains were still unable to cross one another. No signalboxes were erected on the branch line. Open-lever frames were installed at the token exchange points.

New single-storey station buildings were provided in 1882 at Holland Arms, Llangwyllog and Rhosgoch. They were all similar in appearance, constructed of red brick, with bands of white brick above, below and at mid-window height unlike anything else designed by the LNWR. The

Gaerwen

Some Amlwch trains started from Gaerwen and used the bay line which gave cross-platform facilities with trains on the main up line. The station building was on this side, a large red-brick two-storey structure. The main line down platform was spartan by comparison and passengers wishing to travel towards Holyhead had to cross the line either by a footbridge at the Bangor end or over the minor road and the level crossing. The goods yard was off the Amlwch line and, consequently, any freight for the yard had to access the branch first. It was the practice to assemble the second Amlwch goods in the bay platform, as seen here. In May 1949 nearly-new Ivatt Class 2MT 2-6-2T No 41222 has made up a short train and is presumably waiting for a path. The load consists of a privately owned wagon, two three-plank wagons containing hay stackers, and a brake van. Note the simple flower beds. Beyond the footbridge can be seen Gaerwen No 1 signalbox which controls the level crossing, still in situ today. *E. S. Russell*

structures at Llangefni, Llanerchymedd and Amlwch were individually designed and had little similarity to each other, perhaps reflecting the fact that they represented each phase of constructing the line.

When the line lost its passenger services on 4 December 1964 all passing loops were removed.

Gaerwen

Gaerwen station was 6¼ miles from Bangor and opened to traffic in January 1849. The station was some distance away from the village.

The main station building was a two-storey structure built of red brick, located on the main line up side with cross-platform facilities for the branch line which terminated in a bay. There were short canopies over part of each platform which gave some measure of protection. Facilities included a booking hall and an office, a general waiting room, a ladies' waiting room, a parcels office, a porters' room and toilets. Access was off the roadway through the yard. The

bay platform had a short run-round loop. The headshunt ended in stops and had adjoining cattle pens with access into the goods yard.

In the goods yard were three sidings, one of which was used by local coal merchants. There was a spirit store and an agricultural warehouse on site. The entrance to the yard was gated, with a weigh machine and an office.

The branch line was accessed from the main line by a double junction which enabled trains to and from Bangor to work through. Most branch passenger trains commenced from or terminated at the bay platform at Gaerwen.

Once clear of the platform, the branch line opened into a loop which was used for running round. The loop still remains to this day.

At Gaerwen access to the branch was controlled from No 2 signalbox located at the Holyhead end of the station, which survived until 1967. Today (2002), the old No 1 signal cabin works the connection to the Amlwch line which is operated as a long siding but is used mainly to

Holland Arms

Until the advent of the Ivatt Class 2MT 2-6-2Ts after nationalisation, the normal motive power on the Amlwch branch was an LNWR 2-4-2T with 5ft 6in driving wheels, and two non-corridor coaches. Here No 6643 pauses at the station with a train for Bangor. Note that the starter for the line to Llangefni is 'off'; this is misleading, because the station was switched out with the route set permanently for Llangefni and the train staff was for the Gaerwen to Llangefni section. The track in the foreground was the former Red Wharf Bay platform line that by the date of this photograph (27 May 1947) was used for storage only and would be lifted when the Red Wharf Bay line was taken up in 1953. *W. A. Camwell*

1914-18 Ordnance Survey map showing Holland Arms Junction layout. *Crown Copyright*

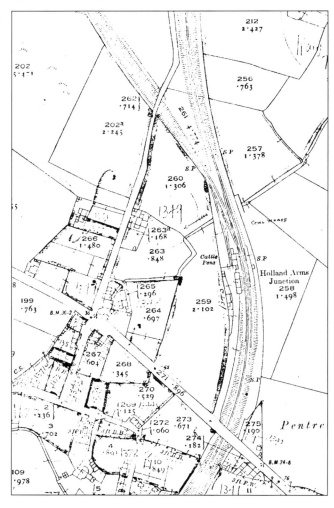

protect the level crossing. The former up platform survives devoid of buildings, although the main line platform edging has been removed. The track in the Amlwch bay line is still intact. Immediately on leaving the station, after two 20-chain curves, the line commences to climb at 1 in 116 for half a mile where it levels off and then falls for a quarter of a mile at 1 in 214 before climbing again at 1 in 112. The gradient levels out at Milepost 1 before falling at 1 in 82/62, easing to 1 in 144 to Holland Arms.

Holland Arms

Holland Arms station was 2¼ miles from Gaerwen and was in the section between Gaerwen and Llangefni. It opened to traffic on 12 March 1865. Initial facilities consisted of a single platform on the down side with a wooden structure that served as a waiting room and a booking office. The LNWR replaced this with a brick-built structure in 1882, similar in design to Llangwyllog and Rhosgoch. It had a small goods yard on the down side beyond the passenger platform.

When the Red Wharf Bay line was built a connection was made with the Amlwch line at Holland Arms and the track layout at the station was modified to accommodate the extra traffic. A line was put in as a spur off the Red Wharf Bay line to serve a passenger platform, specifically for Red Wharf Bay trains. There was no provision for passenger trains to cross here. Passengers for the Red Wharf Bay line were obliged to access the new platform by crossing the tracks at the foot of the ramp at the Llangefni end.

The section between Gaerwen and Llangefni had to be split at Holland Arms to accommodate the trains on the Red Wharf Bay line. It was also desirable to switch out Holland Arms when necessary. The LNWR signalling engineers

Llangefni
The station complex was in a hollow and the part of the line facing the platform was hacked out of rock. A loop line was installed but clearance was tight and it was deemed that no passenger train could occupy the down side loop, although a passenger train could cross a goods train here. The main station passenger platform and buildings were on the up side and comprised a house, station offices and a single platform, which are still there. The goods yard was behind the station front, one side of which bounded the river. An agricultural market was held here every week and the traffic that emanated from here justified a freight train from Menai Bridge yard, purely serving the market. At times of seasonal livestock trains, it was commonplace to have two more trains standing by at Menai Bridge yard ready to make a trip to Llangefni to work away livestock. The single line resumed at the entrance to the goods yard and skirted a rocky bluff. The area is known as 'The Dingle' and a footpath traversed it. *G. H. Platt*

modified equipment to enable the switching in and out facility to be made.

At Holland Arms, a lever frame was mounted flush with the platform, between the main station building and a small wooden goods shed.

The closure of the Red Wharf Bay branch to all traffic in 1950 and the decision to dismantle the line in 1952 resulted in the closure of Holland Arms station to all traffic on 4 August 1952, by which time passenger traffic from the station had all but disappeared. Only deliveries of domestic coal to the local coal merchant made use of the yard. The passenger platform was removed almost immediately after the lifting of the Red Wharf Bay branch was completed in 1953, when the track was realigned through the station and sidings taken up.

Today the station building survives in private hands, owned by a local coal merchant who uses the yard to store his stock and vehicles.

The Amlwch line resumes falling at 1 in 66 for a quarter of a mile before levelling out. There then follows a brief climb for about 200yd before it levels out again for a quarter of a mile. The line then climbs to Llangefni, the first terminus on the branch.

Llangefni
The first station at Llangefni was located a short distance from the present station. It came into use on 26 January 1866.

The present site is located at the northern end of the town but in a relatively convenient position. The single platform is on the up side and contains a stone-built two-storey structure which included the stationmaster's house. Adjoining the house was a single-storey structure that contained a porters' room, a booking office, a booking hall, a general waiting room, a ladies' waiting room, a coal store and a lamp room. A raised open plinth held a standard LNWR 16-lever frame which controlled the loop points, access to the goods yard and signals. The single-line token equipment instruments were located in the station office. The platform faced a rocky outcrop and space was very

Llangefni

It was a fact that the LNWR '17in Coal Engines' had mediocre brakes but three brake vans on a four-vehicle goods was being too cautious! Here LMS Class 2F 0-6-0 No 8159 approaches bridge No 18 over Afon Cefni, overlooked by the public footpath in 'The Dingle'. It is likely that the extra brake vans were being worked one afternoon in late 1937 to Llangefni for the livestock specials needed after the auction of livestock at the market in the goods yard. *G. H. Platt*

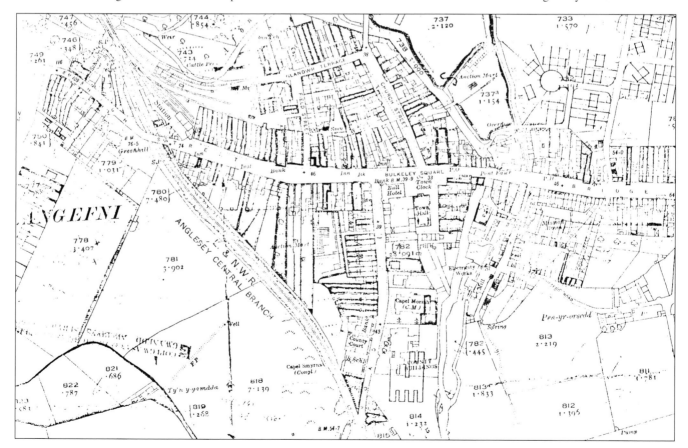

1914-18 Ordnance Survey map showing Llangefni station layout. *Crown Copyright*

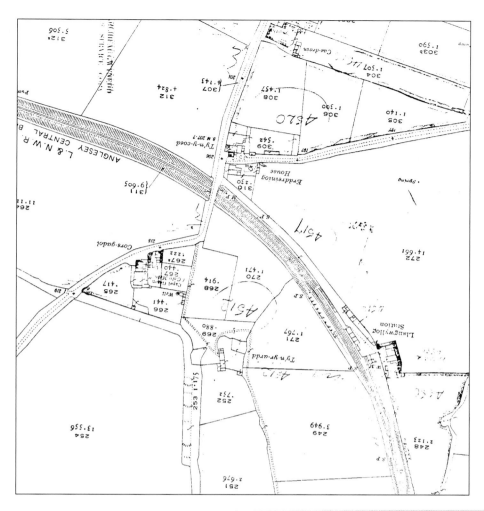

1914-18 Ordnance Survey map
showing Llangwyllog station layout.
Crown Copyright

Llangwyllog

Passenger trains were authorised to
cross another passenger train only at
Llangwyllog, which was
approximately halfway between
Gaerwen and Amlwch. The low
density of trains on the branch meant
that this rarely happened more than a
couple of times a day, although it was
commonplace to see a passenger cross
a freight working here or at other staff
token points along the line. Here
Bangor's Ivatt Class 2MT 2-6-2T
No 41200 pauses at the up platform
whilst an Amlwch-bound train waits.
The porter-signalman hands the long
staff for the section to Llangefni to
the fireman of the Bangor train.
W. A. Camwell

Llanerchymedd

This station was the second temporary terminus of the Anglesey Central Railway until sufficient funds were raised to enable the railway to complete the line to its stated destination. The single-storey brick station building was a modest affair and its one platform was hemmed in by the rocky outcrop facing it, making a run-round loop here impossible. The loop was located off the platform at the Llangefni end, and was passed only for goods trains to use or light engines to run round coaching stock left on the main line. When the line was extended to Amlwch the platform was lengthened. The new section was at a higher level than the original, giving a hump effect. Here an unidentified Ivatt 2-6-2T stands at the platform with a two-coach working for Amlwch. Note the large goods shed. The freight traffic provided most of the station's income and at one time two of the LMS country lorry services were based here. *W. A. Camwell*

limited. A short passing loop was provided on the down side but clearances were such that two passenger trains were not permitted to cross here.

The goods yard was on the up side behind the station buildings. There was a goods shed with one siding terminating in the shed and two sidings outside. Two more lines extended back into the yard, one serving as a coal siding, the other serving cattle pens. There was a stable in the yard, a general store, a weigh machine and an office which completed the inventory. The density of traffic from the yard was such that, in addition to the trains to and from Amlwch, there was a daily freight working from and to Menai Bridge yard which ran every weekday until general freight traffic was withdrawn. The yard adjoined a livestock market and whenever the market was in business, it was normal practice to have an engine and some cattle trucks standing by to carry livestock away after the auction. Peak periods were the spring and autumn sheep and cattle fairs. It was not unknown for three special trains to operate from Llangefni yard on these days in addition to the three regular pick-up goods that normally worked the line.

After the line closed to all but the Octel traffic the goods yard was cleared; Llangefni station house was sold off but still stands, privately owned. The station offices were also sold off and are now owned by Anglesey County Council. On leaving the station the climb then resumes at 1 in 850. It passes through a wooded gorge known as 'The Dingle' where the railway curves around the rocky outcrops, crossing the Afon Cefni several times. The gradient increases to 1 in 67, extending over a mile, before another change of grade to 1 in 147, falling.

Llangwyllog

Llangwyllog station was 7 miles from Gaerwen. It came into being some time after the Anglesey Central Railway line opened to Llanerchymedd. The station was located just over the crest of the 1 in 67 gradient on a falling gradient of 1 in 147 and served a small scattered community. Its establishment was probably due to the fact that it was halfway across Anglesey. Very little passenger traffic was generated from the station.

The station building was of the same design used at Holland Arms and Rhosgoch. It was a single-storey construction on the down side and contained the usual facilities. A goods shed stood on the down platform a short distance from the main station building. The stationmaster had a house on the site but away from the platform on the private access road.

In 1914 a loop was installed at Llangwyllog and the station became a staff token exchange point. The passing loop commenced in a cutting south of the station and extended for about 800ft.

At the Gaerwen end of the platform a raised brick plinth housed an open LNWR frame of 18 levers which controlled the loop points, access to the goods siding on the down side beyond the platform and the signals.

On the up platform a small wooden shed containing rudimentary heating sufficed as a waiting shelter. Passengers crossed the line via a barrow crossing at the southern end.

The goods yard siding ended in a carriage loading ramp; alongside were cattle pens. A local coal merchant had yard space and unloaded his wagons nearer the

Llanerchymedd
The 12.54pm Saturdays Only Amlwch to Bangor working stands at the platform headed by Ivatt Class 2MT 2-6-2T No 41234 in 1961. A member of the station staff talks with the traincrew, possibly exchanging the train staff. A member of the goods yard staff heads down the ramp, shunter's pole in hand, towards the yard. Between the station building and the station nameboard can be seen the small eight-lever frame which controlled the signals. The points controlling the loop were worked from small two-lever frames at the trackside, which were locked by the train staff. *J. S. Gilks*

connection with the main line. The yard contained a weigh machine and office.

Llangwyllog station was sold on closure and is privately owned. The building is now protected from the track by a block wall.

On leaving the station for Llanerchymedd the line falls for about half a mile before resuming the climb to the summit of the line (about 10¼ miles from Gaerwen). After a short stretch on the level, the line then falls for nearly three miles at varying gradients of 1 in 100 to 1 in 96, where the climbing resumes. At 11 miles from Gaerwen the line runs into Llanerchymedd.

Llanerchymedd

Llanerchymedd station was located on a falling gradient of 1 in 100, although the gradient was eased to 1 in 433 through the station. It was 11 miles from Gaerwen. The station was the second temporary terminus of the Anglesey Central Railway. This section of the line was built at a time of financial stringency, reflected in the modest design of station building which was a single-storey red brick structure. The stationmaster had a detached house in the yard.

The platform was on the up side, hemmed in by a rocky outcrop. Trains were unable to cross at the platform, so locomotives had to propel the stock back out of the platform to access a loop in order to run round. When the extension to Amlwch was completed the platform was extended, the line passing under a minor road bridge. There was a flight of steps from the road down to the station but it was little used, the public preferring to walk through the yard.

The station was located in the centre of the village and was well patronised throughout its existence. The main station building contained the usual offices. A 10-lever open frame flush with the platform controlled the loop and signals. A corrugated iron goods shed housed smalls traffic offloaded onto the platform. Llanerchymedd was a staff token exchange station. The instruments for both sections were in the station office.

The station yard contained three sidings. No 1 terminated in front of the larger goods shed, whilst siding No 2 passed through it, terminating near the yard entrance. This section was used by the local coal merchant. No 3 siding served an oil tank, an agricultural feedstuff store and some cattle

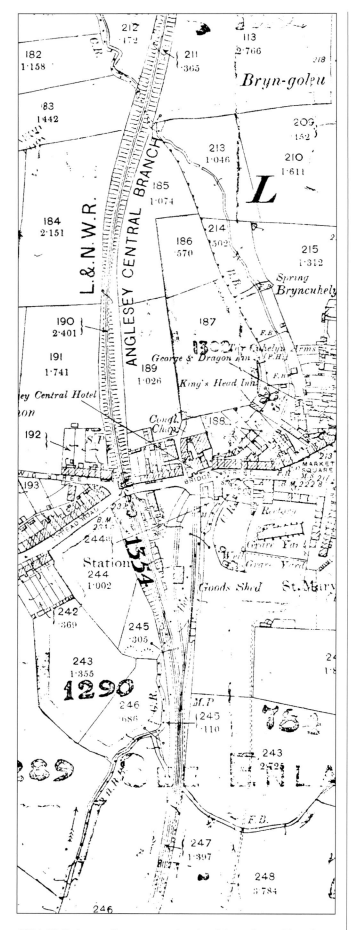

1914-18 Ordnance Survey map showing Llanerchymedd station layout. *Crown Copyright*

pens. The goods yard was gated at the approach and contained a weigh machine and an office.

When the line closed to passenger and freight services in 1964 the goods yard and loop lines were uplifted. The subsidiary store rooms, other buildings and the main goods shed were demolished. The main building was in fair shape and retained but over the years suffered the attentions of local vandals. The local community council decided that the site had potential for development as a small industrial estate and purchased the land and all that remained on it. Today, the station building survives but is derelict. The former agricultural store still stands but is in poor shape. The proposed industrial units never materialised and the site is fenced off.

On leaving the station the line passes under the B5112 road and continues to fall at 1 in 87/192/122 for two miles where it levels out and recommences climbing at 1 in 119/95 for about 1½ miles to Rhosgoch.

Rhosgoch

Rhosgoch station was 14½ miles from Gaerwen and an intermediate halt on the Llanerchymedd to Amlwch section. The station approach was off the public road down a long track. The stationmaster had a house at the station approach.

The platform was on the down side in a shallow cutting. When first opened, the station building was of an unspecified wooden type, but the LNWR replaced it with its single-storey design that had been used elsewhere. A wooden hut at the Gaerwen end of the platform contained a tranship goods shed.

There was a small goods yard beyond the platform which contained two sidings off the main line, access to the yard being controlled by the train staff which unlocked a small two-lever frame. No 1 siding passed through a stone-built goods shed and terminated in a carriage landing platform. No 2 siding had cattle pens adjoining and was used as a coal siding. The station yard, which was gated, contained a weigh machine and an office.

After the line closed to passenger and general freight traffic in 1964 the station building was sold off and is now in private hands. The sidings were uplifted and the goods shed demolished.

About half a mile beyond the station a private siding on the down side was installed to serve an oil tank farm for the Shell petroleum company. The ½-mile-long siding connected with the main line via a trailing connection, access being controlled by the train staff. The siding remains, out of use.

On leaving the siding connection the line descends with long stretches at 1 in 86 and 1 in 77, before levelling out at Amlwch.

Amlwch

Amlwch station was 17¾ miles from Gaerwen. Facilities here were more extensive than at other stations on the line. The line ran into the complex under a minor road bridge. Immediately beyond the bridge on the down side was a single-road brick-built locomotive shed which was demolished in about 1938. Above part of the roof, a water tank was mounted which, however, survived until the end of steam.

The goods yard was also on the down side and contained cattle pens and a brick-built warehouse. There were three

sidings in the yard. No 1 siding passed through the goods
shed and terminated in buffer stops. No 2 siding passed
outside the goods shed and terminated at stops in front of a
store. A 3-ton hand crane stood between No 1 and No 2
sidings. No 3 siding terminated across the goods platform
level with the stops on No 2 siding.

The passenger platform was on the up side, served by a
single track and ending in a loading platform. In 1883/4
Amlwch station was extended, and a canopy provided over
the platform. There was a run-round facility similar in
layout to that at Llanerchymedd, necessitating locomotives
propelling their stock out of the platform in order to run
round. At one time a narrow ticket platform stood on the
loop, in typical LNWR practice, but this fell out of use in
the 1930s.

The loop points and main line signals were controlled
from a 15-lever frame which was located a short distance
from the platform between the ramp and the ticket platform.
For the greater part of its life the frame was open to the
elements although just after nationalisation it was enclosed
in a wooden structure. This was replaced by a brick-built
cabin of non-standard design.

In 1954 a private railway line was installed, linking the
branch with Associated Octel chemical works being built at
Amlwch Port, some half a mile away. The private railway
made a connection opposite the water tank. The main line
was protected by trap points. The private line opened out
into an interchange point, a fan of four lines that converged
before crossing over Queen Street in the town. The line
continued over some scrubland, crossing over another
minor road on the level. Two more level crossings were
effected over minor roads before the works was reached. A
headshunt extended back from the fan by the station,
terminating in buffer stops parallel to the main line.

Until the closure of the branch to passenger traffic in
1964 the Octel tanks traffic was worked to the interchange
sidings by British Railways locomotives. Steam engines
were not allowed into the works, but Associated Octel had
two industrial diesel shunting engines that tripped the
wagons between the sidings and the works. When steam

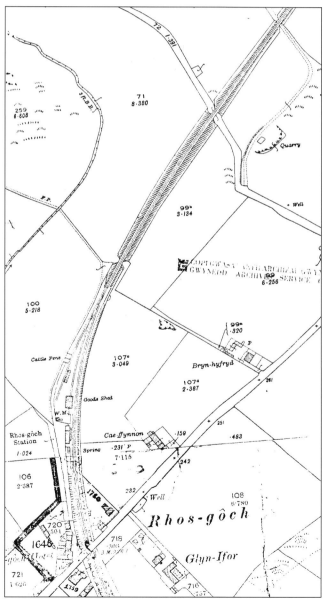

Amlwch

BR Standard Class 2MT 2-6-2T No 84001 pulls away from Amlwch with the 12.45pm Saturdays Only working to Bangor on 10 August 1963. In this last summer of passenger services on the line, the DMUs had migrated to other areas, where the receipts were better, leaving this rural branch line in the hands of pull-push workings. The engine was attached to Llandudno Junction at the time, but was worked by Bangor men. Visible in the yard in front of the goods shed, is an Ivatt tank of the same wheel arrangement as No 84001 which had worked the daily freight trip from Menai Bridge yard and was booked to shunt the yard here. In the foreground can be seen the shunting neck and four lines belonging to the Associated Octel Co. After the passenger traffic ceased, British Railways diesel locomotives were authorised to work over the private line down into the works complex, whereas formerly the works shunter worked the tank wagons between the works and the loop. Consequently, the headshunt and two of the looplines were taken out. The track into the station and goods yard was also removed about this time and the station building was demolished when the town's bypass road was constructed. *T. B. Owen*

Amlwch
Riddles Class 2MT 2-6-2T No 84003 working a two-coach pull-push set pulls out of the platform one Saturday afternoon in 1964 and heads for the water tank through the loop line whilst on layover at Amlwch. It was deemed easier to take the coaches rather than go through the rigmarole of uncoupling and recoupling at the platform. In the yard Ivatt Class 2MT No 41234 shunts the warehouse road. There are a few souls on the platform, probably wondering about this bizarre manoeuvre. Just behind the up starter can be seen the enclosed lever frame. For most of the line's existence this frame was open to the elements. At one time a ticket platform stood where the point rodding lies, but this fell out of use in the 1930s and was demolished just before World War 2.
Norman Kneale

was discontinued, British Railways diesel locomotives were authorised to work the tanks down to the works. The headshunt and two lines were taken out, leaving a single line with one passing loop. After closure in 1964 the track into the station and yard was lifted and the main line cut back to the connection with Associated Octel's private line. Eventually the station building was demolished, the site being truncated by the town bypass, although the former goods shed survives in private hands.

In 1992 Isle of Anglesey Railways Ltd chartered a DMU on four occasions to run trains to a temporary platform at Amlwch as a feasibility exercise. On three occasions the DMU made two trips daily from Bangor, and on August bank holiday Monday ran a special from and to Chester. Loadings were very successful and there was an optimism that the line could be restored to passenger use. In 1993 the rail service to the Octel works was terminated and the traffic transferred to road. Apart from a couple of special excursions, the last one being in February 1994, the line has seen no use. The private line to Associated Octel remains out of use but connected to the branch line. An electronic barrier protecting the bypass road is still in situ but out of use, with the track fenced off on both sides. The crossing over the main street is also out of use, and although the track is still in position to the works, it is very much overgrown. At the works the tracks have been covered over and the works diesel engines isolated.

The project to develop the line as a preservation project ran into difficulties in 1995 and no progress has been made.

Train Working

Traincrew working over the branch was shared between Bangor and Amlwch sheds, until the latter closed in 1931 when all the work was transferred to Bangor. When Bangor shed itself closed in 1965, the Associated Octel traffic was worked from Llandudno Junction shed.

Although the line possessed many sharp radius curves, with several bridges over and under the line, the restrictions on motive power size were governed by traffic needs rather than weight limitations. Apart from the earliest days, and until the advent of the LMS Ivatt design of light 2-6-2T, passenger traffic was in the hands of LNWR locomotives. Freight workings were usually hauled by LNWR 0-6-0 tender engines, worked tender-first out of Bangor.

In LMS days L&Y-design 2-4-2T engines in power Class 3 were tried on the branch but were deemed unsatisfactory. From 1948 the Ivatt design Class 2MT 2-6-2T engines became the regular motive power for both passenger and freight workings over the branch.

In May 1953, an ACV three-car diesel railcar set spent a month on the branch, as part of an assessment of the unit's capabilities. It arrived at Bangor on Friday 15 May at 12.18pm and was put to work immediately. Although this unit was experimental, it was the precursor of things to come. Three years later most of the steam-operated services were taken over by Derby 'Lightweight' two-coach units, which were an instant success.

In the late 1950s and early 1960s, Ivatt and later BR Standard Class 2 2-6-0 tender engines appeared on the freight workings. The reason given for this change was that the modification of the freight engine diagrams increased the time away from adequate water supplies and the powers-that-be erred on the side of caution.

One anomaly, brought about by the shortage of DMUs, was the return to steam-hauled two-coach push-pull sets hauled by BR Standard Class 2MT 2-6-2T locomotives, usually Nos 84003 or 84009, for the summer of 1963, reverting to DMU operation in the winter. The same thing happened in the summer of 1964, with DMUs working the final months of passenger services over the branch.

In 1964 platform clearance trials were undertaken with Stanier Class 4MT 2-6-4T No 42606 which, having proved satisfactory, enabled this type and Class 5 4-6-0 locomotives to work all the freight traffic over the line. When steam was replaced by diesel locomotives, a new

agreement was reached and BR locomotives worked the extra ¼ mile into the Octel works. This practice then persisted until the rail traffic finally ceased in 1994.

A couple of anecdotes connected with the Amlwch branch are worthy of mention. In 1952, during the time of rationing, a certain fireman at Bangor who was attached to No 3 Link had heard various accounts about 'footplate cooking' on the shovel, and declared his intention to perform and show off his culinary skills. He persuaded his wife to let him have bacon, a sausage, a slice of bread and eggs (which were still on ration) together with some tomatoes. It was much talked about at the shed and there was some scepticism about his abilities which was really a wind-up.

The duty worked was the 12.45pm Bangor to Amlwch and return, followed by the 4.4pm Afon Wen. The locomotive was No 41200.

At Amlwch there was some standing time and after propelling the stock back to the loop, the engine ran round and through to the former shed road and took water. After that was done, the fire was cleaned and everything was ready. Our hero washed the shovel with the pet pipe and wiped it with a none-too-clean sweat-rag. In time-honoured tradition he put the rasher of bacon and held it into the fire for a second to get the fat on the shovel, then added the sausage, egg, tomato and bread. All was well until his mate accidentally [?] opened the blower . . !

The language that followed would make a docker blush, even now. Parentage and pedigree were called into question and a normally placid man became a morose evil assassin. Dinner was gone. What could he eat, and with another seven hours to go?

The driver backed No 41200 on to the stock and propelled back into the platform. The guard had informed the platform staff of the culinary activities that should have taken place and had also heard raised voices. Guard and porter advanced on the footplate. Tact was not the guard's strong point.

'Enjoy your meal?' he enquired.

The guard was given chapter and verse about what had happened and told a few facts about the driver which he did not know. He turned pale on hearing such a tirade, and so rude, too, whilst a porter nearby listened intently and grinned broadly. He sped down the platform and picked up the circuit telephone. The news passed down the line with the speed of lightning and the world knew.

A sullen, sulky fireman, pointedly ignoring his driver, attended to his duties. At Llangefni an unwise stationmaster made a reference and then he, too, looked shocked at the response.

At Gaerwen, a chance remark by the signalman at No 2 box about 'hot meals' evoked a mouthful that was not edible but clearly for consumption and distribution. The fireman had lost his rag completely.

At Bangor the train pulled into the up passenger loop to discharge passengers then moved the stock across to the down-side goods loop where he hooked off. The engine pulled forward and set back into the yard in a deafening silence. The fire was cleaned and water taken and not a word passed between driver and fireman. Only dirty looks. They pulled forward to the neck and set back onto a four-coach set on the down passenger loop and awaited time.

Firstly, there was a sound of 'oink, oink', followed by a clucking noise. The shed choir was gathered somewhere, hidden but audible. There were black looks all round. Oaths and expletives emerged from the cab. The driver escaped to somewhere out of range. The fireman contemplated how unwise he had been to even contemplate cooking. He was having a really bad day. Another five hours to go, too, and a tummy rumbling like a thunderstorm in Nantlle Vale. The driver returned but kept himself to himself. After all, he had his pipe and his snap.

Now, the said fireman's wife had taken herself out for the day to Bangor for some shopping and was returning back to Penygroes on this very working. She wandered up to the footplate and enquired, innocently and pleasantly, as to how the meal had gone. It was the last straw. The fireman

Extract from July 1925 LMS timetable for the Gaerwen and Amlwch line.

GAERWEN AND AMLWCH.
Week days only.

			B		B			B						B		B					B		B	B			
Gaerwen ....dep.	5 20	...	8 50	9 20	10 30	...	11 26	...	12 55		1 14	1 30	2 55	3 12	...	4 5	...	5 8	5 40	6 10	7 25	9 15	Runs 10 minutes later on Tuesdays until September 8th
Holland Arms ...... ,,			8 55	9 24	10 35	...	11 31	12 50	1 0		1 19	1 37	3 0	3 17		4 10		5 13	5 45	6 15	7 30	9 19	
Llangefni .... ,,	5 37	...	9 1	9 29	10 41	...	11 37	12 55	1 5		1 25		3 5			4 16		5 50				9 25	
Llangwyllog .... ,,				9 39		...	11 46		1 17				3 14			4 25			5 58			9 34	
Llanerchymedd ... ,,	6 5	...		9 47		...	11 55		1 27				3 22			4 33			6 7			9 43	
Rhosgoch .... ,,	6 22	...		9 56		...	12 4		1 35				3 30			4 42			6 16			9 49	
Amlwch ....arr.	6 35	...		10 5		...	12 13		1 44				3 39			4 51			6 25			9 58	

(Thurs. only columns: 12 50, 12 55; Thursdays excepted: 1 14, 1 19, 1 25; Thurs. only: 1 30, 1 37)

thought she had been informed by others of the disaster and was provoking, so he told her. He said things to her which even in today's liberal climate would have been grounds for divorce. She stormed off and slammed the carriage door in her anger. The fireman realised he had gone too far, this time.

The driver then advised him to go and make his peace with 'she who must be obeyed' for the sake of humanity and probably his own survival. He went into the carriage after her and they were left in peace until departure time. When he returned he was very, very subdued.

Departure time came and they whistled off, sounding for the Caernarfon line as they approached Menai Bridge. They stopped at Menai Bridge and again at Port Dinorwic. Hunger had started to bite and he was fed up and miserable. There was a short wait at Caernarfon and the driver disappeared. The fireman's wife came up to the engine and a few words were exchanged, then she, too, went off, although both she and the driver were back in time for departure. Will Rees arrived from No 2 box with the train staff and they were away again. The regulator was opened briefly and the train lumbered out of the platform and over the scissors crossover, coasting down the 1 in 47, screeching round the check-railed curves under Turf Square, then into Caernarvon Tunnel. On emerging, the driver opened the regulator and the fireman bent his back again. The climb up to Dinas was steady and no speed records were broken, and no word passed between driver and fireman.

At Dinas the peg was off and the driver slowed for entry into the loop. The procession trundled through the platform at the regulation 10mph and the train staff was exchanged for the key token on the trot. A brief halt was made at Llanwnda where no one got off and no one got on.

At Groeslon they pulled up at the platform and the key token was exchanged for the train staff to Penygroes. More misery. More empty stomach. The fireman was wondering just who else would make his life hell about his misfortune.

The guard waved the green flag and they were off, climbing up to Penygroes, where the fireman's wife got off and gave a wave, so domestic relations were back to a manageable level. But what was this? A porter came up to the footplate with two bags of hot chips. Salvation. What bliss! The rest of the run to Afon Wen and return to Bangor was relatively peaceful. The fireman disposed of the engine then got on his motor cycle and phut-phutted off into the distance.

He was under the impression that his wife had phoned up to Penygroes station from Caernarfon and ordered the chips from a nearby chip shop. He duly thanked her when he got home and she, wise woman, said nothing. But it was not she who had come to the rescue.

To that fireman it will come as a great surprise, even now, for him to learn that it was not she but his driver who had ordered the chips and moreover had paid for them. He had had, it would seem, a pang of conscience about what had happened, but was not going to admit it, and had informed the wife what had really happened.

As far as I know, though, the fireman never attempted footplate cooking again!

Another incident is worth setting down. At the public inquiry into the proposal to close the Gaerwen to Amlwch line to traffic in 1964, the panel was sitting in Amlwch and hearing arguments for retention of the line, but things were not going well and rumour had it that the inspector had decided that closure would happen.

Towards the end of the hearing a little old woman clutching a long parcel came up to the inspector and asked him whether the line was going to close. He indicated that it was likely, whereupon she handed him the parcel, turned tail and left.

Mystified he opened it, which was quite heavy, and found inside a Webb & Thompson long train staff for the section Amlwch to Llanerchymedd. There was no explanation. No one could offer any reason how she came to possess such a thing and, more importantly, how the staff had been mislaid.

The explanation was eventually unravelled by a newspaper reporter who had attended the public inquiry.

The lady was then well into her seventies, a well-known and respected member of the Amlwch community. But she had a secret.

Before the war she had been friendly — too friendly — with a Bangor driver who usually worked the goods trip on the line. He was in the habit of visiting her when shunting had finished and there was time to spare. She had an expectation that eventually he would do the decent thing and make an honest woman of her.

Alas, the driver was already married and was having an affair with her. Moreover, he had a roving eye and had recently started a third romance with another Amlwch woman. Our heroine got to learn of this liaison and investigated, watching the driver's movements. One day she saw him pull the engine into the shed road as he always did, then climb down and, after looking round, walk off towards Bull Bay. Since she lived in the other direction, she knew she was not going to have a visit herself that day. She followed him and watched as he was admitted to a house by another lady who was obviously expecting him. He emerged some time later looking very pleased with himself and made his way back to the engine and awaited departure time.

The fireman was aware of what his mate was up to, but was in no position to do anything. After he had finished his duties he went over to the station office and, shortly before departure time, emerged with the train staff which he put on the gauge glass arm, clearly in sight. He then went off the footplate and washed his hands or something. The footplate was unattended.

Our heroine noted that this was the routine for a few days and then she struck. She knew the driver had to have the staff before he set off for Llanerchymedd. He must have told her he would get into trouble, probably sacked, if he ever lost it.

The driver was away with his new inamorata; the fireman put the staff on the gauge glass arm and went off to the toilet. She climbed on the footplate and removed the staff,

taking it home with her. For 30 years she polished that piece of brass and steel.

The fireman duly returned and started to make up his fire. He whistled up for the driver who was a bit later than usual and was out of breath when he got on the footplate. They were late setting off when they pulled out of the yard and onto the main line.

At Llanerchymedd they looked in vain for the staff, which they could not find. They could not get into the loop and could not move at all. The line was blocked, and remained so until the linesman came from Gaerwen by taxi and released the equipment, unblocking the line which had been at a standstill for about three hours.

At the ensuing internal enquiry the driver could not account for what had happened to the staff and got a week's suspension for not checking that the staff was on the engine before departure. He in turn blamed the fireman, but Amlwch staff supported his claim that he had indeed received a staff out of the instrument. Indeed, there was one token missing.

It took 30 years or so for the mystery to be finally untangled.

D80   WEEKDAYS   GAERWEN TO AMLWCH

DOWN

Milcage M	C	Station		5.25 am from Bangor (B)	6.45 am from Bangor (B)	ECS (C) SO		8† from Bangor SX	11.40 am from Bangor (B) SO	12.25 pm from Bangor (B) SO	12.40 pm from Bangor (B) SX	3.50 pm from Bangor (B) SO		5.45 pm from Bangor (B)	8.52 pm from Bangor (B)
				am	am	am		am	am	am	PM	PM	PM	PM	PM
0	0	GAERWEN	dep	5 42	7 6	8†12		9 42	9 47	11 57	12 51	12 56	4 8	6 4	9 8
4	40	Llangefni		5c51	7c15	8 22		9c51	9c56	12c 6	1e 0	1e 5	4e18	6a12	9a16
7	10	Llangwyllog	arr	5 57	7X21	8X*23		9 57	10X2	12 12	1 6	1X11	4 24	6 18	9 22
			dep	5 58	7 24	8*32		9 58	10 3	12 13	1 7	1 17	4 25	6 19	9 23
11	6	Llanerchymedd		6a 6	7a32	8 39		10a 6	10a11	12c22	1a15	1a25	4a33	6a27	9a31
14	47	Rhosgoch		6g16	7a39			10a13	10a18	12a29	1a22	1a32	4a40	6a34	9a38
17	54	AMLWCH	arr	6 24	7 47	8|50		10 21	10 26	12 37	1 30	1 40	4 48	6 42	9 46

ECS column: Until 27th August inclusive — To work 9.35 am from Amlwch

WEEKDAYS   AMLWCH TO GAERWEN

UP

Milcage M	C	Station		(B) SO	(B)	(B) SX		To Bangor (B) SO	To Bangor (B) SO	To Bangor (B) SO	To Bangor (B) SO	To Bangor (B) SX	To Bangor (B)	To Llandudno Jn. (B) SX	To Bangor (B)	To Bangor (B) SO
				am	am	am		am	am	PM	PM	PM	PM	PM	PM	PM
0	0	AMLWCH	dep	6 58	8 5	9 35		10 40	10 55	12 50	2 20	2 25	5 5	7 9	10 0	10 0
3	7	Rhosgoch		7a 7	8a14	9c45		10a49	11a 4	12a59	2a29	2a34	5a14	7c19	10a 9	10a 9
6	48	Llanerchymedd		7a15	8a22	9c54		10c58	11c13	1a 7	2a37	2a42	5a22	7j31	10a17	10a17
10	44	Llangwyllog	arr	7X22	8X29	10X1		11X5	11X20	1X14	2 44	2 49	5 29	7 38	10 24	10 24
			dep	7 23	8 30	10 3		11 5	11 21	1 15	2 45	2 50	5 30	7 39	10 25	10 25
13	14	Llangefni		7a30	8a37	10a10		11a13	11a28	1a22	2a52	2a57	5a37	7c47	10a32	10a32
17	54	GAERWEN	arr	7 37	8 44	10 17		11 20	11 35	1 29	2 59	3 4	5 44	7 54	10 39	10 39

Until 27th August inclusive

Extract from summer 1955 BR passenger timetable for the Gaerwen to Amlwch line.

Red Wharf Bay Branch

Although the first proposed line to Red Wharf Bay failed, the LNWR submitted proposals for two new lines in Anglesey in 1897. The first was planned to connect Menai Bridge and Beaumaris but was soon dropped. The second proposal was originally planned to connect Red Wharf Bay and Benllech with Llanfair PG, to tap the developing tourist traffic. There must have been objections as the proposed connection for the branch moved to Holland Arms on the ACR before the necessary Act of Parliament was drafted. However, when it was obtained on 1 August 1899, the proposed terminus at Benllech, a popular and rapidly developing seaside resort, had been abandoned and

replaced by a proposal to build the terminus at Red Wharf Bay. Even this scheme was modified, and eventually the terminus was constructed about half a mile distant from Red Wharf Bay and about a mile from Benllech, some distance from either place, which was not very convenient for local people.

Construction of the line did not start until June 1907, when a connection was put in at Holland Arms. To save costs the single line was constructed as a light railway, and the first section of 4¾ miles from Holland Arms to Pentraeth was inspected in June 1908. Halts were provided at Ceint and at Rhyd-y-Saint.

Holland Arms
A somewhat fuzzy view of the first train to Pentraeth on 1 July 1908, from a copy in Anglesey Archives: the locomotive is a standard LNWR 2-4-0T, No 1441, its train being specially converted for use on the branch. Official records state that these coaches were modified at Wolverton from old dining and sleeping cars. The coach nearest the camera, a driving trailer, was numbered 79, whilst the trailer coach was numbered 78. Auto-train control at this time was mechanical, involving linkage that passed underneath the coaches to the locomotive. Note the low steps underneath the doors which were necessary because of the low platforms at the intermediate halts. *Anglesey Archives*

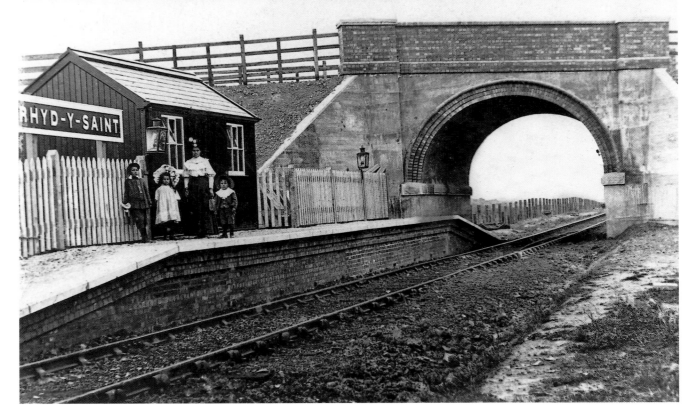

Rhyd-y-Saint
This view was taken shortly after the line was opened to passenger traffic and shows the simple layout. The platform was only 63ft in length and every expense was spared in the station design. The waiting shelter was a standard LNWR 15ft by 7ft hut. A lamp and station nameboard were the extent of the platform furniture. The station was unmanned, the guard acting as conductor and dispensing tickets. Judging by the crowd on the platform, it was rush hour on the line!
Anglesey Archives

The final section of 6¾ miles from Pentraeth to Red Wharf Bay was eventually opened on 24 May 1909. The line contained one intermediate halt at Llanbedrgoch and was single throughout, with no passing loops. It was worked on the 'One Engine in Steam' principle.

This was the last standard gauge branch line to be built in North Wales and the projected passenger traffic failed to materialise. The surge in local bus services after World War 1 reduced revenue still further, and the line lost its passenger services on 22 September 1930.

A daily freight train continued to run until after World War 2, when the service was cut back to three trains a week. However, this failed to support the line and it closed to all traffic on 3 April 1950.

The first demolition train ran on 9 April 1953, and removal of the track to the junction at Holland Arms was completed by 16 October of the same year. Little survives of this branch in 2003 apart from some earthworks, embankments, cuttings and the occasional bridge in the middle of a field!

An interesting letter dated May 1960, found amongst a collection of J. M. Dunn's papers, from Mr R. A. Dane of Peterborough, states that despite closure in 1930 passenger trains continued to work over the branch on Saturdays during summer months because the buses could not cope with the density of tourist traffic from Benllech. This was substantiated by former staff at Bangor MPD who fired on these Saturday workings up to the summer of 1939. It must be remembered that until 1940 the only buses allowed over the Menai suspension bridge and on the island were low-weight 20-seater single-deckers. When Telford's suspension bridge over the Menai was rebuilt during the war, the weight restriction was eased, which permitted heavier vehicles, and in particular single-deck and double-decker buses to work on the island, which had a detrimental effect on any plans to reactivate the branch. The stations as built were of wooden construction and became ramshackle early on and would have needed replacing had passenger services been restored. It was not to be, and as a consequence most of these were demolished after the track had been lifted, although the building and platform at Red Wharf Bay survived trackless into the 1970s. Now, in 2003, nothing survives.

Route Description

Holland Arms

A fuller description of this station can be found in the Gaerwen to Amlwch section of this book.

From the start it was accepted that 'motor' trains (pull-and-push) for passenger services would be the norm, although it is believed that from time to time conventional passenger trains made an appearance. Trains either worked on to Gaerwen or made a slip trip to Llangefni. As there was no loop facility at Holland Arms, Red Wharf Bay trains usually utilised the main platform.

A small wooden hut of LNWR design acted as a shelter on the short platform, but this was removed when the Red Wharf Bay line closed to regular passenger services in 1930.

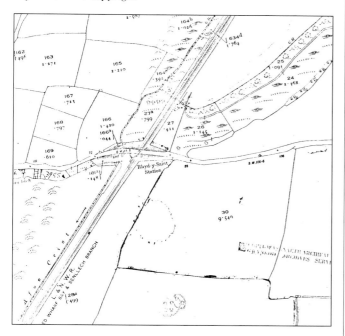

1914-18 Ordnance Survey map showing Rhyd-y-Saint station layout. *Crown Copyright*

Ceint

Ceint was 1 mile 1,300yd from Holland Arms and was an unstaffed halt. From the start traffic expectations were low. It was listed in the timetables as a conditional halt. Ceint consisted of a short platform on the up side with ramps either end. The line was on a rising gradient of 1 in 280. It was located near a crossroads on a minor road and served a scattered community. The line passed underneath a road bridge and passengers were required to access the platform down a flight of steps. The platform itself was 63ft in length, faced in brick with slab edging. Some protection against the elements was provided in the form of a standard LNWR wooden hut. The back of the platform was protected by wooden fencing. The only other facilities were a station nameboard and a single oil lamp in a glass case. The passenger train guard was responsible for ensuring that the long-burning oil lamp was lit as dusk approached and extinguished after the last train had called.

There was no siding nor any provision for freight although small sundries were dealt with by the guard, who also acted as ticket conductor.

When passenger traffic ceased, the building, fencing, steps and platform edging were removed and the site was sealed off. However, the cinder and earth infill remained and could be easily identified for many years later.

Rhyd-y-Saint

Almost identical to Ceint, Rhyd-y-Saint consisted of a single platform, 63ft long with ramps either end, on the down side of the line and in the shadow of a road overbridge that carried a minor road across the track. The platform was faced with brick, the edge was concrete slab and the infill was cinder and earth. The back of the platform was protected by pale and space fencing. A standard LNWR 17ft x 7ft 'portable' hut served as a waiting shelter. Access off the road was down a flight of wooden steps. A standard-design nameboard and single long-burning oil lamp mounted on a wooden post sufficed.

The halt was listed as conditional. Drivers of approaching trains merely slowed in anticipation of an alighting passenger, or had been informed by the guard at Holland Arms that a passenger required to be set down. The guard also acted as ticket conductor here as elsewhere. The site was cleared when the passenger services ceased in 1930.

Pentraeth

This station opened on 1 July 1908. It was approximately four miles from Holland Arms. It was the temporary terminus until the line extended to its final destination. The site was some distance from the village on the hillside and was exposed to the elements. The track was on the level through the station but commenced rising towards Llanbedrgoch on leaving the station.

It was the largest of the intermediate stations on the branch but the facilities were somewhat basic. There was a single all-wood platform on the up side, 120ft long. A cluster of LNWR-design 'portable' huts provided the facilities which included a booking office, a general waiting room and toilets. A ladies' waiting room was added in 1911. A small goods yard with a short run-round loop was provided on the up side, with a loading gauge installed at the centre. Access to the loop was controlled from a small ground frame, locked by the train staff. Two sidings led off the loop: one terminated level with the platform, the other parallel but across an approach track. At the southern end of the loop was a short neck. Despite the provision of a loop, trains could not cross here and the station was not a staff token exchange point on the branch. One of the sidings was used by local coal merchants; the yard included a weigh machine and an office. The second siding ran alongside cattle pens and an unloading platform. A trio of small store huts, one of which was a 16ft x 8ft timber-built goods shed mounted on sleepers, completed the facilities. Access to the goods yard was by a long gated drive off the main Benllech to Amlwch road, east of the bridge by which the railway line crossed over the road.

Two staff were employed here, but with the cessation of passenger services this was reduced to one.

Only up direction goods trains were booked to call here; down freight workings passed through without stopping. The only regular commodity dealt with in the yard was domestic coal and, in season, some livestock traffic.

Llanbedrgoch

The station was less than one mile from the terminus at Red Wharf Bay. The halt came into traffic on 24 May 1909 when the line was extended to Red Wharf Bay. It was located about a mile from the village of the same name, in a cutting over which a minor road from the village to the main A5025 Menai Bridge to Amlwch road crossed the track.

The facilities were very basic, similar to Ceint and Rhyd-y-Saint, consisting of a single platform on the up side, 63ft in length with ramps. The platform was brick faced with concrete slab edging, infilled with cinder. A standard 15ft x 7ft LNWR portable hut provided shelter, there was the inevitable station nameboard and a single long-burning oil lamp mounted on a post sufficed for lighting. Access was off the minor road and down steps. On closure, all the furniture was removed but the brick platform facing remained for several years before it, too, was removed.

223

Red Wharf Bay & Benllech

The terminus of the line was 6¾ miles from Holland Arms and ended in a field.

It is probable that the slump and depression that followed the 1926 General Strike influenced the decision to close the line. The dependence on motor trains, with their limited accommodation, coupled with the need for passengers to change trains at Holland Arms and/or Gaerwen before the main line was reached, did not help matters. Because there was no provision for run-round facilities longer trains could not operate, which merely added to the inevitable decline leading to the closure of the passenger service. The fact that freight traffic continued for another 20 years reinforced the view that it was this traffic that sustained the branch.

Facilities were more extensive than at Pentraeth. The wooden passenger platform was 260ft in length when the line opened although this was cut back to 160ft in 1944. The line terminated in an end-loading carriage platform adjoining the passenger platform. A loop was provided in the approach to the station but this involved propelling the train back out of the platform in order that a locomotive might run round its train. Since passenger trains on the branch were the pull-push type, the facility was used only by goods engines which ran into the station then set back into the loop, where the locomotive detached and ran round its train on the main line.

The goods yard contained three sidings, the shortest of which adjoined a cattle dock and pens with separate road access. The two other sidings bounded a roadway in the yard which led to a timber store adjoining No 1 siding and beyond that a yard crane of 5 tons capacity. No 2 siding was used as a coal siding where merchants bagged their stock straight from the mineral wagons onto their lorries. A weigh machine and an office stood at the entrance to the yard. A loading gauge stood in the yard, and a standard-design platelayer's hut constructed out of creosoted timber, with a brick chimney stack, stood opposite the loop points at the Holland Arms end.

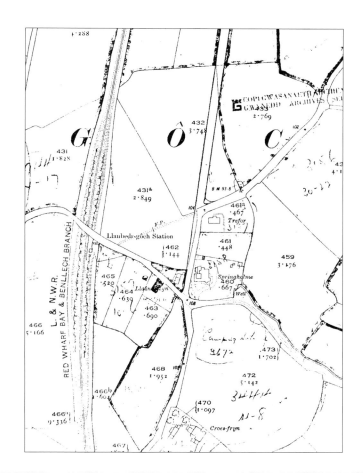

1914-18 Ordnance Survey map showing Llanbedrgoch station layout. *Crown Copyright*

Red Wharf Bay

This view, taken about 1909, shows the platform and buildings at the station. The platform was longer than at all the other stations and terminated at a brick-built end loading ramp. The station was manned by a stationmaster, a porter and two members of staff working in the goods department. An unusual feature was the gradient post opposite the platform, showing the last 40ft of track was on the level! The carriage loading ramp was out of bounds to the public who had to access the station through a wicket gate which led into the station yard. After closure to passenger traffic, the station buildings remained but the station staff was reduced by 50%. Goods traffic continued until 1950 when that, too, was withdrawn. There was no run-round loop provided for passenger trains, as it was intended that auto or pull-push trains would work the line at all times. Goods trains were provided with a loop but it was necessary for such trains to run into the platform road and propel freight stock back to the loop in order that the locomotive could run round. Today the site is overgrown. The buildings were left standing after the track was lifted but gradually decayed and either fell down or were removed as firewood. Nothing remains on site today. *Anglesey Archives*

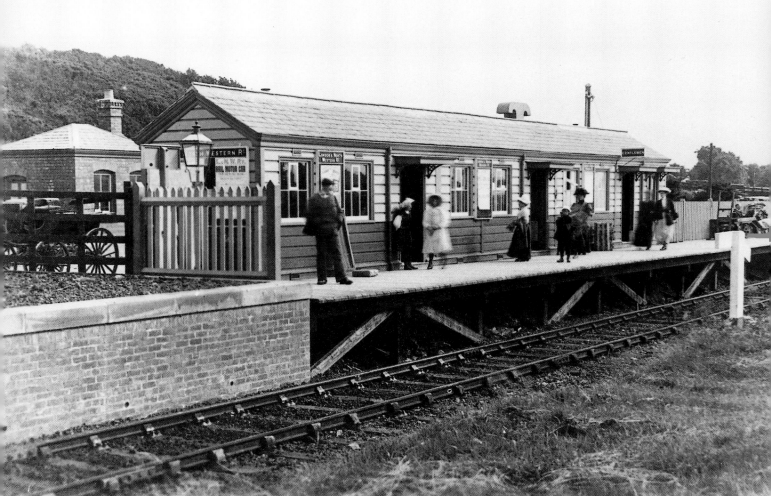

Red Wharf Bay
Ex-LNWR 'Cauliflower' 0-6-0 No 28552 runs into the platform at Red Wharf Bay with the daily goods in April 1945. The largest class of engine authorised to travel over the branch at this time was Class 3, and occasionally ex-L&Y Aspinall Class 27 0-6-0 tender engines worked the daily trip, although the normal engine was one of Bangor shed's LNWR engines, sometimes an 0-6-2T. It would work back to Holland Arms, calling at Pentraeth if there was any traffic to set down or uplift from that station. *G. H. Platt*

Red Wharf Bay
Two LNWR 'Chopper' tanks were transferred to Bangor specifically for working the Red Wharf Bay branch as the motive power for the auto-trains that were specified. Originally, an intermediate trailer was designated part of the unit, but passenger receipts were poor and the intermediate trailer was left out of the formation from very early on. Here No 1001 and the driving trailer constitute the train in early 1909, seen here standing at the terminus. The auto-train working was by mechanical linkage and somewhat inflexible. The locomotive does not yet appear to have been fitted with vacuum-control equipment, which became the accepted method of working pull-push trains. These engines also worked on the Bethesda branch but were considered underpowered and were soon replaced by 2-4-2T engines on both lines. *Bill Rear collection*

In common with other stations on the line, after the passenger service ceased in 1930 the smalls freight traffic was handled by the LMS 'Country Lorry' service that served all the stations and halts and generally covered the district. The lorries were based at Llangefni goods yard.

The wooden buildings and platform were not deemed worth recovering when the line was finally closed and so remained standing in isolation until gradually they disintegrated and were unofficially removed in the 1970s. Today the site is still undeveloped and overgrown but largely undisturbed.

Traffic Working

When the Red Wharf Bay line was constructed it was necessary to upgrade Holland Arms station and facilities to reflect the change of status from that of a convenient passenger and freight place on the line to that of a junction station. Accordingly, it became necessary to split the section of line that existed between Gaerwen and Llangefni and install new single-line train staff token sections, thus enabling trains to work from Gaerwen onto the Red Wharf Bay line. Initially the train staff between Holland Arms was of the miniature type and coloured red. Despite the provision of several staffs in the instruments at either end of the line, the normal method of operation was under the 'One Engine in Steam' arrangement. When passenger services were withdrawn the miniature token instruments were removed and all but one of the miniature train staffs withdrawn. The survivor was retained and used to unlock all the ground frames on the branch.

Traffic consisted of a service of passenger and local freight trains which ran daily, except Sundays. All traffic was worked from Bangor shed. From the commencement of services, the Red Wharf Bay line was worked by 'motor

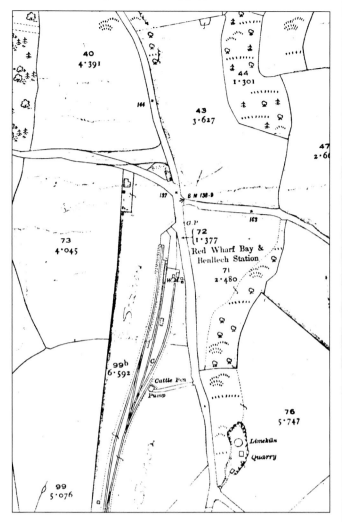

1914-18 Ordnance Survey map showing Red Wharf Bay & Benllech station layout. *Crown Copyright*

trains', for which the LNWR converted two 42ft bogie coaches.

Two 2-4-0 tank engines were fitted out to work the branch. These were Nos 1000 and 1001 and were worked from Bangor to Red Wharf Bay with the locomotive leading, although it is recorded that the locomotive that worked the very first passenger train was No 1441 of the same class. At some stage, possibly before 1915, the 2-4-0 tank engines were replaced by '4ft 6in' 2-4-2Ts. The original two-coach set was replaced by a similar train, but fitted with vacuum-controlled regulator gear.

The line never realised its full potential and consequently, the passenger train service was withdrawn from 22 September 1930. The line remained open for freight traffic, worked on a daily basis out of Menai Bridge until 1944, when the service was reduced to running three days a week only.

The weedkiller train, based at Crewe, made an annual tour of duty to the Bangor area and on 24 June 1947 it paid what was to be its last visit to the line. After spraying up to Amlwch, it was then propelled back to Holland Arms.and then pulled to Red Wharf Bay and then propelled back from there to Holland Arms. On arriving back at Holland Arms it continued to Gaerwen where it reversed onto the down line and sprayed the main line to Holyhead, then spraying the up line back to Bangor, where it was parked up for the night.

On 19 September 1947 the complete closure of the line was contemplated, but it was decided to keep it open, with a reduced overall speed limit of 15mph throughout and motive power restricted to Class 2 freight engines. In all probability, the fact that petrol was still rationed had a lot to do with this decision.

A memo dated 30 March 1950 gave notice of closure of the branch to Red Wharf Bay, to take effect from Monday 3 April 1950. This affected the 9.40am Menai Bridge to Red Wharf Bay, the 12 noon Red Wharf Bay to Gaerwen and the 2.10pm Gaerwen to Menai Bridge (MWFO) workings, together with the retiming of the 12.25pm freight from Menai Bridge to Llangefni, which was advanced by 70 minutes. The cancellation affected Bangor goods guards (turns 110 and 115), and a Bangor locomotive (turns 222 and 221).

The situation was reviewed in May 1950, and in response to a query by G. C. Parslew, who was the District Motive Power Superintendent at Llandudno Junction, Mr Dunn, the Bangor shedmaster, replied on 30 June with the following information:

Bangor Turn No 222. MWFO,
worked by one class LNW 0-6-0 '18in' goods.

Cost of	Period	Total
Engine & men	12 months	£1,658 16s 0d at 26s 7d per hour
Goods Guards at	12 months	£239 4s 0d 3s 10d per hour

Thus armed with the costing figures, a meeting was held at Gaerwen on Tuesday 4 July 1950 when the management side discussed with the staff side the implications of closing the branch to all traffic. The proposal was to close it for a trial period of six months, when the situation would be reviewed. There were the usual arguments on both sides about how the local communities would cope, particularly in bad weather, about the loss of work and employment prospects. It was pointed out that a capital expenditure of £31,000 for re-laying and other engineers' works would be required if it was decided to reopen the branch. Needless to say, the management side had its way and the line remained closed to all traffic.

A memo dated 17 November 1952 informed staff that the Railway Executive had authorised the removal of redundant assets from the branch. The contract for demolition was awarded to Connell of Coatbridge, which advertised for sale 650 tons of rail, 1,500 relayable timber sleepers chaired for 4ft 8½in gauge and a large quantity of timber sleepers suitable for building sites.

A handwritten note in J. M. Dunn's diary dated 9 March 1953 stated that the first train over the branch for three years ran on that day for the commencement of lifting and loading the track, hauled by No 58375. The contractor's foreman told goods guard J. A. Jones that his firm had paid £19,000 for the 6¾ miles of track, and that he had six men on the demolition job which was expected to take nine months to complete.

A locomotive and three wagons worked over the line every third day to the railhead and all material was taken to Gaerwen. The job was completed by Friday 16 October 1953.

21

Special Workings — The 1911 Investiture

The Investiture of the Prince of Wales on Thursday 13 July 1911 called for extraordinary special arrangements for the railways. Their complexity must have been a logistical nightmare, and the range and variety of locomotives and stock that appeared at Caernarfon in that week would have made Caernarfon a rail enthusiasts' paradise.

Prior to the Investiture, Caernarfon station had three through passenger platforms and two passenger bay lines, both on the down side at either end of the main platform, which was designated the 'Up and Down' line platform and which was accessed from the station yard. At the southern end of this platform was the short Llanberis bay which was controlled from No 2 signalbox. It could be accessed only

Caernarfon
This well-known view shows the line up of trains on Investiture day, 13 July 1911. Every platform road was occupied including trains at the temporary wooden platforms. It would seem that the time is late afternoon as most trains are lined up ready for departure towards Menai Bridge and Bangor, the exception being one set of coaches at No 5 platform, (better known as the up & down line) although the stock might have been awaiting a locomotive. According to the official schedule, the departure from this platform line was a guest train for Afon Wen, Criccieth, Portmadoc and Pwllheli and was booked to depart at 4.35pm. The train split at Afon Wen. The booked order of departure in this line-up was, reading from left to right, Platform 1 — 4.30pm Menai Bridge and Bangor shuttle; Platform 2 — 5.15pm Menai Bridge and all stations to Llandudno Junction except Aber; Platform 5 — 4.35pm Afon Wen, Criccieth, Portmadoc and Pwllheli; Platform 3 — 4.50pm all stations to Nantlle; Platform 6 — 4.40pm guest train to Llandudno Junction, Rhyl and Chester. The 'Experiment' class locomotive No 1471 *Worcestershire* was standing at Platform 8 booked to depart at 4.50pm, described as a 'Special Express for Llandudno Junction, Colwyn Bay, Rhyl, Chester and Birmingham'.
Bill Rear collection

off the single line to Llanberis. At the opposite end of the up and down platform was the longer Bangor bay which had an engine release road. There was a through goods loop line in the yard, and storage sidings that ended in buffer stops at the south end of the station.

Special traffic notices were produced by both the Cambrian Railways and the LNWR, giving the timings for the Investiture which covered every aspect of working. All movements at Caernarfon were under the control of Mr Parry, believed to be the stationmaster. The pamphlet (*overleaf*) gave details of all traffic movements along the branch lines and through the station itself.

Because of the intensity and concentration of trains within specific time limits it was necessary to install additional platforms at Caernarfon so temporary platforms were erected in the goods yard.

The numbering of the platforms at Caernarfon was listed as follows (*above right*):

New Platform	Bangor Bay	No 1
Old Platform	Bangor Bay	No 2
Down Platform		No 3
Llanberis Bay		No 4
Up and down Platform		No 5
Up Platform		No 6
New Island Platform	goods yard	No 7
New Island Platform	goods yard	No 8

All platforms were connected by a second temporary footbridge from North Road.

The actual build-up to the Investiture commenced with the first troop train movements on Tuesday 11 July 1911. Specific instructions were given as to the numbering of trains. Additionally, detachments of troops were also sent by ordinary trains. The special trains can be summarised as follows (*below*):

From	Train	Regiment	Carnarvon	via
Chatham	H475	South Wales Borderers	5am	Crewe
Chatham	H476	South Wales Borderers	5.20am	Crewe
Aldershot	H477	Dragoon Guards	6.55am	Crewe
Aldershot	H478	Dragoon Guards	7.20am	Crewe
Ross on Wye	H479	South Wales Borderers	1.10pm	Chester
Conway Morfa	H480	Royal Welch Fusiliers	2.40pm	
Holyhead	26	Seamen	5.10pm	Menai Bridge
Dublin	28	Royal Welch Fusiliers	10pm	Menai Bridge
Dublin	29	Royal Welch Fusiliers	10.20pm	Menai Bridge

From	Train	Regiment	Port Dinorwic	via
Windsor	H481	Life Guards	5.20pm	Chester
Windsor	H482	Life Guards	5.45pm	Chester

Trains H475/6 were South Eastern & Chatham Railway stock and returned empty to Stewarts Lane, London. Trains H477/8 were London & South Western Railway stock which were returned to Crewe. Trains H479/81/2 were GWR stock which returned to Chester. The stock off H480 was booked to work forward to Afon Wen but its subsequent disposal is not given.

The following day, Wednesday 12 July, saw more special train movements. These trains had reporting numbers that were duplicated from the previous day and readers should note this. Note also that some workings were non-military:

Military From	Train No	Regiment	Griffiths Crossing	via
Llanelly		Welsh Regiment	4.50am	Afon Wen
Abergavenny	H475	Monmouth Regiment	5.45am	Chester
Swansea		Welsh Brigade	5.50am	Afon Wen
Pontypool	H476	Monmouth Regiment	6.15am	Chester
Pontypridd	H477	Welsh Regiment	6.45am	Chester
Swansea	H479	Glamorgan Regiment	7am	Chester
Cardiff	H480	Welsh Brigade	7.30am	Chester
Newport	H481	Monmouth Regiment	7.45am	Chester
Shrewsbury	H482	Shropshire Light Infantry	12.55pm	Chester
Birkenhead	H484	Cheshire Regiment	2pm	Chester
Stockport	H486	Cheshire Regiment	2.10pm	Crewe
Hereford	H487	Hereford Regiment	3.10pm	Chester
Denbigh	H488	Denbighshire Regiment	3.50pm	Rhyl
Brecon		South Wales Borderers	4pm	Afon Wen

From	Train	Regiment	Carnarvon	via
Pembroke Dock		Pembroke Yeomanry	6.50am	Afon Wen
Welshpool		Montgomery Yeomanry	2.25pm	Afon Wen
Queensferry	H490	Royal Welch Fusiliers	4.10pm	Rhyl
Gosport	H495	Royal Marines Band	4.20pm	Crewe
Shrewsbury	H491	Shropshire Regiment	4.35pm	Chester
Wrexham	H493	Royal Welch Fusiliers	5.25pm	Chester

Non-military				
From	**Train**	**Organisation**	**Carnarvon**	**via**
Euston	H478	Metropolitan Police	11.15am	Crewe
Euston	H483	Metropolitan Police	12.38pm	Crewe
Euston	H485	Metropolitan Police	1.15pm	Crewe
Chester	H497	Boy Scouts	9.10pm	all stns

Empty stock from the above workings discharging at Griffiths Crossing were first worked empty stock to Caernarfon then worked away, to be stored on the North Wales coast at Holywell embankment, Holywell down refuge siding, Rhuddlan Marsh embankment and on the Foryd Pier line.

Investiture Day

A note in the special notice states that the ordinary train service on the Bangor and Afon Wen lines, the Llanberis branch, the Nantlle branch and the Bethesda branch was suspended and special services run. Certain workings on the Anglesey Central and Red Wharf Bay branches did not operate. On the Blaenau Ffestiniog branch, workmen's service trains would not run but late evening workings normally terminating at Betws y Coed would be extended to Blaenau Ffestiniog.

Advertised excursions were provided from Mold Junction, Denbigh, Corwen, Blaenau Ffestiniog, etc. The table following should give some idea of the intensity of traffic.

The table overleaf dealing with down direction traffic is self-explanatory and needs no further clarification. Other points, however, are of interest and are itemised below.

Due to the short-term difficulty for the LNWR in providing traincrews with knowledge of the lines around Caernarfon, the decision was taken to utilise Cambrian Railways locomotives and staff from Pwllheli and Portmadoc to work over the Carnarvonshire Railway line from Afon Wen. It was agreed that men from these sheds would learn the route to Menai Bridge and to Bangor MPD so that engines could be turned and serviced prior to return

workings. Layover time at Bangor would be lengthy and presumably facilities for traincrews to have a short rest would have been agreed between the companies.

The Cambrian Railways notice No 141 dated 8 July 1911, issued from Oswestry, gives the following information relating to the workings:

Up Direction					
Rep No	**Time**	**From**	**To**	**Due**	**Store at**
42		Brecon	Carnarvon	6.5am	Menai Bridge
37	5.45	Pwllheli	Carnarvon	6.54am	Menai Bridge
35	6.20	Portmadoc	Carnarvon	7.39am	Menai Bridge
36	5.20	Dolgelley	Carnarvon	8.8am	Menai Bridge
38	5.10	Aberystwyth	Carnarvon	9am	Menai Bridge
51	7.30	Aberystwyth	Carnarvon	10.49am	Menai Bridge
39	10.55	Afon Wen	Carnarvon	11.43am	Menai Bridge

The 10.55am from Afon Wen to Caernarvon was shown as 'conditional' and the note on the Cambrian Railways special train notice states that this train will run only if the Pwllheli and Portmadoc trains fail to clear the passengers. There was no provision shown for a return working.

Down Direction — Return Journey				
Rep No	**Time**	**From**	**To**	**Due**
51	5.55pm	Carnarvon	Aberystwyth	9.30pm
42	6.37pm	Carnarvon	Brecon	
38	7.7pm	Carnarvon	Aberystwyth	10.40pm
36	7.38pm	Carnarvon	Dolgelley	10.17pm
35	8.46pm	Carnarvon	Portmadoc	9.56pm
37	9.12pm	Carnarvon	Pwllheli	10.18pm

The return Cambrian Railways excursion workings were timed from Menai Bridge yard where the stock was stored and trains were allowed 15 minutes to run as empty stock to Caernarfon where they were allocated five minutes for loading. Note that the reporting numbers were those ascribed by the LNWR. The Cambrian did not allocate reporting numbers. Departure and arrival times at Brecon were not given.

After the Investiture most of the regiments were worked away on Friday 14 July at various times throughout the day, to fit in with normal traffic movements.

Three Royal trains were scheduled from Caernarfon on Friday 14 July over the Carnarvonshire Railway's line to Afon Wen and thence to Machynlleth. No information is available from the LNWR booklets held but the Cambrian Railways special train notice No 141 states that the first special carrying Royal servants for Machynlleth was followed by a pilot engine followed by the Royal Train. All three trains had a booked stop at Afon Wen which suggests that LNWR engines came off there, and were replaced by Cambrian Railways locomotives, for which 10, five and five minutes per train were allowed. Timings were as follows:

		Servants' Train	Pilot Loco	Royal Train
Carnarvon	dep	3pm	4pm	4.15pm
Afon Wen	arr	3.50pm	4.40pm	4.55pm
	dep	4pm	4.45pm	5pm
Portmadoc	arr	4.15pm	5pm	5.15pm
	dep	pass	pass	5.20pm
Barmouth	pass	4.50pm	5.35pm	5.55pm
Machynlleth	arr	5.45pm	6.25pm	6.45pm

Left:
Cambrian Railways Special Train Notice for the 1911 Investiture.

Below:
LNWR Special Troop Train Notice for the 1911 Investiture.

Right:
LNWR notice for the 1911 Investiture, 'For use of Company's Servants only'.

231

Four locomotives were booked to work the Royal Trains: a single engine for each of the Royal servants' train and the Royal pilot engine and two engines for the Royal Train itself. All four engines were booked off Machynlleth shed and ran light engine to Afon Wen, due to arrive there at 2.25pm, 2.35pm and 2.45pm respectively.

Investiture Day Traffic Movements

Down Direction

Rep No	From	Type	Via	Arr Cnvn	Pfm	Dep	To	Dispose As	Next working/Notes
28	Carnarvon					4.30	Afon Wen	ECS	
3	Birmingham	Excurs	Crewe	4.05	1	4.20	Bethesda	ECS	
1	South Wales	Excurs	Chester	4.38	3	4.45	Glynrhonwy	ECS	
10	Bangor	Mail		5.10	3	5.13	Afon Wen	ord	then 6.25 to Manchester
2	Carnarvon				4	5.30	Llanberis	ECS	
49	Swansea	Excurs	Whitchurch	5.40	3	5.45	Dinas	ECS	11/25
6	Merthyr Tydfil	Excurs	Whitchurch	5.50	3	6.06	Dinas	ECS	11/15
16	Bl. Ffestiniog	Excurs	Llandudno Jn	6.00	2	6.18	Llandudno	ECS	
43	Llandudno	Excurs	Llandudno Jn	6.10	1	6.23	Llandudno	ECS	
7	Bl. Ffestiniog	Excurs	Llandudno Jn	6.20	3	6.27	Nantlle	ECS	then 7.30 from Nantlle
8	Bl. Ffestiniog	Excurs	Llandudno Jn	6.30	3	6.38	Llanberis	ECS	then 7.35 to Carnarvon
9	Mold Junction	Excurs	Denbigh	6.40	3	6.55	Afon Wen	ord	then 8.25 from Afon Wen
48	Corwen	Excurs	Rhyl	6.50	8	7.15	Bangor	ECS	then 8.55 to Afon Wen
11	Sandycroft	Excurs	Rhyl	7.00	1	7.08	Llandudno	ECS	then 9.05 to Carnarvon
14	Llangefni	Excurs	Menai Bridge	7.10	7	7.35	Llandudno Jn	ECS	
13	Bethesda	Excurs	Bangor	7.18	3	8.03	Llanberis	ord	then 8.40 to Carnarvon
18	Holyhead	Excurs	Menai Bridge	7.25	8	7.42	Penmaenmawr	ECS	
12	Bethesda	Shuttle	Bangor	7.35	3	7.40	Penygroes	ord	then 8.15 to Carnarvon
15	Amlwch	Excurs	Menai Bridge	7.43	2	7.58	Penrhyn Siding	ECS	
20	Holyhead	Excurs	Menai Bridge	7.52	7	8.08	Llandudno Jn	ECS	
26	Liverpool	Excurs	Warrington	8.00	1	8.30	Llandudno Jn	ECS	
27	Oswestry	Excurs	Chester	8.10	8		Coal Yard	ECS	
17	Llandudno	Excurs	Llandudno Jn	8.15	3	8.20	Nantlle	ord	then 9.00 to Carnarvon
19	Colwyn Bay	Excurs	Llandudno Jn	8.25	2	8.38	Port Siding	ECS	
45	Rhyl	Excurs	Llandudno Jn	8.33	7		goods yard		then 4/50 to Nantlle
46	Bethesda	Relief	Bangor	8.40	1	8.47	Llandudno	ECS	
21	Llandudno Jn.	Excurs	Bangor	8.48	3	9.01	Nantlle	ord	then 9.40 to Carnarvon
3	Bethesda	Shuttle	Bangor	8.54	3	9.07	Llanberis	ord	then 10.05 to Carnarvon
25	Chester	ordinary	Rhyl	9.02	2	9.30	Rhyl	ECS	
22	Birkenhead	Excurs	Chester	9.08	8	9.20	Llandudno	ECS	
48	Bangor	Special		9.14	3	9.21	Afon Wen	ord	then 11.05 to Carnarvon
23	Colwyn Bay	Special	Llandudno Jn	9.24	3	9.28	Llanberis	ord	then 10.15 to Carnarvon
24	Manchester	Excurs	Chester	9.37	2	9.55	Llandudno	ECS	
16	Llandudno	Relief	Llandudno Jn	9.45	3	9.52	Nantlle	ord	then 10.40 to Carnarvon
53	Chester	Relief	Llandudno Jn	9.55	7	10.10	Penrhyn Siding	ECS	
11	Llandudno	Relief	Llandudno Jn	10.07	8		goods yard	ECS	then 5/55 special
4	Bethesda	Shuttle	Bangor	10.20	3	10.30	Nantlle	ord	then 11.00 to Carnarvon
28	Rhyl	Relief	Llandudno Jn	10.25	7		goods yard	ECS	then 5/25 special
5	Bethesda	Shuttle	Bangor	10.34	3	10.41	Llanberis	ord	
47	Colwyn Bay	Relief	Llandudno Jn	10.45	3	10.50	Dinas	ECS	then spare, as required
29	Chester	Relief	Llandudno Jn	10.55	3	11.16	Dinas	ECS	then spare, as required
44	Llandudno	Special	Llandudno Jn	11.00	8		goods yard	ECS	then 5/10 special
30	Chester	ordinary	Llandudno Jn	11.10	7	11.27	Bangor	ECS	
	Holyhead	Special	Menai Bridge	11.15	1	11.32	Menai Bridge Goods	ECS	
31	Chester	Special	Llandudno Jn	11.45	8				then 4/50 Special Guests
55	London Euston	Special	Crewe	12/15	7				then 5/05 to Euston
	Menai Bridge	Pilot		1/00					
	Royal Train		Menai Bridge	1/22		1/30	Holyhead	ECS	
	2 Royal Train		Menai Bridge	2/02		2/10	Griffiths Crossing	ECS	contained travelling officials
17	Conway Morfa	ECS	Bangor	2/10		4/55			then 4/55 Special Guests
16	Menai Bridge	ECS		2/15	6	4/40			then 4/40 Special Gue
19	Port Dinorwic	ECS		2/35		2/40	Dinas	ECS	then 7/45 to Chester
12	Bangor	ECS		2/50	1	4/30			then 4/30 to Bangor
15	Bangor	ECS		2/55	5	4/35	Portmadoc		

Investiture Day Traffic Movements

Down Direction

Rep No	From	Type	Via	Arr Cnvn	Pfm	Dep	To	Dispose As	Next working/Notes
26	Llandudno Jn	ECS	Bangor	3/10			goods yard		then 6/50 to Liverpool
24	Llandudno	ECS	Llandudno Jn	3/28			goods yard		then 7/30 to Manchester
46	Llandudno	ECS	Llandudno Jn	4/35	1	5/35	Llandudno Jn		stands C'von No 1 @ 3/40pm
15	Carnarvon	Relief			5	4/35	Portmadoc		
45	Carnarvon	Relief			3	4/50	Nantlle		then 5/35 to Carnarvon
2	Carnarvon	Shuttle			4	5/00	Llanberis	ord	then 5/55 to Carnarvon
32	Bangor	Relief		5/05	3	5/09	Portmadoc	Relief	
13	Port Siding	Relief		5/12	3	5/16	Penygroes	Relief	after Royal Train has passed
9	Bangor	ECS		5/20	2	6/00	Llandudno	Shuttle	arr Treborth 4/07
5	Carnarvon				4	5/55	Llanberis	Shuttle	then 6/50 to Carnarvon
8	Bangor	ECS		5/38	1	6/20	Llandudno Jn	Shuttle	
33	Bangor	Special		5/42	3	5/45	Afon Wen	Special	then 7/20 to Carnarvon
51	Menai Bridge	Cambrian		5/50	3	5/55	Aberystwyth	Relief	
12	Bangor	ECS		6/00	2	6/40	Llandudno	Shuttle	
39	Menai Bridge	Cambrian		6/05	3	6/13	Afon Wen	Relief	
52	Bangor	Relief		6/28	3	6/31	Nantlle	Relief	then 7/15 to Carnarvon
42	Menai Bridge	Cambrian		6/34	3	6/37	Brecon	Excurs	
43	Llandudno	ECS	Llandudno Jn	6/45	2	7/20	Llandudno Jn	Shuttle	
23	Bangor	Shuttle		6/50	3	6/55	Nantlle	Shuttle	then 7/40 to Carnarvon
38	Menai Bridge	Cambrian		7/00	3	7/07	Aberystwyth	Excurs	
41	Bangor	Shuttle		7/13	1	7/38	Llandudno Junction	Shuttle	
57	Bangor	Relief		7/25	3	7/28	Penygroes	Relief	then 8/20 to Carnarvon
36	Menai Bridge	Cambrian		7/33	3	7/38	Dolgelley	Excurs	
4	Llandudno Jn.	ECS		7/40	2	7/50	Llandudno Junction	Shuttle	
5	Carnarvon				4	7/40	Llanberis	Shuttle	then 8/25 to Carnarvon
53	Bangor	Relief		7/48	3	7/57	Penygroes	Relief	coaches to Nantlle then as required
14	Llandudno Jn	ECS		7/52	1	8/05	Llandudno Jn	Shuttle	
18	Penmaenmawr	ECS		8/05	7	8/37	Holyhead	Excurs	
40	Bangor	Relief		8/10	3	8/16	Afon Wen	Relief	then 9/35 to Carnarvon
46	Llandudno Jn	ECS		8/15	2	8/45	Llandudno Jn	Shuttle	
10	Bangor	Special		8/21	3	8/25	Afon Wen	Special	then 10/05 to Carnarvon
2	Carnarvon				4	8/26	Llanberis	Shuttle	then 9/20 to Carnarvon
35	Menai Bridge	Cambrian		8/35	3	8/46	Portmadoc	Excurs	
9	Llandudno Jn	ECS		8/40	1	9/15	Llandudno Jn	Shuttle	
8	Llandudno Jn	ECS		8/50	3	8/54	Nantlle	Shuttle	then 9/35 to Carnarvon
37	Menai Bridge	Cambrian		9/05	3	9/12	Pwllheli	Excurs	
5	Carnarvon				4	9/15	Llanberis	Shuttle	then 10/10 to Carnarvon
13	Bangor	Excurs		9/15	3	9/21	Nantlle	Excurs	coaches to Nantlle then as required
12	Llandudno Jn	ECS		9/20	2	9/40	Llandudno Jn	Shuttle	
22	Llandudno	ECS	Llandudno Jn	9/25	8	9/55	Birkenhead	Excurs	
7	Llandudno Jn	Shuttle	Bangor	9/30	1	10/00	Rhyl	Excurs	
54	Bangor	Special		9/46	3	9/50	Afon Wen	Special	
16	Chester	ECS	Llandudno Jn	9/57	7	10/35	Rhyl	Excurs	
43	Llandudno Jn	ECS		10/04	2	10/27	Llandudno Jn	Shuttle	
2	Carnarvon				4	10/05	Llanberis	Shuttle	then 11/00 to Carnarvon
21	Llandudno Jn	ECS		10/10	8	10/50	Mold Junction	Excurs	
4	Llandudno Jn	ECS		10/30	1	10/55	Chester	Relief	
41	Llandudno Jn	ECS		10/49	2	11/05	Rhyl	Shuttle	
23	Bangor	Excurs		10/47	3	10/51	Afon Wen	Excurs	9/55 from Bethesda
20	Llandudno Jn	ECS		11/00	7	11/30	Corwen	Excurs	
4	Carnarvon				4	10/55	Llanberis	Shuttle	
	Llandudno Jn	ord		11/35	3	11/40	Nantlle	ord	
2	Carnarvon				4	11/57	Llanberis	Shuttle	

Note: times are shown following the timetable convention of the time in which a stop denotes am, eg '10.25', and a slash denotes pm, eg '11/35'.

22

Special Workings —
The 1969 Investiture

The 1969 Investiture of Prince Charles, by contrast to the 1911 event, was, from a railway point of view, a very subdued event. It has to be remembered that in 1969 Caernarfon station was very much in terminal decline and the railway authorities were reluctant to spend any money on a station that was already doomed. That the station would have to be smartened up was assumed, but little effort was put into the project.

The fact that the branch lines to Afon Wen and Llanberis had been closed and some track removed, ensured that no

Caernarfon
On Investiture day, Tuesday 1 July 1969, the Royal Train was hauled by a couple of Class 40 locomotives. As a precaution, a third Class 40 was on hand in Caernarfon yard, suitably bulled up should its services be needed, which, as it happened, were not. Here No D207 stands on the up goods loop line from 10.00 until 20.15, just in case! Behind the locomotive on station siding No 3 stands the stock off 1T10 which was the 07.20 Euston to Caernarfon, booked to depart back to Euston at 18.05. *Bill Rear*

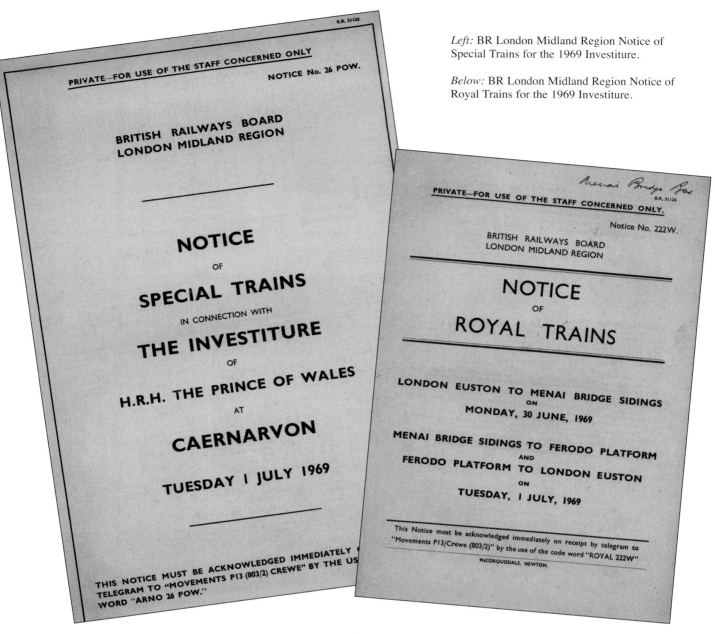

Left: BR London Midland Region Notice of Special Trains for the 1969 Investiture.

Below: BR London Midland Region Notice of Royal Trains for the 1969 Investiture.

extra traffic was possible from those directions. The Afon Wen branch was still in situ as far as Llanwnda, and was earmarked for storing stock on the Investiture day.

In the winter of 1968-9 some engineer's trains were run over the line to establish whether anything needed to be done to make the line safe. In Caernarfon yard the worst decaying structures were removed and redundant track was cleared, but the yard was full of weeds and no attempt was made to smarten up the general environment. Not even a lick of paint was put on the surviving buildings.

The line from Menai Bridge to Caernarfon had been singled in 1965, controlled by a miniature key token for the entire section, and whilst capacity was adequate for normal traffic requirements, it was extremely limited for the Investiture day. The section was 7 miles 8 chains long, and 15 minutes were needed for a passenger train to pass through. In order to double the line capacity it was decided to split the section by creating an intermediate temporary block post at Felin Heli. A small shed, about 4ft x 4ft, was erected underneath a footbridge and contained two miniature single-line token instruments which were wired into the Menai Bridge to Caernarfon circuit and which could be switched in or out as required.

The programme for the day demanded that normal services to and from Caernarfon were suspended. Two Class 40 diesel locomotives departed Crewe for Caernarfon, where they were on standby duties. They were booked to arrive at 8.33am and took up residence in the goods yard. In anticipation that large crowds would travel by rail to attend, three DMU workings comprising six two-car units started from Chester and picked up at every station along the North Wales coast. They were the first to arrive. The first locomotive-hauled special was for railway officials who travelled from Crewe and arrived at Caernarfon at 10.42am. Then came the first of two special guests trains who travelled from Euston and arrived at Caernarfon at 11.21am. Next came three locomotive-hauled workings from Cardiff. The last special guests train to arrive at the royal borough was 1T15, which had departed from Euston at 8.10am and arrived at Caernarfon at 12.30pm. This contained the cream of society such as the Prime Minister, Harold Wilson, the daughters of Richard Nixon, President of the United States of America, etc. The special guests were conveyed to Caernarfon Castle by new Crosville coaches specially brought in for the event. After the ceremony they conveyed the guests back to the station.

Two publications for staff were issued from Crewe. No 26 POW dated 24 June 1969 contained details of the non-royal workings including the specials from Euston 1T10 was E450 power, departing Euston at 07.20 which called at Crewe to change locomotives, becoming D450 (which was a Class 40 locomotive), booked to arrive at Caernarfon at 11.21. The second working was 1T15, another E450 power, running non-stop to Crewe, where another Class 40 locomotive replaced the electric. That train was booked to arrive at Caernarfon at 12.30. Publication notice 222W was the Notice of Royal Trains which covered the outward and return journey and specific instructions.

Motive power for the Royal Train was two Type 4 locomotives (Class 40s) which worked light engine from Crewe diesel depot to Willesden DED on the Monday morning. Two other Type 4 locomotives ran light engine from Willesden DED in the afternoon to Wolverton where they collected the Royal Train and worked it as empty stock to Euston No 1 platform.

The two Royal Train engines departed from Willesden DED at 21.15 for Euston where they attached to the Royal Train, booked to depart at 22.25 for Menai Bridge. A stop was made at Crewe No 1 down through line to change drivers. Menai Bridge sidings were reached at 03.10.

Llandudno Junction traincrews were incensed that they were not involved in any of the special workings. In fact, the men who worked into Caernarfon on that day were all Crewe men who had had to learn the single line from Menai Bridge to Caernarfon and on the Carnarvonshire Railway line to the stabling points.

The day passed off relatively peacefully with few mishaps although a Class 47 locomotive on one of the Cardiff workings that was booked to stable on the Carnarvonshire line got stuck under Turf Square, Caernarfon, near the tunnel and had to be unceremoniously dragged out by one of the standby locomotives. Bowler-hatted inspectors were rampant at all times and all went into panic mode at the sight of a Class 47 stuck down the dip. Eventually they rescued the miscreant and retreated to the safety of the platform. Someone exploded a device near Caernarvon Tunnel but apart from showering some coaches with ballast did no damage.

The empty trains were stabled on the former Afon Wen line in nose-to-tail fashion. The DMUs were first to arrive and proceeded to the end of the line, leaving a small gap between trains. The locomotive-hauled trains followed and, on arrival, detached from their stock and attached to the tail of the one ahead, for the return journey.

Platforming and stabling extract from the Notice of Special Trains for the 1969 Investiture, showing the arrangements in force on the day.

Inward (Down) Direction

Rep No	Type	Power	Time	From	Arr	Notes
0Z00	2 x Light Diesel Locos		06.15	Crewe	08.33	
1T05	DMU	D1	07 30	Chester	09.19	Six 2-cars Stops all stations
1T06	DMU	D1	08.00	Chester	09.49	Six 2-cars Stops all stations
1T07	DMU	D1	08.30	Chester	10.19	Six 2-cars Stops all stations
1T08	Diesel Loco	D450	08.45	Crewe	10.42	BSK, CK, 8-SK, BSK. 363 tons
1T10	Elec to Crewe then	D450	07.20	Euston	11.21	BSK, 2-SO, RK, 2-FO, RK, 2-FO, BSK, Chairman's Saloon. 443 tons
1Z12	Diesel Loco	D450	07.00	Cardiff	11.46	2-SO, RK, 2-SO, BSK, RMB, 3-SO. 340 tons
1Z13	Diesel Loco	D450	07.15	Cardiff	12/03	2-SO, RK, 3-SO, RU, SO, BSK. 310 tons
1Z14	Diesel Loco	D450	07.35	Cardiff	12.15	2-SO, RK, 3-SO, RU, SO, BCK. 310 tons
1T15	Elec to Crewe then	D450	08.10	Euston	12.30	BSK, 2-FO, RK, 4-FO, RK, 2-FO, BFK. 476 tons
1X01	2 Type 4. Royal Train		13.40	M. Bridge	14.00	at Ferodo Platform. 14 vehicles — 597 tons
1X00	2 Type 4 locos		14.45	Ferodo	14.50	Royal Train — Empty Stock to Caernarfon.
2D90	DMU	D1	20.30	Bangor	20.49	One 2-car Special

Outward (Up) Direction

Rep No	Type	Power	Time	From	To	Arr	Notes
1X00	2 Type 4 locos		15.50	Caernarfon	Ferodo	15.55	Royal Train — Empty Stock
1X01	2 Type 4 locos. Royal Train		17.00	Ferodo	Euston	22.10	14 vehicles — 697 tons
1T15	Diesel Loco to Crewe then Elec	D450	17.30	Caernarfon	Euston	21.30	E450 from Crewe. Load — see above
1Z14	Diesel Loco	D450	17.45	Caernarfon	Cardiff	-	arrival time unknown. Load — see above
1T10	Diesel Loco to Crewe then Elec	D450	18.05	Caernarfon	Euston	22.15	E450 from Crewe. Load — see above
1Z13	Diesel Loco	D450	18.18	Caernarfon	Cardiff	-	arrival time unknown. Load — see above
1Z12	Diesel Loco	D450	18.32	Caernarfon	Cardiff	-	arrival time unknown. Load — see above
1T08	Diesel Loco	D450	19.10	Caernarfon	Crewe	21.12	Load — see above
1T07	DMU	D1	19.35	Caernarfon	Chester	21.22	Six 2-cars. Stops all stations
1T06	DMU	D1	19.50	Caernarfon	Chester	21.37	Six 2-cars. Stops all stations
1T05	DMU	D1	20.05	Caernarfon	Crewe	22.50	Six 2-cars. Stops all stations
1Z01	Diesel Loco		20.15	Caernarfon	Crewe	22.25	Return Saloons
2D90	DMU	D1	21.00	Caernarfon	Llandudno Jn	21.40	One 2-car Special

23

Butlin's Traffic

The Butlin's traffic started in 1947 when the holiday camp at Penychain near Pwllheli finally opened for business. Despite the fact that it was situated on a GWR line, the bulk of the traffic came from the northwest of England although some traffic came from Birmingham and other parts of the country.

The LMS and GWR worked in close harmony as the extra traffic was always welcome. It was necessary to enlarge loops on the single lines, particularly on the line from Caernarfon but also along the Cambrian coast.

The LMS extended the passing loops at Dinas, Groeslon, Penygroes, Brynkir and Llangybi. The GWR had extended its platforms at Afon Wen in 1938 in anticipation of the camp opening. In late 1946 it doubled the line from Afon Wen to Penychain and provided extra carriage accommodation at Pwllheli East.

The LMS and later British Railways London Midland Region (Western Division) did not show the train paths in the working timetables, instead listing them in the weekly Programme of Special Trains which was redesignated Special Traffic Notice in the first week of June 1953.

The first reference to Butlin's traffic was given in the Programme of Special Trains dated 5 July 1947 when an entry reads:

> 2.30pm 'Q' Llandudno Jn to Penychain Halt (GW) — To run (8) — 240 tons
> 5.50pm 'Q' light engines (2), Afonwen to Bangor — To run.

The following week (12 July 1947) there were two entries. The first was an ECS working the 7am Llandudno Junction to Penychain (10 coaches — 300 tons) which worked back with the 9.40am Penychain to Manchester Exchange. The second entry showed 7.18am 2 x LE Bangor to Afon Wen, working the 8.50am Penychain to Llandudno Junction.

The following Saturday an additional train ran. This departed Llandudno Junction at 12.15pm to Penychain,

reporting number W249. There was no mention as to whether the coaches returned as empty stock or whether the engines came back light to Bangor. Thereafter, and for the rest of the season, which was short, three trains to the camp on Saturdays sufficed.

The following season saw additional trains working and the season extended. Workings listed in issue 31 of the W1 Programme of Special Trains are as follows:

> 7.50am Manchester Exchange to Rhyl (reporting number W429) to be (10) — 300 tons and extended to Penychain.
> 7.55am 'Q' Emcar, Llandudno Junction to Penychain (WR). To run and depart Llandudno Jn at 7.50am.
> 10.16am 'Q' Warrington to Penychain (WR). To run between Llandudno Jn and Penychain, formed of relief from Stoke (reporting number W569) (10) — 300 tons.
> 11.25am 'Q' Penychain (WR) to Warrington (reporting number W318). To run and be diverted to Coventry, stopping at Nuneaton and all stations to Coventry except Daimler Halt (10) — 300 tons.

The build-up was gradual as the camp became increasingly well known and in its heyday rail traffic dominated the Saturday workings.

In 1949 there was no change to the down direction trains but an additional working was shown departing Penychain at 1.25pm to Chester.

Naturally, August Bank Holiday Monday, which then was the first Monday in the month, was the peak holiday period. The preceding Saturday saw the heaviest concentration of trains to and from the camp. In 1950 the Saturday traffic included those shown in previous years plus a conditional train, the 10.16am from Warrington, which ran on 5 August 1950. The stock was worked back to Llandudno Junction for storage until the following week when it formed the return working.

In 1951 the following additional trains operated on 4 August:

C444	7.50am	Llandudno Jn to Penychain	Emcar	11/330t
W595	8.5am	Manchester Exch to Penychain		10/300t
W325	8.15am	Manchester Exch to Penychain		10/300t
W569	10.16am	Warrington to Penychain		10/300t
W569	9.20am	Stoke on Trent to Penychain		10/300t
	12.20pm	Bangor to Afon Wen extended to Pwllheli		
W636	8.10am	Afon Wen to Birmingham		10/300t
W318	11.25am	Penychain to Coventry		11/330t
S936	12.58pm	Penychain to Llandudno Jn	Emcar	10/300t

Note: The codename 'Emcar' denotes empty stock workings. The figures 10/300t denote 10 coaches weighing 300 tons empty.

The redesigned working timetables commencing 8 June 1953 included some of the regular Saturdays Only Butlin's traffic over the Afon Wen line. However, there were some conditional trains that ran occasionally. These were shown in the Programme of Special Trains notices, the title of which would change to Special Traffic notices after Week 22, and the section Crewe & North which was coded W1 would change to W2 on the same date.

The 1953 summer working timetable shows the following Saturdays Only workings relevant:

6am	ECS	Llandudno Jn to Penychain
7.25am	ECS	Llandudno Jn to Penychain
7.50am	ECS	Llandudno Jn to Penychain
8.5am	W311	Manchester Ex to Penychain
8.15am	W325	Manchester Ex to Penychain
10.15am	W355	Warrington to Penychain
9.35am	W399	Liverpool to Penychain
1.30pm	W467	Llandudno Jn to Penychain
8.50am	W164	Penychain to Stoke on Trent
9.40am	W138	Penychain to Manchester Ex
10.50am	W142	Penychain to Liverpool
11.25am	W318	Penychain to Warrington
12.37pm	ECS	Penychain to Llandudno Jn
2.20pm	ECS	Penychain to Llandudno Jn
4pm	ECS	Penychain to Llandudno Jn

Note: The term 'ECS' denotes empty coaching stock working.

There were light engine movements from Bangor shed to work the Butlin's specials from Penychain to Bangor or Llandudno Junction which were shown in the working timetables.

In 1954 the 7.25am empty stock from Llandudno Junction was replaced by the 6.58am from Holyhead. In the reverse direction the 12.37pm worked to Holyhead instead of Llandudno Junction. Additionally, there was an ECS working, departing Bangor at 9.15am to work a 12.5pm Penychain to Manchester, reporting number W144, which the previous year had been conditional and shown in the Special Traffic notices. The 8.50am to Stoke now departed at 8.45am.

In 1955 the former 6am ECS departure from Llandudno Junction left at 6.5am. Additionally, an empty coach stock working departed Holyhead at 8am, which replaced the 9.15am from Bangor. The Special Traffic Notice for Saturday 23 July also states the following alterations:

7.50am	ECS	Llandudno Jn to Penychain to start from Holyhead
11.25am	W318	Penychain to Warrington extended to Huncoat
12.5pm	W144	Penychain to Manchester diverted to Preston

The 1958 August Bank Holiday Saturday showed little change although W355, the 10.15am Warrington to Penychain, was retimed and started back from Manchester Oxford Road at 9.28am, travelling via Timperley and Arpley.

By 1964 the traffic flow was as follows:

7.18am	ECS	Bangor to Penychain	3J84
7.52am	ECS	Llandudno Jn to Penychain	3J84
9.3am		Bangor to Penychain	2J84
8.5am		Manchester to Penychain	1D10
8.20am		Manchester to Penychain	1D11
9.15am		Liverpool to Penychain	1D26
8.45am		Penychain to Stoke	1K03
9.10am		Penychain to Manchester	1C68
9.48am		Penychain to Manchester	1C71
10.40am		Penychain to Liverpool	1F20
11.25am		Penychain to Warrington	1F03
12.37pm	ECS	Penychain to Holyhead	3D88

This was the last year in which through trains worked beyond Caernarfon. The following year saw the pattern change radically. Trains for Butlin's terminated at Caernarfon and it was necessary for through passengers to be bussed the remaining 20 miles. The organisation was a shambles. Crosville did not want the rail replacement service anyway, and the Butlin's traffic merely compounded things. Old open-platform double-deckers uplifted passengers at Caernarfon station and an hour and a quarter later deposited them at the camp. The traffic was lost in the very first season and thereafter Butlin's traffic resorted to the private car or coaches which provided a guaranteed seat and some comfort, although some trains continued to run from traditional starting points until the line to Caernarfon closed.

1965		**From**		**Coaches/weight**
07.25	1D10	Manchester Exchange	Locomotive-hauled	10/300t
08.20	1D11	Manchester Exchange	Locomotive-hauled	10/300t
10.35	1D26	Liverpool Lime St	Locomotive-hauled	10/300t
12.30	1D24	Warrington Bank Quay	Locomotive-hauled	10/300t
		To		
09.25	1C64	Manchester Exchange	Locomotive-hauled	10/300t
11.20	1C71	Manchester Exchange	Locomotive-hauled	10/300t
13.45	1F03	Warrington Bank Quay	Locomotive-hauled	10/300t
15.10	1F20	Liverpool Lime St	Locomotive-hauled	10/300t

The following year things had changed. One Manchester working had disappeared. Most workings were steam-hauled but the occasional Class 40 appeared.

1966		From		Coaches/weight
08.50	1D11	Manchester Exchange	Locomotive-hauled	10/300t
10.35	1D35	Liverpool Lime St	Locomotive-hauled	10/300t
1230	1D24	Warrington Bank Quay	Locomotive-hauled	10/300t
		To		
11.45	1C71	Manchester Exchange	Locomotive-hauled	10/300t
13.45	1F03	Warrington Bank Quay	Locomotive-hauled	10/300t
15.04	1F20	Liverpool Lime St	Locomotive-hauled	10/300t

In 1967 motive power was still locomotive-hauled but increasingly Class 40 diesel locomotives predominated. The coaching sets were reduced to eight coaches, 250 tons.

1967		From	Due
08.05	1D11	Manchester Exchange	10.50
09.20	1D24	Warrington Bank Quay	11.30
10.40	1D26	Liverpool Lime St	13.33
		To	
11.45	1C71	Manchester Exchange	
13.38	1F03	Warrington Bank Quay	
15.00	1F20	Liverpool Lime St	

The 1968 season saw two of the locomotive-hauled trains replaced by DMUs, usually four two-car sets.

1968		From	Due	Type
08.05	1D11	Manchester Exchange	10.51	DMU
09.22	1D24	Warrington Bank Quay	11.32	D450
10.40	2D83	Liverpool Lime St	13.34	DMU
		To		
11.45	1C71	Manchester Exchange		DMU
13.38	1F03	Warrington Bank Quay		D450
15.00	2F83	Liverpool Lime St		DMU

The last year of Caernarfon station's existence saw four workings to the station that had links to Butlin's traffic. The Warrington working remained loco-hauled to the end. A working from Manchester was reinstated, albeit at a much later time, and was unbalanced. The 16.46 arrival at Caernarfon worked back to Bangor at 17.00 and then worked forward to Crewe.

1969		From	Due	Type
08.40	1D11	Manchester Exchange	11.05	DMU
09.25	1D24	Warrington Bank Quay	11.34	D450
10.40	2D83	Liverpool Lime St	13.32	DMU
13.35	2D99	Manchester Exchange	16.46	DMU
		To		
11.45	1J71	Manchester Exchange		DMU
13.38	1F03	Warrington Bank Quay		D450
14.55	2F83	Liverpool Lime St		DMU

St Asaph
Standard Class 4MT 4-6-0 No 75054 on the Cambrian Radio Cruise near St Asaph, 6 July 1961. The cathedral can be seen in the background. *Bill Rear collection*

St Asaph
Standard Class 4MT 4-6-0 No 75054 on the Cambrian Radio Cruise near Llanerch Park, St Asaph, 20 July 1961.
Bill Rear collection

24

Excursion Services

Regular excursion services were operated along the North Wales coast from the turn of the 20th century, mainly to and from the tourist centres. These included trains from major conurbations — Liverpool, Manchester, etc to the holiday resorts of Rhyl, Colwyn Bay and Llandudno.

Before World War 2 the LMS also operated regular day and evening excursions from diverse places like Amlwch, Bethesda, Caernarfon, Llanberis and Nantlle to Llandudno and Rhyl, and further afield to Belle Vue Manchester, Blackpool and London.

In 1938 some summer seasonal traffic was included in the public timetables. The Conwy Valley line had four additional trains worked during the week between Llandudno and Betws-y-Coed and three on Saturdays.

Prewar, three circuit diagrams for coaches, which included observation coach workings, were listed in the Western Division Diagram of Rolling Stock Working, as follows:

No 1330 — Observation Car (SX)

	Arr	Dep	
	am	am	
Llandudno		10.00	
Blaenau Festiniog	11.25	11.40	A
	pm	pm	
Betws-y-Coed	12.04	1.00	A
Llandudno	1.55	2.10	
Betws-y-Coed	2.52	5.50	
Llandudno	6.45	-	

A — In front

The 10am Llandudno to Blaenau Ffestiniog used normal circuit stock with the observation car attached at the rear of the train, returning with the 11.40am from Blaenau, the coach being at the front immediately behind the engine. The train was due Llandudno at 1.55pm. It then worked to Betws-y-Coed as per diagram. The afternoon trip was

Trefnant
Standard Class 4MT 4-6-0 No 75020 on the North Wales Land Cruise from Pwllheli, near Trefnant, 7 September 1961.
Bill Rear collection

seasonal and worked only between June and September. The observation coach was stored during the winter months. It was not used during World War 2 but reappeared on the Conwy valley line until 1956.

A second observation coach worked between Rhyl and Llanberis in the 1930s until the outbreak of World War 2. It ran at the times shown below.

No 1301 — Vestibule Stock (6B) and Observation Car (196 tons)

	Arr am	Dep am	
Llandudno Jn		8.33	SX
Llandudno	8.42	10.10	SX
Llandudno Jn	10.20	10.24	SX
		pm	
Llanberis	11.31	5.15	SX
	pm		
Llandudno Jn	6.08	6.12	SX
Llandudno	6.20	6.45	FSX
Llandudno Jn	6.55		
	am	am	
Llandudno		10.10	SO
Llandudno Jn	10.20	10.32	SO
	pm	pm	
Llanberis	12B01	12.10	SO
Caernarvon	12.28	3.40	SO A
Bangor	4.02	4.08	SO
Manchester (Ex)	7.12	7.25	SO
Ordsall Lane	7.30		

A — Made up to (11B)
B — Observation car returns 5.30pm to Llandudno

St Asaph
Standard Class 4MT 4-6-0 No 75020 on the Pwllheli to Rhyl land cruise at St Asaph, August 1960. *Bill Rear collection*

LMS Spring Season Excursions, 1925 to North Wales.

Denbigh
Ivatt Class 2MT 2-6-0 No 46425 on the North Wales Radio Land Cruise leaving Denbigh for Corwen, 14 July 1954. *Bill Rear*

No 1302 — Vestibule Stock (6B) and Observation Car (196 tons)			
	Arr	Dep	
		am	
Rhyl		10.20	SX
	pm	pm	
Llanberis	12.01	12.10	SX
Caernarvon	12.28	4.40	SX
Llanberis	5.00	5.30	SX
Rhyl	6.55		

In 1948 the observation car was reintroduced on the Monday to Friday Llandudno to Llanberis excursion which necessitated a reversal at Llandudno Junction. This was repeated in 1949 but in slightly different timings. From June 1950 the working started from and terminated at Rhyl until the service was withdrawn after the 1961 season.

After 1930 the Llanberis line also had a service of local excursion trains running between Caernarfon and Llanberis which was listed in the public timetables. In 1938 there were six such workings, Mondays to Fridays, between May and September, with 10 trains running on Saturdays.

Between 1950 and 1953 there was an attempt to run an additional excursion train over the branch between Llanberis and Caernarfon. The working was as follows:

Excursion Adex W635

	Arr	Dep
	am	am
Rhyl		9.35
Llandudno Jn	10.03	10.05
Bangor	10.37	10.41
Caernarvon	10.56	11.00
Pontrhythallt		11.14
Llanberis	11.22	

Return Adex

	Arr	Dep
	pm	pm
Llanberis		1.00
Pontrhythallt		1.07
Caernarvon	1.20	

Emcar

	Arr	Dep
	pm	pm
Caernarvon		3.30
Pontrhythallt		3.43
Llanberis	3.50	

Return Adex W635

	Arr	Dep
	pm	pm
Llanberis		5.20
Pontrhythallt		5.27
Caernarvon	5.40	5.45
Bangor	6.00	6.05
Llandudno Jn	6.36	6.41
Rhyl	7.08	

The load was seven coaches, 210 tons, which included the observation car.

LMS 1925 Excursions to the Welsh Highland Railway.   LMS 1927 Excursions to the Welsh Highland Railway.

Portmadoc
Ivatt Class 2MT 2-6-0 No 46434 on the North Wales Radio Land Cruise approaching Portmadoc, June 1953.
Bill Rear

The Land Cruise Trains

The Land Cruise trains started operating in 1951 and at first were designated the 'Festival Land Cruise'. Initially it operated on Tuesdays and Thursdays only but after a couple of weeks it was so popular that it operated from Tuesdays to Fridays inclusively until the end of the season.

The train started from and terminated at Rhyl. It followed a circular route along the Vale of Clwyd line to St Asaph and Denbigh, thence over the former Denbigh, Ruthin & Corwen Railway line onto former Great Western metals at Corwen, where a halt was made to take water. It continued to Bala and alongside Llyn Tegid (where the operating instructions stipulated that speed must not exceed 25mph). The climb to Garneddwen summit was steady and then the train coasted down to Dolgellau and on to Barmouth Junction, where it gained the former Cambrian Railways metals, crossing Barmouth viaduct and into Barmouth, where a 90-minute break was taken.

On resuming the cruise, the train proceeded up the Cardigan Bay coast, passing Harlech, Portmadoc and Criccieth, to Afon Wen, where another stop for water was taken. The train then regained London Midland Region metals and climbed the single line to the summit at Pant Glâs, then descended through Penygroes and Groeslon to Caernarfon, to the town's station, where another halt was made for water. There followed a sprint to Menai Bridge and Bangor, then along the North Wales coast to Llandudno Junction, where a halt was made to unload passengers from Llandudno. The cruise then went on to Rhyl where the train terminated.

The concept was instantly popular and a travel-hungry public patronised the cruise, which was exceptionally well marketed by the local agents at Rhyl and Llandudno.

The train was hauled by an LMS Class 2MT '464xx' locomotive which was transferred in for the job. Rhyl men operated the tour throughout and two drivers learnt the road over the Western Region metals as well as the single line from Afon Wen to Bangor, where they were on familiar territory.

The stock used was an assortment of vehicles. According to the rolling stock diagram notice for Friday 10 August to Thursday 16 August 1951, the train was made up of one brake third open coach, four open third coaches and one brake third open coach.

In 1952 a second train was introduced, running Tuesdays to Fridays during the summer season. This started from Llandudno, then ran to Rhyl, where it reversed and followed the same route as the Rhyl train, running about 30 minutes behind the first. A second Class 2MT 2-6-0 engine was transferred in, also worked by Rhyl men. It was decided that the title 'Festival Land Cruise' was by then not appropriate and both trains were named the 'North Wales Radio Land Cruise' at the start of the 1952 season. The coaching sets were made up of six vehicles of assorted vintage. Included in each formation were two brake open

third class coaches formerly part of the 'Coronation Scot' train that toured America in 1939. The rest of the stock was a motley variety of coaches. The 'Radio' element was a commentary that was piped via loudspeakers strategically placed in every coach.

By 1953 the Land Cruise was an established success, and demand for seats exceeded the available capacity. Ever innovative, the cruise trains were rechristened the 'Coronation Land Cruises', but the programme for the year was the same as for the previous years. These trains ran with the reporting numbers W662 for the Rhyl train and W663 for the Llandudno one.

Such was the popularity of this type of facility that the title reverted to 'Radio Land Cruise' for the 1954 season. The Western Region had taken note of the popularity and on 29 June 1954 ran its first train which started from Pwllheli and operated in the reverse direction to the Rhyl and Llandudno trains. The first train consisted of Collett 0-6-0 No 3202 and two LMS corridor coaches. Whilst on the LM Region metals it ran as reporting number W667. The Collett engines were the only class available that did not foul the LM Region loading gauge, although they were ultimately replaced by BR Standard Class 2MT engines of the '78xxx' class.

The LM Region, however, was still unable to satisfy the demand and accordingly operated a third train that ran from Llandudno to Barmouth via Caernarfon and thence followed the same route as the Pwllheli train, terminating back in Llandudno. Its reporting number was W669. This train ran daily Tuesdays to Fridays.

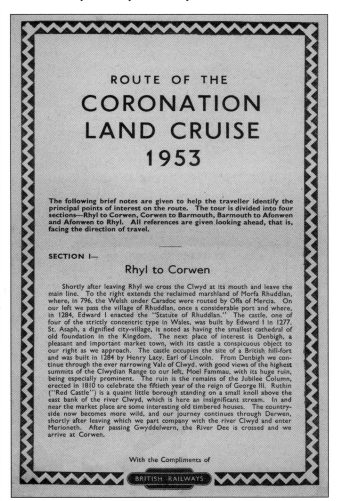

ROUTE OF THE
CORONATION LAND CRUISE 1953

The following brief notes are given to help the traveller identify the principal points of interest on the route. The tour is divided into four sections—Rhyl to Corwen, Corwen to Barmouth, Barmouth to Afonwen and Afonwen to Rhyl. All references are given looking ahead, that is, facing the direction of travel.

SECTION 1—
Rhyl to Corwen

Shortly after leaving Rhyl we cross the Clwyd at its mouth and leave the main line. To the right extends the reclaimed marshland of Morfa Rhuddlan, where, in 796, the Welsh under Caradoc were routed by Offa of Mercia. On our left we pass the village of Rhuddlan, once a considerable port and where, in 1284, Edward I enacted the "Statute of Rhuddlan." The castle, one of four of the strictly concentric type in Wales, was built by Edward I in 1277. St. Asaph, a dignified city-village, is noted as having the smallest cathedral of old foundation in the Kingdom. The next place of interest is Denbigh, a pleasant and important market town, with its castle a conspicuous object to our right as we approach. The castle occupies the site of a British hill-fort and was built in 1284 by Henry Lacy, Earl of Lincoln. From Denbigh we continue through the ever narrowing Vale of Clwyd, with good views of the highest summits of the Clwydian Range to our left, Moel Fammau, with its huge ruin, being especially prominent. The ruin is the remains of the Jubilee Column, erected in 1810 to celebrate the fiftieth year of the reign of George III. Ruthin ("Red Castle") is a quaint little borough standing on a small knoll above the east bank of the river Clwyd, which is here an insignificant stream. In and near the market place are some interesting old timbered houses. The countryside now becomes more wild, and our journey continues through Derwen, shortly after leaving which we part company with the river Clwyd and enter Merioneth. After passing Gwyddelwern, the River Dee is crossed and we arrive at Corwen.

With the Compliments of

BRITISH RAILWAYS

1953 Route of the Coronation Land Cruise.

Denbigh
Standard Class 4MT 4-6-0 No 75054 on the Welsh Chieftain Land Cruise approaching Denbigh from Corwen, 8 September 1960. *Bill Rear collection*

Yet another Land Cruise train was introduced in 1954. This was reporting number W665 and started at Chester at 11.25am, ran to Ruabon and then to Llangollen and Corwen, where the train stood from 12.12pm until 2pm. It reversed direction and worked up the Denbigh, Ruthin & Corwen line, pausing at Gwyddelwern to take water. Water was also taken at Denbigh and brief stops were made at St Asaph, Rhyl, Prestatyn, Holywell Junction and Flint. Arrival back at Chester was 5.36pm. No details of motive power and stock are known and it would seem that the tour was not a success, for it did not reappear in subsequent years.

In 1956 several variations were made. The Western Region Land Cruise ran on Tuesdays and Thursdays, starting at Pwllheli as previously, running along to Cardigan Bay, picking up at Penychain, Afon Wen, Criccieth, Portmadoc, Harlech and Llanbedr, cutting inland at Barmouth Junction running to Corwen, then going over the DR&C to Rhyl, where it reversed and came back along the North Wales coast, cutting inland at Menai Bridge, then passing through Caernarfon to Afon Wen, where it arrived back on Western Region metals at 5.10pm. It stopped at the pick-up points on the Cambrian coast and terminated at Barmouth. The locomotive and stock then worked over the viaduct to Barmouth Junction, where the

engine ran round on the triangle and then took the empty stock back to Pwllheli.

The LM Region Land Cruise went from Llandudno via Rhyl and over the DR&C to Corwen, then continued to Barmouth Junction, where it reversed and proceeded to Aberdovey, arriving there at 1.50pm. It departed at 3.30pm and continued to Barmouth, where a brief halt was taken, then went on to Afon Wen and over the LM metals to Pant Glâs, Caernarfon and back to Llandudno. The cruise starting at Rhyl worked as in previous years.

There was no change to the pattern of Land Cruise trains in 1957 and 1958. In the summer of 1958 the observation coach that was originally attached to the 'Devon Belle' was transferred to the London Midland Region and attached to the Rhyl train. It was initially a success, but by 1959 public tastes were changing and demand was falling off. The reporting numbers changed and the Pwllheli to Rhyl via Barmouth was now (Western Region No) 1940, which worked as before, but on arriving back at Afon Wen proceeded to Barmouth where the whole train turned on Barmouth Junction triangle and headed back empty stock to Pwllheli.

The Rhyl cruise train via Caernarfon and Afon Wen (No 1945) now paused at Criccieth from 11.50am until 12.45pm then ran to Barmouth, pausing only to cross a

Denbigh
Ivatt Class 2MT 2-6-0 No 46445 on the North Wales Radio Land Cruise near Green Bridge, Denbigh, for Corwen, 4 July 1956. *Bill Rear collection*

Pwllheli-bound working, then went on to Barmouth Junction and Corwen, where it took on water, then over the DR&C and back to Rhyl.

A new DMU excursion running on Tuesdays and Wednesdays only and entitled the 'Clwyd Ranger' (reporting number 1955) ran from Llandudno to Corwen over the DR&C, terminating there at 4.20pm. It commenced the return journey at 4.55pm, which did not give much time for the public to enjoy the delights of Corwen.

The Llandudno-based Land Cruise (reporting number 1950) operated to Rhyl, then over the DR&C to Barmouth Junction, where it reversed and headed for Aberdovey as previously, due 1.50pm. Departure was at 3.25pm and was via Barmouth, Afon Wen and Caernarfon. The train had gained a new title in 1959: the 'Cambrian Land Cruise'.

In 1960 the reporting numbers changed again. The Pwllheli Land Cruise via Barmouth was now 1M57, departing at the same times as before and picking up as previously. On regaining Western Region metals it proceeded as before to Barmouth, then turned and went back empty stock to Pwllheli.

The Rhyl Land Cruise, working anticlockwise via Caernarfon and Afon Wen, was reporting number 1V63 and the Criccieth halt was cut out, the break being taken at

Barmouth. It proceeded over the Ruabon line to Corwen and back to Rhyl over the DR&C.

The 'Clwyd Ranger' ran in this year on Tuesdays and Wednesdays. Its reporting number was 1V62. Return departure time was again 4.55pm.

The summer of 1961, the last season that the Land Cruise trains operated, saw a greatly reduced programme. The Pwllheli cruise was discontinued. The former Aberdovey cruise train, running as 1V63, now ran from Rhyl via Caernarfon and Afon Wen and was cut back to Towyn, being due there at 12.55pm. The DR&C line was scheduled for closure and traffic was discouraged; as a result the 'Clwyd Ranger' also disappeared.

In 1954 I had the good fortune to work Land Cruise W663. The circumstances were as follows.

There was a flu epidemic at Rhyl in that summer and I was on a rest day at Crewe. I was asked if I would be willing to work on the cruise from Rhyl, to which I readily agreed. Accordingly, I presented myself at Rhyl MPD on 23 June, booking on at 9.15am. I was to work on the Llandudno train and my driver was Frank Beech, a Rhyl-passed fireman made up for the season.

The regular locomotive should have been No 46428 but this had failed and a replacement was sent from Crewe. This was No 46441 of Carnforth (11A) shed that had just

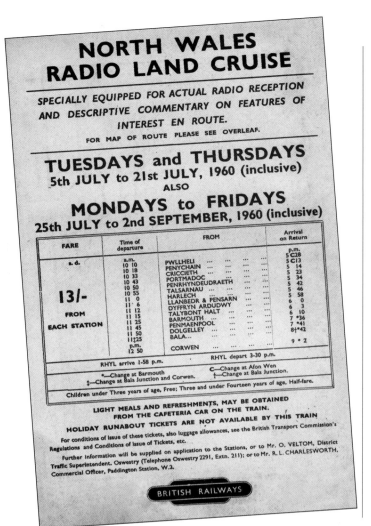

NORTH WALES RADIO LAND CRUISE

SPECIALLY EQUIPPED FOR ACTUAL RADIO RECEPTION AND DESCRIPTIVE COMMENTARY ON FEATURES OF INTEREST EN ROUTE.

FOR MAP OF ROUTE PLEASE SEE OVERLEAF.

TUESDAYS and THURSDAYS
5th JULY to 21st JULY, 1960 (inclusive)
ALSO

MONDAYS to FRIDAYS
25th JULY to 2nd SEPTEMBER, 1960 (inclusive)

FARE	Time of departure	FROM	Arrival on Return
s. d.	a.m.		p.m.
	10 10	PWLLHELI	5 C28
	10 18	PENYCHAIN	5 C13
	10 33	CRICCIETH	5 14
13/-	10 43	PORTMADOC	5 23
	10 50	PENRHYNDEUDRAETH	5 34
	10 55	TALSARNAU	5 42
FROM	11 0	HARLECH	5 46
	11 6	LLANBEDR & PENSARN	5 58
EACH STATION	11 12	DYFFRYN ARDUDWY	6 0
	11 15	TALYBONT HALT	6 3
	11 25	BARMOUTH	6 10
	11 45	PENMAENPOOL	7 *36
	11 50	DOLGELLEY	7 *41
	11†25	BALA...	8†*42
	p.m.		9 2
	12 50	CORWEN	

RHYL arrive 1-58 p.m.	RHYL depart 3-30 p.m.

*—Change at Barmouth   C—Change at Afon Wen
†—Change at Bala Junction and Corwen.   ‡—Change at Bala Junction.

Children under Three years of age, Free; Three and under Fourteen years of age, Half-fare.

LIGHT MEALS AND REFRESHMENTS, MAY BE OBTAINED FROM THE CAFETERIA CAR ON THE TRAIN.

HOLIDAY RUNABOUT TICKETS ARE NOT AVAILABLE BY THIS TRAIN

For conditions of issue of these tickets, also luggage allowances, see the British Transport Commission's Regulations and Conditions of Issue of Tickets, etc.

Further information will be supplied on application to the Stations, or to Mr. O. VELTOM, District Traffic Superintendent, Oswestry (Telephone Oswestry 2291, Extn. 211); or to Mr. R. L. CHARLESWORTH, Commercial Officer, Paddington Station, W.2.

BRITISH RAILWAYS

1960 North Wales Radio Land Cruise.

been out-shopped from Crewe works. The stock was worked from Llandudno and comprised six coaches.

Departure time from Rhyl was 11.4am, four minutes down, but the engine was steaming well and the schedule was easy. The train was full. I understand that passengers were turned away, such was the popularity of the cruise.

We took the slow line out of Rhyl to Foryd Junction and then picked up the staff at Foryd Junction box for Rhuddlan. There was no booked stop until Denbigh, and the token exchanges were taken at a slow pace at Rhuddlan, St Asaph and Trefnant. We had dropped another minute to Denbigh but made up all but one minute by departing after only a minute's halt. At Ruthin we had to cross the up freight from Corwen. The run through Eyarth Gorge was taken at 10mph and was spectacular. The climb to Gwyddelwern was steady but we were not short of steam nor in a hurry. If anything was demanded of this job, it was not to rush. Passengers wanted to see the scenery and not compete in a race.

At Corwen we joined the Western Region and ran into the station nearly five minutes down, but Frank did not seem perturbed. We had 10 minutes booked to take water but made up three minutes as we did not need as much as had been thought.

The run to Bala Junction was leisurely and we kept even time. The run past Llyn Tegid was taken at about 20mph and was very pleasant. At Llanuwchllyn we crossed a passenger train heading for Wrexham and lost a minute waiting for the staff. The climb to Garneddwen was taken at a steady pace and we ran into Drws-y-Nant at 1.13pm. The freight we were booked to cross was already in the loop and we exchanged tokens with only a minute's delay.

Llanwnda
Ivatt Class 2MT 2-6-0 No 46434 on the North Wales Radio Land Cruise departing Llanwnda, July 1953. *Bill Rear*

Groeslon
Standard Class 4MT 4-6-0 No 75054 on the Welsh Chieftain Land Cruise approaching Groeslon near Penygroes, 7 July 1960. *Bill Rear collection*

Eight minutes were then taken to reach Bontnewydd, where we were booked to cross a passenger for Chester. We reached the loop first and dropped two minutes waiting for it. We failed to make up any more time and ran into Barmouth at 1.55pm, three minutes down. Having discharged the passengers, we drew forward and set back into the down-side bay where we took water and attended to the fire.

Departure was on time at 3.15pm. We proceeded at a leisurely pace without stops to Afon Wen, where we were booked to take water. We didn't get held up at Portmadoc level crossing, which was rather unusual! At Afon Wen we had 14 minutes allowed to take water and took the opportunity to clean the fire again, although with a rocking grate this was easy. So far I had not even broken into a sweat!

Departure was at 4.20pm and we climbed steadily to Pant Glâs summit and coasted down the bank to Penygroes, where we arrived one minute early. We were booked to cross the 4.4pm Bangor to Pwllheli, which was running late, and so four minutes were lost awaiting the staff.

We picked up a minute to Caernarfon where we were booked to take water in the local platform. The run to Menai Bridge was easy and we gained a minute. We maintained our one minute early to Llandudno Junction where we pulled into the up local platform and the stock was detached, taken on to Llandudno by a Junction set of men. We went on, light engine to Rhyl, travelling slow line to Colwyn Bay and again from Llandulas to Rhyl. We were back on shed at 6.37pm, two minutes early. After disposing of the locomotive, I made my way to the station and travelled back to Crewe on the cushions, tired but happy.

As far as I am aware, there was only one accident to a Land Cruise train, in about 1958. One of the Rhyl workings travelling from Barmouth to Afon Wen had left Harlech after receiving the key token for the section Harlech to Penrhyndeudraeth. At Ty Gwyn halt the train passed a home signal at danger, which protected the minor road level crossing, and smashed the hand-operated gates. Fortunately, there was no vehicle on the road at the time, and the train made an emergency stop. The lady crossing keeper was adamant that she had not received a signal from Harlech to indicate that the train was on its way and claimed that she was waiting for the bell. The signalman at Harlech claimed he had given a warning signal to the crossing. However, it was never explained why the traincrew did not observe the signal at danger and brake accordingly. The whole incident was hushed up and, since no one was hurt, the incident was allowed to pass into history. The lady crossing keeper came out of it best: she had a good supply of broken timber for domestic use.

Motive power for the Rhyl and Llandudno trains was initially Ivatt Class 2MT tender engines of the '464xx' class. Pwllheli initially used Collett 0-6-0 tender engines and these were originally replaced by BR Standard Class 2MT 2-6-0s of the '78xxx' class. In 1958 the Class 2 engines were deemed to be hard-pressed and the land cruise trains were powered by '75xxx' Class 4MT 4-6-0s.

Denbigh
Ivatt Class 2MT 2-6-0 No 46422 on the North Wales Radio Land Cruise approaching Denbigh from Rhyl, June 1954.
Bill Rear

25

Bangor Motive Power Depot

Motive Power

First reference to a shed at Bangor is about 1857. It was No 21 in the LNWR and had sub-sheds ay Amlwch (21A), Caernarfon (21C) and Llanberis (21L). In LMS days it continued to be known as 21 until 1935 when it was renumbered 7B with Llandudno Junction (7A) as the Concentration depot. In 1952 it became 6H under Chester District.

Caernarfon was a station of some importance until the recession of the 1930s, coupled with the development of public bus services, drew traffic away from the rails and onto the roads. Until 1926 Caernarvon shed worked some important long-distance trains: one Euston job throughout the year with Camden-based 'Claughton' class 4-6-0s, a turn to Chester, another summer season working to Euston, and regular lodging turns to Springs Branch (Wigan) with mineral traffic, returning with coal. The remainder of the work was local, some of which was shared with Bangor. After the General Strike, work was lost, never to be regained, and some men and the Euston jobs were transferred to Bangor shed. The Camden-based 'Claughton' 4-6-0 locomotives, numbered 6026/7/8, were regularly stabled at Caernarfon overnight. There was a minor problem with these locomotives, in that they were too long to be turned on the 42ft turntable, but the problem was overcome by detaching the tender from the locomotive and each was turned separately, being recoupled afterwards. The same procedure was adopted with the tender engine Class G2 0-8-0 used on the Springs Branch job. After 1926 the locomotives were changed at Bangor. As the work diminished, the remaining duties were local in nature, and consisted mainly of trips between Bangor, Llanberis and Afon Wen, although the top job was worked as a lodging turn to Mold Junction with a Class 4F 0-6-0.

In LNWR days 0-6-0 tender engines were used for both passenger and freight workings on the branch but the removal of the turntable at Afon Wen put an end to the practice. Small tank engines, in pairs, then worked the branch and alternated with Bowen Cooke 4-6-2T engines which were drafted in to work over the line in the mid-1930s.

In the summer of 1937 two Fowler 2-6-4T engines were allocated to Bangor and put to work on the line, with immediate success, but were transferred away at the commencement of the winter duties. They were replaced by Fowler and Stanier 2-6-2T engines, but the limited water capacity and indifferent steaming performance of these engines proved a retrograde step, resulting in the loads being reduced, a situation not remedied until 8 July 1946 when Stanier 2-6-4T Nos 2460 and 2628 started to work on the line. On 11 January 1947 Fairburn 2-6-4Ts Nos 2258 and 2261 were received new, followed by 2260 on the 13th, and 2259 on the 24th of the same month, replacing four 2-6-2T engines. On 17 February 1947 Ivatt 2-6-2T No 1200 was received new from Crewe Works, followed by 1201 on 3 March. These replaced 6710 and 6926, which moved to other sheds in the district, but which reappeared at Bangor from time to time. No 42460 was the first engine to receive its new British Railways number in May 1948. The following month saw another 2-6-4T arrive — No 2662 — standing in for 2260 which went to Crewe Works on 21 June and stayed until October, the same month that 1201 was transferred to 4D. However, four new Ivatt 2-6-2Ts, Nos 41221/2/3/4, arrived in November, together with Nos 40087 and 143, replacing some of the older LNWR engines. The larger engines worked the Afon Wen line, whilst the Class 2 tanks spent most of their days on the Amlwch and Bethesda branches. During this same period (1946-8) Bangor had three Stanier Class 5P5F 2-6-0 engines for its main line work, Nos 2948/51/84, and Fowler Class 4F 0-6-0s Nos 4305/4445, which spent their days working the Nantlle and Llanberis goods jobs. Class 2P No 524 was used for the Chwilog milk turn, whilst the remainder of the allocation consisted of sundry types of various vintages and pedigrees. On 23 May 1949, two more 2-6-4Ts were received — Nos 42660 and 42617 — whilst the Stanier 2-6-0s were sent to Bescot on 21 June and replaced by Class 5 4-6-0 No 4913, and No 45417 on 23 June and No 5144 the following day. No 41200 was sent to Ipswich for trials on the Aldeburgh branch on 28 June, returning to Bangor via Crewe works on 16 November. (It again went to Ipswich on 11 May 1950, finally returning in August to Bangor, where it was to remain, apart from periodic visits to the works, until withdrawn.) September saw Nos 41221/2 transferred to Barrow and Bletchley respectively. June 1950 saw the seasonal increase with Fairburn 2-6-4Ts Nos 42156/7 followed by Stanier 2-6-4T No 42588 on 8 July. Two more 2-6-4Ts appeared briefly in early August, No 42552 from 3D and No 42599 from 9A, both returning home on the 15th of the same month. No 42660 departed in September, leaving the winter complement of 2-6-4Ts standing at 10 locomotives for eight jobs. The following July saw No 42062 from 5D and No 42350 from 6A drafted in for the month, and No 41287 was received new. No 46430 arrived from Rhyl on 21 September 1951 and stayed for three weeks. Dwindling traffic saw some of the older locomotives disappear over the succeeding months; some were transferred and some cut up. By July 1952 the allocation consisted largely of modern locomotives and it is worth listing the allocation in full:

Class 1PT	2-4-2T	46701, 46604 (to 6G on loan)
Class 2MT	2-6-2T	41200, 41223, 41230, 41233, 41239, 41287, 41324
Class 3MT	2-6-2T	40132
Class 4MT	2-6-4T	42156, 42157, 42258, 42259, 42260, 42261, 42455, 42460, 42588, 42617, 42628.
Class 4F	0-6-0	44305, 44445
Class 5MT	4-6-0	44913, 45144, 45417
Class 3F	0-6-0	52119, 52162, 52230, 12269
Class 2F	0-6-0	58375
Class 2F	0-6-2T	58903

Another change came in April 1954 when four Fairburn 2-6-4Ts were exchanged for four Fowler engines of the same class. Nos 42258-61 went to Gourock in exchange for Nos 42415-8. The allocation for August 1954 was as follows:

Class 3MT	2-6-2T	40102
Class 2MT	2-6-2T	41200, 41212, 41223, 41230, 41233, 41239, 41324
Class 4MT	2-6-4T	42156, 42157, 42178, 42415, 42416, 42417, 42418, 42444, 42455, 42460, 42588, 42617
Class 4F	0-6-0	44305, 44445
Class 5MT	4-6-0	44913, 45144, 45417
Class 3F	0-6-0	52119, 52230, 52269
Class 2F	0-6-0	58394

In October 1956 there was a wholesale clear-out of most of the LMS old-design 2-6-4T locomotives, which were replaced by a batch of BR Standard Class 4MT 2-6-4Ts.

The allocation was as follows:

Class 3MT	2-6-2T	40003
Class 2MT	2-6-2T	41200, 41230, 41233, 41239
Class 4MT	2-6-4T	42415, 42416, 80087, 80088, 80089, 80090, 80091, 80092, 80094, 80095
Class 4F	0-6-0	44305, 44445
Class 5MT	4-6-0	44913, 45144, 45417
Class 3F	0-6-0	52119, 52230, 52269
Class 0F	0-4-0T	51221 (in store)

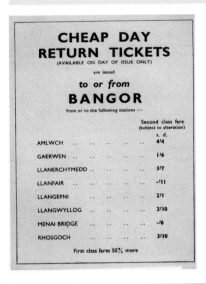

Train fares between Bangor and Amlwch, for June-September 1956

Timetable of 'Diesel Passenger Trains' for 11 June 1956- 16 September 1956.

BANGOR TO AMLWCH

The services will be worked by Diesel trains except where otherwise shown :—

WEEKDAYS ONLY

					SX† am	SX am	SO† am	SO am	SO† am	SX pm	SO pm	pm	† pm	pm	pm
BANGOR	dep.	5 25	6 40	9 15	..	9 23	..	11 40	12 35	12 40	3 50	5 35	..	8 52
Menai Bridge	,,		6 43	9 19	..	9 29	..	11 44	12 39	12 44	3 54	5 39		
Llanfair	Z ,,	..	..	9 24	..	9 33	..	..	12 44	12 49	3 59	5 44		9 00
Gaerwen	arr.	5 36	6 54	9 30	..	9 39	..	11 54	12 50	12 50	4 05	5 50		9 06
,,	dep.	5 40	6 55	..	9 40	..	9 45	11 57	12 51	12 56	4 06	..	6 02	9 07
Llangefni	,,	5 50	7 04	..	9 49	..	9 54	12 06	1 00	1 05	4 15		6 11	9 16
Llangwyllog	,,	5 58	7 15	..	9 57	..	10 02	12 14	1 08	1 16	4 23	..	6 19	9 24
Llanerchymedd	,,	6 06	7 23	..	10 05	..	10 10	12 22	1 16	1 24	4 31		6 27	9 32
Rhosgoch	,,	6 13	7 30	..	10 12	..	10 17	12 29	1 23	1 31	4 38		6 34	9 39
AMLWCH	arr.	6 21	7 38	..	10 20	..	10 25	12 38	1 31	1 39	4 46		6 42	9 47

AMLWCH TO BANGOR

The services will be worked by Diesel trains except where otherwise shown :—

WEEKDAYS ONLY

					† am	SO† am	SO† am	SX am	SO am	SO† pm	pm	pm	† pm	pm	SX pm	SO pm
AMLWCH	dep.	6 52	8 06	..	9 35	..	10 40	10 55	12 50	2 00	5 05	..	7 13	10 00	10 00
Rhosgoch	,,	6 59	8 13	..	9 44	..	10 48	11 03	12 58	2 07	5 13	..	7 20	10 08	10 08
Llanerchymedd	,,	7 06	8 20	..	9 53	..	10 56	11 10	1 06	2 15	5 21	..	7 28	10 16	10 16
Llangwyllog	,,	7 14	8 29	..	10 02	..	11 04	11 18	1 14	2 23	5 29	..	7 37	10 24	10 24
Llangefni	,,	7 21	8 36	..	10 09	..	11 11	11 25	1 21	2 30	5 36	..	7 46	10 31	10 31
Gaerwen	arr.	7 31	8 46	..	10 17	..	11 21	11 35	1 29	2 40	5 46	..	7 56		10 41
,,	dep.	7 32	..	8 50	..	11 22	11 42	1 31	2 41	..	6 01	7 58	..	10 42
Llanfair	Z ,,	..	..	8 55	10 25	..	10 30	11 47	2 46	..	6 06	8 03		
Menai Bridge	,,	7 40	..	9 00	10 35	11 30	11 52	1 41	2 51	..	6 11	8 08		
BANGOR	arr.	7 44	..	9 05	10 40	11 35	11 57	1 46	2 55	..	6 16	8 12	10 52	10 53

SO—Saturdays only. SX Saturdays excepted. Z—For other trains, Bangor to Gaerwen see public timetables. † —STEAM train.

252

The allocation for August 1958 was as follows:

Class 3MT	2-6-2T	40071, 40132, 40136, 40185
Class 2MT	2-6-2T	41200, 41230, 41233, 41234, 41239
Class 4MT	2-6-4T	42478, 42482, 42494, 42538, 42586, 42604, 42611, 42627, 80059, 80087, 80088, 80089, 80090, 80094, 80095
Class 4F	0-6-0	44305, 44445
Class 5MT	4-6-0	44913, 45144, 45417
Class 3F	0-6-0T	47511, 47588
Class 0F	0-4-0T	47006
Class 2MT	2-6-0	78057

With the closure of the Afon Wen, Amlwch, Llanberis and Nantlle lines in 1963-4, work at Bangor was drastically reduced and some locomotives were transferred elsewhere. The writing was on the wall for the shed, and it closed on 12 June 1965. The final allocation and subsequent fate of its locomotives were as follows:

Class 2MT 2-6-2T

41200 to 6G	Scrapped 10/65
41204 to 6C	Scrapped 4/67
41233 to 9B	Scrapped 12/65
41234 to 8G	Scrapped 4/67
41241 to 10G	Preserved Keighley & Worth Valley Railway

Class 5MT 4-6-0

44821 to 6J	Scrapped 12/67
45145 to 6J	Scrapped 2/68
45223 to 6J	Scrapped 7/67
45298 to 6J	Scrapped 2/68
45345 to 6J	Scrapped 9/68

Class 2MT 2-6-0

78003 to 1A	Scrapped 9/67
78032 to 1A	Scrapped 1/66
78058 to 1A	Scrapped 9/67
78059 to 1A	Preserved Bluebell Railway

Class 4MT 2-6-4T

80131	Scrapped 7/65

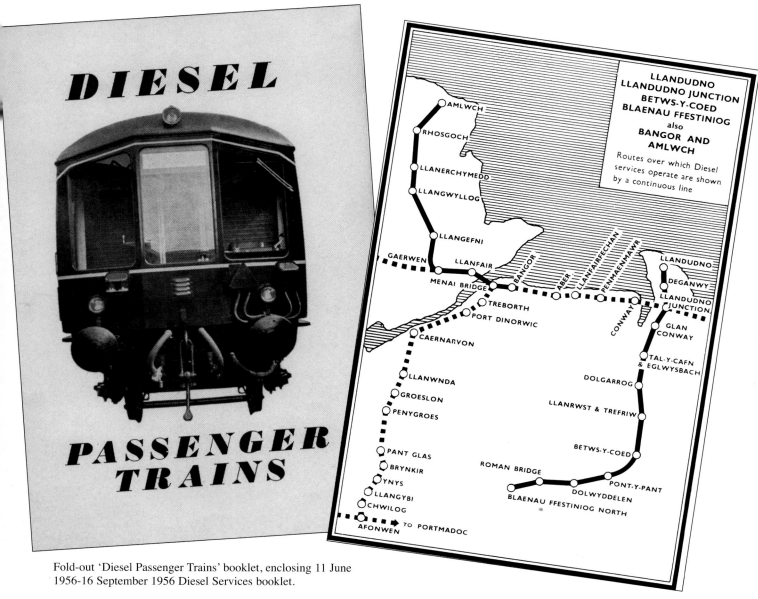

Fold-out 'Diesel Passenger Trains' booklet, enclosing 11 June 1956-16 September 1956 Diesel Services booklet.

Index

254